The Retirement Researcher's Guide Series

How Much Can I Spend in Retirement?

A Guide to Investment-Based Retirement Income Strategies

Wade D. Pfau,
Ph.D., CFA

Library of Congress Cataloging-in-Publication Data:
Pfau, Wade D., 1977–
  How Much Can I Spend in Retirement? A Guide to Investment-Based Retirement Income
    Strategies / Wade D. Pfau.
      pages cm
  Includes index.
ISBN [978-1-945640-02-5] (paperback) - ISBN [978-1-945640-03-2] (ebook)

Library of Congress Control Number: 2017914698
McLean Asset Management Corporation, McLean, VIRGINIA

1. Retirement Planning. 2. Financial, Personal. I. Title.

Cover Design: Mineral Interactive
Graphics and Layout: Watermark Design Office
Printed in the United States of America

To Yasue.

TABLE OF CONTENTS

PREFACE

How much can you spend in retirement? Naturally, this is a very important question for those approaching their retirement date. Essentially, if you wish to retire one day, you are increasingly responsible for figuring out how to save during your working years and convert your savings into sustainable income for an ever-lengthening number of retirement years.

It is not an easy task, but it is manageable.

This guide focuses on sustainable spending from investments, which is an important piece of any retirement plan. People want to know if they have saved enough to be able to fund their lifestyle in retirement. In this book, I explain the findings of a large body of financial planning research regarding sustainable spending from investment portfolios in the face of a variety of retirement risks.

I start by discussing classic studies from the financial planner's approach to retirement income planning using safe withdrawal rates based on historical data. William Bengen's 1994 study gave us the concept of the SAFEMAX, which is the highest sustainable spending rate from the worst-case scenario observed in the US historical data. The Trinity study added portfolio success rates from the historical data for different spending strategies. Both studies suggest that for a thirty-year retirement period, a 4 percent inflation-adjusted withdrawal rate using a 50–75 percent stock allocation should be reasonably safe.

Next, I investigate the implications of the many assumptions incorporated in these classic studies. The underlying assumptions matter. Several factors suggest that the estimates about sustainable spending provided by traditional studies are too optimistic, such as:

- US historical data is not sufficiently representative of what may happen in the future,
- the portfolios of real-world investors may underperform compared to the underlying index returns,
- retirees may not wish to invest as aggressively as the traditional studies recommend, and
- there is no desire to build in a safety margin or bequest at the end of the thirty-year time horizon.

However, other factors suggest that sustainable spending may be even higher than traditional studies imply. Reasons for this include:

- actual retirees may tend to reduce their spending with age,
- they may build more diversified portfolios than used in the basic research studies,
- real-world retirees may be willing to adjust spending for realized portfolio performance, and
- some retirees may have the capacity and tolerance to accept higher portfolio failure probabilities because they have other sources of income from outside their portfolios.

Retirees need to weigh the consequences between spending too little and spending too much—that is, being too frugal or running out of assets.

This book is about implementing what I call the "probability-based" school of thought for retirement planning. It is especially relevant for people who plan to fund their retirements using an investment portfolio and those who are hesitant about using income annuities or other insurance products. I will explore annuities and insurance more extensively in later volumes, but for now, we have plenty to discuss within the world of sustainable spending from an investment portfolio in retirement.

I welcome your feedback and questions.
You can reach me at wade@retirement researcher.com.

As a final note, I have avoided including footnotes to make the book more readable and give it a less academic feel. Each chapter ends with a "Further Reading" list that includes the bibliographic information for resources mentioned.

Wade Pfau
Bryn Mawr, PA

How Much Can I Spend in Retirement?

ACKNOWLEDGEMENTS

Writing a book is a major endeavor, and I have been helped along the way by countless individuals. First and foremost, I would like to thank my colleagues at McLean Asset Management for providing the vision and resources to make this book possible. In particular, I'm grateful for the leadership and willingness of Alex Murguia and Dean Umemoto to build a firm that can turn my research on retirement income planning into practical solutions for real-world retirees. I would also like to thank the entire advisory and social-media team at McLean: Kevin Brawner, Athena Chang, Rob Cordeau, Jason Dye, Bob French, Paula Friedman, Joel Gemmell, Danielle Jordan, Christian Litscher, Kyle Meyer, Robert Papa, Mark Witaschek, and Jessica Wunder.

The team at Mineral Interactive has also provided invaluable help in preparing this book and building my Retirement Researcher website. Thank you to Jud and Kim Mackrill, Zach McDonald, Johnny Sandquist, Rebecca Tschetter, and everyone else there who has contributed to this effort.

I am also deeply indebted to Don and Lynne Komai and the Watermark Design Office for their assistance in developing the layout and design for this book.

Furthermore, I am grateful to the American College of Financial Services for their leadership and focus on retirement income planning, particularly Bob Johnson, Michael Finke, David Littell, and Jamie Hopkins.

When it comes to retirement income planning, I wish to thank countless other practitioners and researchers who have helped me along the way. A partial list must include Bill Bengen, Bill Bernstein, David Blanchett, Jason Branning, J. Brent Burns, Bill Cason, Curtis Cloke, Jeremy Cooper, Dirk Cotton, Harold Evensky, Francois Gadenne, Jonathan Guyton, David Jacobs, Robert Huebscher, Stephen Huxley, Michael Kitces, Manish Malhotra, Moshe Milevsky, Aaron Minney, Dan Moisand, Kerry Pechter, Robert Powell, John M. Prizer, Jr., Dick Purcell, Bill Sharpe, Joe Tomlinson, Bob Veres, Steve Vernon, and the editorial team at the Journal of Financial Planning.

Finally, I wish to thank everyone who has read and participated at RetirementResearcher.com since 2010.

CHAPTER 1

Overview of Retirement Income Planning

Without the relative stability provided by earnings from employment, retirees must find a way to convert their financial resources into a stream of income that will last the remainder of their lives. Two trends complicate this task. First, people are living longer, so those retiring in their sixties must plan to support a longer period of spending. Second, traditional defined-benefit pensions are becoming less common. Pensions once guaranteed lifetime income by pooling risks across a large number of workers, but few employees have access to them today. Instead, employees and employers now tend to contribute to various defined-contribution pensions like 401(k)s, where the employee accepts longevity and investment risk and must make investment decisions. 401(k) plans are not pensions in the traditional sense, as they shift the risks and responsibility to employees rather than employers.

If you've been saving and accumulating, you need to know what to do with your pot of assets on reaching retirement. It is not an easy task, but it is not impossible.

My goal is to help guide you along the right path to building an efficient retirement income strategy. Ultimately, this is something you may seek to do on your own, but as an informed participant in the financial services profession, I will also offer suggestions on how to obtain help if you decide to seek further assistance.

It is important to note from the outset that retirement income planning is still a relatively new field. Wealth management has traditionally focused on accumulating assets without applying further thought to the differences that happen after retirement. To put it succinctly, retirees experience reduced capacity to bear financial market risk once they have retired. The standard of living for a retiree becomes more vulnerable to enduring permanent harm as a result of financial market downturns.

While it is relatively new, retirement income planning has emerged as a distinct field in the financial services profession. It continues to suffer from growing pains as it gains recognition, but increased research and brainpower in the field have benefited those planning for retirement and retirees alike. It is now clear that the financial circumstances facing retirees are not the same as for preretirees, calling for different approaches from traditional investment advice for wealth accumulation.

A mountain-climbing analogy is useful for clarifying the distinction between accumulation and distribution, as the ultimate goal of climbing a mountain is not just to make it to the top; it is also necessary to get back down. The skill set required to get down a mountain is not the same as that needed to reach the summit. In fact, an experienced mountain climber knows that it is more treacherous and dangerous to climb down a mountain. On the way down, climbers must deal with greater fatigue; they risk falling farther and with greater acceleration when facing a downslope compared to an upslope; and the way our bodies are designed makes going up easier than coming down.

The Mountain Climbing Analogy for Retirement

Exhibit 1.1

Distribution—the retirement phase when you are pulling money from your accounts rather than accumulating wealth—is much like descending a mountain. The objective of a retirement saver is not just to make it to the top of the mountain, which we could view as achieving a wealth accumulation target. The real objective is to safely and smoothly make it down the mountain, spending assets in a sustainable manner for as long as you live.

◉ The Retirement Researcher Manifesto

As I have attempted to summarize the key messages and themes that have underscored my writing and research going into this book, I find that the following eight guidelines serve as a manifesto for my approach to retirement income planning. Much of my writing concerns how to implement these guidelines into a retirement income plan.

1. Play the long game. A retirement income plan should be based on planning to live, not planning to die. A long life will be expensive to support, and it should take precedence over death planning. Fight the impatience that could lead you to choose short-term expediencies carrying greater long-term cost. This does not mean, however, that you sacrifice short-term satisfactions to plan for the long term. Many efficiencies can be gained from a long-term focus that can support a higher sustained standard of living for as long as you live.

You still have to plan for a long life, even when rejecting strategies that only help in the event of a long life. Remember, planning for average life expectancy is quite risky—half of the population outlives their expectancy. Planning to live longer means spending less than otherwise. Developing a plan that incorporates efficiencies that will not be realized until later can allow more spending today in anticipation of those efficiencies. Not taking such long-term, efficiency-improving actions will lead to a permanently reduced standard of living.

2. Do not leave money on the table. The holy grail of retirement income planning is finding strategies that enhance retirement efficiency. I define efficiency as follows: if one strategy allows for more lifetime spending and a greater legacy value for assets relative to another strategy, then it is more efficient. Efficiency must be defined from the perspective of how long you live. Related to point 1, a number of strategies can enhance efficiency over the long term (but not necessarily over the short term) with more spending and more legacy. One simple example for tax planning in retirement is taking IRA distributions or harvesting capital gains to generate enough income to fill the 0 percent marginal tax bracket.

3. Use reasonable expectations for portfolio returns. A key lesson for long-term financial planning is that you should not expect to earn the average historical market returns for your portfolio. Half of the time, realized returns will be less. As well, we have been experiencing a period of historically low interest rates, which unfortunately provides a clear mathematical reality that at least bond returns are going to be lower in the future. This has important implications for those who have retired (these implications are relevant for those far from retirement as well, but the harm of ignoring them is less than for retirees). At the very least, dismiss any retirement projection based on 8 or 12 percent returns, as the reality is likely much less when we account for portfolio volatility, inflation, and a desire to develop a plan that will work more than half the time and in today's low interest rates.

4. Be careful about plans that only work with high market returns. A natural mathematical formula that applies to retirement planning is that higher assumed future market returns imply higher sustainable spending rates. Bonds provide a fixed rate of return when held to maturity, and stocks potentially offer a higher return than bonds as a reward for their additional risk. But a "risk premium" is not guaranteed and may not materialize. Retirees who spend more today because they are planning for higher market returns than available for bonds are essentially "amortizing their upside." They are spending more today than justified by bond investments, based on an assumption that higher returns in the future will make up the difference and justify the higher spending rate.

For retirees, the fundamental nature of risk is the threat that poor market returns will trigger a permanently lower standard of living. Retirees must decide how much risk to their lifestyle they are willing to accept. Assuming that a risk premium on stocks will be earned and spending more today is risky behavior. It may be reasonable behavior for the more risk tolerant among us, but it is not a behavior that will be appropriate for everyone. It is important to think through the consequences in advance.

5. Build an integrated strategy to manage various retirement risks.
Building a retirement income strategy is a process that requires determining how to best combine available retirement income tools in order to meet retirement goals and to effectively protect against the risks standing in the way of those goals. Retirement risks include longevity and an unknown planning horizon, market volatility and macroeconomic risks, inflation, and spending shocks that can derail a budget. Each of these risks must be managed by combining different income tools with different relative strengths and weaknesses for addressing each of the risks. There is no single solution that can cover every risk.

6. Approach retirement income tools with an agnostic view. The financial services profession is generally divided between two camps: those focusing on investment solutions and those focusing on insurance solutions. Both sides have their adherents who see little use for the other side. But the most efficient retirement strategies require an integration of both investments and insurance. It is potentially harmful to dismiss subsets of retirement income tools without a thorough investigation of their purported role. In this regard, it is wrong to describe the stock market as a casino, to lump income annuities together with every other type of annuity, and to dismiss reverse mortgages without any further consideration.

For the two camps in the financial services profession, it is natural to accuse the opposite camp of having conflicts of interest that bias their advice, but each side must reflect on whether their own conflicts color their advice. On the insurance side, the natural conflict is that insurance agents receive commissions for selling insurance products and may only need to meet a requirement that their suggestions be suitable for their clients. On the investments side, those charging for a percentage of assets they manage naturally wish to make the investment portfolio as large as possible, which is not necessarily in the best interests of their clients who are seeking sustainable lifetime income and proper retirement risk management. Meanwhile, those charging hourly fees for planning advice naturally do not wish to make their recommendations so simple that they forego the need for an ongoing planning relationship. It is important to overcome these hurdles and to rely carefully on what the math and research show. This requires starting from a fundamentally agnostic position.

7. Start by assessing all household assets and liabilities. A retirement plan involves more than just financial assets. The retirement balance sheet is the starting point for building a retirement income strategy. This has been a fundamental lesson from various retirement frameworks, such as Jason Branning and M. Ray Grubbs's Modern Retirement Theory, Russell Investments' funded ratio approach, and the household balance sheet view of the Retirement Income Industry Association. At the core of these different methodologies is a desire to treat the household retirement problem in the same way that pension funds treat their obligations. Assets should be matched to liabilities with comparable levels of risk. This matching can either be done on a balance sheet level, using the present values of asset and liability streams, or it can be accomplished on a period-by-period basis to match assets to ongoing spending needs. Structuring the retirement income problem in this way makes it easier to keep track of the different aspects of the plan and to make sure that each liability has a funding source. This also allows retirees to more easily determine whether they have sufficient assets to meet their retirement needs, or if they may be underfunded with respect to their goals. This organizational framework also serves as a foundation for choosing an appropriate asset allocation and for seeing clearly how different retirement income tools fit into an overall plan.

Exhibit 1.2 provides a basic overview of potential assets and liabilities to consider.

Exhibit 1.2	Basic Retirement Assets and Liabilities
	Retirement Balance Sheet
Assets	**Liabilities**
Human Capital • Continuing Career • Part-time Work Home Equity Financial Assets • Checking Accounts • Brokerage Accounts • Retirement Plans Insurance & Annuities Social Capital • Social Security • Medicare • Company Pensions • Family & Community	Fixed Expenses • Basic Living Needs • Taxes • Debt Repayment Discretionary Expenses • Travel & Leisure • Lifestyle Improvements Contingencies • Long-Term Care • Health Care • Other Spending Shocks Legacy Goals • Family • Community & Society

8. Distinguish between technical liquidity and true liquidity. An important implication from the retirement balance sheet view is that the nature of liquidity in a retirement income plan must be carefully considered. In a sense, an investment portfolio is a liquid asset, but some of its liquidity may be only an illusion. Assets must be matched to liabilities. Some, or even all, of the investment portfolio may be earmarked to meet future lifestyle spending goals. Curtis Cloke describes this in his Thrive University program for financial advisors (which I have attended twice) as allocation liquidity. Retirees are free to reallocate their assets in any way they wish, but the assets are not truly liquid, because they must be preserved to meet the spending goal. While a retiree could decide to use these assets for another purpose, doing so would jeopardize the ability to meet future spending. In this sense, assets are not as liquid as they appear.

This is different from free-spending liquidity, in which assets could be spent in any desired way because they are not earmarked to meet existing liabilities. True liquidity emerges when there are excess assets remaining after specifically setting aside what is needed to meet all of the household liabilities. This distinction is important because there are cases when tying up part of one's assets in something illiquid, such as an income annuity, may allow for the household liabilities to be covered more cheaply than could be done when all assets are positioned to provide technical liquidity. In simple terms, an income annuity that pools longevity risk may allow lifetime spending to be met at a cost of twenty years of the spending objective, while self-funding for longevity may require setting aside enough from an investment portfolio to cover thirty to forty years of expenses. Because risk pooling and mortality credits allow for less to be set aside to cover the spending goal, there is now greater true liquidity and therefore more to cover other unexpected contingencies without jeopardizing core spending needs. Liquidity, as it is traditionally defined in securities markets, is of little value as a distinct goal in a long-term retirement income plan.

◉ The Retirement Income Challenge

The process of building a retirement income strategy involves determining how to best combine retirement income tools to optimize the balance between meeting various retirement goals and effectively protecting your goals from retirement risks. Building an optimal strategy is a process, and there is no single right answer. No one approach or retirement income product works best for everyone. Different people will approach the problem in different ways, as some will feel affinity for solutions connected with managing withdrawals from an investment portfolio, while others will begin from a desire to build income guarantees. The objective becomes to flesh out the details for how each income tool could contribute, quantify the advantages and disadvantages of different strategies, and determine how to best combine the income tools into an overall plan.

Exhibit 1.3 shows the retirement income planning problem as a series of concentric circles. I call it the retirement income challenge. The innermost circle summarizes the overall process for retirement income. At the center, we must combine income tools to best meet goals and balance risks.

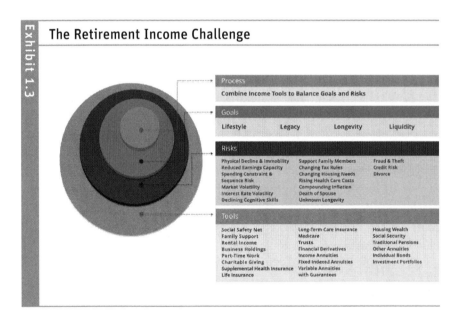

Exhibit 1.3

The Retirement Income Challenge

Process
Combine Income Tools to Balance Goals and Risks

Goals
Lifestyle   Legacy   Longevity   Liquidity

Risks
Physical Decline & Immobility   Support Family Members   Fraud & Theft
Reduced Earnings Capacity   Changing Tax Rules   Credit Risk
Spending Constraint &   Changing Housing Needs   Divorce
Sequence Risk   Rising Health Care Costs
Market Volatility   Compounding Inflation
Interest Rate Volatility   Death of Spouse
Declining Cognitive Skills   Unknown Longevity

Tools
Social Safety Net   Long-Term Care Insurance   Housing Wealth
Family Support   Medicare   Social Security
Rental Income   Trusts   Traditional Pensions
Business Holdings   Financial Derivatives   Other Annuities
Part-Time Work   Income Annuities   Individual Bonds
Charitable Giving   Fixed Indexed Annuities   Investment Portfolios
Supplemental Health Insurance   Variable Annuities
Life Insurance   with Guarantees

Possible goals are listed in the next concentric circle. The third circle lists risks confronting those goals. The final circle shows available income tools for building a retirement income plan. Much of what follows in this chapter is about fleshing out the details of this exhibit.

Financial Goals for Retirement

It is important to clarify the goals for a retirement income plan, as different income tools are better suited for different goals. Retirement plans should be customized to each person's specific circumstances. Each retiree should seek to meet specific financial goals in a way that best manages the wide variety of risks that threaten those goals. The primary financial goal for most retirees relates to their spending: maximize spending power (lifestyle) in such a way that spending can remain consistent and sustainable without any drastic reductions, no matter how long the retirement lasts (longevity). Other important goals may include leaving assets for subsequent generations (legacy) and maintaining sufficient reserves for unexpected contingencies that have not been earmarked for other purposes (liquidity). Lifestyle, longevity, legacy, and liquidity are the four Ls of retirement income.

Changing Risks in Retirement

It is important to understand from the very outset how changing risks are primarily what separate retirement income planning from traditional wealth management. Retirees have less capacity for risk, as they become more vulnerable to a reduced standard of living when risks manifest. Those entering retirement are crossing the threshold into an entirely foreign way of living. These risks can be summarized in seven general categories, listed in Exhibit 1.4.

Exhibit 1.4

Retirement Risks

- Reduced earnings capacity
- Visible spending constraint
- Heightened investment risk
- Unknown longevity
- Spending shocks
- Compounding inflation
- Declining cognitive abilities

1. Reduced earnings capacity

Retirees face reduced flexibility to earn income in the labor markets as a way to cushion their standard of living from the impact of poor market returns. One important distinction in retirement is that people often experience large reductions in their risk capacity as the value of their human capital declines. As a result, they are left with fewer options for responding to poor portfolio returns.

Risk capacity is the ability to endure a decline in portfolio value without experiencing a substantial decline in your standard of living. Prior to retirement, poor market returns might be counteracted with a small increase in the savings rate, a brief retirement delay, or even a slight increase in risk taking. Once retired, however, people can find it hard to return to the labor force and are more likely to live on fixed budgets.

2. Visible spending constraint

At one time, investments were a place for saving and accumulation, but retirees must try to create an income stream from their existing assets—an important constraint on their investment decisions. Taking distributions amplifies investment risks (market volatility, interest rate volatility, and credit risk) by increasing the importance of the order of investment returns in retirement.

It can be difficult to reduce spending in response to a poor market environment. Portfolio losses could have a more significant impact on standard of living after retirement, necessitating greater care and vigilance in response to portfolio volatility. Even a person with high risk tolerance (the ability to stomach market volatility comfortably) would be constrained by his or her risk capacity.

The traditional goal of wealth accumulation is generally to seek the highest returns possible in order to maximize wealth, subject to your risk tolerance. Taking on more risk before retirement can be justified, because many people have greater risk capacity at that time and can focus more on their risk tolerance. However, the investing problem fundamentally changes in retirement.

Investing during retirement is a rather different matter from investing for retirement, as retirees worry less about maximizing risk-adjusted returns and worry more about ensuring that their assets can support their spending goals for the remainder of their lives. After retiring, the fundamental objective for investing is to sustain a living standard while spending down assets over a finite but unknown length of time. The spending needs that will eventually be financed by the portfolio no longer reside in the distant future. In this new retirement calculus, views about how to balance the trade-offs between upside potential and downside protection can change. Retirees might find that the risks associated with seeking return premiums on risky assets loom larger than before, and they might be prepared to sacrifice more potential upside growth to protect against the downside risks of being unable to meet spending objectives.

The requirement to sustain an income from a portfolio is a new constraint on investing that is not considered by basic wealth maximization approaches such as portfolio diversification and modern portfolio theory (MPT). In MPT, cash flows are ignored, and the investment horizon is limited to a single, lengthy period. This simplification guides investing theory for wealth accumulation. When spending from a portfolio, the concept of sequence-of-returns risk (the order that market returns arrive) becomes more relevant, as portfolio losses early in retirement will increase the percentage of remaining assets withdrawn to sustain an income. This can dig a hole from which it becomes increasingly difficult to escape, as portfolio returns must exceed the growing withdrawal percentage to prevent further portfolio depletion. Even if markets subsequently recover, the retirement portfolio cannot enjoy a full recovery. The sustainable withdrawal rate from a retirement portfolio can fall below the average return earned by the portfolio during retirement.

3. Heightened investment risk

As we just discussed, retirees experience heightened vulnerability to sequence-of-returns risk when they begin spending from their investment portfolio. Poor returns early in retirement can push the sustainable withdrawal rate well below that which is implied by long-term average market returns.

The financial market returns experienced near your retirement date matter a great deal more than you may realize. Retiring at the beginning of a bear market is incredibly dangerous. The average market return over a thirty-year period could be quite generous, but if you experience negative returns in the early stages when you have started spending from your portfolio, withdrawals can deplete wealth rapidly, leaving a much smaller remainder to benefit from any subsequent market recovery, even with the same average returns over a long period of time. What happens in the markets during the fragile decade around the retirement date matters a lot.

The dynamics of sequence risk suggest that a prolonged recessionary environment early in retirement without an accompanying economic catastrophe could jeopardize the retirement prospects for particular groups of retirees. Some could experience much worse retirement outcomes than those retiring a few years earlier or later. It is nearly impossible to see such an instance coming, as devastation for a group of retirees is not necessarily preceded or accompanied by devastation for the overall economy.

4. Unknown longevity
The fundamental risk for retirement is unknown longevity, which is summarized in the question, "How long will your retirement plan need to generate income?" The length of your retirement could be much shorter or longer than the statistical life expectancy. A long life is wonderful, but it is also costlier and a bigger drain on resources. Half of the population will outlive their statistical life expectancy, and that number is only increasing as scientific progress constantly increases the number of years we can expect to live. For many retirees, the fear of outliving resources may exceed the fear of death.

5. Spending shocks
Unexpected expenses come in many forms, including:

- unforeseen need to help family members,
- divorce,
- changes in tax laws or other public policy,
- changing housing needs,
- home repairs,
- rising health-care and prescription costs, and
- long-term care.

Retirees must preserve flexibility and liquidity to manage unplanned expenses. When attempting to budget over a long retirement period, it is important to include allowances for such contingencies.

6. Compounding inflation

Retirees face the risk that inflation will erode the purchasing power of their savings as they progress through retirement. Low inflation may not be noticeable in the short term, but it can have a big impact over a lengthy retirement, leaving retirees vulnerable. Even with just 3 percent average annual inflation, the purchasing power of a dollar will fall by more than half after twenty-five years, doubling the cost of living.

Sequence-of-returns risk is amplified by greater portfolio volatility, yet many retirees cannot afford to play it too safe. Short-term fixed-income securities might struggle to provide returns that exceed inflation, causing these assets to be quite risky in a different sense: they may not be able to support a retiree's long-term spending goals. Low-volatility assets are generally viewed as less risky, but this may not be the case when the objective is to sustain spending over a long time horizon. Even low levels of inflation can create dramatic impacts on purchasing power over a long period of time. Retirees must keep an eye on the long-term cumulative impacts of even low inflation and position their assets accordingly.

7. Declining cognitive abilities

Finally, a retirement income plan must incorporate the unfortunate reality that many retirees will experience declining cognitive abilities, which will hamper portfolio management and other financial decision-making skills. For the afflicted, it will become increasingly difficult to make sound portfolio investments and withdrawal decisions in advanced ages.

In addition, many households do not equally share the management of personal finances. When the spouse who manages the finances dies first, the surviving spouse can run into serious problems without a clear plan in place. The surviving spouse can be left vulnerable to financial predators and other financial mistakes. Survivors often become more exposed to fraud and theft.

While liquidity and flexibility are important, retirees should also prepare for the reality that cognitive decline will hamper the portfolio management skills of many as they age, increasing the desirability of advanced planning and automation for late-in-life financial goals.

● Retirement Income Tools

Retirement plans can be built to manage varying risks by strategically combining different retirement income tools. As a result, retirement income planning is now emerging as a distinct field.

Total-Return Investment Portfolios

Making systematic withdrawals from a well-diversified investment portfolio is a common way to obtain retirement income. Systematic withdrawals do not protect a retiree from longevity risk or sequence-of-returns risk and may only protect from inflation risk when asset returns can keep up with inflation. This approach has its benefits, such as the potential to keep your nest egg growing so you can leave a large inheritance, as well as a sense of technical liquidity that could become true liquidity if markets perform well. A total-return approach is particularly vulnerable to declining cognitive abilities, as it requires complex financial decision-making to manage distributions and investments.

Individual Bonds

Leaving behind the purely total-return perspective, another viable option is to hold fixed-income assets to their maturity to guarantee upcoming retiree expenses. Often, this will be done to support short-or medium-term spending, with a more aggressive investment portfolio with higher expected returns and growth to be deployed for expenses in the long term.

Holding bonds to their maturity can keep you from selling them at a loss, which may help alleviate sequence-of-returns risk. Individual bonds do not provide longevity protection, however. While they may provide technical liquidity, selling them early to use for other contingencies could result in capital losses as well as the loss of assets that had been earmarked to cover future spending. Traditional bonds will be exposed to inflation risk, but Treasury Inflation-Protected Securities (TIPS) can be used to lock in the purchasing power of money in real terms.

As for the risk of declining cognitive abilities, managing the bond and investment portfolio may still be complicated, but the bonds can provide additional behavioral benefits. Knowing that income is accounted for over the next several years can help retirees stay the course and not sell off their stock positions in a panic after a market decline. Retirees can take comfort in the knowledge that there will be time for their stocks to recover before they must be sold. By using bonds to provide income for a fixed number of years, it may also be easier for retirees to understand why the overall asset allocation is what it is. Individuals may not be clear why their portfolio has 60 percent stock funds and 40 percent bond funds, but if they instead think in terms of how building a bond ladder with 40 percent of their assets allows for eight years of income, for instance, then the nature of their asset allocation choice may be clearer.

Income Annuities, Traditional Pensions, and Other Annuity Types

Partially annuitizing your assets can also provide an effective way to build an income floor for retirement. Income annuities, as opposed to individual bonds, provide longevity protection by hedging the risks associated with not knowing how long you will live. Fixed annuities can be real or nominal, and the initial payments can begin within one year (single-premium immediate annuities or SPIAs) or be deferred to a later age (deferred-income annuities, or DIAs). Some employers still offer traditional defined-benefit pensions, which can also be treated as an income annuity. Though income annuities only represent about 4 percent of total annuity sales, they are the type of annuity that is of the utmost importance as a retirement income tool.

Deciding whether to annuitize, when to annuitize, how much to annuitize, and whether to build a ladder of annuities over time are all important questions. Annuities protect from longevity and sequence-of-returns risk, and they can protect from inflation risk if a real annuity is purchased. Because income continues automatically, they also provide protection for cognitive decline. David Laibson, a professor at Harvard University, refers to income annuities as "dementia insurance." They help manage many risks, but they provide no growth potential, and life-only versions will not support an inheritance by themselves. In general, they are also not liquid if more funds are needed for unplanned contingencies. However, partial annuitization combined with investments can be an effective way to create true liquidity on the balance sheet.

Income annuities represent only a small percentage of total annuity sales. Countless types of annuities can be used for many different purposes.

Deferred fixed annuities can act as an alternative to CDs or savings accounts; investment-only deferred variable annuities can provide a source of tax-deferred savings during the accumulation phase; and fixed indexed annuities (a newer name for equity indexed annuities), immediate variable annuities, and deferred variable annuities with guarantee riders can all provide various combinations of guaranteed income, liquidity, and upside growth potential. Related nonannuity investment options include the ability to have an income guarantee rider on an investment portfolio and the use of financial derivatives to generate the same types of outcomes as some types of annuities on your own.

Social Security

Social Security is the ultimate form of an income annuity, and it is generally one of the largest assets on the retirement balance sheet. For a high-earning couple, the present value of lifetime Social Security benefits could exceed $1 million. Social Security provides protection from inflation, longevity, and sequence-of-returns risk, as well as providing survivor benefits. Retirement benefits can begin as early as age sixty-two, but the benefits grow through age seventy if you wait. If you view lost benefits from ages sixty-two to sixty-nine as a premium to buy a larger annuity starting at seventy, delaying Social Security can be viewed as the best annuity money can buy. It offers a better deal than any commercial providers. Because Social Security income continues automatically over time, it also provides protections for cognitive decline. The only risk Social Security does not help manage is spending shock, as you cannot borrow against your future benefits to obtain greater liquidity today.

Housing Wealth

The other major asset for most households, outside of investment portfolios and Social Security, is home equity, or housing wealth. Housing wealth can be used in a variety of ways in retirement. If care is taken to choose housing that will allow for aging in place, then housing can provide inflation protection and some protection for the uncertain costs related to long-term care. With cognitive or long-term care needs, housing could be used to put off institutional living, and then housing wealth could be redeployed to cover the costs of institutional living when it becomes necessary. With a reverse mortgage, home equity can become a liquid buffer asset which can help reduce exposure to sequence-of-returns risk or cover unexpected contingencies.

Long-Term Care Planning

One of the largest spending shocks facing a retired household is the need for ongoing long-term care. A retirement income plan must account for this, and various tools are available to help control the impacts of long-term care costs on family wealth.

The four main options for meeting long-term care needs include:

- self-funding,
- Medicaid,
- traditional long-term care insurance, and
- new hybrid insurance products that combine long-term care coverage with an annuity or life insurance.

Planning in advance for long-term care needs can help control the impact of spending shocks and cognitive decline.

Other Assets, Insurance, and Income Sources

A hodgepodge of other retirement income tools can also be a valuable source of support for retirement. Decisions made about Medicare or other health insurance can help mitigate the risks of large health-care spending shocks throughout retirement. Part-time work, to the extent that it is feasible, can help support a more fulfilling lifestyle while also providing a source of income to help mitigate risks related to market returns. An active mind may also help limit the onset of cognitive difficulties.

Another source of support is social capital: the ability to obtain help from family members, the community, and the social safety net. Access to these opportunities can help mitigate harms related to the various retirement risks. Other potential assets that are less exposed to market risk and may be available to support retirement goals include life insurance, business holdings, and rental income from real estate.

◎ Insurance versus Investments

As I mentioned before, retirement income planning has emerged as a distinct field in the financial services profession. But due in part to its relatively new status, the best approach for building a retirement income plan remains elusive. Two fundamentally different philosophies for retirement income planning—which I call "probability-based" and "safety-first"—diverge on the critical issue of where a retirement plan is best served: in the risk/reward trade-offs of an equity portfolio, or in the contractual guarantee of insurance products. The fundamental question asks which type of strategy can best meet the retirement income challenge of combining retirement income tools to meet goals and manage risks.

Those favoring investments (the probability-based) rely on the notion that the market will eventually provide favorable returns for most retirees. Though stock markets are volatile, stocks can be expected to outperform bonds over a reasonable amount of time. The investments crowd considers upside potential from a portfolio to be so significant that insurance solutions can only play a minimal role. Why needlessly cut off the upside? In addition, the investments side feels a general unease about relying on the long-term prospects of insurance companies or bond issuers to meet contractual obligations. Perhaps not fully understanding the implications of how sequence-of-returns risk differs from market risk, the probability-based school believes that in the rare event that the performance for the equity portfolio does not materialize, an economic catastrophe will sink insurance companies as well. This volume specifically focuses on the probability-based approach.

Meanwhile, those favoring insurance (safety-first) believe that contractual guarantees are reliable and that staking your retirement income on the assumption that favorable market returns will eventually arrive is emotionally overwhelming and dangerous. The insurance side is clearly more concerned with the implications of market risk than those favoring investments, believing that even with a low probability of portfolio depletion, a retiree gets only one opportunity for a successful retirement. At the very least, they say, essential income needs should not be subject to the whims of the market. The safety-first school views investment-only solutions as undesirable because the retiree retains all the longevity and market risks, which an insurance company is in a better position to manage.

But retirement income planning is not an either/or proposition. We must step away from the notion that either investments or insurance alone will best serve retirees. Each tool has its own advantages and disadvantages. An entire literature on "product allocation" has arisen, showing how a more efficient set of retirement outcomes can be obtained by combining investments with insurance.

The Advantages and Disadvantages of Investments in Retirement

With investment solutions, a more comfortable lifestyle may be maintained if you are willing to invest aggressively in the hope of subsequently earning higher market returns to support a higher income rate. Should decent market returns materialize and sufficiently outpace inflation, investment solutions can be sustained indefinitely. Portfolio balances are also liquid in the technical sense that they are accessible to a retiree, not locked away as part of a contractual agreement such as an annuity. Upside growth could also support a larger legacy and provide liquidity for unexpected expenses.

However, the dual impact of sequence of returns and longevity risk leaves you open to the possibility of being unable to support your desired lifestyle over the full retirement period. These are risks a retiree cannot offset easily or cheaply in an investment portfolio. Investment approaches seek to reduce sequence and longevity risk by having the retiree spend conservatively. Retirees spend less to avoid depleting their portfolio through a bad sequence of returns in early retirement, and because they must be prepared to live well beyond their life expectancy. The implication is clear: should the market perform reasonably well in retirement, the retiree will significantly underspend relative to their potential and leave an unintentionally large legacy.

At the same time, longevity protection (the risk of outliving savings) is not guaranteed with investments, and sufficient assets may not be available to support a long life or legacy. A "reverse legacy" could result if the portfolio is so depleted that the retiree must rely on others (often adult children) for support. This is particularly important in light of the ongoing improvements in mortality. On the whole, retirees of today will live longer and have to support longer retirements than their predecessors. For healthy individuals in their sixties, we are approaching the point where forty years must replace thirty years as a conservative planning horizon.

Retirees experience reduced risk capacity as they enter retirement. Their reduced flexibility to earn income leaves them more vulnerable to forced lifestyle reductions resulting from the whims of the market. A probability-based strategy could backfire.

Investment assets may also be less liquid than they appear. Though they are technically liquid, a retiree who spends assets that were meant to cover spending needs later in life may find that those later needs can no longer be met.

Additionally, with age come declining cognitive abilities, which make it increasingly difficult to manage investment and withdrawal decisions required for a systematic withdrawal strategy. However, these concerns may be offset by allowing a trusted family member to handle your finances or working with a professional financial planner.

The Advantages and Disadvantages of Insurance in Retirement

Insurance companies pool sequence and longevity risks across a large base of retirees—much like a traditional defined-benefit pension—allowing for retirement spending that is more closely aligned with average long-term fixed-income returns and longevity. This could support a higher lifestyle than what is feasible for someone self-managing these risks by assuming low returns and a longer time horizon.

Guarantees can also provide peace of mind for your lifestyle that leads to a less stressful and more enjoyable retirement experience. Overly conservative retirees become so concerned with running out of money that they spend significantly less than they could. A monthly annuity payment can provide the explicit permission to spend and enjoy retirement. A dependable monthly check from an annuity can also simplify life for those with reduced cognitive skills or for surviving spouses who may be less experienced with regard to financial matters.

The primary benefit of the safety-first, insurance-based approach is longevity protection, as it provides a guaranteed income for as long as you live. It hedges longevity risk and calibrates the planning horizon to something much closer to life expectancy. Those who fall short of life expectancy subsidize the income payments for those who outlive it (known as "mortality credits"). Both groups enjoy higher spending because they have pooled the longevity risk and do not have to plan based on an overly conservative time horizon. This higher income also provides flexibility to spend less than possible and maintain more reserves to manage inflation risk.

A death benefit can be created with life insurance to provide a specific legacy amount. Additionally, an income annuity dedicates assets specifically toward the provision of income, allowing other assets to be earmarked specifically for growth. This can allow for a larger legacy, especially when the retiree enjoys a long life and more of his or her income is supported by the annuity's mortality credits.

But many retirees may be significantly underfunded and may not be able to reach their goals even after pooling risks. Though income annuities can guarantee a lifestyle, they lack the ability to provide upside potential on their own, and inflation-protected versions are costly. In such cases, individuals may need to rely on the growth potential of their investments to achieve retirement goals and protect against inflation. Though risky, some retirees may tolerate those disadvantages and conclude that the loss of upside potential is not worth the sacrifice.

Liquidity could also be a problem with insurance solutions when unexpected expenses arise. While some annuity products offer liquidity, there is generally a high cost for this flexibility. Efforts to gain liquidity can undermine the true advantages of annuitization. Partial annuitization helps free up other assets on the balance sheet from having to support spending needs, and this combination can work to provide a greater amount of true liquidity. As for a legacy, though the death benefit in an insurance contract may grow over time, it is unlikely to keep pace with inflation. Also, income annuities do not offer legacy benefits without additional riders, which reduce the power of mortality credits.

◉ Two Philosophies for Retirement Income Planning

Within the world of retirement income planning, the siloed nature of financial services between investments and insurance leads to two opposing philosophies about how to build a retirement plan. There is an old saying that if the only tool you have is a hammer, then everything starts to look like a nail. This tendency is alive as those on the investments side tend to view an investment portfolio as a solution for any problem, while those on the insurance side tend to view insurance products as the answer for any financial question.

While we have just reviewed the general benefits and disadvantages of the general categories of investments and insurance, it is worthwhile to dig deeper into how the two schools distinctly approach the retirement income challenge in an effort to bridge the gap between these two philosophies. Ultimately, we can integrate both philosophies into a comprehensive strategy that can promote more efficient overall retirement income planning and support more income and legacy.

As I said before, I distinguish the opposing schools as either *probability-based* (investments) or *safety-first* (insurance). Understanding the distinctions and thought processes of both schools is important; discussions about retirement income planning can become quite confusing. Each individual investor must ultimately identify which school can best support his or her financial and psychological needs for retirement.

Indeed, advocates of the two schools view retirement income planning differently. They provide opposite answers for basic questions such as:

- Can people effectively prioritize among different financial goals in retirement?
- What is the best way to invest financial assets for retirement income?
- Is there a sustainable spending rate from a portfolio of volatile assets?
- What role do income annuities play in a retirement income strategy?

As a basic introduction to these schools, a simple litmus test can be applied. Monte Carlo simulations are often used in financial planning contexts to gain a better understanding of the viability of a financial plan in the face of market and longevity risks. Suppose a Monte Carlo simulation identifies a retirement plan's chance of success as 90 percent. Both sides of the debate might accept this as the correct calculation from the software, but they will have dramatically different interpretations of what to do with this number.

For probability-based thinkers, a 90 percent chance is a more than reasonable starting point, and the retiree can proceed with the plan. It has a high likelihood of success, and that's enough for them. If future updates determine that the plan might be on course toward failure, a few changes, such as a small reduction in spending, should be sufficient to get the plan back on track.

Those identifying with the safety-first school, however, will not be comfortable with this level of risk, focusing instead on the 10 percent chance of failure. They make a distinction between essential expenses and discretionary expenses and seek a solution that practically eliminates the possibility of failure for meeting essential expenses. Jeopardizing success, they say, is only reasonable for discretionary expenses.

Financial service professionals and retirees should understand which school they most identify with and to what extent their own thinking might incorporate views from each school. Consumers of the financial services profession must understand whether they and their advisor are speaking the same language. Advisors able to communicate effectively from both sides will be more likely to deliver successful retirement income outcomes.

The Probability-Based School of Thought

Of the two approaches, the probability-based school of thought is probably the more familiar to the public and financial professionals. Its roots grow from research completed by California-based financial planner William Bengen in the 1990s. Bengen sought to determine the safe withdrawal rate from a financial portfolio over a long retirement. Though the term *safe withdrawal rate* uses the word *safe*, it is not part of the safety-first approach. The probability-based school uses "safe" in a historical context. The probability-based approach is more closely associated with the traditional concepts of wealth accumulation and investment management.

Probability-based models tend to focus on this concept of safe withdrawal rates, a concept that is rather foreign to the safety-first school of thought. Safe withdrawal rates are about systematic withdrawals from a volatile portfolio. The question is: how much can retirees withdraw from their savings, which are invested in a diversified portfolio, while still maintaining sufficient confidence that they can safely continue spending without running out of wealth?

In the early 1990s, William Bengen read misguided claims in the popular press that average portfolio returns could guide the calculation of sustainable retirement withdrawal rates. If stocks average 7 percent after inflation, then plugging a 7 percent return into a spreadsheet suggests that retirees could withdraw 7 percent each year without ever dipping into their principal. Bengen recognized the naïveté of ignoring the real-world volatility experienced around that 7 percent return, and he sought to determine what would have worked historically for hypothetical retirees at different points. He used data extending back to 1926 for US financial markets for his research, which introduced the concept of "sequence-of-returns risk" to the financial planning profession.

The problem he set up is simple: a new retiree makes plans for withdrawing some inflation-adjusted amount from his or her savings at the end of each year for a thirty-year retirement period. For a sixty-five-year-old, this leads to a maximum planning age of ninety-five, which Bengen felt was reasonably conservative. What is the highest withdrawal amount as a percentage of retirement date assets that, with inflation adjustments, will be sustainable for the full thirty years? He looked at rolling thirty-year periods from history (1926 to 1955, 1927 to 1956, etc.). He found that with a 50/50 asset allocation to stocks and bonds (the S&P 500 and intermediate-term government bonds), the worst-case scenario experienced in US history was for a hypothetical 1966 retiree who could have withdrawn 4.15 percent at most. Thus was born what is known as the "4 percent rule."

Bengen's work pointed out that sequence-of-returns risk will reduce safe, sustainable withdrawal rates below what is implied by the average portfolio return. Its popularity has coalesced into what we are calling the probability-based approach. It will be the focus of this book.

Next, we'll discuss probability-based answers to some basic retirement income planning questions.

How are goals prioritized?

The idea of using a safe withdrawal rate, as implied by the 4 percent rule, is that people don't retire until they have accumulated a sufficient level of assets that can meet their entire lifestyle goal by spending from their portfolio at the determined safe withdrawal rate. For instance, if someone seeks to spend $40,000 per year from his or her portfolio and is comfortable with spending at an initial 4 percent rate from assets, then the wealth accumulation target to allow retirement to commence is:

Wealth = Spending/Withdrawal Rate = 40,000/0.04 = $1,000,000

According to probability-based advocates, people identify lifestyle spending needs that must be met to fulfill the standard of living they have in mind for retirement. If they are unable to meet these lifestyle spending goals, they will view their retirement as a failure. Thus, the emphasis is on minimizing the probability of failure (or, conversely, maximizing the probability of success) for the overall lifestyle goal without concern for the potential magnitude of those failures when they happen. If retirees are generally more sensitive to the probability of meeting their goals than to the magnitude of their shortfall, then it hardly matters if they can spend only one-quarter or one-half less than their goal, because their lifestyle is severely diminished either way.

As suggested by the naming of the probability-based school, the objective is to develop a plan that will maximize the probability of success for meeting the overall lifestyle goal. For aggressive goals, an aggressive asset allocation may maximize success with the hope that an outsized return premium for stocks can be earned above bonds. Financial planners such as Michael Kitces and Jonathan Guyton argue that it is difficult for people to differentiate between essential needs and discretionary expenses, and that real people are not as blasé about meeting their "wants" (as opposed to needs) as safety-first advocates assume.

What is the investment approach?
The probability-based approach is based closely on the concepts of maximizing risk-adjusted returns from the perspective of the total portfolio. Asset allocation during retirement is generally defined in the same way during the accumulation phase—using modern portfolio theory (MPT) to identify a portfolio on the efficient frontier in terms of single-period trade-offs between risk and return. Different volatile asset classes that are not perfectly correlated are combined to create portfolios with lower volatility. The efficient frontier identifies the asset allocation combinations with the highest probability-weighted arithmetic average return (often called "expected return" in finance literature) for an acceptable level of

year-by-year volatility (often called "risk"). This is an assets-only analysis, and the investor's spending needs are not part of the decision calculus for determining asset allocation. In addition, inputs for the efficient frontier are generally estimated from historical data. With MPT, investors aim to maximize wealth by seeking the highest possible returns given their capacity and tolerance for risk over a specific time horizon.

For retirement planning, spending and asset allocation recommendations are based on historical or Monte Carlo simulations of failure rates in order to mitigate the risk of wealth depletion inherent in drawing down a portfolio of volatile assets. The failure rate is the probability that wealth is depleted before death or before the end of the fixed time horizon, which stands in for a maximum feasible lifespan. Asset allocation decisions are generally guided by what can minimize the failure rate in retirement. Advocates of the probability-based approach take this as license to use more aggressive asset allocations than seen elsewhere (such as the rule of thumb that bond allocation should be equal to one's age).

Advice from Bengen and subsequent studies is to have a stock allocation between 50 and 75 percent, but as close as possible to the higher end. Probability-based advocates are generally more optimistic about the long-run potential of stocks to outperform bonds and provide positive real returns, so investors are generally advised to take on as much risk as they can tolerate in order to minimize the probability of failure.

Probability advocates generally see little value in income annuities. Income annuities have no upside potential, a cost these advocates view as too high regardless of the safety the income annuity provides. Especially with today's low interest rates, building a lifetime floor in such a way can be seen as unnecessarily expensive. Income annuities may protect a person from destitution, but, probability-based advocates argue, they could also lock out the ability to enjoy the higher quality of life people desire for their retirement.

Most retirees will not have saved enough to safely immunize their entire lifestyle spending goals through only bond ladders and income annuities while still maintaining sufficient remaining wealth to create a liquid contingency fund for unexpected expenses. If a retiree's desired withdrawal rate is above what can be generated with the bond yield curve, a bond portfolio will not be able to meet his or her spending goals. Bonds would actually become a drag on the portfolio, as they offer no chance at the types of returns needed to fund the retiree's desired lifestyle. It is the same if the spending goal exceeds what can be obtained with an income annuity. Equity exposure moves retirees away from the guarantee that their plan will work, but it might provide the only opportunity for them to meet all their aspirations. This aspect of probability maximization through a diversified portfolio is why we refer to this school of thought as "probability-based."

What is the safe withdrawal rate from a diversified portfolio of volatile assets? Users of safe withdrawal rates generally treat 4 percent as a reasonably safe worst-case sustainable withdrawal rate for a thirty-year retirement period, although they acknowledge that a new worst-case scenario could force that number lower. Bengen now speaks regularly about 4.5 percent as the safe withdrawal rate, a result of also including small-capitalization stocks in the portfolio mix. He is confident that US history provides a good guide about worst-case scenarios, since his analysis period includes the Great Depression, a world war, and the stagnation of the 1970s.

If people can meet lifestyle goals using a safe withdrawal rate determined from history, they can be reasonably confident about their retirement, too. Also, in all but this worst-case scenario—so the argument goes—retirees will enjoy further upside as the portfolio grows when using a conservative withdrawal rate.

Regarding upside, Kitces and Bengen both reference—as a statement of confidence in safe withdrawal rates—the fact that in 96 percent of the US historical simulations, the value of assets remaining after thirty years was higher than the retirement date amount (although this is not adjusted for inflation). Ultimately, the idea is to retire when you can meet your spending goals from your portfolio using what you consider to be a safe withdrawal rate.

The Safety-First School of Thought

The safety-first school of thought was originally derived from academic models of how people allocate their resources over a lifetime to maximize lifetime satisfaction. Academics have studied these models since the

1920s to figure out how rational people make optimal decisions. In the retirement context, the question to be answered is how to get the most lifetime satisfaction from limited financial resources. It is the basic fundamental question of economics: how do you optimize in the face of scarcity? In more recent history, Nobel Prize winners such as Paul Samuelson, Robert Merton, Franco Modigliani, and William Sharpe have explored these models.

Safety-first comes from a more academic foundation, so it is often described with mathematical equations in academic journals. As a result, it has been slow to enter the public consciousness. The safety-first approach is probably best associated with Professor Zvi Bodie from Boston University, whose popular books such as *Worry-Free Investing* and *Risk Less and Prosper* have brought these ideas alive to the public. Michael Zwecher's Retirement Portfolios is also an excellent resource written for financial professionals about this school of thought.

How are goals prioritized?
Advocates of the safety-first approach view prioritization of retirement goals as an essential component of developing a good retirement income strategy. The investment strategy aims to match the risk characteristics of assets and goals, so prioritization is a must.

Prioritizing goals has its academic origins in the idea of utility maximization. As people spend more, they experience diminishing marginal value with each additional dollar spent. The spending required to satisfy basic needs provides much more value and satisfaction to someone than the additional spending on luxuries after basic needs are met. Retirees should plan to smooth spending over time to avoid overspending on luxuries in one year and being unable to afford essentials later.

In developing Modern Retirement Theory, financial planner Jason Branning and academic M. Ray Grubbs created a funding priority for retiree liabilities. Essential needs are the top priority, then a contingency fund, funds for discretionary expenses, and a legacy fund. They illustrate these funding priorities with a pyramid. Building a retirement strategy requires working from the bottom to properly fund each goal before moving up to the next. There is no consideration of discretionary expenses or providing a legacy until a secure funding source for essential needs and contingencies is in place.

What is the investment approach?
Traditionally, investing in the accumulation phase has built on the tools of modern portfolio theory (MPT) and portfolio diversification to find a suitable balance between investment returns and the volatility of those returns. Investors seek strategies that will support the highest expected wealth, subject to the investor's tolerance and capacity to endure downward fluctuations in the portfolio value. But this was never the complete story. In 1991, Nobel laureate and MPT founder Harry Markowitz wrote in the first issue of *Financial Services Review* about how MPT was never meant to apply to the investment problems of a household. Rather, it was for large institutions with indefinite lifespans and no specific spending objectives for the portfolio. This should have been a eureka moment for the entire retirement income industry, but MPT is still misapplied today.

People have finite lifespans. The purpose of saving and investing is to fund spending during retirement. MPT does not address this more complicated issue. The alternative is asset-liability matching, which focuses more holistically at the household level and also emphasizes hedging and insurance. In simple terms, hedging means holding individual bonds to maturity, and insurance means using income annuities as a solution for longevity and market risk.

With asset-liability matching, investors are not trying to maximize their year-to-year returns on a risk-adjusted basis, nor are they trying to beat an investing benchmark. The goal is to have cash flows available to meet spending needs as required, and investments are chosen in a way that meets those needs. Assets are matched to goals so that the risk and cash-flow characteristics are comparable. For essential spending, Modern Retirement Theory argues that funding must be with assets meeting the criteria of being "secure, stable, and sustainable." Funding options can include defined-benefit pensions, bond ladders, and income annuities. In this regard, another important aspect of the investment approach for the safety-first school is that investing decisions are made in the context of the entire retirement balance sheet. This moves beyond looking only at the financial portfolio to consider also the role of human and social capital. Examples of human and social capital include the ability to work part-time, pensions, the social safety net, and so on.

An important point is that volatile assets are seen as inappropriate for basic needs and the contingency fund. Stated again, the objective of investing in retirement is not to maximize risk-adjusted returns, but first to ensure that basics will be covered in any market environment and then to invest for additional upside. Volatile (and hopefully, but not necessarily, higher returning) assets are suitable for discretionary expenses and legacy, in which there is some flexibility about whether the spending can be achieved.

Asset allocation, therefore, is an output of the analysis, as the entire retirement balance sheet is used and assets are allocated to match appropriately with the household's liabilities. Asset-liability matching removes the probability-based concept of safe withdrawal rates from the analysis, since it rejects relying on a diversified portfolio for the entire lifestyle goal.

The idea is to first build a floor of very low-risk guaranteed income sources to serve your basic spending needs in retirement. The guaranteed income floor is built with Social Security and any other defined-benefit pensions, and through the use of your financial assets to do things such as building a ladder of TIPS or purchasing an income annuity. Not all of these income sources are inflation adjusted, and you need to make sure the floor is sufficiently protected from inflation, but this is the basic idea.

Once there is a sufficient floor in place, you can focus on upside potential. With any remaining assets, you can invest and spend as you wish. Since this extra spending (such as for nice restaurants, extra vacations, etc.) is discretionary, it won't be the end of the world if you must reduce spending at some point. You still have your guaranteed income floor in place to meet your basic needs no matter what happens. With this sort of approach, withdrawal rates hardly matter.

What is the safe withdrawal rate from a diversified portfolio of volatile assets?
The general view of safety-first advocates is that there is no such thing as a safe withdrawal rate from a volatile portfolio. A truly safe withdrawal rate is unknown and unknowable. Retirees only receive one opportunity to obtain sustainable cash flows from their savings and must develop a strategy that will meet basic needs no matter the length of life or the sequence of postretirement market returns and inflation. Retirees have little leeway for error, as returning to the labor force might not be a

realistic option. Volatile assets like stocks are not appropriate when seeking to meet basic retirement living expenses. Just because a strategy did not fail over a historical period does not ensure it will always succeed in the future.

The objective for retirement is first to build a safe and secure income floor for the entire retirement planning horizon, and only after that should you include more volatile assets that provide greater upside potential and accompanying risk. In terms of this floor for essentials and contingencies, pensions, bond ladders, and income annuities should take the lead. Failure should not be an option when meeting basic needs. Thus, income annuities serve as a fundamental building block for retirement income.

Income annuities are especially valuable because of their ability to provide longevity protection through the provision of mortality credits. People do not know their age of death in advance. They can learn about their remaining life expectancy, but that is just a projection of the average outcome, and there is a surprisingly large distribution of actual lifespans around the average. Individual retirees cannot self-insure to protect from longevity risk, and without annuitization they are obliged to plan for a long lifespan.

The annuity provider, however, can pool longevity risk across a large group of retirees, and those who die earlier than average subsidize payments to those who live longer than average. These are mortality credits. Because the annuity provider can pool the longevity risk, they are able to make payments at a rate much closer to what would be possible when planning for remaining life expectancy. A retiree seeking to self-annuitize must assume a time horizon extending well beyond life expectancy (such as thirty years with the 4 percent rule), to better hedge against the consequences of living beyond his or her planning age. A retiree must spend less when on the self-annuitize path.

◉ Retirement Income Strategies

This discussion of the two schools of thought highlights that retirement income planning is a field in flux. Exhibit 1.5 illustrates this matter with just a sampling of different retirement income planning techniques used in practice today. The exhibit includes thirty-six possibilities, which I have

Exhibit 1.5

Retirement Income Strategies

Probability-Based Approaches

Total Returns / Constant Spending	Total Returns / Variable Spending	Time Segmentation
Safe Withdrawal Rates (W. Bengen, Trinity Study, M. Kitces)	Fixed Percentage Withdrawals (W. Bengen)	Age Banding (S. Basu)
Safe Savings Rates (W. Pfau, inStream)	Desired and Maximum Distribution with Spending Rules (inStream)	Asset Dedication (J. Burns; S. Huxley)
Cash Flow Management (H. Evensky, D. Katz)	Decision Rules and Guardrails (J. Guyton, W. Klinger)	Income Discovery (M. Malhotra)
Rising Equity Glide path (M. Kitces, W. Pfau)	Floor and Ceiling (W. Bengen)	Wealth 2K (D. Macchia)
	IRS RMD Rule (A. Webb, W. Sun)	
	PMT Formula (D. Blanchett, L. Frank, J. Mitchell, M. Waring, L. Siegel)	
	Target Percentage Adjustment (D. Zolt)	
	Endowment Spending Policies	
	Actuarial Approach (K. Steiner)	

Safety-First Approaches

Utility Maximization / Dynamic Programming	Locked-In (Lifetime) Flooring	At-Risk Flooring
Product Allocation and Efficient Frontiers (M. Milevsky, P. Chen, Morningstar, M. Warshawsky, W. Pfau)		
Bequest Value vs. Shortfall Value (J. Tomlinson)	Dimensional Managed DC (R. Merton, Z. Bodie)	R-MAP (M. Lonier)
Spending on the Planet Vulcan (M. Milevsky and H. Huang)	Household Balance Sheet Management (M. Zwecher, RIIA)	
Lifecycle Finance (P. Samuelson, R. Merton, Z. Bodie, L. Kotlikoff)	Modern Retirement Theory (J. Branning, M. Ray Grubbs)	Funded Ratio Management (Russell Investments)
Financial Guidance Theory (H. Markowitz)	Safety-First Goals-Based Approach (Z. Bodie, R. Toqqu)	
ESPlanner (L. Kotlikoff)	TIPS & Deferred Income Annuities (S. Gowri Shankar, S. Sexauer et al.)	
Financial Engines (W. Sharpe, J. Scott, J. Watson)	Floor-Leverage Rule (J. Scott, J. Watson)	
Dynamically Adapting Asset Allocation and Withdrawal Rates (J.P. Morgan)	Thrive Distribution (C. Cloke)	
Asset Allocation Calculator (G. Irlam)	Liability Matching Portfolios (W. Bernstein)	

attempted to differentiate in part by whether they have characteristics more similar to the probability-based or safety-first philosophy.

Many more strategies could be listed in the "Total Returns/Variable Spending" category, as it seems almost every financial services company is developing a retirement income strategy these days. Most of the excluded strategies would be difficult to distinguish from what is already on the list, though.

My aim is to simplify this list by narrowing down the options to some core attributes that can serve as best practices. I have studied all of these different approaches and tried to draw what is best from each to build an overall framework to guide retirement income planning.

Ultimately, I believe Exhibit 1.6 provides a proper summary of how to approach the retirement income problem. This exhibit draws on attributes from the safety-first approach to consider the entire retirement balance sheet and to match assets and liabilities. It is most inspired by ideas found within Modern Retirement Theory, the household balance sheet view,

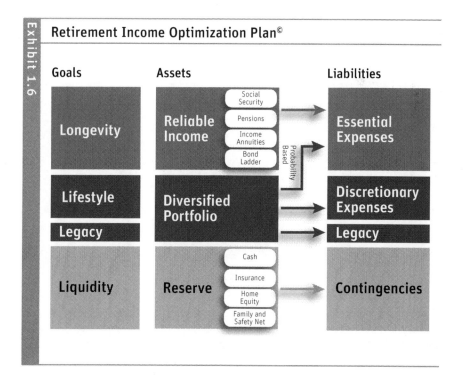

Exhibit 1.6

Retirement Income Optimization Plan©

Goals	Assets		Liabilities
Longevity	Reliable Income	Social Security / Pensions / Income Annuities / Bond Ladder	Essential Expenses
Lifestyle	Diversified Portfolio		Discretionary Expenses
Legacy			Legacy
Liquidity	Reserve	Cash / Insurance / Home Equity / Family and Safety Net	Contingencies

Probability Based

funded ratio management, and product allocation. At the same time, this approach is not overly regimented and includes both probability-based and safety-first plans, as the relative sizes of the reliable income and diversified portfolio boxes can be adjusted to create a plan that meets the psychological needs of the individual implementing it.

The remainder of this book is about implementing the probability-based approach in practice. This book is relevant for those who plan to fund their retirements using an investment portfolio, and who are hesitant about using income annuities or other insurance products. I will explore the safety-first approach more extensively in a later volume to be published as part of the Retirement Researcher's Guide Series.

Further Reading

Bodie, Zvi, and Michael J. Clowes. 2003. *Worry-Free Investing: A Safe Approach to Achieving Your Lifetime Financial Goals.* Upper Saddle River, NJ: Financial Times Prentice Hall. [http://amzn.to/2mWqdUG]

Bodie, Zvi, and Rachelle Taqqu. 2012. *Risk Less and Prosper: Your Guide to Safer Investing.* Hoboken, NJ: John Wiley. [http://amzn.to/2sjgBFT]

Branning, Jason K., and M. Ray Grubbs. 2010. "Using a Hierarchy of Funds to Reach Client Goals." *Journal of Financial Planning* 23 (12): 31–33.

Kitces, Michael. 2011. "What Happens if You Outlive Your Safe Withdrawal Rate Time Horizon?" *Nerd's Eye View* (blog).

Zwecher, Michael J. 2010. *Retirement Portfolios: Theory, Construction, and Management.* Hoboken, NJ: John Wiley. [http://amzn.to/2uOcbRA]

CHAPTER 2

Sustainable Spending Rates with Fixed Returns and Known Longevity

One of the most hotly contested debates in personal finance is over the safe withdrawal rate for retirement. How much can you expect to spend sustainably from your investments? This question can drive you to madness, perhaps because it brings up a fundamental reality about our existence: we cannot predict the future, especially when it comes to financial markets. We also do not know how long we will live. What do we need to do to be safe?

The problem with trying to determine a sustainable spending rate from an investment portfolio is that retirees must manage a number of different types of risk when deciding how much to spend. The three basic risks for retirees are longevity risk, market risk, and spending shocks. Longevity risk relates to not knowing how long one will live and, therefore, how long wealth must last. Market risk relates to the possibility that poor market returns deplete available wealth and reduce the sustainable standard of living. Spending shocks are surprise expenses from outside the planned budget, such as for long-term care and major health expenses, which require a pool of contingency assets beyond what are being used to support the expected portion of living expenses. Retirement will be cheaper with some combination of a shorter life, strong market returns, and few spending shocks. But retirement could become quite expensive when a long life is combined with poor market returns and significant spending shocks.

To better understand what is at stake, let's take a step back to first focus only on how sustainable spending relates to a known retirement length and a fixed portfolio return. We will not worry yet about longevity risk, market volatility, or spending shocks, because there is still a lot we can learn with a simple framework when lifespan and market returns are fixed and known.

We can use a basic spreadsheet program, such as Microsoft Excel, or a business calculator to understand the basic relationships between sustainable spending, time horizon, and an investment return. All of our analysis about systematic withdrawals will fundamentally tie into a few basic formulas. First, using the notation of Microsoft Excel, the PMT formula allows us to calculate the sustainable amount of spending in retirement. This formula is defined as:

$$=PMT(rate,nper,pv,fv,type)$$

The variable *rate* is the assumed investment return in decimal form, *nper* is the number of periods (I usually think in terms of years) that the nest egg should last, *pv* is the amount you have saved at retirement, and *fv* is the amount you wish to be able to take out for a legacy at the end of retirement (counterintuitively, it needs to have a negative sign if you want to have money left over at the end). It is more conservative to set *type* to a value of 1 to reflect that you will take your distributions at the start of each time period. For instance,

$$=PMT(0.0133,30,1000000,0,1)$$

will provide you with an answer of $40,109, meaning if you assume an inflation-adjusted compounding investment return of 1.33 percent, want your money to last thirty years, start with $1 million, want to end up with $0, and take your distributions at the start of each year, then you can sustainably spend $40,109, with subsequent inflation adjustments for your yearly spending amount. I say that inflation adjustments are allowed because I am thinking of the 1.33 percent return as a real or after-inflation return. As a percentage of initial assets, that is just slightly above a 4 percent spending rate.

With all else being equal, if you increase the value of *rate* (your investment return), then you can increase the sustainable spending amount. For instance, replace 1.33 percent with 7 percent in the function, and the spending answer jumps to $75,314. This represents a 7.53 percent withdrawal percentage from initial assets. Perhaps surprisingly as well, with a 7 percent return assumption, if you wanted to fully preserve the purchasing power of your initial retirement portfolio after thirty years (which requires putting in a value of -1000000 for *fv*), the sustainable spending rate falls only to 6.54 percent.

Another formula in Excel is NPER, which provides a variation on this theme. It works the same way as PMT, but in this case you input how much you wish to spend, and the formula tells you how long your money will last. Moshe Milevsky suggested in his article "It's Time to Retire Ruin (Probabilities)" from the March/April 2016 issue of the *Financial Analysts Journal* that this formula will be a good starting point for understanding how our spending assumptions impact portfolio sustainability (though he actually expressed the formula in terms of calculus, rather than as an Excel function). NPER is expressed as:

=NPER(rate,pmt,pv,fv,type)

So, reflecting the first problem we investigated above,

=NPER(0.0133,-40109,1000000,0,1)

will give us an answer of thirty years. With a 1.33 percent real return, we can spend an inflation-adjusted $40,109 from a $1 million portfolio sustainably for thirty years and be left with nothing at the end of that period.

If we wished to spend $80,000 and keep the other assumptions, NPER would inform us that our portfolio would only last for 13.6 years before depletion. Milevsky likes to start with this formula because he believes it provides a more useful reality check about a spending plan. Will the portfolio last for as long as you intend? In the context of sustainable spending from available assets, the only way to increase the portfolio's longevity is to assume a higher investment return or a lower spending amount. Increasing the return assumption by too much endangers the plan, as it will become increasingly difficult for that return to be met in practice.

Incidentally, the RATE function in Excel works in the same basic way as these two formulas, instead telling us the rate of return we would require to meet our *pmt* spending objective for *nper* years. If the implied rate of return is seemingly too high, this formula makes clear that either the level of spending must be reduced or spending will not last for as long as desired.

These formulas provide useful starting points to understand retirement spending because they clearly link spending amounts, rates of return, and time horizons. This is the heart of the sustainable spending problem: spend more, and your money will not last as long. But these fundamentally important links are easy to lose sight of later when we enter the world of the "4 percent rule" for retirement spending.

With these functions, the task becomes to determine appropriate values for the underlying inputs. How much do we want to be able to spend? How long should our spending strategy work? What is a reasonable rate of return assumption for our portfolio? How much should we try to leave at the end of the time horizon? We have to answer these questions within the context of retirement risk: how likely is it that we outlive our planning age, and what happens if the market returns are less than we assumed?

The answer, invariably, is that spending will have to be reduced at some point later in retirement. We must also consider the impact of a potential spending reduction in terms of how much it lowers our standard of living. With enough income sources from outside the portfolio and with greater flexibility to adjust spending in response to market performance, we may be more willing to accept potential late-in-life reductions for our portfolio spending.

Returning to an earlier example, we saw that a 7 percent rate of return would allow for a 7.53 percent initial spending rate for a thirty-year retirement. That was the state of analysis in the mid-1990s when William Bengen came onto the scene and his research led him to coin the 4 percent spending rule. If the long-term average real compounding return from the stock market is 7 percent, does that really mean you can safely use a 7.5 percent withdrawal rate from a 100 percent stocks portfolio without worrying about running out of wealth for thirty years? No, it does not.

Stocks do not earn their average real return each year. Some years they go up, and some years they go down, as recent investors know all too well. For a retiree who is taking distributions from savings, the sequence of market returns matters. If a retiree's portfolio drops in value during the early retirement period, portfolio withdrawals will dig a further hole. Climbing out of this hole becomes increasingly difficult, even if a subsequent market recovery arrives. This is sequence-of-returns risk. Sequence risk amplifies the impact of traditional investment volatility, meaning that the *rate* assumption in the above formulas has to be further reduced to improve the odds that the plan will work.

The debate today is over whether Bengen took the analysis far enough to provide a sufficiently conservative projection for the safe withdrawal rate. Is a thirty-year planning horizon appropriate for today's retirees? Is it appropriate to assume retirees can annually rebalance and maintain a rather aggressive stock allocation and precisely earn the underlying market returns net of fees and taxes? While a 4 percent spending rate represents the worst-case outcome using US historical data, how do we reflect that we have very little experience with what happens when people retire at times when interest rates are at such low levels as today, while stock market valuations are also well above their historical averages? On the other hand, inflation is also quite low now. What implications does this have? How does spending flexibility impact all of this analysis? We will consider these matters throughout.

◉ Choosing a Portfolio Return Assumption

For a lifetime financial plan, the most intuitive way to express a portfolio return assumption is as an inflation-adjusted compounding return. Unfortunately, this is not the most common way returns are expressed. A quick review of the steps needed to arrive at a real compounded return for a portfolio, as well as other adjustments that may be needed to create a properly conservative portfolio return assumption, is in order. This will provide a backdrop for reasonable returns to anchor to in later exhibits.

I will illustrate the process by first focusing on the compounded real returns generated historically since 1926 by a 50/50 asset allocation to large-capitalization US stocks (the S&P 500) and intermediate-term US government bonds (ITGB). This is displayed in Exhibit 2.1.

Exhibit 2.1

Components of Portfolio Return Assumptions

	S&P 500	ITGB
Average (Arithmetic) Return	12.0%	5.3%
<- impact of volatility ->		
Compounded Return	10.0%	5.1%
<- impact of inflation ->		
Real Compounded Return	6.9%	2.2%
<- impact of asset allocation ->		

Portfolio Characteristics Based on Historical Data

50/50 Portfolio Real Arithmetic Return	5.6%
50/50 Portfolio Real Compounded Return	5.1%
50/50 Annual Volatility	10.7%
<- impact of current interest rates ->	
Real Yield on 5-Year TIPS (January 2017)	0.1%

Portfolio Characteristics Adjusted for Current Interest Rates

50/50 Portfolio Real Arithmetic Return	3.5%
50/50 Portfolio Real Compounded Return	2.7%
50/50 Annual Volatility	10.7%

Source: Own calculations from Stocks, Bonds, Bills, and Inflation data provided by Morningstar and Ibbotson Associates, covering 1926–2016. Other potential adjustments suggested to these numbers for real-world investors include for taxes, investment fees, investor over- or underperformance relative to these benchmark indexes, and a desire to have greater confidence than an average outcome.

For the period from 1926 through 2016, Morningstar data reveals that the S&P 500 enjoyed an average (arithmetic) return of 12 percent, while intermediate-term government bonds earned 5.3 percent.

When simulating long-term financial plans, we also have to account for volatility and the lack of symmetry in outcomes for positive and negative returns. We calculate the compounded returns over time to account for this volatility. The S&P 500 compounded return fell to 10 percent, while the compounded real return for the less volatile bonds fell only slightly to 5.1 percent. These compounded returns express the growth rate for a portfolio over a number of years, while the larger arithmetic average returns represent the growth rate only for a single year. Compounded returns are smaller than the arithmetic returns because a portfolio loss must be followed by a greater portfolio gain in order to get back to the same starting point. For instance, if a portfolio loses 50 percent of its value, then from this new lower point it must gain 100 percent (not 50 percent) to get back to its initial starting level. At least one popular radio host likes to imply that his listeners' stock portfolios will grow at 12 percent, but this is a misunderstanding on his part. It is the compounded return, not the arithmetic return, that matters for the long-run growth of a portfolio.

But we are still not done. Next, we must remove inflation so the numbers allow for a better understanding of purchasing power growth. Real returns will be less, because they preserve the purchasing power of wealth over time. The real compounded returns fell to 6.9 percent and 2.2 percent, respectively. Though not shown in the exhibit, the real historical arithmetic returns for stocks and bonds were 8.9 percent and 2.4 percent, respectively.

The next step is to consider asset allocation. Though many articles about long-term investing will assume 8 or 12 percent returns, this implicitly suggests that the investor holds 100 percent stocks. That will rarely be the case, especially for retirees. Consider, instead, a retiree with a 50/50 portfolio rebalanced annually. For the historical data, the estimated arithmetic real return from the 50/50 portfolio was 5.6 percent, and the standard deviation for returns was 10.7 percent. The compounded real return was 5.1 percent for a 50/50 portfolio.

For some, the 5.1 percent real return might be a properly adjusted starting point for a portfolio return assumption to project retirement outcomes. We are getting closer. However, there are still a number of further adjustments we must consider to provide realistic expectations about what may happen in retirement, such as incorporating taxes on interest and dividends, accounting for the fact that today's interest rates are much lower than historical averages, accounting for the impact of investment management fees, and considering the possibility of outperformance or underperformance with respect to the underlying market indexes.

Also of utmost importance is making a downward adjustment to increase the probability that the assumed return will be met. For a best guess about the forward-looking compounded real return, there is still a 50 percent chance that the actual realized return will be lower. Retirees generally focus on building a plan with a high probability of success, which implicitly means they must assume a lower return than average. How should we adjust our return assumptions to account for this aspect of risk? This is an important matter that we will revisit in the next chapter.

For the time being, Exhibit 2.1 does also include a further adjustment for today's low interest rate environment. With a yield to maturity of 0.1 percent on five-year Treasury Inflation-Protected Securities (TIPS) at the start of 2017, the real interest rate as I write is about 2.1 percent less than the historical average compounded real return on intermediate-term government bonds. Accounting for lower interest rates but maintaining the same historical premium that stocks have earned above bonds, the exhibit provides an arithmetic real return of 3.5 percent and a compounded real return of 2.7 percent for a 50/50 portfolio with the same historical volatility. These returns are much less than 8 to 12 percent, and they should serve as the anchor for choosing a realistic fixed-return assumption.

◉ Choosing the Planning Age (Length of Retirement)

Longevity risk—the risk of running out of assets before running out of time—is fundamental to retirement. We know about the distribution of longevity for the overall population, but an individual cannot know in advance precisely where he or she will fall in the distribution. The length of your retirement could be much shorter or longer than your statistical life expectancy. Half of the population will outlive their median life expectancy—some will live far beyond it. A long life is wonderful, but it is expensive. For how long should you build your retirement plan to last?

In a probability-based world, the available means for an individual to manage longevity risk is to choose a conservative planning horizon for which there is a sufficiently low probability to outlive. This will require spending less so that available assets can be drawn out for a longer period of time. The probability of surviving to advanced ages is low. Individuals must determine how low of spending they are willing to accept today in their effort to plan for a longer life and better ensure that they will not deplete their assets before death.

As a first step to measuring longevity risk, it is important to understand what the data says about mortality and survivorship rates. Different data sources provide different longevity estimates for several key reasons:

1. From what age is life expectancy being measured?

Life expectancy at birth is the most familiar number, though it is of little relevance for someone reaching retirement. If you have reached age sixty-five, then an obvious point to note is that you did not die prior to age sixty-five. As obvious as it might be, this is important information. Your life expectancy conditional upon reaching age sixty-five is not the same as your life expectancy at birth. As you age, your remaining life expectancy increases. The remaining number of years one can expect to live decreases, but not on a one-to-one basis with age. This matter leads individuals to underestimate how long they may live in retirement, and we must keep in mind from which age life expectancy is being measured.

2. Is life expectancy calculated from current year mortality rates or projected future mortality rates?

Probably the most commonly used source of mortality data is the Social Security Administration's (SSA) Period Life Tables. A period life table makes calculations about remaining lifetimes using the mortality data from one year. For instance, calculations for the life expectancy of a sixty-five-year-old would use the year's mortality rates for different ages in that one year. How many seventy-year-olds died that year? Eighty-year-olds? And so on. This method has the advantage of using actual data without requiring any sort of projections, but it is bound to underestimate life expectancies on account of the persistent trends of increasing life expectancies over time.

Exhibit 2.2 provides period life table historical data from the Centers for Disease Control to show remaining life expectancies for males and females at different points in history. Between 1950 and 2010, the additional remaining years expected after age sixty-five increase by 4.9 years for males and 5.3 years for females. Much of these gains took place more recently. Over the course of twenty years—from 1990 to 2010—males reaching sixty-five added 2.6 more years, while females could expect 1.4 more years. Though demographers debate extensively whether humans have reached

Exhibit 2.2

Historical Data for Remaining Life Expectancy at Age 65

	Male	Female
1950	12.8	15.0
1960	12.8	15.8
1970	13.1	17.0
1980	14.1	18.3
1990	15.1	18.9
2000	16.0	19.0
2010	17.7	20.3

Source: Centers for Disease Control
http://www.cdc.gov/nchs/data/hus/2011/022.pdf

the peak of our potential longevity, or whether we are on the verge of seeing someone make it to 150, it is reasonable for planning purposes to at least expect such longevity trends to continue. If longevity improves by about one year per decade, today's thirty-five-year-olds could expect to live three years longer than today's sixty-five-year-olds.

Instead of using period life tables, a better alternative is to use a cohort life table, which tracks mortality for the same individual over time. When a sixty-five-year-old in 2017 turns eighty-five in 2037, his mortality rate at eighty-five will most likely be lower than that of an eighty-five-year-old in 2017. A cohort life table uses projections for future mortality improvements when calculating life expectancies. Cohort life tables will project longer lives and are surely a better choice for considering longevity when building a retirement income plan. A practical implication is that if you are basing your own longevity on how long your parents lived, then you are probably underestimating it by ignoring the persistent improvements over time.

3. What is the underlying population for which mortality and survivorship is being calculated?

It may seem natural to base calculations on the aggregate US population—as is done with the Social Security Administration life tables—but clear socioeconomic differences have been identified in mortality rates. Higher income levels and more education both correlate with longer lifespans.

This may not be a matter of causation (i.e., more income and education cause people to live longer), but perhaps some underlying personality trait leads some people to have a more long-term focus, and that in turn may lead them to seek more education and practice better health habits. The very fact that you are reading this somewhat technical tome on retirement income suggests you probably have a longer-term focus and can expect to live longer than the average person.

In this case, mortality data based on population-wide averages will underestimate your longevity. This is not because I think my readers are all from Lake Wobegon (where everyone is above average); rather, it is because of the important links between income, education, long-term planning, and health. Not everyone will live longer, as unfortunate accidents and illnesses will inevitably befall some along the way. But in a statistical sense, my average reader will live longer than the average person.

The Society of Actuaries (SOA) produced the 2012 Individual Annuity Mortality tables that I think will best reflect the situation for my readers. Their mortality data is for annuity purchasers, who tend to live longer than average. Those with significant illnesses tend to avoid buying annuities. The data also reflects estimates for future mortality improvements and is not based only on the situation in one year.

Exhibit 2.3 helps clarify the distinction between different mortality data sets by showing some key numbers estimated from the Social Security life table and the Society of Actuaries data. I focus on the probability of survival from age sixty-five for males, females, and at least one member of a same-aged couple for different combinations of gender. I also provide life expectancy estimates from age sixty-five for each of these groups.

In terms of remaining life expectancy at sixty-five, the Society of Actuaries data generally shows individuals living about four to five years longer. With SSA data, men can expect to live 17.8 more years to 82.8, while women can expect 20.3 more years to 85.3. For an opposite-sex couple, the longest-living member can expect 24.1 more years to age 89.1, on average. Incidentally, these numbers are 22.7 years for two males and 25.3 years for two females. Meanwhile, with the SOA data, men are looking at life expectancies of 87.6, women of 89.3, and 93.6 for the longest-living member of an opposite-sex couple.

Exhibit 2.3

Longevity Statistics for 65-Year-Olds Using Two Data Sources

		Male	Female	At Least One Member of a Couple		
				One Male, One Female	Two Males	Two Females
Social Security 2013 Periodic Life Table						
Probability of Living to Age:	70	91%	94%	99%	99%	100%
	75	79%	85%	97%	96%	98%
	80	63%	73%	90%	86%	92%
	85	43%	55%	74%	67%	80%
	90	22%	33%	48%	39%	55%
	95	7%	13%	20%	14%	25%
	100	1%	3%	4%	2%	6%
Remaining Life Expectancy		17.8	20.3	24.1	22.7	25.3
Society of Actuaries 2012 Individual Annuity Mortality with Projected Improvements for a 2017 Start Date						
Probability of Living to Age:	70	95%	96%	100%	100%	100%
	75	89%	91%	99%	99%	99%
	80	80%	84%	97%	96%	97%
	85	66%	71%	90%	88%	92%
	90	45%	52%	74%	70%	77%
	95	22%	29%	45%	39%	50%
	100	6%	10%	16%	12%	20%
Remaining Life Expectancy		22.6	24.3	28.6	27.7	29.4

Exhibit 2.3 also illustrates longevity risk by showing the probability of survival to different ages beyond sixty-five. For instance, with SSA data, 91 percent of men are still alive by age seventy (i.e., 9 percent did not live to their seventieth birthday), 63 percent are still alive at eighty, and 22 percent are still alive at ninety. With retirement planning, the trouble is knowing what age to plan for, as this distribution is quite wide.

But more relevant for readers—again because the data reflects people with more similar backgrounds as well as projected improvements in mortality—

are the numbers from the SOA data, with mortality improvements projected for a starting year of 2017. The probability of a sixty-five-year-old reaching age ninety-five is 22 percent for males, 29 percent for females, and 45 percent for at least one member of an opposite-gender couple.

In 1994, William Bengen chose thirty years as a conservative planning horizon for a sixty-five-year-old couple when he discussed sustainable retirement spending. But as mortality improves over time, this planning horizon is becoming less conservative. A thirty-year time horizon is not so conservative when we look at data that better reflects higher earning and more highly educated individuals.

Exhibit 2.4 illustrates this longevity risk for a sixty-five-year-old who builds a retirement plan using a thirty-year planning horizon. Again, the probability of outliving this time horizon is not insignificant. The probability of a sixty-five-year-old reaching age ninety-five is 22 percent for male annuitants, 29 percent for female annuitants, and 45 percent for at least one member of an opposite-gender annuitant couple. Longevity risk is the risk of living longer than anticipated and not having the resources to sustain spending for a longer lifetime.

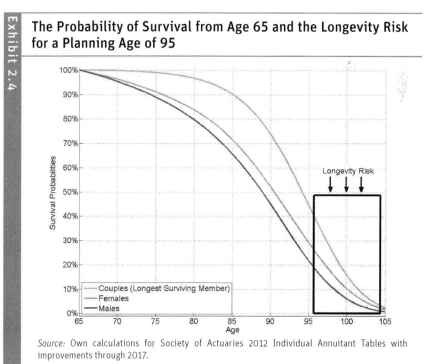

The Probability of Survival from Age 65 and the Longevity Risk for a Planning Age of 95

Source: Own calculations for Society of Actuaries 2012 Individual Annuitant Tables with improvements through 2017.

Next, Exhibit 2.5 uses survival data to calculate the distribution for the actual age of death for sixty-five-year-olds. This is the probability that each age will serve as your last. The exhibit helps highlight the uncertainties around longevity risk. For instance, 10 percent of males will have died by 74.3, the median age is 88.9, and 10 percent are still alive by 98.4. The corresponding numbers for females are 75.8, 90.5, and 100.1. These wide ranges can make planning difficult.

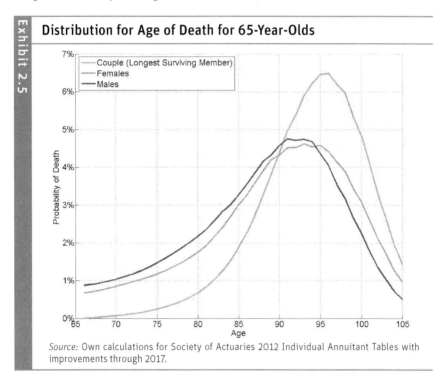

Exhibit 2.5

Distribution for Age of Death for 65-Year-Olds

Source: Own calculations for Society of Actuaries 2012 Individual Annuitant Tables with improvements through 2017.

Continuing with the theme of longevity being conditional on age, Exhibit 2.6 shows how median remaining longevity evolves with age. For each additional year of life, remaining longevity reduces by a fraction of a year. For a male at sixty-five, median remaining longevity is about twenty-four years, but at age eighty-nine, longevity has not fallen to zero. It is still about five years.

Exhibit 2.7 makes a similar point, with results expressed as the median age of death by age, rather than median remaining life expectancy. Longevity continues to increase as one survives into advanced ages.

Exhibit 2.6

Remaining Longevity (Median) by Age

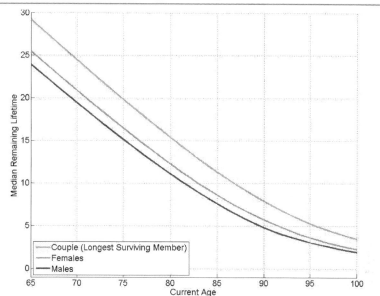

Source: Own calculations for Society of Actuaries 2012 Individual Annuitant Tables with improvements through 2017.

Exhibit 2.7

Median Age of Death by Age

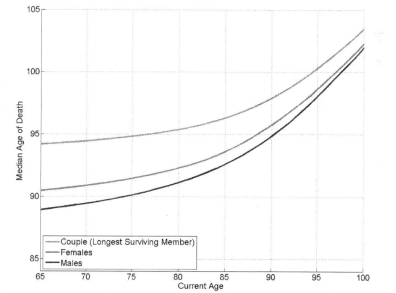

Source: Own calculations for Society of Actuaries 2012 Individual Annuitant Tables with improvements through 2017.

What planning age should a sixty-five-year-old retiree choose when building a retirement income plan? This is a personal decision to be based partly on objective characteristics: gender, smoking status, health status and history, family health history, and other socioeconomic characteristics that correlate with mortality. It is also partly based on an individual's answers to more subjective questions: how do you feel about outliving your investment portfolio, and what would be the impact on your standard of living if you outlived your portfolio? In a 2011 article, Moshe Milevsky and Huaxiong Huang define longevity risk aversion as the attitude one has regarding the possibility of living longer than expected and outliving one's financial resources. Beyond the objective information available about mortality, longevity risk aversion is what will drive a retiree's decision about an appropriate planning age.

> **The Longevity Illustrator, www.longevityillustrator.org**
>
> Though the longevity estimates are more fine-tuned and will differ a bit from the data source I use in relevant examples, the Longevity Illustrator from the Society of Actuaries and the American Academy of Actuaries is a free resource that readers may wish to utilize. It provides longevity estimates based on gender, age, smoking status, and an overall evaluation of health. This allows for a bit more fine-tuning for your individual situation. The Longevity Illustrator accounts for the three concerns expressed earlier: longevity is expressed conditional on already living to a particular age, longevity is based on projections for future mortality improvements, and longevity is based on an appropriate self-selected population (as you have chosen) with more similar mortality characteristics.

An individual's longevity risk aversion determines how he or she will evaluate the trade-off between how a higher planning age improves the odds that a plan will work and how it reduces the sustainable spending amount. As an example, let us consider a sixty-five-year-old female who decides that her appropriate planning horizon is the age for which there is only a 10 percent chance she might live even longer. Assuming the Society of Actuaries mortality data is the correct objective mortality data to apply for her case, she can use this to decide on a percentile of the longevity distribution. For instance, if she is willing to accept a 10 percent chance she will live beyond her planning horizon, then her appropriate planning age is one hundred. Precisely, there is a 10 percent chance she will live beyond age 100.1. She plans for thirty-five years of retirement spending from sixty-five through ninety-nine, with an assumption she will pass away on her one hundredth birthday. We might assume this is the planning age that she is comfortable using with respect to her longevity risk aversion and then build her financial plan around this.

There is no one-size-fits-all answer about the appropriate planning age. This requires careful thought about whether it is reasonable to plan for more or less than typical life expectancies. You also need to make a decision about how much you are willing to risk outliving your wealth by choosing a shorter horizon and a higher withdrawal rate. For retirees who are self-managing their longevity risk, the idea is to choose a sufficiently long time horizon that one is unlikely to outlive, and to then ensure that one's plan can work for this long. Those with greater longevity risk aversion, which is the fear of outliving their resources, will seek a higher planning age with a lower probability to outlive. Individuals pick planning ages that are sufficiently conservative to reflect their personalized concerns about outliving their wealth. Choosing planning ages based on only a 10 percent chance for outliving may be a reasonable baseline assumption. I have described the basic framework for making the decision.

● Sustainable Spending Rates for Varying Return and Longevity Assumptions

We now have sufficient context to look more closely at the relationship between sustainable spending, investment returns, and time horizon. This analysis will help illustrate the impact of three important matters:

1. What happens to sustainable spending rates as the planning horizon changes,
2. What happens to sustainable spending rates as the fixed investment return changes, and
3. What happens to sustainable spending rates if we build in a constraint to preserve wealth and not accept complete portfolio depletion at the end of the planning horizon.

This analysis will assume inflation-adjusted investment returns, which will allow the sustainable spending rate to be defined as a percentage of the assets available to spend at the initial retirement date, with that spending amount then adjusting for the realized inflation experience in subsequent years. However, readers could treat the investment returns as nominal, in which case the spending rates represent spending that does not adjust for inflation.

Exhibit 2.8 begins the analysis with planning horizons of ten to fifty years, real compounded investment returns of 0 to 6 percent, and an objective of depleting wealth by the end of the planning horizon. In looking at this exhibit, the sustainable spending rates for a 0 percent real return should be intuitive. With no returns, spending 10 percent of initial assets will deplete the portfolio in ten years, spending 5 percent will deplete the portfolio in twenty years, and so on. Without real investment growth, longer time horizons continue pushing the sustainable spending rate lower. As we move down the rows, we see that obtaining returns on the underlying portfolio naturally allows the spending rate to increase. For longer time horizons, spending rates continue to decline, but at a slower rate as returns increase. In other words, long horizons allow for relatively more investment growth to better stabilize spending. For instance, with a 5 percent real return, the sustainable spending rate is 12.3 percent over ten years and 5.2 percent over fifty years.

To provide context, the level return required to duplicate spending supported by the traditional 4 percent rule can also be found in Exhibit 2.8: it uses a spending horizon of thirty years and allows wealth to be depleted at the end of the horizon. With these circumstances, a 1 percent fixed-return supports a 3.8 percent spending rate, and a 2 percent fixed return supports a 4.4 percent spending rate. We can therefore understand that the level real compounded return that supports the 4 percent rule fell somewhere between 1 and 2 percent. This aligns with what we found earlier using the PMT formula: the 4 percent spending rate matches a real investment return of 1.3 percent.

While the allowance for wealth depletion characterizes the baseline assumption used in retirement income planning, Exhibit 2.9 moves us in the direction of preserving assets for indefinite use. Whereas Exhibit 2.8 allowed all assets to be depleted at the end of the planning horizon,

Exhibit 2.8

Sustainable Spending Rates for Different Planning Horizons and Investment Returns

Objective: Deplete All Assets at End of Planning Horizon

		Planning Horizon (in Years)				
		10	20	30	40	50
Inflation-Adjusted Investment Return	0%	10.0%	5.0%	3.3%	2.5%	2.0%
	1%	10.5%	5.5%	3.8%	3.0%	2.5%
	2%	10.9%	6.0%	4.4%	3.6%	3.1%
	3%	11.4%	6.5%	5.0%	4.2%	3.8%
	4%	11.9%	7.1%	5.6%	4.9%	4.5%
	5%	12.3%	7.6%	6.2%	5.6%	5.2%
	6%	12.8%	8.2%	6.9%	6.3%	6.0%

Exhibit 2.9

Sustainable Spending Rates for Different Planning Horizons and Investment Returns

Objective: Preserve 50% of Wealth (Inflation-Adjusted) at End of Horizon

		Planning Horizon (in Years)				
		10	20	30	40	50
Inflation-Adjusted Investment Return	0%	5.0%	2.5%	1.7%	1.3%	1.0%
	1%	5.7%	3.2%	2.4%	2.0%	1.8%
	2%	6.4%	4.0%	3.2%	2.8%	2.5%
	3%	7.1%	4.7%	3.9%	3.6%	3.3%
	4%	7.9%	5.5%	4.7%	4.4%	4.2%
	5%	8.5%	6.2%	5.5%	5.2%	5.0%
	6%	9.2%	6.9%	6.3%	6.0%	5.8%

Exhibit 2.9 includes an objective to preserve 50 percent of assets (in inflation-adjusted terms) at the end. The intuition is most basic with a 0 percent return. With the desire to keep half of the initial wealth (adjusted for inflation), sustainable spending rates are cut in half. Now 5 percent is only sustainable for ten years, and 1 percent lasts fifty years. As return assumptions increase, the degree of differences between the two exhibits gets smaller. For instance, with a 5 percent real return, the sustainable spending rate over fifty years falls from 5.2 percent to 5 percent. This small reduction to sustainable spending reflects just how sensitive remaining wealth is to small differences in spending rates over longer periods of time, at least when returns are high. Within the context of the 4 percent rule, real compounded returns would need to be a bit above 3 percent to sustain a 4 percent initial spending rate over thirty years with an additional objective to preserve 50 percent of the purchasing power of the initial retirement wealth.

Finally, Exhibit 2.10 includes the objective that the full inflation-adjusted purchasing power of the initial wealth must be preserved at the end of the planning horizon. With 0 percent returns and a desire to preserve the portfolio, the sustainable spending rate is obviously 0 percent regardless

Exhibit 2.10

Sustainable Spending Rates for Different Planning Horizons and Investment Returns

Objective: Preserve 100% of Wealth (Inflation-Adjusted) at End of Horizon

		Planning Horizon (in Years)				
		10	20	30	40	50
Inflation-Adjusted Investment Return	0%	0.0%	0.0%	0.0%	0.0%	0.0%
	1%	1.0%	1.0%	1.0%	1.0%	1.0%
	2%	2.0%	2.0%	2.0%	2.0%	2.0%
	3%	2.9%	2.9%	2.9%	2.9%	2.9%
	4%	3.8%	3.8%	3.8%	3.8%	3.8%
	5%	4.8%	4.8%	4.8%	4.8%	4.8%
	6%	5.7%	5.7%	5.7%	5.7%	5.7%

of the planning horizon. Nothing can be spent, because the portfolio would be unable to make up the difference. As for other investment returns, sustainable spending rates fall a bit below the investment return due to the assumption that spending is taken from the portfolio at the start of each year. For instance, regardless of horizon, the sustainable spending rate is 4.8 percent when the return is 5 percent. The investment return must be a bit higher than the spending rate so the portfolio balance can return to its initial level by year-end. Had spending been taken at the end of each year, the spending rate would equal the investment return, as you could indefinitely sustain a plan that spent each year's investment return.

It is important to fully internalize how dependent spending rates are on investment returns and the planning horizon. Naturally, lower returns support less spending. This is a key lesson to keep in mind for the subsequent discussion. We next move away from the assumption about fixed market returns in order to further consider the impact of market volatility on a retirement spending plan.

Further Reading

Milevsky, Moshe A. 2016. "It's Time to Retire Ruin (Probabilities)." *Financial Analysts Journal* 72 (2): 8–12.

Milevsky, Moshe A., and Huaxiong Huang. 2011. "Spending Retirement on Planet Vulcan: The Impact of Longevity Risk Aversion on Optimal Withdrawal Rates." *Financial Analysts Journal* 67 (2): 45–58.

Society of Actuaries and American Academy of Actuaries. 2016. "The Longevity Illustrator." [http://www.longevityillustrator.org]

CHAPTER 3

Spending from Volatile Investments and Sequence-of-Returns Risk

Retirees spending from investment portfolios face market risk. Market volatility causes investment returns to vary over time. Market volatility is further amplified by the growing impact of sequence-of-returns risk in retirement. This is the heightened vulnerability individuals face regarding the realized investment portfolio returns in the years around their retirement date—it adds to the uncertainty in retirement by making retirement outcomes more contingent on a shorter period of investment returns. The financial market returns experienced near retirement matter a great deal more than most people realize. Even with the same average returns over a long period of time, retiring at the start of a bear market is very dangerous; wealth can be rapidly depleted as withdrawals are made from a diminishing portfolio, leaving less wealth to benefit from any subsequent market recovery.

Though sequence-of-returns risk is related to general investment risk and market volatility, it differs from general investment risk. The average market return over a thirty-year retirement period could be quite generous. But if negative returns are experienced when you start spending from your portfolio, you will face a difficult hurdle to overcome even if the market offers higher returns later in retirement.

The dynamics of sequence risk suggest that a prolonged recessionary environment early in retirement could jeopardize the retirement prospects for a particular cohort of retirees. That scenario does not imply a large-scale economic catastrophe. This is a subtle but important point. Some retirees could experience very poor retirement outcomes relative to those retiring a few years earlier or later.

Sustainable withdrawal rates can fall below what would be expected for average market returns over long periods of time, because the ordering of those returns matters. Poor early returns followed by strong later returns can still derail a retirement plan. It is worthwhile to further quantify the impact of sequence risk on retirement spending. This chapter focuses on investment volatility and its impact on retirement outcomes.

◉ Wealth Glide Paths and Current Withdrawal Rates

First, let us return to a simple example using a fixed-return assumption. From 1926 through 2016, the compounded inflation-adjusted return for a 50/50 portfolio of the S&P 500 and intermediate-term government bonds was 5.1 percent. Using this as a fixed-return assumption for a thirty-year retirement period with the PMT formula, the sustainable initial spending rate is 6.3 percent. Subsequent spending from this base could be adjusted for inflation, and the portfolio would last for precisely thirty years.

Exhibit 3.1 shows the glide path for remaining wealth over the thirty-year retirement period for this spending strategy. It also shows the "current withdrawal rate" over these thirty years. This is worth emphasizing, as a common misconception about the "4 percent rule" is that it means you withdraw 4 percent of what remains each year. That is not what happens with a constant spending strategy.

The initial withdrawal rate is 6.3 percent in the exhibit, creating a baseline spending of $6.30 from a $100 initial portfolio. As retirement progresses, the inflation-adjusted withdrawal amount remains at $6.30. But the percentage of the remaining portfolio balance this represents will change as remaining wealth changes. In other words, the current withdrawal rate changes over time. In the exhibit, the wealth glide path shows a reduction in wealth over time, which increases the current withdrawal rate until it reaches 100 percent as the last of the wealth is spent in year thirty. In this example, the real portfolio value decreases throughout retirement, increasing the necessary withdrawal rate from what remains. Growing wealth, on the other hand, would allow the current withdrawal rate to decrease over time.

Next, Exhibit 3.2 provides a way to understand sequence risk and investment volatility by showing the glide path for remaining wealth

Exhibit 3.1

Wealth Glide Path and Current Withdrawal Rates over a 30-Year Retirement

For a 5.1% Real Return and 6.3% Initial Withdrawal Rate

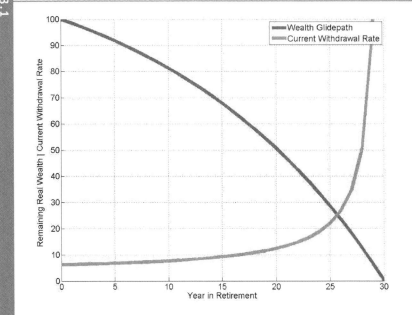

for a 6.3 percent initial withdrawal rate with a 50/50 asset allocation for each of the sixty-two rolling historical thirty-year periods we have available since 1926. Historical outcomes vary greatly. In some cases, remaining wealth is entirely depleted within the first fifteen years of retirement. In other cases, real wealth has doubled after thirty years of retirement. This variation of outcomes is triggered by the different sequence of investment returns experienced by hypothetical individuals who otherwise behave in the same way, but who retire at different times in US history.

The actual historical outcomes vary greatly for reasons outside the control of these hypothetical retirees. They all use the same retirement withdrawal strategy, but their experiences with that strategy could be good or bad through no fault of their own. This is the randomness created by sequence risk. Some retirees will be able to spend more aggressively than others based on the luck of the market returns they experience in retirement.

Exhibit 3.2

Wealth Glide Path over a 30-Year Retirement

For a 6.3% Initial Withdrawal Rate, 50/50 Asset Allocation, Inflation Adjustments

Using SBBI Data, 1926–2016, S&P 500 and Intermediate-Term Government Bonds

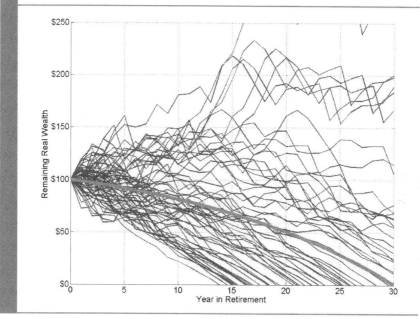

Exhibit 3.3 provides another reflection about the historical volatility of outcomes shown previously. Instead of defining results in terms of remaining wealth, Exhibit 3.3 provides the current withdrawal rates as time progresses. When wealth grows, the necessary withdrawal rate declines. When wealth decreases, the necessary withdrawal rate increases. This exhibit helps illuminate how sequence-of-returns risk works, as an increasing withdrawal rate creates pressure on the portfolio. Portfolio returns must exceed the withdrawal rate to prevent further portfolio declines, and this exhibit shows how once withdrawal rates exceed about 10 percent, they tend to shoot up rather dramatically afterward.

● Lifetime Sequence-of-Returns Risk

As we are starting to see, individual investors are vulnerable to the sequence of market returns experienced over their investing lifetimes.

Exhibit 3.3

Current Withdrawal Rates over a 30-Year Retirement

For a 6.3% Initial Withdrawal Rate, 50/50 Asset Allocation, Inflation Adjustments
Using SBBI Data, 1926–2016, S&P 500 and Intermediate-Term Government Bonds

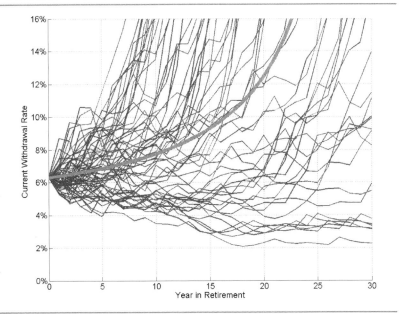

Individuals who behave in exactly the same way over their careers—saving the same percentage of the same salary for the same number of years—can experience disparate outcomes based solely on the specific sequence of investment returns that accompanies their career and retirement. Peak vulnerability is reached at the retirement date, when returning to the labor force becomes increasingly difficult and a postretirement market drop can be devastating. Actual wealth accumulations and sustainable withdrawal rates will vary substantially among retirees, as these outcomes depend disproportionately on the shorter sequence of returns just before and after the retirement date.

In other words, individuals are the most vulnerable when their wealth is likely the largest it has ever been, in absolute terms, due to the sequence of returns. Two investors may enjoy the same average return on their investments but could still experience divergent outcomes based on the sequence in which returns arrive. This can impact both those who are saving and contributing to their portfolio, and those who are withdrawing a constant stream of cash flows from their portfolio.

Historical simulations based on overlapping periods reveal how sequence of returns can create differing outcomes for otherwise identical investors. We'll look at the life of one individual investor we'll call Adam. The only unknown Adam faces with regard to his retirement planning is what his specific sequence of market returns will be. This simplifies reality, as Adam is not saddled with uncertainty in his future employment status and salary.

Adam saves for retirement during the final thirty years of work, and he earns a constant real income in each of these years. For thirty years, he puts away a fixed savings rate of 15 percent of his income at the end of each year. The wealth accumulation achieved at retirement is defined as a multiple of Adam's constant real salary. In other words, if the wealth accumulation is 10×, then Adam had savings equal to ten times his salary upon reaching retirement. A $100,000 salary means a $1 million portfolio. In this simplified world, Adam does not worry about health risks, disability, or potential involuntary job loss. He can continue work over the next thirty years earning a constant inflation-adjusted salary.

Adam retires at the start of the thirty-first year, and his retirement lasts thirty years. Withdrawals are made at the beginning of each year during retirement. The withdrawal amount is defined as the percentage of retirement date assets withdrawn (e.g., 4 percent), and this amount adjusts for inflation in subsequent years. The maximum sustainable withdrawal rate over thirty years is the initial percentage of assets withdrawn in the first year. That amount is adjusted for inflation in subsequent years, and the portfolio balance reaches zero at the end of the thirtieth year of retirement. For simplicity's sake, portfolio administrative and planning fees are not charged, and taxes are not deducted.

The historical characteristics for the 50/50 portfolio include a 5.6 percent real arithmetic mean, volatility of 10.7 percent, and a real compounded return of 5.1 percent. If the historical average compounded return could be fixed at 5.1 percent without volatility, a 15 percent savings rate for thirty years would result in retirement date wealth equal to 10.1 times salary. Exhibit 3.4 shows the historical wealth accumulations based on actual rolling periods of the historical data. Though Adam could expect (on average) a wealth accumulation equal to 10.1 times his salary, the historical outcomes ranged from a minimum of 5.2 times if he retired in 1982 to a maximum of 17.4 times if he retired in 2000. Despite saving in the same way from identical salaries and using the same 50/50 asset allocation, one Adam was able to save more than 3.3 times as much as the other. These are very different outcomes, again, for individuals who otherwise behaved in identical ways and were only exposed to a different sequence of market returns during their working years.

Even individuals whose careers largely overlap may still experience different outcomes. For instance, retirees in 1973 and 1975 had twenty-eight of their thirty working years overlap, but the 1975 retiree reached retirement with 36 percent less real wealth than the 1973 retiree. William Bernstein, in his 2012 e-book, *Ages of the Investor,* used waterfalls to describe the large drops in wealth accumulations that may follow wealth peaks, explaining how some individuals might unwittingly just miss

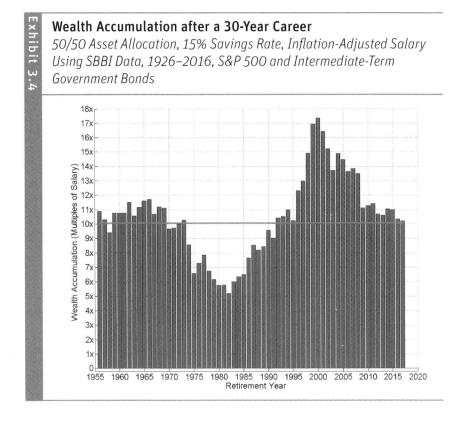

Exhibit 3.4

Wealth Accumulation after a 30-Year Career
50/50 Asset Allocation, 15% Savings Rate, Inflation-Adjusted Salary Using SBBI Data, 1926–2016, S&P 500 and Intermediate-Term Government Bonds

their opportunity to reach their wealth target after thirty years, and subsequently may find that working for much longer does not get them back to where they had hoped to be. This is sequence-of-returns risk in the context of the accumulation phase, as people are more vulnerable to the returns experienced when their portfolios are larger. A given percentage change has a bigger impact on absolute wealth, and a large drop in the portfolio value could counterbalance all of the capital gains earned for most of the early part of your career.

The sequence-of-returns problem occurs even more harshly for retirees using a constant inflation-adjusted spending strategy. With compounded returns of 5.1 percent, retirees could expect to withdraw 6.3 percent of their retirement date assets, adjust this for inflation, and have their wealth last for precisely thirty years. But because of return volatility, the actual maximum sustainable withdrawal rates vary greatly over time. In Exhibit 3.5, sustainable withdrawal rates from the rolling historical data ranged from 4 percent (in 1966) to 9.8 percent (in 1982). The variance between these sustainable withdrawal rates is based simply on the luck of the draw regarding the postretirement return sequence.

Next, Exhibit 3.6 attempts to give a clearer picture of how sequence-of-returns risk impacts both the accumulation and distribution phases. The exhibit is based on statistical regression analysis, which determines how much of the outcome (wealth accumulation or sustainable withdrawal rate) can be explained by the returns experienced in each year of the life cycle. The exhibit isolates the impact of each year's return on lifetime outcomes using a larger sample of one hundred thousand Monte Carlo simulations based on a 50/50 portfolio with the same characteristics as the historical data. For the first thirty years (when individuals are saving), the percentage of the final wealth accumulation at the retirement date grows from year one through year thirty. With wealth accumulations at insignificant levels in the early part of one's career, the early returns have very little impact on the absolute level of wealth accumulated at the end of the savings period. But as retirement approaches, a given percentage return produces an increasing impact on the final wealth value in absolute terms, leaving individuals particularly vulnerable to these later returns. Simply put, later market returns impact more years of contributions.

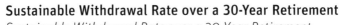

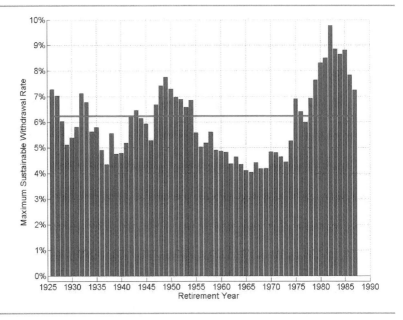

Exhibit 3.5

Sustainable Withdrawal Rate over a 30-Year Retirement

Sustainable Withdrawal Rate over a 30-Year Retirement
50/50 Asset Allocation, Inflation-Adjusted Spending
Using SBBI Data, 1926–2016, S&P 500 and Intermediate-Term
Government Bonds

In years thirty-one through sixty, during the retirement distribution phase, the exhibit shows the impact of each year's return on the maximum sustainable withdrawal rate. The return in year thirty-one represents the first year of retirement; this initial return explains almost 14 percent of the final outcome for retirees. Retirees are extremely vulnerable to what happens just after they retire. This result would hold even more so with the human capital considerations of the real world, as it is increasingly difficult to return to the workforce after you retire. Sustainable withdrawal rates are disproportionately explained by what happens in the early part of retirement. Returns from later in retirement have minimal impact, as the outcome for that retirement (high or low sustainable spending) was already set in motion earlier.

Sequence-of-returns risk affects individuals throughout their entire investing lives. Individuals from different birth cohorts who otherwise

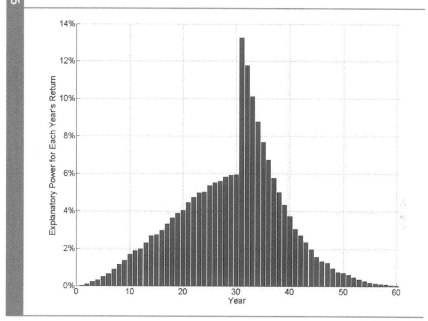

Lifetime Sequence-of-Returns Risk
50/50 Asset Allocation, Inflation-Adjusted Spending
100,000 Monte Carlo Simulations Based on SBBI Data, 1926–2016,
S&P 500 and Intermediate-Term Government Bonds

Exhibit 3.6

behave in identical ways may experience dramatically different wealth accumulations and sustainable withdrawal rates. These outcomes are unpredictable.

Strategies using a volatile portfolio to target a wealth accumulation goal or to sustain a constant spending strategy expose individuals to much greater risk than you might expect when thinking about an average return that might apply to someone investing over a sixty-year time horizon.

◉ Investment Risk versus Sequence Risk

Another way to understand how sequence risk amplifies investment risk is to consider how historical withdrawal rates would have varied based on the actual sequence of historical returns and on the average compounded return over each thirty-year period in history. To illustrate this, we will first look at the rolling compounded investment returns over thirty-year periods for the same 50/50 portfolio described before.

Exhibit 3.7 represents investment risk (aka market risk) as distinct from sequence-of-returns risk. Average returns over different thirty-year rolling periods fluctuate. They range from about 3 percent for the period starting in 1952 to roughly 7 percent for the period starting in 1982. Note that rolling thirty-year returns never fell too close to the 1.3 percent compounded real

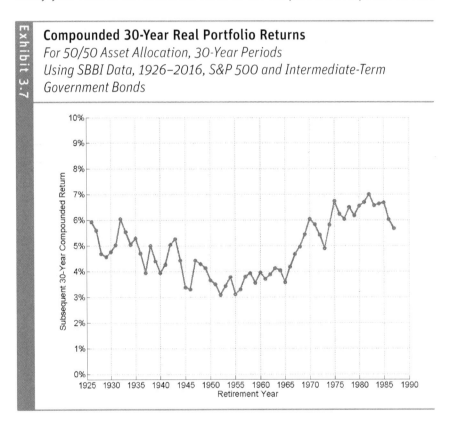

Exhibit 3.7

Compounded 30-Year Real Portfolio Returns
For 50/50 Asset Allocation, 30-Year Periods
Using SBBI Data, 1926–2016, S&P 500 and Intermediate-Term Government Bonds

return that would trigger a maximum sustainable spending rate of 4 percent. We can think about this volatility for compounded returns over a thirty-year period as the general investment risk facing retirees. However, sequence-of-returns risk has not been factored in yet, so this is not the whole story.

Exhibit 3.8 demonstrates the specific impact of sequence risk compared to more general investment risk by showing historical withdrawal rates for two sets of return assumptions. The lighter curve shows withdrawal rates assuming that the fixed compounded returns shown in the previous exhibit were earned without any market volatility within each thirty-year period. These numbers represent a simple PMT calculation: with withdrawals taken at the start of the year and a fixed compounded portfolio return for the next thirty years, what spending rate would deplete the portfolio in the thirtieth year?

Because the average investment returns fluctuate, the hypothetical sustainable withdrawal rates also fluctuate. Nonetheless, they remain within a range of about 2.5 percentage points. They do not fall below 5 percent, and they are a little above 7.5 percent at their highest. These would be sustainable withdrawal rates if the average compounded returns over thirty years were all that mattered.

Exhibit 3.8

Comparing Sustainable Withdrawal Rates Implied by Fixed Real Compounded Returns

With Sustainable Withdrawal Rates Supported by Actual Sequences of Returns

For 50/50 Asset Allocation, 30-Year Retirement, Inflation Adjustments Using SBBI Data, 1926–2016, S&P 500 and Intermediate-Term Government Bonds

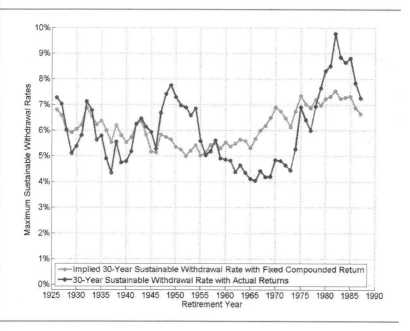

The darker curve in the exhibit represents the actual sustainable withdrawal rates over those thirty-year periods, as previously shown in Exhibit 3.5. What matters for calculating the actual withdrawal rates is not just an average portfolio return, but also the specific sequence of returns. Actual withdrawal rates are more volatile and include greater downside after accounting for sequence risk—the withdrawal rate fell as low as 4 percent for a 1966 retiree. On the other hand, greater upside potential exists as well—a 1982 retiree could have used a 9.8 percent withdrawal rate. Retirees can indeed be adversely affected in ways that dig deeper than the investment risk associated with the average return experienced over a long retirement.

◎ Reverse-Engineering Fixed-Return Assumptions

Taking distributions from an investment portfolio amplifies the impacts of portfolio volatility, making retirement income planning particularly tricky when systematic portfolio distributions tend to be the primary income source for retirees. In financial planning, it is common to use software based on Monte Carlo simulations to show a distribution of potential outcomes for a financial plan by calculating how the plan performs with different sequences of random market returns.

This contrasts with developing a financial plan using a fixed-return assumption in a spreadsheet. Implied investment returns are usually not shown with Monte Carlo simulation output in financial planning software, but they exist underneath the hood. The mistake that is frequently made with a spreadsheet, I worry, is that the choice of return assumptions will reflect a "best guess" about future market returns. This is one of the matters I said we would come back to when describing how to assemble a portfolio return assumption in Exhibit 2.1. This best guess would correspond with only a 50 percent chance for success. Financial planning software generally focuses on having a financial plan work with odds greater than a coin flip. The "best guess" return assumption must be reduced to have greater than a 50 percent confidence that the financial plan will work.

Which implied portfolio return supports a 90 percent chance for success? We have to reverse engineer Monte Carlo simulations to find out. The implied return will be lower than the average returns inputted in the simulation, and I find support for appropriate portfolio return assumptions for the postretirement period being more conservative than for the preretirement period.

Consider three scenarios:

1. An individual investing a lump-sum amount for thirty years,
2. An individual saving a fixed percentage of a constant inflation-adjusted salary at the end of each year over a thirty-year accumulation period, and
3. An individual withdrawing the maximum sustainable constant inflation-adjusted amount from a portfolio at the start of each year over a thirty-year retirement period.

Exhibit 3.9 provides the distribution of results for the simulations. These simulations are based on a standard 50/50 portfolio using historical Morningstar data for the S&P 500 and intermediate-term government bonds. For the lump-sum investment, the numbers represent the distribution of average compounded returns over one hundred thousand thirty-year periods. For the accumulation phase, the distribution of outcomes is for the internal rate of return for the final wealth accumulation when making thirty annual contributions. For the retirement phase, the distribution of results is for the internal rates of return on the portfolio when withdrawing the maximum sustainable amount over a thirty-year period with distributions taken at the start of each year.

In all three cases, the median return was close to 5.1 percent, which was the assumed compounded return input (given the 5.6 percent arithmetic return and 10.7 percent volatility) for the simulations. However, after thinking about it, most retirees would probably shy away from using this number to develop a financial plan with a fixed return in a spreadsheet. The probability the median return can be achieved is only 50 percent. When choosing a number to plug into a spreadsheet, a conservative retiree might be more comfortable using something like the return in the twenty-fifth percentile—or even the tenth—of the distribution. These numbers would correspond to 75 or 90 percent probabilities of success, respectively, for a financial plan created with planning software. I worry that this point is too often forgotten. People tend to think in terms of an average return rather than a more conservative return that would provide a better chance for the plan to work.

Exhibit 3.9

Distribution of Compounded Real Returns over 30 Years
Distribution of Compounded Real Returns over 30 Years
Monte Carlo Simulations for a 50/50 Asset Allocation
Based on SBBI Data, 1926–2016, S&P 500 and Intermediate-Term
Government Bonds

	Lump Sum	Accumulation	Retirement
1st Percentile	0.7%	0.2%	−0.1%
5th Percentile	2.0%	1.7%	1.3%
10th Percentile	2.7%	2.4%	2.1%
25th Percentile	3.8%	3.7%	3.4%
Median	5.1%	5.2%	4.9%
75th Percentile	6.4%	6.6%	6.6%
90th Percentile	7.6%	7.9%	8.3%
95th Percentile	8.3%	8.7%	9.3%
99th Percentile	9.7%	10.2%	11.4%
Mean	5.1%	5.2%	5.1%
Std. Deviation	1.9%	2.1%	2.5%

Source: Own calculations with one hundred thousand Monte Carlo simulations for thirty-year periods. Portfolio returns are lognormally distributed with a 5.6 percent arithmetic real return and 10.7 percent volatility.

Financial planning software does not usually show the implied returns, but Exhibit 3.9 does just that through a reverse-engineering process. With the lump-sum investment, the compounded real return at the twenty-fifth percentile is 3.8 percent over thirty years. For an accumulator, the twenty-fifth percentile return is 3.7 percent, while it is 3.4 percent for the retiree. At the tenth percentile, realized compounded real returns were 2.7 percent for the lump-sum investment, 2.4 percent for the accumulator, and 2.1 percent for the retiree. These numbers are naturally lower to provide a greater chance of success, and sequence-of-returns risk pushes these numbers even lower for accumulators and retirees than with the lump-sum investment that does not experience sequence risk. The volatility of outcomes increases as we transition from a lump sum (standard deviation of 1.9 percent) to accumulation (2.1 percent) to retirement (2.5 percent).

Financial planning software based on Monte Carlo simulations generally presents its results in terms of a probability for success. For instance, retirees may aim for a 90 percent rate of success or higher. An implied rate of return on the portfolio is connected to a given probability of success, though Monte Carlo simulations generally do not express their output in this way. Higher rates of success would be connected with lower portfolio returns, since this return hurdle must be exceeded by the portfolio for the financial plan to be successful. In this discussion, I am tackling Monte Carlo from a different direction—using Monte Carlo simulations first to get a rate of return for the portfolio, then to simulate a financial plan using a fixed rate of return. Conservative investors will want to work with lower assumed returns, implying a need to save more today. The exhibit provides insight about appropriately conservative adjustments for return assumptions.

Individuals accumulating or spending assets will have different experiences than someone using a lump-sum investment. Accumulation effectively places greater importance on the returns earned late in your career when a given return impacts more years of contributions. This is sequence-of-returns risk as it applies in the accumulation phase. With greater importance placed on a shorter sequence of returns, we should expect a wider distribution of outcomes.

As for retirement, the impacts are even bigger as sequence risk further amplifies the impact of investment volatility. Retirees experience heightened sequence-of-returns risk when funding a constant spending stream from a volatile portfolio. While you may not be withdrawing more money, as your portfolio declines, your withdrawals become a larger percentage of your remaining assets. This digs a hole for your portfolio that can be difficult to emerge from. The distribution of internal rates of return during retirement will be even wider because of the heightened importance placed on the shorter sequence of postretirement returns. A conservative retiree seeking a return assumption for retirement should use a lower value than for preretirement.

Not only does sequence risk widen the distribution of outcomes in retirement, but retirees also experience less risk capacity. With less time and flexibility to make adjustments to their financial plans, retirees who experience portfolio losses after leaving the workforce can experience a devastating impact on remaining lifetime living standards.

This is another reason why individuals may want to use different return assumptions pre- and postretirement. For example, a conservative individual might be willing to use the twenty-fifth-percentile return during accumulation (calibrated to a 75 percent chance for success) but only the tenth percentile during retirement (90 percent chance). If the individual were comfortable with the arithmetic real return and volatility of 5.6 percent and 10.7 percent, this would suggest using a 3.7 percent compounded real return assumption in the spreadsheet for accumulation and a 2.1 percent compounded real return assumption in the spreadsheet for retirement, even though the "best guess" about the ongoing compounding return the retiree will experience is 5.1 percent.

Because of sequence-of-returns risk, conservative investors will want to use lower fixed-return assumptions than just the compounded return assumed for a lump-sum investment. Sequence-of-returns risk is relevant for both the accumulation and retirement phases. Assumed returns should be lower in both cases. The impact is even greater for retirement. Conservative individuals will not want to use the "expected return" for their portfolios when developing lifetime financial plans. This is a really important point to remember and internalize when working in environments that require a fixed-return assumption without an accompanying volatility.

◉ Four Approaches to Managing Sequence-of-Returns Risk in Retirement

Attempting to sustain a fixed living standard using distributions from a portfolio of volatile assets is an inefficient retirement income strategy. This is a unique source of sequence risk. Four general techniques for managing sequence risk in retirement are highlighted in Exhibit 3.10.

1. Spend Conservatively

The first option for managing sequence risk in retirement is to spend conservatively. Retirees want to keep spending consistent on an inflation-adjusted basis throughout retirement. With a total-returns investment portfolio, an aggressive asset allocation provides the highest probability of success if the spending level is pushed beyond what bonds can safely support and annuities are not otherwise considered. The primary question with this strategy is how low spending must be to ensure a sufficient probability of success. Combining an aggressive investment portfolio with

Exhibit 3.10

Approaches for Managing Sequence-of-Returns Risk in Retirement

1. Spend conservatively

2. Maintain spending flexibility

3. Reduce volatility (when it matters most)

   Build a retirement income bond ladder

   Build a lifetime spending floor with income annuities

   Ensure a rising equity glide path in retirement

   Use funded ratio to manage asset allocation

   Use financial derivatives to cut downside risks

4. Buffer assets—avoid selling at losses

   Cash reserve to fund near-term expenses

   Cash value of life insurance

   Line of credit from HECM reverse mortgage

concerns of outliving your assets means spending must be conservative. Ultimately, fearful retirees may end up spending less with an aggressive investment strategy than they might have had they focused more on fixed-income assets. This aggressive portfolio/conservative spending strategy can be rather inefficient, as the safety-first school argues that there is no such thing as a safe spending rate from a volatile investment portfolio. While this approach seeks to mitigate sequence-of-returns risk, it can actually increase it, as there is no lever to provide relief after a market decline. The only solution is to sell more shares to keep spending consistent. Conservative spending will be covered more in depth in chapters 4 and 5.

2. Maintain Spending Flexibility

The next approach keeps the aggressive investment portfolio of the prior strategy while allowing for flexible spending. Sequence risk is mitigated here by reducing spending after a portfolio decline, thereby allowing more to remain in the portfolio to experience any subsequent market recovery.

At the extreme, Dirk Cotton demonstrated at his Retirement Café blog that a strategy of withdrawing a constant percentage of remaining assets eliminates sequence-of-returns risk. Just like investing a lump sum of assets, the order of returns no longer matters. Such a strategy results in volatile spending amounts, so most practical approaches to flexible retirement spending seek to balance the trade-offs between reduced sequence risk and increased spending volatility by partially linking them to portfolio performance. Chapter 6 discusses flexible spending strategies more deeply.

3. Reduce Volatility (When It Matters Most)
A third approach to managing sequence-of-returns risk is to reduce portfolio volatility, at least when it matters the most. A portfolio free of volatility does not create sequence-of-returns risk. Essentially, individuals should not expect constant spending from a volatile portfolio. Those who want upside (and, thus, accept volatility) should be flexible with their spending and should make adjustments. Retirees can reduce volatility in several ways, at least on the downside, and at least when the volatility could have the largest impact.

Spending can be kept constant if the portfolio is derisked. To really get constant spending, you should look to hold fixed-income assets to maturity or use risk-pooling assets like income annuities. Consider, for instance, traditional defined-benefit pension systems that can reduce volatility's impact on the pensioner's income. Defined-benefit pensions provide a way to pool the sequence-of-returns risk across separate birth cohorts, thus reducing exposure. Individuals are entitled to benefits based on their contributions into the system, not market performance. With defined-benefit pensions, some individuals will receive less than they might have by investing on their own, but others will receive more. In this regard, defined-benefit pensions are essentially a separate asset class that most investors should find very valuable, as pensions diversify sequence of returns across time and allow them to collect income based more closely on the average returns over long periods.

Other approaches to reducing downside risk (volatility in the undesired direction) could also be considered. For instance, a rising equity glide path in retirement could start with an equity allocation that is even lower than typically recommended (in safe withdrawal rate research literature) at the start of retirement, but then slowly increase the stock allocation over time. This can reduce the probability and the magnitude of retirement failures. This approach reduces vulnerability to early retirement stock market declines that cause the most harm to retirees. Asset allocation could also be managed with a funded ratio approach, in which more aggressive asset allocations are used only when sufficient assets are available beyond what is necessary to meet retirement spending goals. Finally, financial derivatives or income guarantee riders can be used to place a floor on how low a portfolio may fall by sacrificing some potential upside.

4. Buffer Assets—Avoid Selling at Losses

The final category of approaches to managing sequence risk is to have other assets available outside the financial portfolio to draw from after a market downturn. Returns on these assets should not be correlated with the financial portfolio, since the purpose of these buffer assets is to support spending when the portfolio is otherwise down. An old strategy in this category is to maintain a separate cash reserve, perhaps with two or three years of retirement expenses, separate from the rest of the investment portfolio. While this is a safe approach, one disadvantage is that the cash reserve could have otherwise been invested to seek higher returns than cash provides. Cash can be a drag on the portfolio, and in recent years more attention has focused on other alternatives. In a sense, though, cash reserve strategies are just another type of a time segmentation strategy, which are discussed extensively in chapter 7. The two main alternatives discussed are to use the cash value of permanent life insurance policies as a reserve, and to open a line of credit with a reverse mortgage to serve as a reserve. I discuss the latter strategy extensively in my previous book, *Reverse Mortgages: How to Secure Your Retirement with a Reverse Mortgage*.

Further Reading

Bernstein, W. J. 2012. *The Ages of the Investor: A Critical Look at Life-Cycle Investing (Investing for Adults)*. Efficient Frontier Publications. [http://amzn.to/2s495L2]

Cotton, Dirk. 2013. "Clarifying Sequence of Returns Risk (Part 2, with Pictures!)." *Retirement Café* (blog), September 20.

Pfau, W. D. 2014. "The Lifetime Sequence of Returns: A Retirement Planning Conundrum." *Journal of Financial Service Professionals* 68 (1): 53–58.

Technical Appendix: **Key Data Sources and Methods Used**

Throughout the book, I draw from three historical data sources.

Most commonly, I use the Stocks, Bonds, Bills, and Inflation data provided by Morningstar and Ibbotson Associates. This data source provides monthly US market returns since 1926 for large-capitalization and small-capitalization stocks, as well as a variety of Treasury bond indexes and a corporate bond index. This is the data source used by William Bengen to formulate the 4 percent rule. Access to this data requires a subscription.

A second data source that I use when discussing stock market valuations is the data collected by Yale professor and Nobel laureate Robert Shiller. On his website, he freely provides monthly updates on US large-capitalization stock returns, dividends, and earnings, as well ten-year Treasury bond yields. This data is available since 1871, making it the longest available data series commonly used for retirement income research. It is also the only data source that is available for free.

Third, when I discuss the international experience of safe withdrawal rates, I rely on Morningstar's Global Returns Dataset. Total returns for stocks, long-term government bonds, and short-term government bonds are available on an annual basis since 1900 for twenty developed-market countries. Morningstar also offers this data set on a subscription basis.

There are three ways that these data sets are generally used to study retirement questions. The simplest method to test a retirement plan is to build a spreadsheet and see how it works assuming a fixed rate of return. In this case, the data may be used to calculate historical average returns for different asset classes, which are then incorporated into the spreadsheet. This approach is also known as deterministic modeling, as there is no randomness in the future outcome. The financial plan could, for example, assume a long-term return on stocks of 10 percent, and that would be the assumed return for each year with no variability over time.

Deterministic approaches are overly simplified because they do not account for volatility (unless the reverse-engineering approach described in this chapter is applied) and therefore miss the impact of sequence-of-returns risk. The basic approach of assuming a fixed return reflecting the best guess one can make about future market returns leads to a retirement plan with only a 50 percent chance to work. The outcomes are too optimistic and could lead a retiree down an unsustainable path.

A second alternative is to use "historical simulations" from rolling periods of the data. The outcomes for a thirty-year retirement could be studied using each possible thirty-year period available in the data. It was with this approach that William Bengen developed the 4 percent rule.

Third, Monte Carlo simulations provide an alternative that is now widely used in financial planning software. The simulations are used to develop sequences of random market returns fitting predetermined characteristics, in order to test how financial plans will perform in a wider variety of good and bad market environments. The use of Monte Carlo tools has increased considerably over the past decade, which can likely be attributed to lower computing costs, increased recognition that returns are random, and desires to provide more robust financial plans. A thousand or more simulations could be created to test the robustness of a retirement plan in many market environments.

Monte Carlo simulations can be created for different asset classes or for an overall portfolio. With the asset class approach, one defines the arithmetic average return, the volatility for that return, and the correlations with other asset classes. Random draws are then taken from multivariate normal or lognormal distributions sharing these characteristics. By combining the arithmetic mean with volatility, the resulting simulated returns will display the appropriate compounded return. Historical data is commonly used to set these input characteristics. Most financial planning software works in this way.

With Monte Carlo simulations, though, the sky is the limit about what types of assumptions can be used to prepare the assumptions guiding the simulations. For instance, one could assume "fat tail" distributions that allow for more extreme market outcomes, or one could incorporate serial correlation, which allows simulated returns to also be related to their past values.

My efforts to build Monte Carlo simulations that more adequately reflect the low interest rate environment at the present have led me to build assumptions for serial correlation and low initial bond yields into my analysis. For the Monte Carlo simulations I use in this book, the capital market expectations connect the historical averages from Robert Shiller's data set with the current market values for inflation and interest rates. This makes allowances for the fact that interest rates and inflation are currently lower than their historical averages, but it also respects historical averages and does not force returns to remain low for the entire simulation.

Exhibit 3A.1 provides summary statistics for the historical data, which guides the Monte Carlo simulations for investment returns. A Cholesky decomposition is performed on a matrix of the normalized values for the risk premium, bond yields, home prices, bills, and inflation. A Monte Carlo simulation is then used to create error terms for these variables, which preserve their contemporaneous correlations with one another. Then the variables are simulated with these errors using models that preserve key characteristics about serial correlation.

With the correlated error terms, inflation is modeled as a first-order autoregressive process starting from 1.7 percent inflation at the end of 2016 and trending toward its historical average of 2.9 percent over time with its historical volatility. Bond yields are similarly modeled with a first-order autoregression with an initial seed value of 2.45 percent, representing the yield for ten-year Treasury bonds at the start of 2017. Next, home prices and the risk premium are both modeled as random walks around their

Exhibit 3A.1 — Summary Statistics for US Returns and Inflation Data, 1890–2016

Correlation Coefficients

	Arithmetic Means	Geometric Means	Standard Deviations	Stocks Returns	Risk Premium	Bond Yields	Bond Returns	Home Prices	Bills	Inflation
Stock Returns	10.7%	9.2%	18.1%	1.0	0.99	0.05	0.06	0.15	-0.09	0.06
Risk Premium	6.1%	4.5%	18.2%	0.99	1.0	-0.09	-0.01	0.13	-0.20	0.03
Bond Yields	4.6%	–	2.4%	0.05	-0.09	1.0	0.52	0.13	0.85	0.22
Bond Returns	4.8%	4.6%	6.6%	0.06	-0.01	0.52	1.0	-0.06	0.33	-0.09
Home Prices	3.4%	3.2%	7.1%	0.15	0.13	0.13	-0.06	1.0	0.05	0.39
Bills	4.4%	–	3.0%	-0.09	-0.20	0.85	0.33	0.05	1.0	0.15
Inflation	2.9%	2.8%	5.3%	0.06	0.03	0.22	-0.09	0.39	0.15	1.0

Source: Calculated using data from Robert Shiller's website.

historical averages and with their historical volatilities. Bond returns are calculated from bond yields and changes in interest rates, assuming a bond mutual fund with equal holdings of past ten-year Treasury issues. Stock returns are calculated as the sum of bond yields and the simulated equity risk premium over yields. Exhibit 3A.2 shows the simulated median outcomes for the key variables using one hundred thousand simulations. As can be seen, stock and bond returns start lower but trend upward, on average, toward their historical averages.

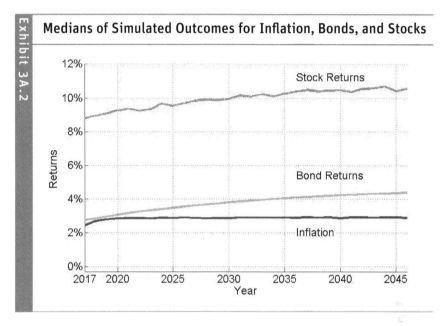

Medians of Simulated Outcomes for Inflation, Bonds, and Stocks

CHAPTER 4

Managing Sequence Risk by Spending Conservatively

For a retiree seeking a stable annual spending amount that adjusts for inflation, what is a sustainable spending trajectory defined as an initial withdrawal rate from retirement date assets? This chapter and the next focus on how low spending must be to achieve an acceptable probability of plan success when using a volatile investment portfolio to fund a stable spending stream.

⊙ William Bengen's SAFEMAX

For sustainable spending from an investment portfolio, William Bengen's work is the next natural stop on our journey. William Bengen's seminal study in the October 1994 *Journal of Financial Planning*, "Determining Withdrawal Rates Using Historical Data," helped usher in the modern area of retirement withdrawal rate research by codifying the importance of sequence-of-returns risk. The problem he set up is simple: a newly retired couple plans to withdraw an inflation-adjusted amount from their savings at the end of every year for a thirty-year retirement period. What is the highest annual sustainable percentage of retirement date assets that can be withdrawn with inflation adjustments for a full thirty years?

To answer this question, Bengen obtained a copy of Ibbotson Associates' *Stocks, Bonds, Bills, and Inflation* yearbook, which provides monthly data for a variety of US asset classes and inflation since January 1926. He decided to investigate using the S&P 500 index to represent the stock market and intermediate-term government bonds to represent the bond market.

He constructed rolling thirty-year periods from this data (1926 through 1955, then 1927 through 1956, and so on), using a technique called "historical simulations." He calculated the maximum sustainable withdrawal rate for each rolling historical period. Such an approach helps illustrate the role of market volatility in a way that assuming a constant portfolio return does not. Though he did not create the following illustration, his spreadsheet calculations would provide something similar to what is seen in Exhibit 4.1.

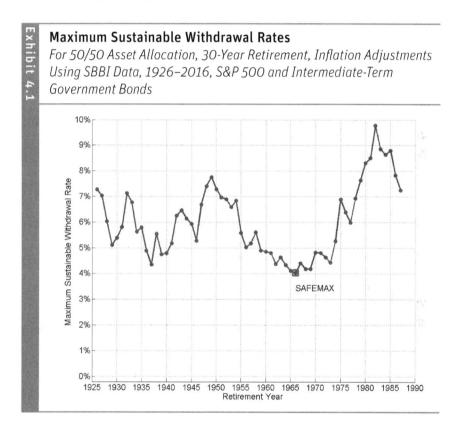

Exhibit 4.1

Maximum Sustainable Withdrawal Rates
For 50/50 Asset Allocation, 30-Year Retirement, Inflation Adjustments Using SBBI Data, 1926–2016, S&P 500 and Intermediate-Term Government Bonds

To bring greater realism to the discussion of safe withdrawal rates in retirement, he focused his attention on what he later called the "SAFEMAX"—the highest sustainable withdrawal rate for the worst-case retirement scenario in the historical period. With a 50/50 allocation for stocks and bonds, the SAFEMAX was 4.15 percent, and it occurred for a new hypothetical retiree in 1966 who experienced the 1966–1995 market returns. Searching for this "worst-case scenario" puts the focus on spending conservatively.

The highest sustainable withdrawal rate was only a little more than 4 percent in spite of the fact that from 1966 to 1995, a 50/50 portfolio provided a 4.7 percent average inflation-adjusted return. With this simple average, the compounded real growth rate for the portfolio in these thirty years was 4.2 percent after accounting for the impacts of volatility. If the portfolio could have grown at a fixed 4.2 percent for thirty years, someone withdrawing funds at the end of the year would have been able to use a sustainable withdrawal rate of 5.9 percent of initial assets. Why was the withdrawal rate barely over 4 percent?

We saw earlier that a 1.3 percent return assumption is needed to make the 4 percent rule work. The further amplifying effects of sequence risk on investment volatility made it seem like the compounded return was only 1.3 percent for retirees that year, instead of the actual 4.2 percent. The difference between the 4.15 percent and 5.9 percent spending rates is another illustration of the specific impact of market returns sequence in that thirty-year period. The early part of the 1966 retiree's retirement was a tough time, with market losses in 1966, 1968, and 1973–74. This early period set the course for sustainable spending and caused spending to fall below what was implied by the average over the whole period. The markets boomed in the second half of this retirement period, but by then it was too late. The portfolio was already on an unsustainable trajectory, leading to the lowest withdrawal rate in this historical period.

Bengen showed that, historically, a 4 percent initial withdrawal turned out to be much more realistic than higher numbers found when ignoring market volatility. Hence, 4 percent became the rule of thumb for retirement withdrawals.

For the following discussion, I mostly will use the same assumptions as Bengen's original research, with one exception: I assume retirees make their withdrawals at the start of each year, while Bengen assumes end-of-year withdrawals. I think withdrawals at the start of the year are more realistic, since retirees need the funds in order to be able to spend them, and this assumption causes my SAFEMAX to be 4.03 percent, compared to Bengen's 4.15 percent.

⊙ Asset Allocation for Safe Withdrawal Rates

One other important factor from William Bengen's original study is asset allocation. In particular, he recommended that retirees maintain a stock allocation of 50–75 percent, writing in his 1994 article, "I think it is appropriate to advise the client to accept a stock allocation as close to 75 percent as possible, and in no cases less than 50 percent."

Exhibit 4.2 illustrates of how Bengen reached this conclusion by showing the time path of maximum sustainable withdrawal rates for different asset allocations. It is hard to see exactly what is going on in the 1960s, but the general idea is that higher stock allocations tended to support higher withdrawal rates, with little in the way of downside risk. The SAFEMAX does not appear to be that much lower with higher stock allocations, though the potential for upside with higher stock allocations is quite striking as higher sustainable withdrawal rates are possible with all but the worst-case outcomes.

Exhibit 4.2

Maximum Sustainable Withdrawal Rates
For Various Asset Allocations, 30-Year Retirement, Inflation Adjustments
Using SBBI Data, 1926–2016, S&P 500 and Intermediate-Term Government Bonds

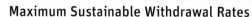

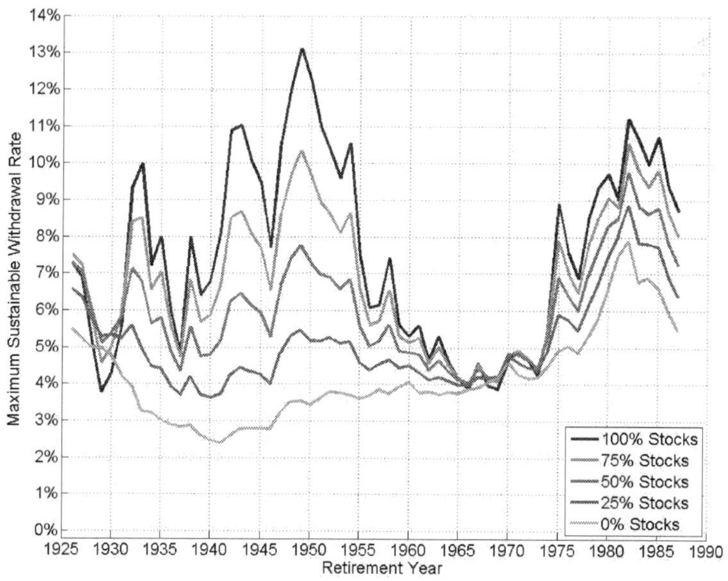

Exhibit 4.3

Connection between SAFEMAX and Stock Allocation
30-Year Retirement, Inflation Adjustments
Using SBBI Data, 1926–2016, S&P 500 and Intermediate-Term
Government Bonds

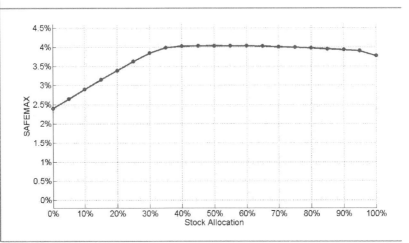

This point can be seen more clearly in Exhibit 4.3, which shows the SAFEMAX across the range of stock allocations. Low stock allocations resulted in lower SAFEMAXs, with an all-bonds portfolio falling below 2.5 percent. But there is a sweet spot between about 35 percent stocks and 80 percent stocks where higher stock allocations have no discernable impact on the SAFEMAX. A 4 percent withdrawal rate tended to work no matter what stock allocation was chosen in this range. On the downside, retirees would have been just as well-off with 80 percent stocks as with 35 percent stocks.

Why, then, did William Bengen recommend 50–75 percent stocks? The answer lies in Exhibit 4.4, which shows the median remaining inflation-adjusted real wealth after thirty years as a multiple of retirement date wealth when using a 4 percent withdrawal rate. In this exhibit, we can see a general upward trajectory in remaining wealth as the stock allocation increases. In the average case, retirees using at least 45 percent stocks would have found that the real inflation-adjusted value of their portfolio remained after thirty years. And with higher stock allocations, wealth tended to continue to grow in the median outcome. So while Exhibit 4.3 shows little in the way of downside spending risk with higher stock allocations, Exhibit 4.4 shows that there is plenty of upside potential available with higher stock allocations, which justifies Bengen's recommendation.

Exhibit 4.4

Connection between Median Remaining Real Wealth after 30 Years and Stock Allocation

For a 4% Withdrawal Rate, Inflation Adjustments
Using SBBI Data, 1926–2016, S&P 500 and Intermediate-Term
Government Bonds

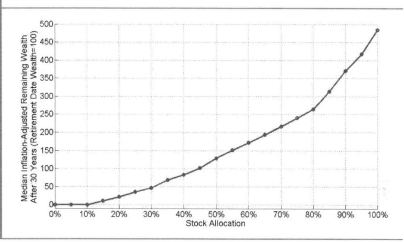

⊙ The Trinity Study and Portfolio Success Rates

Following Bengen, another of the classic studies in the field of financial and retirement planning is the "Trinity study," a nickname for the article "Retirement Spending: Choosing a Sustainable Withdrawal Rate," by Philip L. Cooley, Carl M. Hubbard, and Daniel T. Walz (all professors at Trinity University in Texas). It appeared in the February 1998 issue of the *Journal of the American Association of Individual Investors.*

This research followed the same methodology used by William Bengen in his 1994 article. What was different in the Trinity study was the shift in emphasis away from William Bengen's SAFEMAX, or the highest withdrawal rate possible in the worst-case scenario from history, toward the idea of "portfolio success rates." An unfortunate side effect of this redirection is that the meaning of these portfolio success rates has been widely misinterpreted by the public.

There was one important difference in the assumptions between William Bengen's work and the Trinity study, which I think furthered some of the misunderstandings about the latter study. This difference regards the choice of bond indexes. While Mr. Bengen's original research combined the S&P 500 index with intermediate-term government bond returns, the Trinity study used long-term high-grade corporate bond returns instead. The different choice for bonds explains why the worst-case scenario for Mr. Bengen (his SAFEMAX) was a withdrawal rate of 4.15 percent, but the original Trinity study found that a 4 percent withdrawal rate only had a 95 percent success rate. With more volatile corporate bonds, the sustainable withdrawal rate dipped slightly below 4 percent in 1965 and 1966. This led people to hear that the 4 percent rule has a 95 percent chance for success, though that is true only in the historical data. It does not imply that today's retirees will enjoy the same chance for success. Nonetheless, a 95 percent chance for success has a special meaning in statistics about providing a good level of confidence, so it easy to misunderstand this point. The 4 percent rule became further entrenched.

Since keeping volatility low is just as important as obtaining high returns, I do think it makes more sense to use intermediate-term government bonds than to use corporate bonds. The updated results for the Trinity study provided in Exhibit 4.5 follow Mr. Bengen's choice and include the assumption that withdrawals are made at the start of the year rather than the end of the year.

William Bengen's research gave us the SAFEMAX, which he defined as the highest sustainable withdrawal rate in the worst-case scenario from rolling periods of the historical data. The Trinity study went a step further by tallying up the percentage of times that withdrawal rates fell below or above certain levels. They calculated these portfolio success rates for different withdrawal rates, for different time horizons, and for different asset allocations.

For instance, what is the success rate for a 5 percent inflation-adjusted withdrawal rate over a thirty-year period with a 50/50 asset allocation? To answer, note that there are sixty-two rolling thirty-year periods starting between 1926 and 2016. These rolling thirty-year periods begin in the years 1926 through 1987. We do not yet fully know the thirty-year results for more recent starting periods. Of these sixty-two rolling periods, we can refer back to Exhibit 4.1 and count the number of times that the historical surviving withdrawal rate was at least 5 percent. The answer is forty-three times. That means the portfolio success rate is 100 × 43 / 62 = 69%. This is shown in the exhibit, along with a variety of other permutations.

Exhibit 4.5

Portfolio Success Rates

Inflation-Adjusted Withdrawals For Various Withdrawal Rates, Asset Allocations, and Retirement Durations Using Ibbotson's Stocks, Bonds, Bills, and Inflation Data, 1926–2016, S&P 500 and Intermediate-Term Government Bonds

	3%	4%	5%	6%	7%	8%	9%	10%
100% Stocks								
15 Years	100	100	100	90	79	69	66	55
20 Years	100	100	92	82	72	63	49	40
25 Years	100	99	82	72	63	54	40	28
30 Years	100	94	77	66	55	42	35	21
35 Years	100	91	75	58	51	35	25	12
40 Years	100	88	69	54	37	29	21	10
75% Stocks								
15 Years	100	100	100	97	82	71	60	48
20 Years	100	100	94	81	69	54	46	26
25 Years	100	100	84	69	58	46	28	12
30 Years	100	98	77	58	47	35	13	3
35 Years	100	93	68	54	37	23	4	2
40 Years	100	92	63	42	29	6	2	0
50% Stocks								
15 Years	100	100	100	100	84	71	51	36
20 Years	100	100	99	79	63	42	28	6
25 Years	100	100	85	60	43	22	7	1
30 Years	100	100	69	45	24	10	2	0
35 Years	100	96	58	32	7	4	2	0
40 Years	100	87	42	15	0	0	0	0
25% Stocks								
15 Years	100	100	100	99	77	58	39	19
20 Years	100	100	94	64	47	22	8	1
25 Years	100	100	66	43	22	9	1	0
30 Years	100	87	44	19	10	3	0	0
35 Years	100	65	21	7	5	2	0	0
40 Years	98	44	8	0	0	0	0	0
0% Stocks								
15 Years	100	100	99	90	64	39	23	13
20 Years	100	94	76	40	26	11	3	0
25 Years	97	79	37	25	9	3	0	0
30 Years	82	44	21	10	3	0	0	0
35 Years	70	26	7	5	2	0	0	0
40 Years	62	10	0	0	0	0	0	0

This is the Trinity study in a nutshell. It is a collection of similar calculations made for all the different scenarios shown. What we can generally observe is that success rates increase for lower withdrawal rates, shorter time horizons, and higher stock allocations. We can also see how sensitive results are to withdrawal rates, as for instance with thirty-year horizons and a 50/50 portfolio, the success rate is 100 percent with a 4 percent initial withdrawal rate, and it falls to 69 percent with a 5 percent withdrawal rate, and only 45 percent with a 6 percent withdrawal rate.

As well, I know of at least one nationally syndicated radio show host who talks about an 8 percent withdrawal rate being safe with a 100 percent stock portfolio. The Trinity study does help clarify the wackiness of this notion. After twenty-five years, it's a coin flip about whether any assets are left for someone following that strategy in the historical data.

Again, it is important to be clear that these success rates are based on US history. It is faulty logic to think that these are the success rates applying to new retirees today. The particular situation today is that interest rates are so low relative to history, and this is a very important matter when assessing the viability of different withdrawal strategies. Remember the initial lesson: lower returns imply lower spending. So while I know that the Trinity study is still quite popular in practice, I would suggest a lot of extra caution for anyone seeking to plan their retirements using its numbers. Before discussing this point further, it is worthwhile to discuss Monte Carlo simulations as another alternative for studying the question of safe withdrawal rates.

◉ Monte Carlo Simulations versus Historical Simulations

A second classical approach to studying retirement withdrawal rates is to use Monte Carlo simulations that are parameterized to the same historical data used in historical simulations. This can be done either by randomly drawing past returns from the historical data to construct thirty-year sequences of returns (a process known as "bootstrapping"), or by simulating returns from a statistical distribution (usually a multivariate normal or lognormal distribution) that matches the historical parameters for asset returns, standard deviations, and correlations. Simply put, Monte Carlo simulations provide a way to develop sequences of random market returns fitting predetermined characteristics, in order to test how financial plans will perform in a wider variety of good and bad market environments.

Financial planner Lynn Hopewell implored the financial advisory profession to adopt Monte Carlo simulation tools in his seminal 1997 article in the *Journal of Financial Planning*. He argued forcefully against merely developing spreadsheets for financial plans based on average input assumptions or by testing the robustness of plans with worst-case scenarios. He said those approaches do not provide probabilities of outcomes, and it is still difficult to know how to develop a financial plan, save, and spend using such limited analysis. Today, Monte Carlo analysis is at the heart of most financial planning software programs that aim to test the feasibility of financial plans.

Monte Carlo simulations have a number of advantages over their historical simulations counterparts used in the analysis for Bengen's work and the Trinity study. First, Monte Carlo allows for a wider variety of scenarios than the rather limited historical data can provide. Between 1926 and 2016, there are only sixty-two rolling thirty-year periods, and these are not independent periods since they share so many overlapping data points. Meanwhile, it is not uncommon to see a Monte Carlo simulation study based on ten thousand or more simulated paths for financial market returns. This provides an opportunity to observe a wider variety of return sequences that support a deeper perspective about possible retirement outcomes.

Also, because of the way overlapping periods are formed with historical simulations, the middle part of the historical record plays a disproportionately important role in the analysis. With data since 1926 and for thirty-year retirement durations, 1926 appears in one rolling historical simulation, while 1927 appears in two (for the 1926 and 1927 retirees). This pattern continues until 1955, which appears in thirty simulations (the last year for the 1926 retiree through the first year for the 1955 retiree). The years 1955 through 1987 all appear in thirty simulated retirements, with 1988 appearing in twenty-nine simulations, through 2016, which only appears in one simulation (as the final year of retirement for the 1987 retiree). This overweighted portion of the data (1955–1987) coincides with a bear market for bonds.

In contrast, Monte Carlo simulations treat each data point as equally important. This has implications for portfolio success rates with different asset allocations. Essentially, bonds will have more opportunity to shine with Monte Carlo. In addition, with many more simulations we can expect some scenarios where a particular spending strategy will not work even when it always worked in the same historical data that drives the simulations. Monte Carlo simulations of the 4 percent rule based on the same underlying data as historical simulations tend to show greater relative success for bond-heavy strategies, less relative success for stock-heavy strategies, and lower optimal stock allocations.

Exhibit 4.6 compares the portfolio success rates for varying asset allocations when using a 4 percent withdrawal rate over thirty-year periods. Withdrawals of 4 percent did not fail in the historical period for stock allocations between 40 and 70 percent. Bond-heavy portfolios experienced much lower success rates, though, with a bonds-only portfolio providing success in 44 percent of the historical simulations. With Monte Carlo simulations based on the same historical data, retirees would be encouraged to hold some stocks, but success rates of over 90 percent are possible with stock allocations of only 20 percent. The highest success rates occur in the range between 30 and 60 percent stocks.

Exhibit 4.6

Portfolio Success Rates for a 4% Withdrawal Rate
30-Year Retirement, Inflation Adjustments
Using SBBI Data, 1926–2016, S&P 500 and Intermediate-Term
Government Bonds

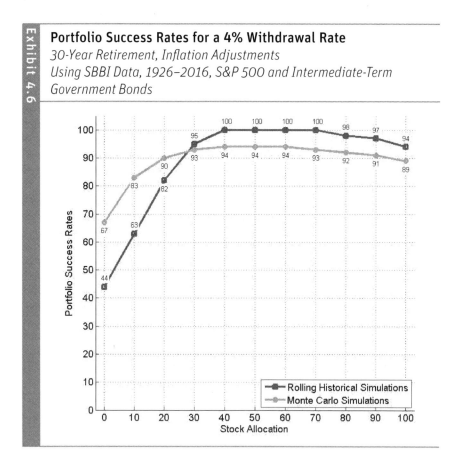

A downside for Monte Carlo simulations is that they do not reflect other characteristics of the historical data not incorporated into the assumptions. For instance, most Monte Carlo simulations used by financial planners do not incorporate mean reversion guided by market valuations, though the US historical record has generally exhibited such behavior. Also, Monte Carlo simulations that do not include "fat tails" in the distribution of returns may not create extreme low or high returns as frequently as seen in reality. However, these two factors may partly offset one another. The lack of mean reversion makes it more likely that extreme returns will happen repeatedly, creating the same overall effect as more extreme one-time returns.

Which brings us to the next point: the results of Monte Carlo simulations are only as good as the input assumptions, though when thinking about future retirements, historical simulations are likely to be even more disadvantaged by this issue. Monte Carlo simulations can be easily adjusted to account for changing realities for financial markets. I described my preferred approach in the technical appendix to chapter 3. Overall, the advantages of Monte Carlo simulations likely more than make up for any deficiencies when compared to the results we obtain using historical simulations.

◉ Capital Market Expectations, Asset Allocation, and Safe Withdrawal Rates

While still within the realm of exploring classical studies about sustainable spending, we should look at an alternative way to frame the results and analysis. That is, rather than asking for the probability of success associated with a particular withdrawal rate, we could also calculate the highest sustainable withdrawal rate linked to a particular probability of success. This discussion is based on my article "Capital Market Expectations, Asset Allocation, and Safe Withdrawal Rates," which was published in the January 2012 issue of the *Journal of Financial Planning*.

There, I presented results for Monte Carlo simulations based on the same historical data that has guided my discussion thus far. For various retirement durations and acceptable failure rates, this method provides details about maximum sustainable withdrawal rates and optimal asset allocations.

Exhibit 4.7

Sustainable Withdrawal Rates Allowing for 10% Failure Probability

For a 30-Year Retirement, Inflation Adjustments
Efficient Frontier Based on SBBI Data, 1926–2016, S&P 500 and
Intermediate-Term Government Bonds

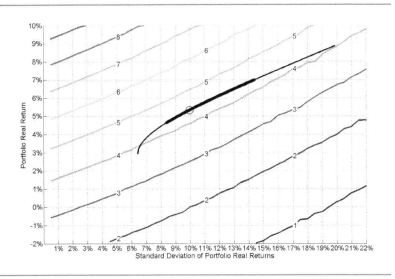

Exhibit 4.7 shows how sustainable withdrawal rates relate to the expectations about portfolio returns and volatilities when the allowed failure rate is set at 10 percent and the retirement horizon is set at thirty years. As we move toward the upper left-hand corner of the exhibit, higher sustainable withdrawal rates are supported through combinations of higher portfolio returns and lower portfolio volatilities. We can observe the lines in the exhibit that map out different withdrawal rates and how returns and standard deviations offset each other in order to maintain the same withdrawal rate.

The efficient frontier of asset allocations generated from the historical data, when combining large-capitalization stocks (S&P 500) with intermediate-term government bonds, is included in this exhibit. The points on this curve represent the highest possible returns for a given level of volatility, or the lowest volatility achievable with a given return. It is the standard formulation for an efficient frontier used in modern portfolio theory, but it is overlaid on a graph that provides information about how different points on the frontier impact sustainable spending rates.

The asset allocation that maximizes the sustainable withdrawal rate of 4.4 percent is identified with a circle. In addition to the optimal asset allocation, the range of points on the efficient frontier (representing a range of asset allocations) that allow for a withdrawal rate within 0.1 percentage points of the maximum are highlighted with a thicker line.

But what *is* the optimal asset allocation, and what range of asset allocations perform nearly as well as the optimal allocation? Though the exhibit does not allow us to see this directly, these answers are provided more clearly in Exhibit 4.8, which shows results for a wide variety of retirement durations and failure rates in the same sort of way as the Trinity study. For the case just discussed—a thirty-year retirement with a 10 percent acceptable failure rate—the third column indicates a maximum sustainable withdrawal rate of 4.4 percent with these conditions. The next set of columns shows that the optimal asset allocation to achieve this 4.4 percent withdrawal rate is 45 percent stocks and 55 percent bonds. This is a fixed asset allocation held throughout retirement with annual rebalancing.

The last four columns demonstrate the range of allocations in which one could expect to do nearly as well with a withdrawal rate within 0.1 percent of the maximum. Any stock allocation between 34 and 71 percent would support a withdrawal rate of 4.3 percent.

The exhibit further shows, unsurprisingly, that sustainable withdrawal rates are higher for shorter retirement durations and higher allowable failure probabilities. In addition, the optimal stock allocation tends to increase both for longer retirement durations and higher allowed failure probabilities. This suggests that the upside potential from stocks is increasingly important to sustaining a longer retirement, and that an acceptance of greater lifestyle risk (the risk of portfolio depletion) allows for more aggressive behavior in relation to a higher spending rate and stock allocation.

A wide range of asset allocations often support withdrawal rates that are nearly as high as the optimal allocation. This exhibit provides clear evidence that lower stock allocations can compete with higher stock allocations in retiree portfolios, even when the results are based on the excellent performance of stocks found in the US historical record.

Withdrawal Rate and Asset Allocation Guidelines for Retirees
Inflation-Adjusted Withdrawals For Various Withdrawal Rates,
Asset Allocations, and Retirement Durations
Monte Carlo Simulations Based on SBBI Data, 1926–2016, S&P 500
and Intermediate-Term Government Bonds

4.8

Retirement Duration (Years)	Failure Rate (%)	Withdrawal Rate (%)	Optimal Asset Allocation (%)		For Withdrawal Rates within 0.1% of Maximum			
			Stocks	Bonds	Range Stocks		Range Bonds	
					Min	Max	Min	Max
10	1	8.9	21	79	11	31	69	89
10	5	9.7	26	74	15	36	64	85
10	10	10.2	29	71	19	45	55	81
10	20	10.8	44	56	27	72	28	73
15	1	6.1	21	79	12	32	68	88
15	5	6.8	29	71	19	45	55	81
15	10	7.2	44	56	21	52	48	79
15	20	7.8	56	44	43	80	20	57
20	1	4.7	21	79	13	36	64	87
20	5	5.3	30	70	19	48	52	81
20	10	5.7	45	55	27	57	43	73
20	20	6.4	71	29	44	92	8	56
25	1	(3.9)	(25	75)	17	38	62	83
25	5	(4.5)	(36	64)	21 — 53 MAX		47	79
25	10	4.9	45	55	29	68	32	71
25	20	5.6	86	14	53	93	7	47
30	1	3.4	26	74	19	44	56	81
30	5	4.0	44	56	24	57	43	76
30	10	4.4	45	55	34	71	29	66
30	20	5.1	86	14	56	96	4	44
35	1	3.1	30	70	19	44	56	81
35	5	3.6	44	56	26	61	39	74
35	10	4.1	56	44	36	80	20	64
35	20	4.8	86	14	60	100	0	40
40	1	2.8	31	69	20	44	56	80
40	5	3.4	48	52	29	62	38	71
40	10	3.8	56	44	42	80	20	58
40	20	4.6	87	13	61	100	0	39

Our initial draw is projected at 37K ÷ 1.1mll = 3.36%

This exhibit has several advantages over the corresponding Trinity study shown before, despite being based on the same underlying data. Exhibit 4.8 uses Monte Carlo simulations, which, as I mentioned earlier, count each year of the historical data equally. It is not subject to the bias against bonds in the historical simulations resulting from an overweighting of the middle historical years. The information is more directly useful than portfolio success rates, as the exhibit directly links acceptable failure rates with maximum withdrawal rates and optimal asset allocation.

The results also fit better with real-world investing. With reduced risk capacity and tolerance, stock allocation recommendations for retirees tend to be lower than the 50–75 percent suggested in historical simulation studies. The exhibit shows how a wide range of asset allocations work nearly as well as the optimum. And since the exhibit is based on Monte Carlo simulations, it can be easily customized to allow changing capital market expectations and asset class choices. Indeed, this was my objective for writing the initial research article. I wished to provide the opportunity for readers to see how their own assumptions would impact sustainable spending rates. Users of the article would not be beholden to the assumptions and choices made by the authors of various research articles. The underlying exhibit remains the same, but you are free to develop your own efficient frontiers and map these onto the exhibit to observe the implications for retirement spending.

Further Reading

Bengen, William P. 1994. "Determining Withdrawal Rates Using Historical Data." *Journal of Financial Planning* 7 (4): 171–180.

Cooley, Philip L., Carl M. Hubbard, and Daniel T. Walz. 1998. "Retirement Savings: Choosing a Withdrawal Rate That Is Sustainable." *American Association of Individual Investors Journal* 20 (2): 16–21.

Hopewell, Lynn. 1997. "Decision Making Under Conditions of Uncertainty: A Wakeup Call for the Financial Planning Profession." *Journal of Financial Planning* 10 (5).

Pfau, Wade D. 2012. "Capital Market Expectations, Asset Allocation, and Safe Withdrawal Rates." *Journal of Financial Planning* 25 (1): 36–43.

CHAPTER 5

The Impact of Changing Bengen's Assumptions

Many of the assumptions used in Bengen's research that led to the 4 percent rule are overly simplistic for real-world retirees. The next several chapters explore what happens when various assumptions change. This chapter maintains a focus on conservative spending from a volatile investment portfolio, and later chapters will further relax even these aspects. Exhibit 5.1 provides a list of the key assumptions we investigate in greater detail.

William Bengen's 1994 study and the Trinity study were only meant to serve as starting points. Bengen in particular has subsequently made several advances and addendums to his initial work. He has been joined by numerous other researchers working to expand the body of knowledge about sustainable retirement spending.

Simplifying assumptions were used in early research, as the purpose was to provide a more realistic assessment of sustainable spending than found when assuming a fixed average investment return. But these studies subsequently took on a life of their own. The 4 percent rule has been widely adopted by the popular press and financial planners as an appropriate rule of thumb for retirees. The 4 percent rule is so widely ingrained in the culture as a universal standard that people commonly think it must apply to any retirement length. Indeed, people are often surprised to learn it is specifically designed for a thirty-year retirement. The 4 percent rule wasn't necessarily meant to apply to eighty-five-year-olds, nor can it be safely used by early retirees who leave the workforce by age forty.

Exhibit 5.1

Assumptions for the 4% Rule

Basic Assumption for 4% Rule	What Else to Consider	Covered in Chapter	Spending Impact
US historical data provides sufficient precedence for future outcomes.	International data is not as favorable for the 4% rule. _Yes –_	5	⬇
	Current low interest rate and high stock market valuation environment is unprecedented. _Yes –_	5	⬇
	Safe savings rates.	5	⬆ ⬇
Retirees earn underlying market index returns.	Investment fees reduce returns relative to indexes. _Our fees low_	5	⬇
	Real-world investors tend to underperform market indexes.	5	⬆ ⬇
Retirees draw from a total-return investment portfolio, spending both portfolio income and principal.	Retirees focus on portfolio income and reach for yield. _No_	5	⬇
	Retirees may use individual bonds to meet upcoming expenses. _No_	7	⬆ ⬇
Retirement portfolio is tax-free or tax-deferred.	Retirement assets may be held in taxable portfolio, which reduces compounding growth potential. _No_	5	⬇
Retirees are willing to deplete portfolio entirely by planning age.	Retirees seek a safety margin for remaining wealth or wish to provide a legacy. _Yes –_	5	⬇
Retirees seek constant inflation-adjusted spending in retirement. They automatically adjust spending each year for inflation and do not voluntarily reduce spending as they age or adjust withdrawals in response to realized financial market returns.	Real retirement spending tends to decline throughout retirement (except for health costs); it may exhibit a "spending smile" pattern over time. _Yes+_	5	⬆
	Retirees may have flexibility to make spending adjustments in response to market performance.	6	⬆
	Retirees may have sufficient income sources outside the portfolio that they need not pay much attention to maintaining a constant portfolio spending amount. _Yes+_	8	⬆
30 years represents a sufficient retirement planning horizon.	Depending on age, health, household composition, and longevity risk aversion, the appropriate planning horizon could be more or less than 30 years. _Less +_	5	⬆ ⬇
Retirement portfolios include two asset classes and a fixed stock allocation of 50–75% to minimize portfolio failure.	Broader diversification beyond two asset classes is possible. _Yes +_	5	⬆
	Retiree risk aversion may prevent holding at least 50% stocks throughout retirement. _Yes –_	5	⬇
	The asset allocation glide path may not be fixed in retirement (rising or declining equity glide paths).	5	⬆ ⬇

The basic philosophy and assumptions behind the 4 percent rule include that the objective is to meet an overall lifestyle spending goal. Retirees are assumed to desire smooth spending, but they also have an appetite for market volatility. Retirees do not voluntarily reduce spending as they age or adjust withdrawals in response to realized financial market returns. Withdrawals are constant, inflation-adjusted amounts.

Failure in retirement is defined as not meeting the overall spending goal for the full assumed retirement time horizon. The underlying objective is to keep the failure rate (the probability of portfolio depletion) at a reasonably low level. For market risk management, retirees use a diversified portfolio focused on total returns with spending from income and principal. Historically, 50–75 percent stocks maximizes the probability of plan success. For longevity risk management, retirees assume a planning horizon sufficiently beyond life expectancy. The 4 percent rule is calibrated specifically to a thirty-year horizon. For management of spending shocks, retirees focus on precautionary savings. As the 4 percent rule is calibrated to be sustainable in the worst case from US history, it otherwise preserves assets that could potentially be deployed for contingencies in other cases.

Basic assumptions also include that retirees earn the precise underlying investment returns net of any fees for a fixed asset allocation with annual portfolio rebalancing. The investment portfolio is either tax deferred or tax free. The two financial assets are large-capitalization stocks (S&P 500) and intermediate-term US government bonds. Finally, the 4 percent rule assumes the US historical experience is sufficiently representative of what future retirees may expect for their own retirements. We will start with this assumption and then continue to work our way through the assumptions to see how alternative approaches would impact our guidelines about sustainable spending from investments.

◎ Is US Historical Data Sufficiently Representative?

Changing some of the most important assumptions used in the early studies will impact the advisable course of action for current and prospective retirees. To begin, we should determine whether US historical data is sufficiently representative to have a clear idea of forward-looking safe spending rates. How relevant is the US historical record?

Classic safe withdrawal rate studies are largely based on the Ibbotson Associates' *Stocks, Bonds, Bills, and Inflation* (SBBI) data, which outlines total returns for US financial markets since 1926. This should be a concern for several important reasons. First, the time period is too short to develop a wide perspective of possible outcomes. Looking at thirty-year retirements, there have only been about three independent observations since 1926. Even for studies with data reaching back to 1871, less than five independent thirty-year periods are available.

Second, this time period also coincides with the rise of the United States as a world superpower. The twentieth century was a rather remarkable and unparalleled era in the United States from the perspective of any country at any point in history. The US economic engine grew and produced extraordinarily during these years, which could give us overinflated estimates of how high the spending rates and stock allocations can safely extend for future retirees. Markets may behave differently in the future, so simply extrapolating the past experience of the United States is problematic.

As William Bernstein pointed out in part 3 of his "Retirement Calculator from Hell" series, post-1926 United States was fortunate to avoid experiencing any truly destructive political, economic, or military crises, which can wipe out a retiree's wealth. A casual look through world history, though, suggests that such crises occur altogether too frequently. Focusing solely on investment risk over a thirty- or forty-year retirement while excluding these other risks will result in overconfidence. For this reason, Bernstein suggests it is meaningless to think about portfolio success rates above 80 percent.

Even if basing the analysis on this extraordinary period is otherwise sensible, current market conditions still outweigh the past events when developing sustainable spending rates. Rather than using historical averages to define our capital market expectations, we should be thinking about realistic assumptions based on what is possible for investors considering present conditions. Though forecasting is hard, clues to better ground us in the current reality can be found by looking at the current term structure of interest rates and stock market valuations.

More generally, we have little basis for knowing how suitable our simulation input assumptions truly are. Will our assumptions be representative of future financial market returns? Small changes in assumptions for portfolio returns and volatility can create a large impact on sustainable retirement spending, as efforts to test assumptions with the PMT and NPER formulas clearly show.

The International Experience of the 4 Percent Rule

An argument in support of the 4 percent rule is that the post-1926 US historical period included a number of calamitous market events (Great Depression, Great Stagnation of the 1970s, etc.). As such, the argument goes, it is hard to imagine an even more dire situation awaiting future retirees. The historical success of the 4 percent rule suggests that we can reasonably plan for its continued success in the future.

But from a global perspective, asset returns enjoyed a particularly favorable climate in the twentieth-century United States, and to the extent that the United States may experience a more typical outcome in the twenty-first century, present conceptions of safe withdrawal rates may be less safe. Prospective retirees must consider whether they are comfortable basing retirement decisions on the impressive but perhaps anomalous numbers found in historical US data. In planning for retirements in the future, it is unclear whether asset returns of this century will continue to be as favorable as they were in the twentieth century, or whether savers and retirees should plan for something closer to the average international experience.

My first foray into researching personal retirement planning—"An International Perspective on Safe Withdrawal Rates: The Demise of the 4% Rule?" (published in the December 2010 *Journal of Financial Planning*)— was a study of the sustainability of the 4 percent rule in other developed-market countries. The study is based on a data set providing financial market returns since 1900 for twenty developed-market countries plus GDP-weighted world and world ex-US indexes. The data is from the Dimson-Marsh-Staunton Global Returns Dataset provided by Ibbotson and Morningstar.

From an international perspective, a 4 percent withdrawal rate has been problematic. In the original article, to avoid claims of bias that I chose an asset allocation that exaggerated the risk of the 4 percent rule, I used a rather generous and unrealistic "perfect foresight assumption." For each country and in each retirement year, I used the asset allocation for local market investors (between stocks, bonds, and bills) that supported the highest withdrawal rate. In many cases, though not all, this meant using 100 percent stocks.

Using the updated data set through 2015 and the perfect foresight assumption, the calculated SAFEMAX meets or exceeds 4 percent in Sweden (4.5 percent), Canada (4.4 percent), New Zealand (4.1 percent), Denmark (4.1 percent), and the United States (4 percent)—only five of the twenty countries. In seven countries, the perfect foresight assumption yields a SAFEMAX below 2 percent for hypothetical retirees investing in their local markets.

The perfect foresight assumption is quite unrealistic, though. As mentioned, the optimal asset allocation is often 100 percent stocks, which is too aggressive for most retirees, and of course no one knows the best asset allocation in advance. For this reason, it is worthwhile to focus on a more plausible 50/50 retirement asset allocation. In terms of the SAFEMAX, 50 percent stocks and 50 percent bills generally outperforms 50 percent stocks and 50 percent bonds in the data set. For bonds, the additional returns over bills failed to compensate for their additional volatility in a retirement income plan, so I will further consider results for the stocks and bills case. Bengen used intermediate-term government bonds—which seem to hold a sweet spot in the trade-off between returns and volatility—to yield the highest sustainable spending. But this bond option is not available in the Global Returns Dataset. For what is available, bills work better than long-term bonds for the aforementioned reason that their lower volatility helps more than the lower return hurts. The results for the 50/50 asset allocation can be seen in Exhibit 5.2.

With a 50/50 asset allocation in this data set, the 4 percent rule survived in Canada (4.0 percent) and came very close in the United States (3.9 percent). Even allowing for a 10 percent failure rate, 4 percent made the cut only in Canada, the United States, New Zealand, and Denmark. In half of the countries, the SAFEMAX fell below 3 percent. World War II–era Japan, in particular, faced the sort of crisis suggested by William Bernstein, as the SAFEMAX was only 0.3 percent for 1937 retirees. The 4 percent rule would have supported expenditures for only three years.

Exhibit 5.2

Maximum Sustainable Withdrawal Rates for Retirees
Global Returns Dataset, 1900–2015
Asset Allocation: 50% Stocks and 50% Bills

	SAFEMAX	SAFEMAX Year	10th Percentile	Withdrawal Rate = 4%		Withdrawal Rate = 5%	
				# Years in Worst Case	% Failures within 30 Years	# Years in Worst Case	% Failures within 30 Years
Canada	4.0%	1937	4.6%	29	1%	19	40%
United States	**3.9%**	**1937**	**4.4%**	**28**	**2%**	**18**	**39%**
New Zealand	3.8%	1935	4.1%	27	8%	18	40%
Denmark	3.7%	1937	4.2%	25	7%	19	59%
World Portfolio	3.5%	1937	3.9%	22	15%	16	56%
Australia	3.4%	1937	3.7%	21	16%	15	38%
United Kingdom	3.4%	1937	3.8%	22	23%	16	46%
Switzerland	3.1%	1915	3.4%	19	32%	13	59%
Sweden	3.1%	1914	3.8%	19	14%	13	47%
South Africa	3.0%	1937	3.8%	21	15%	17	29%
Norway	3.0%	1939	3.1%	17	45%	12	66%
World Ex-US	3.0%	1937	3.5%	19	25%	15	48%
Netherlands	2.8%	1941	3.8%	17	21%	13	62%
Ireland	2.8%	1937	3.2%	19	36%	14	62%
Spain	2.2%	1936	2.6%	12	51%	10	83%
Belgium	1.5%	1914	1.9%	9	48%	7	64%
Finland	1.3%	1917	1.8%	6	40%	5	52%
Germany	1.0%	1914	1.3%	3	53%	3	68%
France	0.8%	1943	1.3%	7	71%	6	82%
Italy	0.8%	1940	1.1%	5	76%	4	83%
Japan	0.3%	1937	0.3%	3	36%	3	44%
Austria	0.1%	1914	0.1%	5	62%	4	75%

Note: Assumptions include a thirty-year retirement duration, no investment fees, constant inflation-adjusted withdrawal amounts, and annual rebalancing.

Meanwhile, hyperinflation in Austria led hypothetical retirees at the start of World War I to only sustain a 0.1 percent withdrawal rate from their portfolio. Shockingly, the 4 percent rule would have failed more than half of the time for countries including Spain, Germany, France, Italy, and Austria. Italians attempting to use the 4 percent rule in their domestic financial markets would have actually faced failure in 76 percent of the historical periods (24 percent success). The exhibit also shows results for a 5 percent withdrawal rate, and failures rates are substantially higher than for 4 percent. Even if the 4 percent rule could somehow be deemed safe, there is clearly not much room for error when seeing how quickly failure rates rise for 5 percent withdrawals. It is somewhat of an understatement to suggest that the results in this exhibit do not portray the 4 percent rule in a positive light.

Keep in mind also that I am only looking at the twenty developed-market countries in the data set, with data going back to 1900. Travel back in time to 1900, though, and ask people to put together a list of twenty developed-market countries for the twentieth century, and you would probably find frequent mention of countries like Argentina, Russia, and China, among others. As those countries never made the data set, even the results I describe here include a degree of survivorship bias.

Thus far, the international data set has revealed sustainable spending rates that fall well below what has been observed with only US historical data. Exhibit 5.3 provides further insight into how the SAFEMAX is impacted by asset allocation. For each stock allocation, the perfect foresight assumption is allowed to guide an optimal asset allocation for bonds and bills, which allows for outcomes slightly different than what was seen in Exhibit 5.2 when only bills were used. While withdrawal rates were often less, this exhibit does, nonetheless, support Bengen's original argument in favor of aggressive asset allocations. For eighteen of the twenty countries, as well as the world and world ex-US, the highest SAFEMAX was obtained with at least 50 percent stocks. Only Switzerland (20 percent stocks) and Sweden (40 percent stocks) witnessed the highest SAFEMAX with less than 50 percent stocks. Especially for the countries with the lowest sustainable spending rates, aggressive stock allocations helped. The seven countries with the lowest SAFEMAX could achieve these only with stock allocations of 80 percent or higher. Because of inflation, nominal bonds were even riskier than stocks for retirement portfolios in those countries.

Exhibit 5.3

Maximum Sustainable Withdrawal Rate for Thirty Years
By Percentage Allocation to Stocks, Combined with the Optimal Bond/
Bill Allocation for the Remainder, Global Returns Dataset, 1900–2015

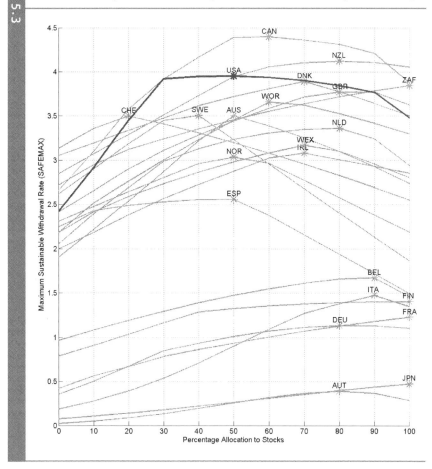

From the perspective of a US retiree, the question is this: will the future provide the same asset return patterns as in the past, or should Americans expect lower asset returns to levels more in line with the experiences of other countries? International readers should keep in mind that the 4 percent rule is based on US historical data, and mileage has varied quite dramatically for other countries. It may be tempting to hope that asset returns in the twenty-first-century United States will continue to be as spectacular as in the last century, but, as John Bogle cautioned his readers in his 2009 book *Enough*, it is important not to count on this happening.

The Importance of Market Conditions at the Retirement Date

For those presently reaching retirement, this leads to a second concern beyond that suggested by the international data. US financial markets have entered uncharted waters now in regard to the low bond yields and high stock market valuations facing investors.

Classic safe withdrawal rates studies such as Bengen's and the Trinity study investigate sustainable withdrawal rates from rolling periods of the historical data, giving us an idea of what would have worked in the past. For a thirty-year retirement period, we can learn about the historical sustainable withdrawal rates beginning up to thirty years ago (i.e., 1987). The question remains whether those past outcomes provide reasonable expectations for the future.

This is worth repeating, as it is important to remember and easy to forget. When looking at thirty-year retirements with historical simulations, we can only consider retirements beginning up to the 1980s. Due to sequence-of-returns risk, recent market conditions only show up at the end of these retirements and have little bearing on their outcomes. This matter extends beyond academic interest, as market conditions have witnessed historical extremes in recent years, in terms of both low interest rates and high stock market valuations.

The general problem with attempting to gain insights from historical outcomes is that future market returns and withdrawal rate outcomes are connected to the current values of the sources for market returns.

As John Bogle describes in his brilliant 2009 book *Enough*, these sources include income, growth, and changing valuation multiples. Future stock returns depend on dividend income, growth of underlying earnings, and changes in valuation multiples placed on earnings. If the current dividend yield is below its historical average, then future stock returns will also tend to be lower. When price-earnings multiples are high, markets tend to exhibit mean reversion, so relatively lower future returns should be expected. Exhibit 5.4 shows that stock market valuations have been high for much of the past twenty years, relative to the period until 1987 for which we know the outcomes from simulated thirty-year retirements.

Exhibit 5.4

Robert Shiller's Cyclically Adjusted Price-Earnings Ratio (PE10)
In January of Each Year, 1880–2017

Source: Robert Shiller's data
(http://www.econ.yale.edu/~shiller/data.htm).

Returns on bonds, meanwhile, depend on the initial bond yield and subsequent yield changes. Mathematically, if interest rates stay the same, then current interest rates will reflect the subsequent return on bonds. Low bond yields will tend to translate into lower returns due to less income and the heightened interest rate risk associated with capital losses if interest rates rise. This relationship is very tight. Exhibit 5.5 shows that recent retirees have been dealing with low interest rates. We do not have much experience in the historical record with this type of interest rate environment, as the early 1940s was the only other period where ten-year Treasuries fell to the 2 percent range.

Our earlier discussion about the PMT formula makes clear that sustainable withdrawal rates are intricately related to the returns provided by the underlying investment portfolio. With sequence-of-returns risk, the returns experienced in early retirement will weigh disproportionately on the final outcome. Current market conditions are much more relevant than historical averages. Past historical success rates are not the type of information that

Exhibit 5.5

10-Year Treasury Yields at the Start of Each Year, 1871–2017

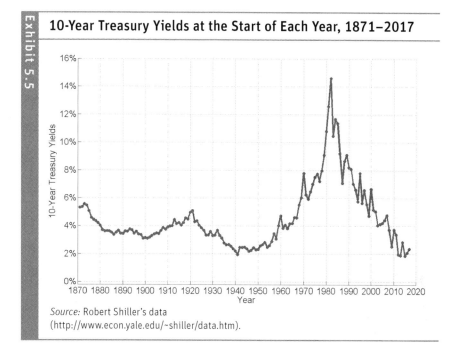

Source: Robert Shiller's data
(http://www.econ.yale.edu/~shiller/data.htm).

current and prospective retirees need for making withdrawal rate decisions. While the original Trinity study concluded that the 4 percent rule has a 95 percent chance for success, that only means the 4 percent rule succeeded in 95 percent of the rolling historical thirty-year periods. New retirees should not count on the same 95 percent chance that the 4 percent rule will work for them.

This is a matter where Monte Carlo simulations are able to shine, by allowing simulations to begin from today's starting point rather than incorporating historical outcomes generated from completely different market environments.

Let's consider outcomes for sustainable spending rates using the Monte Carlo simulations with the low interest rate world of today as a starting point for the simulations. This is the simulation approach described in the technical appendix to chapter 3. We will not make any additional adjustments to reflect the high stock market valuation level, but we will preserve the historical equity premium that stocks have earned above bonds. So when bond yields are low, stock returns must be less as well, as there is no particular reason to believe that stocks would offer even higher premiums above bonds than they have done in the past. On average, these simulations allow bond yields (and therefore stock and bond returns) to wander upward toward historical averages over time to reflect the unlikelihood that interest rates would remain low for the next thirty years or longer. But interest rates could remain low, and some simulations account for this; there is just an upward trend on average.

Exhibit 5.6 provides a way to compare the success rates for the 4 percent rule using Monte Carlo simulations that reduce bond yields at the start of retirement. This is compared with simulations calibrated to historical averages, as well as with the results of rolling period historical simulations. This exhibit makes clear that the low interest rate environment creates additional stresses for the 4 percent rule that were not apparent in Monte Carlo simulations calibrated to historical data with higher bond yield assumptions than are available today. For a 50/50 asset allocation to stocks and bonds, these simulations indicate that the 4 percent rule

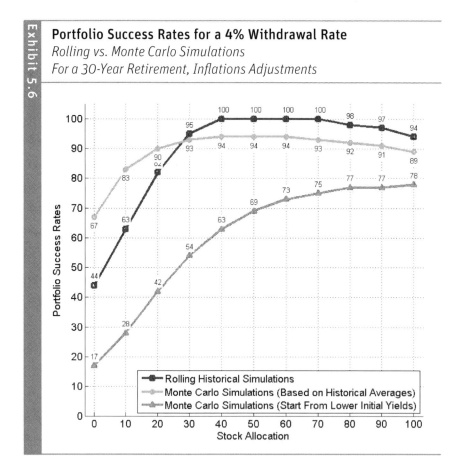

Exhibit 5.6

Portfolio Success Rates for a 4% Withdrawal Rate
Rolling vs. Monte Carlo Simulations
For a 30-Year Retirement, Inflations Adjustments

has a 69 percent chance of success instead of a 94 percent chance. The 4 percent rule may work for today's retirees, but it is far from a sure bet or a "safe" spending strategy.

With lower stock allocations, the 4 percent rule is less likely to work, because it places demands on spending above what today's interest rate environment can easily support. It is magical thinking to believe that bonds can earn higher rates of return than implied by today's low interest rate environment. Returning to the issue of sequence-of-returns risk for retirees, the early returns matter disproportionately in determining sustainable spending outcomes. Success is also less for higher stock allocations because of the assumption that the historical equity premium is maintained on top of a lower bond yield, resulting in lower overall stock returns during the early part of retirement when returns matter the most.

Exhibit 5.7 provides further details by plotting failure rates (instead of success rates) for different withdrawal rates and asset allocations, using the same Monte Carlo simulations that reflect the lower interest rate environment of today. Failure for a 3 percent withdrawal rate hovers at about 10 percent for stock allocations between 40 and 100 percent. This suggests that in a lower interest rate world, a 3 percent withdrawal rate reflects something closer to a chance of success that a 4 percent withdrawal rate historically provided over the broad range of historical market environments. With higher withdrawal rates, failure rates increase accordingly. In addition, when spending rises above what the bond yield curve is able to support, bonds will tend to lock in failure. This explains why the 100 percent stock allocations support the lowest failure rates when spending rates are 4 percent or more. Aggressive allocations provide a type of "Hail Mary pass" that creates the only possible way for higher spending rates to work, but the odds for such success are not favorable; high spending rates are fundamentally unsustainable.

The previous discussion focused on low interest rates without accounting for any future impact from high stock market valuations. The risk premium that stocks earn above bonds was kept at its historical level. Exhibit 5.8 shows the type of risks created by the combination of high stock market valuations and low interest rates. In this case, we can observe the impact of both factors on sustainable retirement spending by looking to historical data rather than relying on Monte Carlo simulations.

Exhibit 5.7

Failure Probabilities for Inflation-Adjusted Withdrawal Strategies
Over a 30-Year Retirement Horizon
Monte Carlo Simulations Starting from Current Market Conditions

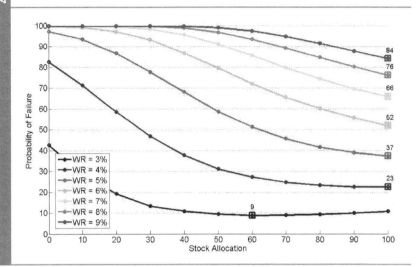

An alternative way to view the historical data is to go beyond merely *considering* past withdrawal rate outcomes, by instead calculating how past outcomes relate to retirement date values of the underlying sources of returns. We can find a way to investigate these implications by following the approach described in 1998 by John Campbell and Robert Shiller, in their article "Valuation Ratios and the Long-Run Stock Market Outlook." They found useful predictive power in estimating the relationship between Shiller's PE10 and the subsequent ten-year real return for stocks. Returns tend to be lower after high valuation periods and vice versa.

Sustainable withdrawal rates from a diversified portfolio including stocks can be expected to share this relationship with market valuations. Using a statistical method called "multivariate regression analysis," we can analyze the relationship between the maximum sustainable withdrawal rate over a thirty-year retirement with a 50/50 asset allocation to stocks and bonds, and the values of Shiller's PE10 and the ten-year Treasury rate at the start of those retirements. The statistical analysis results in this equation:

Predicted Withdrawal Rate = 12.15 – 2.47 × log(PE10) + 0.05 × Bond Yield
Explanatory power: 55 percent

Exhibit 5.8

Actual and Predicted Maximum Sustainable Withdrawal Rates

For 50/50 Asset Allocation, 30-Year Retirement Period
Estimated for Years 1881–1987, Explanatory Variables:
PE10 and 10-Year Treasury Rate

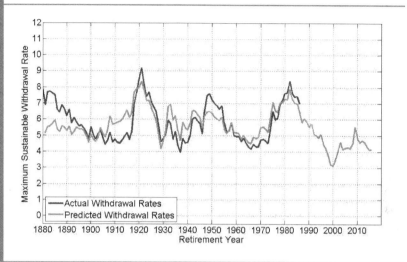

This equation informs us that the sustainable withdrawal rate in retirement can be expected to fall as PE10 is higher and as interest rates are lower. The precise numbers in this equation were estimated from the historical relationship between sustainable spending rates and these variables. We take the natural logarithm of PE10 in order to fit a more precise curve for the relationship between market valuations and spending rates.

Exhibit 5.8 shows the historical sustainable spending rates from 1881 to 1987 using Shiller's data for large-capitalization stocks and ten-year Treasuries. With this data, a hypothetical 1937 retiree saw a historical SAFEMAX of 3.95 percent. This is slightly different from previous results we discussed, as the data set and bond index are different. Every data set is a little different.

The exhibit also provides the estimates developed through the aforementioned equation for the entire time period through the start of 2017. Until 1987, we can compare the relationship between the predictions and the actual values and see it is close. The two variables (PE10 and interest rates) can explain 55 percent of the fluctuations in the historical spending rates. We do not yet know what the thirty-year sustainable spending rates will be after 1987, but we can use this equation to estimate sustainable spending for more recent years, as we know the values of PE10 and the ten-year Treasury rate at the start of those years. We can estimate a sustainable withdrawal rate from any point in time by using the current values for these variables. For instance, in January 2017, PE10 was about 28.2, and the ten-year Treasury was 2.45 percent. Plugging these into the fitted equation gives us:

$$Predicted\ Withdrawal\ Rate\ for\ January\ 2017\ Retirees =$$
$$12.15 - 2.47 \times log(28.2) + 0.05 \times 2.45 = 4.02\%$$

According to this model, the best guess we can make for the sustainable spending rate for a new retiree in 2017 is 4.02 percent. While this is almost identical to the historical SAFEMAX, it is important to emphasize that this is *not* an estimate of the "safe" withdrawal rate. The actual withdrawal rate is *not* a conservative estimate about a safe withdrawal rate; rather, it is the best guess based on the historical relationship between withdrawal rates, market valuations, and interest rates. It could end up being more or less (we won't know which for another thirty years). This estimated withdrawal rate has a 50 percent chance for success. To be conservative, a lower withdrawal rate is required to account for the additional random fluctuations from outside the model. This analysis further confirms the idea that the 4 percent withdrawal rate cannot be treated as safe for retirees in today's market environment. A 4 percent withdrawal rate should never be treated as an almost guaranteed annuitization rate from one's assets, and this is especially true for today's retirees.

These exercises about looking at the impacts of interest rates and market valuations illustrate that assumptions about future returns matter a great deal. This reemphasizes what we could already learn with the PMT formula. As has been the theme thus far, arbitrarily basing Monte Carlo simulations on historical averages may lead to overly optimistic results. Unfortunately, we do not know what the future will bring, and, ultimately, retirees should remain cautious and flexible.

◉ Safe Savings Rates

The relationship between stock market valuations and sustainable spending rates has even greater implications for retirement planning when we consider how the preretirement savings phase and the postretirement withdrawal phase can be linked through the stock market valuation level at retirement. When considered as a whole, the historical data show that, though the relationship is not perfect, the lowest sustainable spending rates (which give us our conception of the safe withdrawal rate) tend to occur after prolonged bull markets. Prolonged bear markets during the accumulation phase tend to allow for much larger spending rates in retirement. This tendency motivates a fundamental rethink of probability-based retirement planning, as worrying about the "safe" withdrawal rate combined with a "wealth accumulation target" is distracting and potentially harmful.

Rather, it is better to think in terms of a "safe savings rate" that has demonstrated success in financing desired retirement expenditures for overlapping historical periods (or with Monte Carlo simulations) including both the accumulation and distribution phases. Put another way, someone saving at his or her "safe savings rate" can expect to finance intended expenditures with as much confidence as we give the 4 percent rule (i.e., it worked in historical data), regardless of the person's actual wealth accumulation and withdrawal rate. This approach has actually supported lower withdrawal rates in recent years that are more reasonable in a low-yield, high-valuation world.

Thus far, we have focused on sustainable spending rates for retirement. It is worth taking a moment to understand how this links to preretirement savings. I define the traditional approach to retirement planning as a four-step process:

Step 1: Estimate the withdrawals needed from financial assets to pay for planned retirement expenses after accounting for Social Security, any defined-pension benefits, and other income sources. Define these planned retirement expenses as a replacement rate (RR) from preretirement salary.

Step 2: Decide on a withdrawal rate (WR) you feel comfortable using based on what has been shown to be sufficiently capable in the historical data.

Step 3: Determine the wealth accumulation (W) you wish to achieve by retirement, defined as W = RR / WR.

Step 4: Determine the savings rate you need during your working years to achieve this wealth accumulation goal.

In my research on safe savings rates published in the May 2011 *Journal of Financial Planning*, "Safe Savings Rates: A New Approach to Retirement Planning over the Lifecycle," I suggest the following retirement planning process as a replacement:

Step 1: Same as step 1 above.

Step 2: Decide on a savings rate you feel comfortable using as determined by what can sufficiently finance your desired retirement expenditures as based on historical data.

If you save responsibly throughout your career, you will likely be able to finance your expenditures regardless of what withdrawal rate this implies. Of course, a caveat must be included that the safe savings rate is merely what has been shown to work in rolling periods from the historical data. The same caveat applies to the safe withdrawal rate. Either rate may need to be revised upward or downward in the future. It must also be clear that my findings about safe savings rates are not one-size-fits-all. I merely illustrate the principles at work by focusing on the case of a particular stylized individual. Real people will vary in their income and savings patterns, consumption smoothing needs, desired retirement expenditures, and asset allocation choices. Through my role as chief planning strategist at inStream Solutions, we have built a safe savings rates module as a planning option in the software for financial advisors to use with their clients. This allows for analysis of more general cases.

The case study I use to illustrate the safe savings rate concept is someone saving for retirement during the final thirty years of her career, and she earns a constant real income in each of these years. A fixed savings rate determines the fraction of this income she saves at the end of each of the thirty years. Savings are deposited into an investment portfolio, which is allocated to an annually rebalanced 50/50 portfolio of the S&P 500 and shorter-term bills. Retirement begins at the start of the thirty-first year and is assumed to last for thirty years. Altogether, the accumulation and decumulation life cycle is sixty years.

Withdrawals are made at the beginning of each year during retirement. The underlying 50/50 asset allocation remains the same during retirement, as does the annual rebalancing assumption. Withdrawal amounts are defined as a replacement rate from final preretirement salary. I assume that the baseline individual wishes to replace 50 percent of her final salary with withdrawals from her accumulated wealth. This 50 percent is more than it may initially seem, as it is only the part from retirement savings. Social Security benefits and any other income sources will be added on top of this. In addition, after retiring, she no longer has to save for retirement or contribute to Social Security, which increases the replacement rate with respect to what could have been spent before retirement. Withdrawal amounts are then adjusted each year for the previous year's inflation. A particular savings rate was successful if it provided enough wealth at retirement to sustain thirty years of withdrawals without having the account balance fall below zero. Actual wealth accumulations and withdrawal rates may vary substantially for different hypothetical individuals from different starting points in history.

Using Robert Shiller's data, I can consider eighty-seven different thirty-year careers followed by thirty-year retirements for retirement dates from 1901 to 1987. In Exhibit 5.8, we saw the historical sustainable spending rates using this data. Exhibit 5.9 shows these outcomes again, along with historical minimum required savings rates to reach a traditional wealth accumulation goal. The savings rates turn Bengen's SAFEMAX calculations on their head in order to calculate a savings rate in isolation from the following retirement period. I calculate the minimum necessary fixed savings rate required over a thirty-year career to achieve a wealth accumulation target at the retirement date. I consider a person wishing to replace 50 percent of her final salary with withdrawals from her accumulated wealth. She wishes to play it safe and hopes to save enough that her desired expenditures represent a 4 percent withdrawal rate from her accumulated wealth. Therefore, she must accumulate wealth that is 12.5 (= 50/4) times her final salary. As indicated before, I treat this as an example of traditional retirement planning advice.

Exhibit 5.9 shows the path of minimum necessary savings rates (MSRs) for thirty-year careers to achieve the fixed wealth accumulation goal. These MSRs are volatile and can be quite high. They were over 30 percent for new retirees between 1918 and 1922 and in 1980–1982. Interestingly, the

Exhibit 5.9

**Minimum Necessary Savings Rate to Accumulate
12.5× Final Salary & Maximum Sustainable Withdrawal Rate**
*For 50/50 Asset Allocation, 30-Year Work Period,
30-Year Retirement Period*

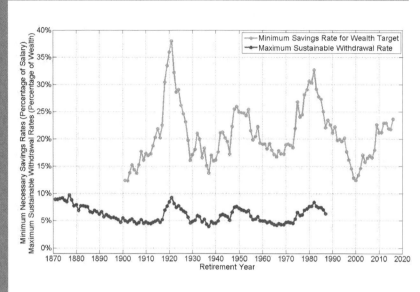

pattern of these MSRs closely follows that of the corresponding maximum sustainable withdrawal rates (MWRs) for each retirement year. For instance, the largest MSR of 38 percent occurs for someone retiring in 1921, the same year we see the largest MWR of 9.2 percent. In addition, retirement years that experienced relative lows for MWRs also experienced relative lows for MSRs. The MSR for 1929 was 16.1 percent, 13.8 percent for 1937, and 16.7 percent for 1966. These retirement years experienced MWRs of 4.6 percent, 4 percent, and 4.2 percent, respectively. More recently, the 2000 retiree enjoyed the lowest MSR in history. This individual only needed to save a fixed 12.5 percent of her annual salary (coincidentally) over a thirty-year career to be able to retire with accumulated wealth equal to 12.5 times her final salary. We will not know the corresponding MWR for the 2000 retiree until the end of 2029.

Exhibit 5.10 shows us that 87 percent of the variation in MWRs can be explained by MSRs. This exhibit also shows that the link between MSRs and MWRs is the market valuation level at the retirement date. Market valuations are represented by the ten-year average of real earnings divided

Exhibit 5.10

Relationship between Valuations, Savings Rates, and Withdrawal Rates

For 50/50 Asset Allocation, 30-Year Work Period, 30-Year Retirement Period

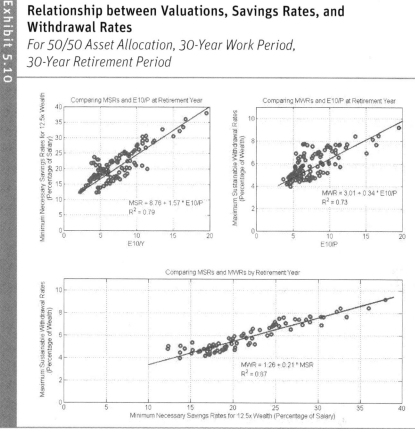

by the real stock market index value at the beginning of the retirement year (E10/P). This is just the inverse of Shiller's PE calculation. When this smoothed earnings yield is low, the stock market tends to be overvalued as a result of a recent run-up in stock prices. Stock price appreciation helps the worker reach her wealth accumulation goal with a lower savings rate. At the same time, a highly valued stock market at the retirement date—as represented by the low smoothed earnings yield—also correlates with a lower subsequent MWR for the new retiree. This point is covered more thoroughly in the previous section.

Now we are ready to integrate the working and retirement phases to determine the savings rate needed to finance the planned retirement expenditures for rolling sixty-year periods from the data. The baseline individual wishes to withdraw an inflation-adjusted 50 percent of her final salary from her investment portfolio at the beginning of each year for thirty years. Prior to

Exhibit 5.11

Minimum Necessary Savings under Isolated and Integrated Approaches

For 50/50 Asset Allocation, 30-Year Work Period,
30-Year Retirement Period, 50% Replacement Rate

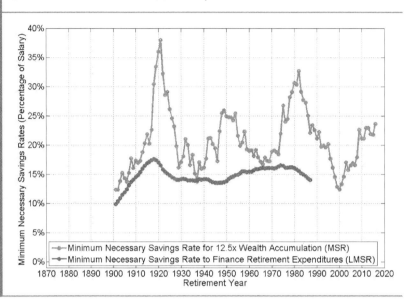

retiring, she earns a constant real salary over thirty years, and her objective is to determine the minimum necessary savings rate to be able to finance her desired retirement expenditures. Her asset allocation during the entire sixty-year period is 50/50 for stocks and short-term fixed-income assets.

Exhibit 5.11 provides these results, showing both the savings rate needed to accumulate 12.5 times final salary (the MSR described above) and the life-cycle-based minimum savings rate (LMSR) needed to finance desired expenditures. The LMSR curve provides my idea about the "safe savings rates." From rolling historical periods, they represent the minimum necessary savings rate for the accumulation phase to pay for the desired retirement expenditures. In the context of Bengen's original study, the maximum value of the LMSR curve (17.6 percent in 1918) becomes the SAFEMIN savings rate from a lifetime perspective that corresponds to Bengen's SAFEMAX withdrawal rate. Had the baseline individual used a fixed 17.6 percent savings rate, she would have always saved enough to finance her desired retirement expenses, having barely accomplished this in the worst-case retirement year of 1918.

Retirement planning in the context of the LMSR curve is less prone to making large sacrifices in order to follow a conservative strategy. In the context of safe withdrawal rates, if someone used a 4 percent withdrawal rate at a time that would have supported an 8 percent withdrawal rate, she is sacrificing 50 percent of the spending power from her savings (her overall spending reduction would be less after including Social Security and other income sources). But in the context of safe savings rates, if someone saved at a rate of 17.6 percent at a time when she only needed to save 9.9 percent (this is the lowest LMSR value, occurring for the 1901 retiree), she is sacrificing 7.7 percent of her annual salary as surplus savings. She will usually also find that she still has funds remaining after a thirty-year retirement period, but she was indeed able to afford her desired expenditures.

The safe savings rate concept has several advantages over traditional planning with regard to individuals who seem to be falling behind or soaring ahead of retirement goals. When retiring after a bear market, individuals using the safe savings rate will have still fallen far behind their traditional wealth accumulation targets. Though the SAFEMIN savings rate was shown to always have worked, these seemingly low wealth accumulations may have discouraged someone from continuing to save, or may have caused someone to needlessly delay retirement.

On the other hand, in recent years, wealth accumulations have been high. They exceeded 12.5 times final earnings between 1997 and 2007. Those saving for retirement during this time may have achieved traditional wealth targets earlier than expected, which may have caused people to either cut back on their savings or even retire early, while postretirement market conditions may result in a lower than expected sustainable withdrawal rate. This is of particular concern for recent retirees who may be overly reliant on the notion that a 4 percent withdrawal rate is safe. The unprecedented bull market of the 1990s would have allowed the 2000 retiree to finance her planned retirement expenditures using a withdrawal rate of only 2.8 percent, a number which could be more in line with reality for more recent retirees.

Safe *savings* rates provide a resolution to the "safe withdrawal rate paradox," which David Jacobs and Michael Kitces developed independently (see Further Reading). Consider the following. At the start of 2008, Person

A and Person B both have accumulated $1 million. Person A retires and uses the 4 percent rule to determine she can withdraw an inflation-adjusted $40,000 for the entirety of her retirement. In 2008, both Person A and Person B's portfolios drop to $600,000. Person B retires in 2009, and the 4 percent rule suggests she can withdraw an inflation-adjusted $24,000. The paradox is that these seemingly similar individuals experience such different retirement outcomes. To resolve the paradox, I am suggesting we shift the focus away from the safe withdrawal rate and instead toward the savings rate that will safely provide for the desired retirement expenditures. Had both these individuals saved in accordance with the "safe savings rate," they would both likely be able to withdraw the same desired amounts, even though they would be using different withdrawal rates.

◉ Do Retirees Earn Underlying Market Index Returns?

Another optimistic assumption of classic safe withdrawal rate studies is that retirees are able to precisely earn the underlying index returns. Three truths dispute that idea:

1. Investing costs may reduce returns below the benchmark levels,
2. Many investors may make behavioral and timing mistakes of buying high and selling low, and
3. Actively managed funds do not precisely match the underlying benchmarks.

In reality, many investors may experience investment returns that lag behind the annually rebalanced and indexed portfolios enjoyed by the hypothetical retiree used in the safe withdrawal rate studies.

It is important to consider the impact of account underperformance relative to benchmarks. In Exhibit 5.12, I consider the impact of 1 percent annual account underperformance relative to the index returns, with every other assumption matching my discussion of William Bengen's work on the SAFEMAX. These assumptions include withdrawals taken at the start of the year, annual rebalancing from a 50/50 portfolio of stocks and bonds, a thirty-year retirement, and inflation-adjusted withdrawal amounts. The exhibit shows the pure Bengen results and the results when annual returns are one percentage point less than the underlying indexes.

In both cases, 1966 retirees are the source of our SAFEMAX. With the index returns, a 1966 retiree could sustain withdrawals over thirty years using a 4.03 percent withdrawal rate. With 1 percent underperformance, the SAFEMAX fell by 0.47 percentage points to 3.56 percent. From the perspective of the SAFEMAX, 1 percent underperformance would have resulted in reduced potential spending power of 11.9 percent. Across the historical period, underperformance caused the maximum sustainable withdrawal rates to fall on average by 0.65 percentage points, or 10.9 percent of spending power.

Despite common misconceptions, a one-to-one trade-off between underperformance and withdrawal rates does not exist. As the portfolio decreases in size, underperformance impacts a smaller amount of wealth, while real withdrawal amounts for retirement spending do not change. This explains why the 4 percent rule did not become the 3 percent rule in response to the underperformance.

It is important to emphasize that this 1 percent underperformance should not necessarily be viewed as fund management or advisory fees. Doing that would confuse the reality that most investors, on their own, would not be in a position to earn the underlying benchmark index returns. Evidence on investor behavior suggests that investor returns trail behind overall market performance even net of investment costs.

Market Mistiming

Generally, investors tend to increase stock allocations near a market peak and then panic and decrease allocations after a market drop. Vanguard has estimated that the behavioral coaching provided by financial advisors to help their retirees stick with a financial plan could add 1.5 percent of additional returns for an investor per year on average over time (their study is discussed further in chapter 9). Even after advisory fees, the net return earned by the investor could be higher than otherwise. In this regard, sustainable spending numbers derived from an analysis that assumes investors always stay the course and rebalance regularly to their aggressive asset allocation throughout retirement may be far from reality for most retirees.

Exhibit 5.12

Maximum Sustainable Withdrawal Rates (MWRs)

Cases: (1) Earn Underlying Index Returns, (2) Underperform Index by 1% Annually For 50/50 Asset Allocation, 30-Year Retirement Duration, Inflation Adjustments Using SBBI Data, 1926–2016, S&P 500 and Intermediate-Term Government Bonds

Year	MWR (Pure)	MWR (1% Less)	Difference	Year	MWR (Pure)	MWR (1% Less)	Difference
1926	7.28	6.47	0.81	1958	5.61	4.90	0.71
1927	7.03	6.24	0.79	1959	4.91	4.29	0.62
1928	6.03	5.35	0.68	1960	4.86	4.25	0.61
1929	5.12	4.54	0.58	1961	4.81	4.21	0.60
1930	5.39	4.79	0.60	1962	4.38	3.83	0.55
1931	5.81	5.16	0.65	1963	4.64	4.07	0.57
1932	7.13	6.34	0.79	1964	4.34	3.82	0.52
1933	6.78	6.02	0.76	1965	4.11	3.62	0.49
1934	5.63	5.00	0.63	1966	4.03	3.56	0.48
1935	5.79	5.14	0.65	1967	4.41	3.9	0.51
1936	4.91	4.36	0.55	1968	4.18	3.7	0.48
1937	4.35	3.87	0.48	1969	4.19	3.73	0.46
1938	5.55	4.95	0.60	1970	4.83	4.31	0.52
1939	4.75	4.24	0.51	1971	4.81	4.3	0.51
1940	4.80	4.30	0.50	1972	4.64	4.16	0.48
1941	5.19	4.65	0.54	1973	4.44	4.00	0.44
1942	6.26	5.62	0.64	1974	5.27	4.76	0.51
1943	6.47	5.81	0.66	1975	6.9	6.25	0.65
1944	6.15	5.52	0.63	1976	6.4	5.81	0.59
1945	5.93	5.32	0.61	1977	5.99	5.44	0.55
1946	5.28	4.73	0.55	1978	6.93	6.30	0.63
1947	6.69	6.00	0.69	1979	7.64	6.96	0.68
1948	7.42	6.64	0.78	1980	8.31	7.56	0.75
1949	7.76	6.93	0.83	1981	8.5	7.73	0.77
1950	7.29	6.49	0.80	1982	9.77	8.87	0.90
1951	6.97	6.18	0.79	1983	8.85	8.01	0.84
1952	6.89	6.09	0.80	1984	8.64	7.80	0.84
1953	6.59	5.80	0.79	1985	8.80	7.94	0.86
1954	6.84	6.00	0.84	1986	7.84	7.05	0.79
1955	5.59	4.89	0.70	1987	7.25	6.53	0.73
1956	5.03	4.39	0.64	1988 +	30 Years of Data Not Yet Available		
1957	5.18	4.53	0.65				

Note: SAFEMAXs are boxed.

What happens to sustainable spending if retirees change their asset allocation at inopportune times? That is, what if retirees increase their stock allocation to chase returns after valuations have risen and then become fearful and lower their stock allocation after valuations have already fallen? Retirees could take any number of arbitrary actions in this regard.

These hypotheticals are much easier to understand with numbers attached to them, so I created an example of an asset allocation strategy in which a retiree maintains a 50 percent stock allocation when Shiller's PE10 is between two-thirds and four-thirds of its historical median up to that point in time. When values exceed the four-thirds threshold, the recent market gains embolden the retiree to increase her stock allocation to 75 percent. When market valuations drop to less than two-thirds of historical numbers, she panics and switches to a 0 percent stock allocation. When market valuations return to the middle range, she switches back to a 50 percent stock allocation.

When tested on Robert Shiller's historical data since 1871, this strategy typically lowers sustainable withdrawal rates compared to a fixed 50/50 allocation. For this data set, the fixed 50 percent stock allocation supported a SAFEMAX of 3.95 percent. The SAFEMAX fell to 3.06 percent with the behaviorally driven asset allocation strategy. There were twenty-nine starting years in which the sustainable spending rate fell below 4 percent. Exhibit 5.13 provides these historical spending rates.

Retirees clearly would have been harmed historically by having their emotions lead them to deviate from their strategic asset allocation. This is an important consideration, because to the extent that individuals do not successfully stick with an asset allocation over time, the hypothetical retiree used to derive the 4 percent rule is irrelevant to real individual outcomes. To the extent that advisors can help retirees better approach the ideal outcomes for the hypothetical retiree used in safe withdrawal rate studies, the discussion of portfolio performance falling below a benchmark return should generally not be interpreted as an impact of advisory fees. Without the better outcomes supported by advisory fees, retirees may be left in an even worse position.

Exhibit 5.13

Maximum Sustainable Withdrawal Rates
50% Stock Allocation and Market Mistiming Asset Allocation,
30-Year Retirement

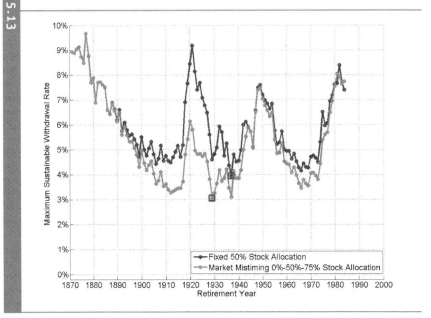

● Should Retirees Use a Total-Return Investment Portfolio?

Total-return investing focuses on building diversified portfolios from stocks and bonds to seek greater long-term investment growth. By focusing on total return, the objective over the long run is to produce a greater and steadier amount of income relative to what could be obtained by investing for income by focusing solely on interest and dividends to support spending without the need for principal drawdown. Nonetheless, investing for income is quite popular in practice. Many do-it-yourself retirees and advisors recommend investing for and living off of income in retirement, shifting away from a total-return perspective. Such methods have yet to receive much academic scrutiny, as it is difficult to obtain good data on historical returns for portfolios that tilt toward higher-yielding subsectors of the market.

Colleen Jaconetti, a senior investment analyst at Vanguard, has taken care to discuss the issues and pitfalls that come with investing for income. She spoke with the American College on these matters in an interview that is available online (see Further Reading). I will summarize her key points here.

A retirement income strategy can be based on one of two things: total return or income. In some cases, these strategies are the same. If your asset allocation is designed from a total-return perspective and you can live off the income provided by the portfolio and other income sources from outside the portfolio (e.g., Social Security), then everything is fine.

The problem is what to do when the total-return portfolio does not generate the desired income. In such a situation, a total-return perspective would have you maintain your strategic asset allocation while consuming your principal. With an income perspective, the last thing you want to do is consume your principal, so you would instead rearrange your investments to provide enough income so you wouldn't have to sell any assets to meet spending needs. In other words, you chase higher yields than a total market portfolio (capitalization-weighted on all investable assets) can provide. Often this means either shifting to higher-yielding dividend stocks, or shifting your bond holdings in the direction of either greater maturity or increased credit risk.

Shifting away from a total market portfolio comes with risk. For higher dividend stocks, the investment portfolio becomes less diversified relative to the total stock market. Dividend-based approaches tend to overweight value stocks relative to the broad market. Portfolios become more concentrated as the top ten holdings in a dividend fund take up a much higher percentage of the total fund. It is also important to remember that dividend stocks are not bonds, so the value of these assets is highly correlated with the stock market. A stock downturn can decimate the portfolio value of dividend stocks.

Also, the misconception persists that higher dividends result in higher returns. In fact, the value of the portfolio drops by the amount of the dividend. Total wealth is not affected by a dividend payment. Actually, the dividend may be taxed at a higher income tax rate rather than the capital gains rate, diminishing after-tax returns with dividends. Higher-yielding dividend stocks have historically provided about the same total return as lower dividend stocks before considering taxes.

As for higher-yielding bonds, the idea is to shift toward longer maturity bonds or bonds with greater credit risk. First, switching to higher-yielding, longer-term bonds leaves investors more exposed to capital losses if interest rates increase. Long-term bond prices are more volatile. With current low yields, a small increase in interest rates will result in capital losses that cancel out the higher interest income. Consider that in January 2017, one-year Treasury bills were yielding 0.89 percent, and thirty-year Treasury bonds were yielding 3.04 percent (let's also assume a coupon rate of 3.04 percent to simplify the analysis). If the thirty-year bond is sold after one year, its return consists of the coupon payments matching 3.04 percent of principal plus any capital gain or loss. If interest rates for thirty-year bonds rose just eleven basis points to 3.15 percent, the capital loss experienced would reduce the total return to the same level as the Treasury bill. A bigger interest rate increase would lead the thirty-year bond to underperform. A capital loss can offset the additional yield with just a small rate increase for long-term bonds, wiping out their potential higher returns.

As for higher-yielding corporate bonds, this leaves investors more exposed to default risk; when the stock market drops, corporate bond prices tend to do the same, as increased default risk works its way into higher interest rates. This credit risk must be considered alongside any potential for increased yields.

As Jaconetti concluded her interview, she summarized the matter perfectly: by reaching for yield, investors trade higher current income for a greater risk to future income. This risk must be accepted when moving away from a total-return portfolio.

◉ Is Any of the Retirement Portfolio in a Taxable Account?

Most research on sustainable spending rates assumes spending is either from a tax-free account such as a Roth IRA or a tax-deferred account such as a traditional IRA. In the latter case, spending is assumed to be gross of taxes, as any taxes due must be paid from the distributions.

For a taxable account, sustainable spending rates would be negatively impacted by the need to pay ongoing taxes for interest, dividends, any capital gains distributions from mutual funds, and realized capital gains or losses when assets are sold. This reduces the potential for compounding growth. Because the tax situations of individuals will vary so greatly in terms of tax rates, interest and dividends supported by the portfolio, and the cost basis of the taxable account, it is impossible to create one general number for a sustainable spending rate from a taxable account. This is an area, though, where William Bengen has extended his research to provide some guidance.

In his 2006 book on sustainable spending rates, *Conserving Client Portfolios during Retirement*, William Bengen attempted to estimate the impact of taxes on spending. He estimated that increasing the marginal income tax rate by 25 percent would approximate the impact of capital gains taxes. For instance, someone in a 25 percent tax bracket could estimate the impact of taxes using a 31.25 percent tax rate to approximate the total income tax liability.

Based on his historical SAFEMAX of 4.15 percent, Bengen provides comparisons for different effective tax rates. For a 20 percent effective tax rate (implying a marginal income tax rate of 16 percent), Bengen estimates that the SAFEMAX fell from 4.15 percent to 3.67 percent (a 12 percent decrease in spending power). If the effective tax rate is 35 percent, the SAFEMAX drops to 3.38 percent. With a 45 percent effective tax rate, the SAFEMAX is 3.2 percent. As tax rates increase, the stock allocation required to maximize spending increases as well. That 3.2 percent SAFEMAX number, for instance, requires a 90 percent stock allocation. One final point is that these new withdrawal rate numbers represent numbers net of taxes. Meanwhile, for a tax-deferred account, a SAFEMAX of 4.15 percent with a 25 percent tax rate would reduce the net spending rate to 3.11 percent.

While I cannot provide generalized numbers to show the impact of ongoing taxes on sustainable spending, basic estimates show that the impact can be substantial.

◉ Is the Retiree Willing to Plan for Complete Portfolio Depletion?

Traditional safe withdrawal rate literature regularly assumes that retirees will choose a withdrawal rate that will leave precisely no wealth at the end of the retirement period. Retirees cling to inflation-adjusted withdrawal amounts, which leaves them playing a game of chicken as their wealth plummets toward zero. In addition, these hypothetical retirees do not make any adjustments for the fact that as their final planned year of retirement approaches, they are increasingly likely to live longer than the age they have planned for. The classical assumptions also present retirees with no particular desire to leave a bequest, an estate, an inheritance, or whatever you may like to call it. The objective of the classical studies is to get a handle on the maximum sustainable withdrawal rate from a portfolio of volatile assets over a thirty-year retirement period without worrying about whether anything will still be left at the end. When we talk about using a safe withdrawal rate, we are describing a situation in which remaining wealth is potentially allowed to fall to zero at the end of the planning horizon.

The safe withdrawal rate approach is meant to typically provide leftover funds at the end of the time horizon when not in a worst-case scenario. But the analysis will be different if we specifically incorporate a desire that our worst cases still preserve some assets at the end of the time horizon. I aim to investigate how withdrawal rate decisions may change when retirees specifically incorporate a desire to leave a bequest, which I will summarize here as either maintaining the nominal value of retirement date wealth at the end of the thirtieth year, or maintaining the real value of retirement date wealth at the end of the thirtieth year. The value of wealth may decline and rebound in the interim, as I am only checking the value of wealth after the thirtieth year.

I am using the same assumptions as described in my discussion of William Bengen's SAFEMAX:

- withdrawals at the start of the year,
- annual rebalancing from a 50/50 portfolio of large-capitalization stocks and intermediate-term government bonds,
- a thirty-year retirement, and
- inflation-adjusted withdrawal amounts.

Exhibit 5.14 shows the maximum sustainable withdrawal rates by retirement year for three scenarios:

1. The classic case in which wealth is depleted after thirty years,
2. The case in which the nominal value of retirement date wealth is preserved after thirty years, and
3. The case in which the real inflation-adjusted value of retirement date wealth is preserved after thirty years.

With the classical wealth depletion assumption and a 50/50 asset allocation, the worst-case scenario withdrawal rate (SAFEMAX) of 4.03 percent fell to the 1966 retiree. Switching to an objective to preserve nominal wealth after thirty years, the SAFEMAX falls to 3.77 percent. The 4 percent rule would have been too aggressive to preserve nominal wealth at four historical starting points (though after thirty years of inflation, that wealth may not have a whole lot of purchasing power left).

When people say they want to preserve the value of their wealth, they are probably implicitly thinking in terms of preserving the real purchasing power of their wealth, even if they do not articulate as much. People tend to suffer from "money illusion," in which they think in terms of nominal dollars when they really mean to consider the real purchasing power of dollars. The next column in the exhibit shows the maximum sustainable withdrawal rates that will preserve the real value of wealth after the thirtieth year. The 4 percent withdrawal rate accomplishes this in 58 percent of the historical simulations (thirty-six out of sixty-two rolling periods). The SAFEMAX for this case happened for 1965 retirees who could only use 2.72 percent to preserve the real value of their retirement date wealth.

Exhibit 5.15 expresses this information in a different way by identifying the amount of wealth remaining after thirty years in both nominal and real terms (retirement date wealth = $100) when using a 4 percent withdrawal rate with a 50/50 asset allocation and all of the other standard assumptions. As I mentioned before, 1966 retirees got the SAFEMAX of 4.03 percent, and we can see that the real value of their wealth after thirty years is $3.40. Since a real withdrawal of $4.00 will be taken in year thirty-one, the 4 percent rule fails over a thirty-one-year horizon for the 1966 retiree.

On the other end of the spectrum is the 1982 retiree. In nominal terms, wealth would have grown to more than ten times its retirement date value, and even in real terms the value of wealth more than quadrupled over thirty years with a 4 percent withdrawal rate.

In the 58 percent of cases that real wealth grows after thirty years of spending with the 4 percent rule, this exhibit better clarifies the degree of this wealth growth. One could also calculate the current withdrawal rate

Exhibit 5.14

Maximum Sustainable Withdrawal Rates (MWRs)

Cases: (1) Wealth Depletion, (2) Preserve Nominal Value of Retirement Date Wealth, and (3) Preserve Real Value of Retirement Date Wealth
For 50/50 Asset Allocation, 30-Year Retirement Duration, Inflation Adjustments Using SBBI Data, 1926–2016, S&P 500 and Intermediate-Term Government Bonds

Year	MWR (Wealth Depletion)	MWR (Preserve Nominal Wealth)	MWR (Preserve Real Wealth)	Year	MWR (Wealth Depletion)	MWR (Preserve Nominal Wealth)	MWR (Preserve Real Wealth)
1926	7.28	6.41	5.99	1958	5.61	5.18	3.92
1927	7.03	6.15	5.69	1959	4.91	4.49	3.26
1928	6.03	5.10	4.55	1960	4.86	4.51	3.41
1929	5.11	4.32	3.80	1961	4.81	4.45	3.29
1930	5.39	4.61	4.07	1962	4.38	4.07	3.02
1931	5.81	5.09	4.49	1963	4.64	4.34	3.30
1932	7.13	6.53	5.91	1964	4.34	4.06	3.06
1933	6.77	6.20	5.45	1965	4.11	3.81	**2.72**
1934	5.63	5.08	4.37	1966	**4.03**	3.79	2.88
1935	5.79	5.26	4.57	1967	4.41	4.18	3.33
1936	4.90	4.37	3.69	1968	4.18	3.97	3.22
1937	4.35	**3.77**	3.03	1969	4.19	4.01	3.35
1938	5.55	5.00	4.30	1970	4.83	4.64	4.02
1939	4.75	4.23	3.50	1971	4.81	4.61	3.96
1940	4.80	4.24	3.38	1972	4.64	4.42	3.70
1941	5.18	4.66	3.78	1973	4.44	4.19	3.41
1942	6.25	5.72	4.87	1974	5.27	5.03	4.32
1943	6.46	5.91	5.12	1975	6.90	6.63	5.95
1944	6.14	5.51	4.61	1976	6.40	6.11	5.40
1945	5.93	5.18	3.97	1977	5.99	5.69	4.99
1946	5.28	4.62	3.42	1978	6.93	6.62	5.92
1947	6.68	6.01	4.95	1979	7.64	7.24	6.38
1948	7.41	6.62	5.44	1980	8.31	7.87	7.10
1949	7.76	6.94	5.64	1981	8.50	8.02	7.30
1950	7.29	6.52	5.10	1982	9.77	9.24	8.52
1951	6.97	6.25	4.76	1983	8.85	8.29	7.56
1952	6.89	6.11	4.35	1984	8.64	8.09	7.40
1953	6.59	5.93	4.29	1985	8.80	8.24	7.55
1954	6.84	6.24	4.67	1986	7.84	7.21	6.50
1955	5.59	5.02	3.45	1987	7.25	6.62	5.90
1956	5.03	4.56	3.20	1988 +	30 Years of Data Not Yet Available		
1957	5.18	4.76	3.50				

Note: SAFEMAXs are boxed.

Exhibit 5.15

Remaining Wealth after 30 Years (Measured in Nominal and Real Terms)

Using a 4% Withdrawal Rate and Retirement Date Wealth = 100
50/50 Asset Allocation, Inflation Adjustments for Withdrawals
Using SBBI Data, 1926–2016, S&P 500 and Intermediate-Term
Government Bonds

Year	Nominal Wealth	Real Wealth	Year	Nominal Wealth	Real Wealth
1926	380.2	254.9	1958	372.4	95.8
1927	345.6	227.4	1959	221.0	55.4
1928	219.9	137.7	1960	245.9	59.9
1929	141.1	85.0	1961	227.7	53.8
1930	178.8	106.0	1962	125.5	28.1
1931	251.6	138.1	1963	218.5	48.1
1932	525.5	257.1	1964	124.6	27.1
1933	481.2	209.8	1965	38.9	8.3
1934	298.6	129.3	1966	15.8	3.4
1935	338.4	147.0	1967	179.1	38.4
1936	169.5	75.0	1968	89.3	19.1
1937	60.8	26.7	1969	106.9	23.5
1938	284.7	124.7	1970	448.1	103.0
1939	146.4	60.5	1971	404.7	95.6
1940	144.1	56.6	1972	291.4	68.8
1941	226.1	84.5	1973	180.5	43.4
1942	420.6	163.5	1974	527.2	134.8
1943	448.3	184.3	1975	1090.8	307.0
1944	340.8	139.8	1976	820.6	239.4
1945	257.0	98.9	1977	671.7	198.6
1946	196.5	68.9	1978	948.0	291.8
1947	399.8	154.8	1979	895.9	288.9
1948	430.9	173.6	1980	980.5	357.9
1949	459.2	177.9	1981	940.9	375.8
1950	430.8	150.3	1982	1081.9	463.9
1951	413.9	134.8	1983	871.9	377.1
1952	371.2	113.9	1984	849.8	375.0
1953	396.3	112.6	1985	849.4	383.8
1954	476.6	131.2	1986	614.7	286.1
1955	281.8	74.4	1987	515.0	240.6
1956	221.5	56.4	1988 +	30 Years of Data Not Yet Available	
1957	279.8	70.7			

after thirty years as the $4.00 real spending divided by the remaining real wealth. The withdrawal rate is higher when wealth is less and lower when wealth is greater. When meeting a spending goal with the 4 percent rule, the withdrawal rate for the 1982 retiree after thirty years has fallen to 0.86 percent. On the other hand, for a 1966 retiree the withdrawal rate would rise to 100 percent for the next year beyond thirty as the last of the wealth is spent.

◉ What Are Reasonable Spending Patterns for Retirees?

An important simplifying assumption in William Bengen's research is that retirees spend constant inflation-adjusted amounts throughout retirement. This behavior may be at odds with the actual spending patterns of many retirees. An exploration of the data should give us an idea of how people actually change their spending during retirement.

A well-known early example of spending changes over time for retirees can be found in Michael Stein's 1998 book, *The Prosperous Retirement: Guide to the New Reality*. Stein says retirement happens in three phases, popularly known as the Go-Go, Slow-Go, and No-Go years of retirement. He found retirement spending to be greatest in the early active phase of retirement through age seventy-five. In these Go-Go years, discretionary expenses for things such as travel and restaurants are high, and retirement spending tends to keep pace with inflation. Between the ages of seventy-five and eighty-five, retirees enter a transition phase (Slow-Go) in which they become less active and reduce discretionary expenditures. Spending no longer keeps pace with inflation and may even decline on a nominal basis. Finally, after age eighty-five, retirees enter the No-Go years, which are signified by a much more modest spending budget whose growth will generally also trail consumer price inflation.

The idea that spending declines throughout retirement obtained further support in an article Ty Bernicke published in the June 2005 issue of the *Journal of Financial Planning* called "Reality Retirement Planning: A New Paradigm for an Old Science." Bernicke used evidence from the Consumer Expenditure Survey (CES) to show that those aged seventy-five and older spend less than those aged sixty-five to seventy-four, who in turn spend less than those aged fifty-five to sixty-four (these are population-wide averages by age group). To account for spending decreases, Bernicke described a tug-of-war for retirees: though their spending increases over time with inflation, they voluntarily spend less as they age. For instance, retirees may lose the desire or ability to go on vacations or restaurants as they age, resulting in fewer expenditures.

Exhibit 5.16 provides updated data from the most recent CES, conducted in 2015. With the updated data, we can observe the trends highlighted by Bernicke. In terms of average annual household expenditures, homes with a reference person aged seventy-five and older spent 23 percent less than households aged sixty-five to seventy-four, and households aged sixty-five to seventy-four spent 15.8 percent less than fifty-five- to sixty-four-year-olds. The exhibit also provides spending broken down

Exhibit 5.16

Spending in the Consumer Expenditure Survey, 2015

	Under 25 years	25–34 years	35–44 years	45–54 years	55–64 years	65–74 years	75 years and older
Average Annual Expenditures	**$32,797**	**$52,062**	**$65,334**	**$69,753**	**$58,781**	**$49,477**	**$38,123**
Food at home	$2,543	$3,539	$4,944	$4,713	$4,200	$3,803	$2,859
Food away from home	$2,347	$3,097	$3,900	$3,693	$2,792	$2,411	$1,702
Alcoholic beverages	$250	$543	$697	$547	$574	$451	$244
Housing	$11,328	$18,305	$22,204	$21,160	$18,188	$16,465	$14,253
Apparel and services	$1,271	$1,864	$2,584	$2,605	$1,596	$1,331	$698
Transportation	$6,320	$9,777	$10,945	$11,781	$10,024	$8,028	$5,228
Health care	$978	$2,770	$3,873	$4,669	$5,112	$5,715	$5,814
Entertainment	$1,354	$2,475	$3,192	$3,317	$3,323	$3,005	$1,728
Personal care	$406	$611	$818	$821	$714	$608	$526
Reading	$38	$86	$95	$106	$115	$157	$199
Education	$2,572	$1,123	$1,178	$2,659	$1,162	$294	$221
Tobacco and smoking	$230	$364	$383	$465	$401	$259	$142
Miscellaneous	$198	$628	$1,142	$1,041	$849	$989	$779
Cash contributions	$397	$874	$1,664	$2,395	$2,066	$2,273	$2,306
Insurance	$24	$127	$317	$475	$482	$397	$243
Pensions and Social Security	$2,540	$5,879	$7,399	$9,305	$7,181	$3,289	$1,182

Source: Consumer Expenditure Survey, US Bureau of Labor Statistics, August 2016.

into various categories. Comparing those seventy-five and older to the younger retiree age group (sixty-five to seventy-four), we see substantial decreases in spending for food away from home, alcohol, apparel and services, transportation, entertainment, and education. As most have left the workforce, contributions to pension funds and Social Security decreased substantially as well. The only categories that increased were cash contributions, which represents gifts to family, friends, or charity; health care; and reading.

The next exhibit provides a different view of the same data, with expenditure categories broken down by the percentage of overall household expenditures by age group. Expenditure shares grow for ages seventy-five and older in the categories of housing, health care, and cash contributions. For these averages, Bernicke's suggestion about retirement spending holds; expenditures decrease in a number of discretionary categories. Housing and health-care expenses may not always decline, but the average growth in these categories is more than offset by expenditures in other categories. Suggesting that retirees should plan for constant inflation-adjusted spending may overestimate the retirement savings that many households will require for a successful retirement. On average, spending declines with age.

That being said, any conclusions drawn from the CES data should be tempered considerably. For instance, inflation is higher in some spending categories than others. The previous analysis misses this because it considers spending between different age groups in the same year. The CES data shows that health-care spending, for instance, tends to rise over time for given age groups even after adjusting for inflation. Health care has a higher inflation rate than overall consumer price inflation. Ten years later, when the sixty-five-to-seventy-four group joins the ranks of seventy-five and older, we should expect higher health-care spending. By looking at different age groups in the same year, we miss this. It is important to follow the same households over time to be confident that spending declines with age.

Another issue is that even if spending declines on average, certain households may experience rising expenditures with age and would be ill-suited by planning with a general assumption that spending will decline. The CES data represents average trends, but conservative plans will call for preparations beyond what happens in the average outcome.

Exhibit 5.17

Spending Shares in the Consumer Expenditure Survey, 2015

	Under 25 years	25–34 years	35–44 years	45–54 years	55–64 years	65–74 years	75 years
Average Annual Expenditures	$32,797	$52,062	$65,334	$69,753	$58,781	$49,477	$38,123
Food at home	7.8%	6.8%	7.6%	6.8%	7.1%	7.7%	7.5%
Food away from home	7.2%	5.9%	6.0%	5.3%	4.7%	4.9%	4.5%
Alcoholic beverages	0.8%	1.0%	1.1%	0.8%	1.0%	0.9%	0.6%
Housing	34.5%	35.2%	34.0%	30.3%	30.9%	33.3%	37.4%
Apparel and services	3.9%	3.6%	4.0%	3.7%	2.7%	2.7%	1.8%
Transportation	19.3%	18.8%	16.8%	16.9%	17.1%	16.2%	13.7%
Health care	3.0%	5.3%	5.9%	6.7%	8.7%	11.6%	15.3%
Entertainment	4.1%	4.8%	4.9%	4.8%	5.7%	6.1%	4.5%
Personal care	1.2%	1.2%	1.3%	1.2%	1.2%	1.2%	1.4%
Reading	0.1%	0.2%	0.1%	0.2%	0.2%	0.3%	0.5%
Education	7.8%	2.2%	1.8%	3.8%	2.0%	0.6%	0.6%
Tobacco and smoking	0.7%	0.7%	0.6%	0.7%	0.7%	0.5%	0.4%
Miscellaneous	0.6%	1.2%	1.7%	1.5%	1.4%	2.0%	2.0%
Cash contributions	1.2%	1.7%	2.5%	3.4%	3.5%	4.6%	6.0%
Insurance	0.1%	0.2%	0.5%	0.7%	0.8%	0.8%	0.6%
Pensions and Social Security	7.7%	11.3%	11.3%	13.3%	12.2%	6.6%	3.1%

Source: Consumer Expenditure Survey, US Bureau of Labor Statistics, August 2016.

Retirement Spending Smile

A more recent contribution to the retirement spending debate is David Blanchett's May 2014 article from the *Journal of Financial Planning*, "Exploring the Retirement Consumption Puzzle." Blanchett's "puzzle" concerns how spending tends to decrease both at and during retirement. While this again reflects the average outcome, Blanchett's data set provides some ability to follow the same households over time throughout retirement. He uses real household survey data from the Health and Retirement Study to track the inflation-adjusted spending for retired households between 2001 and 2009. This helps correct for problems present when focusing on the spending of different age groups at the same point in time.

Blanchett observes a "retirement spending smile" that varies slightly for retirees with different household spending levels. The following exhibit provides Blanchett's spending smile for a retiree who begins retirement with expenditures of $100,000. On average, this household can expect to experience declining real expenditures through age eighty-four, when real spending reaches a trough of $74,146. This reflects a nearly 26 percent drop in real expenditures. After this point, average real expenditures increase, though they do not necessarily exceed their initial retirement levels until retirees reach their midnineties. I produced these calculations using Blanchett's own equation, which relates changes in annual retirement spending to age and the expenditure target at the start of retirement.

Exhibit 5.18

Blanchett's Retirement Spending Smile
The Estimated Path of Real Retirement Spending for a $100,000 Initial Budget at 65 vs. Constant Inflation-Adjusted Spending Strategy

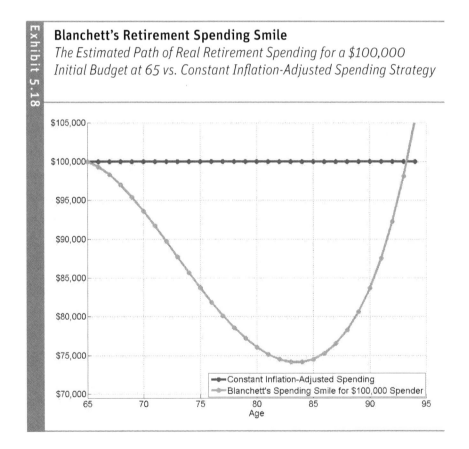

Blanchett observes that the spending smile reflects the same types of outcomes we have described thus far. At the start of retirement, retirees spend more as they enjoy traveling, eating out, and other types of discretionary expenses. As they continue to age, retirees tend to slow down and spend less. However, while discretionary expenses are declining, health costs tend to rise, and at some point later in retirement, these rising health costs offset reductions in other spending categories. Exhibit 5.19 provides a further illustration of this process.

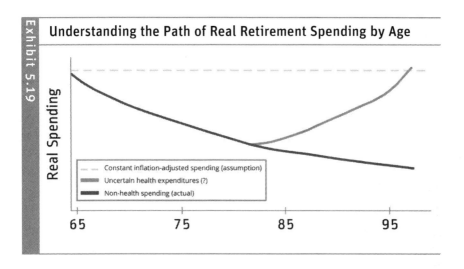

Exhibit 5.19

Understanding the Path of Real Retirement Spending by Age

Real Spending

- Constant inflation-adjusted spending (assumption)
- Uncertain health expenditures (?)
- Non-health spending (actual)

65   75   85   95

The assumption of constant inflation-adjusted spending, according to Blanchett's article, will lead individuals to oversave for retirement. The easiest way to understand this is to simply explore historical sustainable spending rates for different retirement spending patterns. In Exhibit 5.20, I provide the time path of historical sustainable spending rates for both constant inflation-adjusted spending and the retirement spending smile I showed in Exhibit 5.18. As seen earlier, for a thirty-year retirement and 50/50 portfolio, 4.03 percent represents the historical worst-case sustainable spending rate using Bengen's preferred data set. With the spending smile, the initial spending rate can increase to account for subsequent spending declines. In this case, the worst-case initial spending rate rose to 4.73 percent. For retirees basing their spending on these historical worst-case numbers, the retirement smile pattern would allow retirement to begin with almost 15 percent less accumulated wealth than otherwise on account of this higher sustainable withdrawal rate.

Exhibit 5.20

Maximum Sustainable Withdrawal Rates (MWRs)

Cases: (1) Blanchett's Retirement Spending Smile, (2) Constant
Inflation-Adjusted Spending Strategy For 50/50 Asset Allocation,
30-Year Retirement Duration, Inflation Adjustments
Using SBBI Data, 1926–2016, S&P 500 and Intermediate-Term
Government Bonds

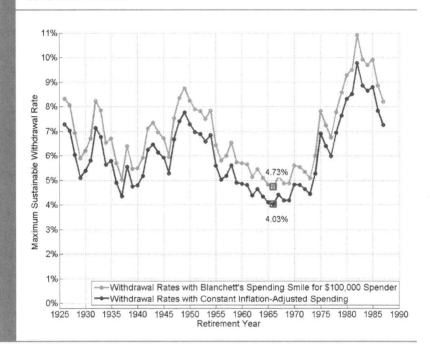

This makes clear that retirement spending patterns are an important component of deciding on a sustainable spending rate. Constant inflation-adjusted spending is a simplifying and conservative assumption.

Age Banding

Another important contribution in the study of retirement spending patterns is Somnath Basu's 2005 article "Age Banding: A Model for Planning Retirement Needs," from the *Journal of Financial Counseling and Planning*. Though it provided a comprehensive retirement planning framework, I want to focus specifically on the findings that cover postretirement spending patterns.

For simplicity's sake, Basu divided a thirty-year retirement into three ten-year intervals. Rather than assuming a constant rate of inflation for expenses during retirement, he divided spending into four general categories: taxes, basic needs, health care, and leisure. Within these categories, he investigated the spending patterns by age and made allowances for differential inflation rates between these categories. For instance, he noted that retirees spend more on leisure in the early part of retirement and more on health in the later part of retirement.

Exhibit 5.21 details how the approach works in four spending categories and three time segments (sixty-five to seventy-four, seventy-five to eighty-four, and eighty-five to ninety-four). The numbers are not calibrated closely to data but are illustrative for a typical retiree.

Exhibit 5.21

An Age Banding Illustration

	Inflation Rate	Lifestyle Adjustment Factor at Age 65	Lifestyle Adjustment Factor at Age 75	Lifestyle Adjustment Factor at Age 85
Taxes	3%	0.5	1.0	1.0
Basic Living	3%	0.7	0.8	0.9
Health Care	7%	1.15	1.2	1.25
Leisure	7%	1.5	0.5	0.25

Source: Adapted from the Stylized Example in Somnath Basu's "Age Banding: A Model for Planning Retirement Needs."

Taxes: The inflation rate for taxes is 3 percent. At age sixty-five, the lifestyle adjustment factor for taxes is an assumed drop to 50 percent of their preretirement level, as payroll taxes are no longer paid and taxable income may be less. The lifestyle adjustment factors are iterative—a value of one at age seventy-five means tax amounts will not change relative to real values at age sixty-five; they only grow with inflation. The same is the case for taxes at eighty-five. Overall, taxes drop by 50 percent at retirement but then stay at this same inflation-adjusted level.

Basic Living Expenses: Basic living expenses—always adjusted for 3 percent annual inflation—are assumed to fall by 30 percent at retirement, then another 20 percent at age seventy-five, and another 10 percent at age eighty-five. Thus, by eighty-five, real spending on basic expenses has fallen to about 50.4 percent of its preretirement level ($0.7 \times 0.8 \times 0.9 = 0.504$).

Health Care: Health care has an inflation rate of 7 percent instead of 3 percent. Health-care expenses also increase with age, adjusting upward by 15 percent at sixty-five, 20 percent at seventy-five, and another 25 percent at eighty-five. By eighty-five, real health expenses are assumed to be 3.7 times larger than their preretirement value ($1.15 \times 1.2 \times 1.25 \times 1.07^{20} / 1.03^{20} = 3.7$), assuming a somewhat simplified overall inflation rate of 3 percent.

Leisure: Like health care, leisure carries an inflation rate of 7 percent. It increases by 50 percent at retirement as retirees set out to enjoy their new freedoms, then drops by 50 percent at seventy-five and another 75 percent at age eighty-five. By eighty-five, even with the higher inflation rate, leisure spending is only 40 percent of its preretirement level in terms of the overall price index ($1.5 \times 0.5 \times 0.25 \times 1.07^{20} / 1.03^{20} = 0.4$).

By capturing both the differential inflation rates and the changing dynamics by age, age banding provides a useful tool for planning long-term retirement budgets. With this approach, however, it is not obvious that retirement spending will decline with age. It may, but rapid growth in health-care expenses could lead to an overall increase in spending needs at the highest ages.

Four Types of Retirement Spenders

One final study should be considered to help shed light on retirement spending patterns and which default assumptions could be appropriate for different types of retirees. In August 2015, J.P. Morgan Asset Management released a study about retirement spending by Katherine Roy and Sharon Carson titled "Spending in Retirement." Their data set provides a "big data" analysis of 613,000 US households led by people fifty-five or older who were estimated by the researchers to have managed most of their household finances through banking services at Chase (debit and credit cards, paying mortgages through a bank account, etc.). In analyzing the expenditures for their diverse consumer base, they outlined four retirement spending profiles and an additional category of miscellaneous individuals. These are the profiles they found:

Foodies (39 percent of households): The largest category of the population tends to be fairly frugal in retirement, with the lowest overall spending. The category name comes from the fact that 28 percent of their expenditures are in the food and beverage category, including purchases at large box stores or online retailers. Foodies tend to have lower housing expenditures, as they have paid off their mortgage and have limited property taxes. Foodies also tend to spend less as they age. The authors conclude that while foodies should separately account for health expenditures, they can otherwise reasonably plan for their spending to decrease as they continue through retirement. As will be clearer after describing the other categories, foodies may be the only group that can plan to be reasonably well served by a retirement spending smile expenditure pattern.

Homebodies (29 percent of households): This group tends to spend much more on housing in retirement than others. Some may still have a mortgage, but even for homebodies without mortgages, there can be significant expenses for property taxes, ongoing maintenance, repairs, furnishings, and utilities. Homebodies may be maintaining a large home, and their expenses may be more likely to keep pace with inflation. For instance, as homebodies age, they may require greater expenditures on home maintenance and chores for activities they are no longer able to manage on their own. For homebodies, getting a sense of future retirement expenses can require making clear plans about future housing: When will the mortgage be paid? Is there a second home that may be sold? What portion of the budget consists of property taxes and utility bills? What are future plans for downsizing or further renovating the home?

Globetrotters (5 percent of households): This category of households spends much more on travel and has the highest overall expenditures of any category. Globetrotters represent 11 to 13 percent of households with at least $1 million of investment assets. Spending does not seem to decline much with age: the proportion of globetrotters in the population stays consistent at the age seventy-five-plus range, and expenditures on travel are also the highest for this age group. The authors conclude that globetrotters should probably work from the assumption that their retirement spending will keep pace with inflation, making it more dangerous for them to plan in advance to follow a retirement spending smile type of pattern.

Health-care spenders (4 percent of households): For this group, health-care expenditures reflect 28 percent of income. Expenditures include Medicare-related expenses and prescription costs. As health-care expenses tend to rise faster than the overall inflation rate, those who are part of this category must take care to adequately project their health-care expenses. The forces that create the upward spending tick in the retirement spending smile could happen sooner, and overall spending could increase faster than average consumer inflation.

Snowflakes (24 percent of households): The remaining households reflect more unique types of experiences that cannot be categorized more generally.

And so, what is the best baseline assumption to use: constant inflation-adjusted spending, decreased spending, or a retirement spending smile? This is a big question that is still not fully resolved. We need to track individual households over time in order to better see the variety of spending patterns and how they relate to personal characteristics of the household. What percentage of households voluntarily reduce their spending? What percentage are forced to increase spending due to entering a nursing home or experiencing large medical bills? Are their personal characteristics linked to different spending patterns that could help retirees find better assumptions? For instance, higher net worth retirees may have much larger discretionary expenses when they enter retirement, while more typical retirees may find that most of their spending is for essential needs, which will not be reduced and must adjust with inflation. The research by Roy and Carson moves the furthest in analyzing these sorts of questions, but one would still be hard-pressed to develop a personalized spending plan based on their findings. A clear point, though, is that those who plan for greater expenses related to travel, housing, or health care should expect their spending needs to keep closer pace with inflation.

Spending may decline, so I would not fault anyone for using assumptions of gradual real spending declines such as 10 percent or even 20 percent over the course of retirement. But pending further research developments, I would avoid moving too far in the reduced spending direction as a baseline assumption. Though the inflation-adjusted withdrawal assumption could be improved, it builds in reasonable conservatism and may not be too far off as a baseline for many retirees, even if the *average* retiree experience suggests otherwise.

With regard to constant inflation-adjusted spending patterns, there are two significant further issues that we will consider in later chapters. Chapter 6 considers the possibility that retirees may maintain flexibility to adjust spending in response to market fluctuations. We consider a number of different dynamic or variable spending strategies that have been proposed as alternatives to the basic assumption of constant inflation-adjusted spending. Chapter 8 further explores why retirees may have the flexibility to adjust spending by also considering household resources, such as Social Security and other pension income, held outside the investment portfolio. An increased capacity to maintain their lifestyle by relying on alternative income sources in the face of market volatility can allow retirees to be more aggressive with their portfolio spending and worry less about supporting constant inflation-adjusted withdrawals.

◎ What Is the Appropriate Planning Age for Retirees?

In chapter 2, we considered how sustainable spending relates to the retirement planning horizon and found that a longer horizon means spending less in order to sustain the available resources. We extend that discussion here within the context of Bill Bengen's analysis of the 4 percent rule.

The 4 percent rule is specifically based on a planning horizon of thirty years (so an eighty-five-year-old is not necessarily limited to a 4 percent spending rate). It gets its name from its suggested spending rate for the *first year* of retirement. Beyond that, the spending rate evolves to compensate for inflation, and portfolio returns guide the amount of remaining financial assets.

How long will your retirement last? The impossibility of answering this question with any long-term accuracy is one of the key challenges of planning a retirement income strategy. The nature of longevity risk is that we know our life expectancy, but it is based on an average with a great deal of variability.

Two general approaches exist to deal with this unknown element of longevity:

1. Planning for fixed retirement durations that are generally somewhere beyond life expectancy, and

2. Making plans that specifically incorporate survival rates by age into the calculations.

The former method is the most common (the 4 percent rule's fixed thirty-year horizon uses this method) and easiest to work with, but both approaches have their strengths.

Planning for a Fixed Retirement Horizon

Planning for a specific retirement time horizon begins by selecting a horizon you are unlikely to outlive and then developing a plan that covers the entire period. The horizon should be greater than life expectancy, as retirees have a 50 percent chance of living beyond the average.

In 1994, Bill Bengen considered thirty years to be a reasonable planning horizon for sixty-five-year-old couples, resulting in a planning age of ninety-five. Many people use different planning ages, such as 100 or 105. Those who are either younger or older than sixty-five may need to plan for more or less than thirty years. Even sixty-five-year-olds may wish to plan for different retirement durations depending on how conservative they wish to be and how fearful they are of outliving their investment portfolio. A sixty-five-year-old planning to live to 100 or 105 would need to plan for a thirty-five or forty-year horizon.

The assumed retirement duration is of utmost importance. Retirement simulations based on longer time horizons will guide optimal retirement income solutions toward:

*   lower withdrawal rates,
*   higher stock allocations, and
*   a stronger case for guaranteed income retirement products.

Writing in Harold Evensky and Deena Katz's *Retirement Income Redesigned*, Bob Curtis makes a convincing case for fixed horizons. He argues that longevity is not a "probability problem" but a "possibility problem," adding, "What possible sense does it make to tell your client that she can spend more money now because you're assuming in *some* of the Monte Carlo iterations that she'll die early? How does a person die 'some of the time?'"

It is a good question. But at the same time, does it make sense to lower spending now so you can plan to spend just as much at one hundred as at age sixty-five, despite the low chance of living to one hundred? The answer is *yes* and *no*. It truly depends on your unique preferences regarding these trade-offs.

The conservative approach is to plan for a longer horizon by spreading out distributions from your portfolio. You will have to spend less and most likely leave a larger than planned bequest. Traditional safe withdrawal rate studies ignore this risk entirely, instead focusing solely on minimizing failure. On the other hand, planning for a shorter horizon could leave you exposed to overspending, which means you could outlive your wealth. For some, the risk of cutting spending and missing out on enjoying hard-earned wealth outweighs the risk of overspending. The impact of this risk varies from person to person depending on the value each would get from additional spending.

Exhibit 5.22 explores the impact of retirement length on sustainable withdrawal rates. Using historical data since 1926 and all of the baseline assumptions—including a 50/50 allocation to large-capitalization stocks and intermediate-term government bonds—the exhibit shows Bill Bengen's SAFEMAX withdrawal rate for retirement horizons between five and forty years. We saw before that the SAFEMAX for a thirty-year retirement is 4.03 percent. This exhibit illustrates a curve in which the SAFEMAX declines, but at a decreasing rate, as the retirement duration increases. The historical SAFEMAX for forty years reduces to 3.72 percent.

Next, Exhibit 5.23 shows the specific spending rates for a variety of asset allocations and retirement lengths. It also shows the withdrawal rates implied by the required minimum distribution (RMD) rates set by the IRS for tax-deferred retirement accounts. The requirements apply after age 70.5, but those with inherited IRAs may have to withdraw at earlier ages using these rules, so the government provides RMDs for younger ages as well. Including the RMD withdrawal rates in this exhibit allows us to compare historical SAFEMAXs and RMDs for different time horizons. These are lined up in the exhibit to imply a planning age of one hundred.

Exhibit 5.22

Relationship between SAFEMAX and Retirement Duration
for a 50/50 Asset Allocation, Inflation-Adjusted Spending Using SBBI Data, 1926–2016, S&P 500 and Intermediate-Term Government Bonds

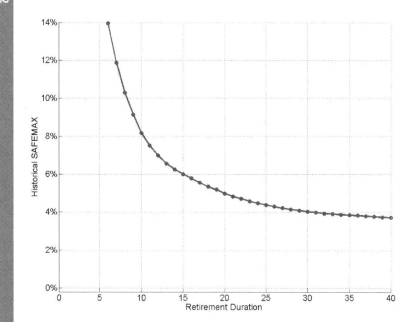

We can observe a number of important points about asset allocation with this table. For instance, a 100 percent bond allocation supports a higher withdrawal rate than a 100 percent stock allocation until the time horizon is thirteen years. Beyond that point, 100 percent stocks supports a higher withdrawal rate than 100 percent bonds. With shorter time horizons, bonds more effectively lock in a goal at a higher withdrawal rate with less risk. But as the horizon lengthens, the amount that can be safely supported with bonds declines. Eventually, stocks are able to support more spending despite their greater volatility.

Nonetheless, diversification is important. A 50/50 asset allocation always supports a higher SAFEMAX than 100 percent stocks at all time horizons, and it supports a higher SAFEMAX than 100 percent bonds after a time horizon of six years.

Exhibit 5.23

Varying SAFEMAXs by Retirement Duration and Asset Allocation
Inflation-Adjusted Spending
Using SBBI Data, 1926–2016, S&P 500 and Intermediate-Term
Government Bonds

Retirement Duration	100% Stocks	75% Stocks	50% Stocks	25% Stocks	0% Stocks	RMDs	Age
1	100	100	100	100	100	14.93	99
2	38.51	41.82	44.40	45.52	46.08	14.08	98
3	23.53	25.85	27.93	28.78	29.12	13.16	97
4	16.12	19.10	20.68	21.04	21.24	12.35	96
5	12.84	15.57	16.82	16.86	16.86	11.63	95
6	10.89	12.90	13.96	14.12	13.85	10.99	94
7	9.41	10.96	11.86	12.16	11.66	10.42	93
8	8.60	9.55	10.29	10.73	10.08	9.80	92
9	7.89	8.56	9.14	9.61	8.90	9.26	91
10	7.10	7.68	8.16	8.55	7.93	8.77	90
11	6.54	7.06	7.50	7.83	7.08	8.33	89
12	6.13	6.61	6.99	7.27	6.36	7.87	88
13	5.78	6.22	6.56	6.81	5.77	7.46	87
14	5.53	5.94	6.25	6.38	5.30	7.09	86
15	5.30	5.71	6.01	5.98	4.91	6.76	85
16	5.08	5.51	5.78	5.67	4.57	6.45	84
17	4.88	5.26	5.55	5.40	4.26	6.14	83
18	4.73	5.07	5.34	5.16	4.01	5.85	82
19	4.58	4.92	5.18	4.94	3.78	5.59	81
20	4.42	4.78	4.98	4.75	3.56	5.35	80
21	4.28	4.66	4.82	4.58	3.39	5.13	79
22	4.16	4.56	4.70	4.43	3.24	4.93	78
23	4.08	4.46	4.57	4.30	3.10	4.72	77
24	4.01	4.38	4.47	4.17	2.98	4.55	76
25	3.95	4.30	4.38	4.06	2.86	4.37	75
26	3.89	4.22	4.29	3.97	2.76	4.20	74
27	3.85	4.16	4.22	3.87	2.66	4.05	73
28	3.83	4.10	4.15	3.78	2.57	3.91	72
29	3.80	4.05	4.09	3.70	2.48	3.77	71
30	3.77	3.99	4.03	3.62	2.40	3.65	70
31	3.75	3.95	3.99	3.54	2.33	3.60	69
32	3.73	3.92	3.94	3.47	2.26	3.50	68
33	3.71	3.89	3.91	3.40	2.20	3.40	67
34	3.70	3.87	3.88	3.34	2.14	3.31	66
35	3.68	3.85	3.85	3.28	2.08	3.23	65
36	3.67	3.83	3.83	3.21	2.03	3.14	64
37	3.66	3.81	3.80	3.14	1.98	3.06	63
38	3.65	3.78	3.77	3.09	1.93	2.99	62
39	3.63	3.76	3.74	3.03	1.88	2.91	61
40	3.62	3.74	3.72	2.98	1.83	2.84	60

We can also see a rule of thumb developing about the historical SAFEMAXs for a 50/50 portfolio as they relate to the time horizon. The SAFEMAX is about 8 percent for ten-year horizons, 6 percent for fifteen, 5 percent for twenty, and 4 percent for thirty years.

Exhibit 5.24 provides a visual comparison between the SAFEMAX for a 50/50 asset allocation calibrated to a planning age of one hundred, and the RMD rules. These curves are relatively close together, but the RMDs become more conservative as you approach age one hundred. This makes sense, since as you approach the planning age, it becomes increasingly likely that you will live beyond it. RMDs are also more conservative until about age seventy-five, implying lower spending than historical SAFEMAXs for the early part of retirement. Using the RMD rules to set withdrawal rates for each year of retirement presents a viable alternative to using constant inflation-adjusted withdrawal amounts. I will return to this topic in the next chapter when I discuss variable spending strategies. The lesson for now is

Exhibit 5.24

Connection between SAFEMAX with Planning Age of 100 and RMDs for a 50/50 Asset Allocation, Inflation-Adjusted Spending Using SBBI Data, 1926–2016, S&P 500 and Intermediate-Term Government Bonds

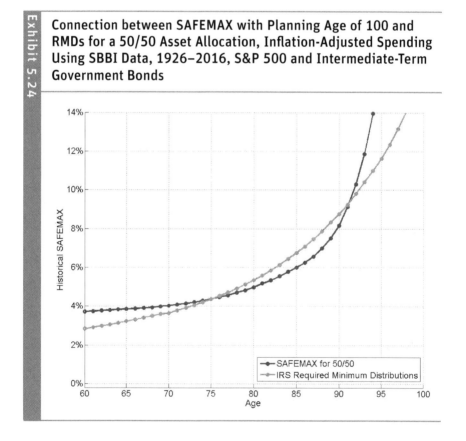

that the assumed retirement horizon is a very important consideration for deciding on a withdrawal rate.

Planning with Mortality Data

The second general approach to dealing with the question of longevity and sustainable spending is to leave the concept of planning horizons behind and simply incorporate survival probabilities into calculations. Failure is really only failure if wealth is depleted while you are still alive, not just over an arbitrarily long time period. Implications of using mortality data directly include:

- a shorter average retirement duration than the standard thirty years,
- higher withdrawal rates for a given probability of failure,
- a lower allocation to stocks, and
- mixed results for the role of lifetime income guarantees, with shorter average retirements but some extremely long ones in the tail of the distribution.

The argument for using survival probabilities is that assuming a remaining lifespan of thirty years or longer for a typical person retiring at age sixty-five results in needless underspending. In this view, the probability of running out of financial assets should be defined as the probability of running out of financial assets *before death,* rather than within an arbitrarily long period of time. This creates competing risks for what comes first: death or financial portfolio depletion.

Dirk Cotton and his coauthors studied these competing risks in a 2016 article titled "Competing Risks: Death and Ruin," in the *Journal of Personal Finance.* They found that retirement could generally be divided into three phases:

1. A low-risk period in early retirement with few portfolio failures and few deaths,
2. A middle period beginning around age eighty in which portfolio failures dominate, and
3. A late period starting in one's early to midnineties when death becomes more likely than portfolio failure.

In other words, for those whose portfolios survive through the middle part of retirement, death becomes a more imminent likelihood than a late-life portfolio depletion.

The American Academy of Actuaries and the Society of Actuaries created the Longevity Illustrator to help users develop personalized estimates for their longevity based on a few questions about age, gender, and health. Exhibit 5.25 provides these numbers for sixty-five-year-old males and females based on their health assessment and smoking status.

In practical terms, most individuals will probably be best served by using fixed time horizons that are sufficiently conservative to reflect their personal concerns about outliving their wealth. Generally, choosing planning ages for the tenth percentile from this exhibit is a reasonable approach for many. Those who are more concerned about the implications

Exhibit 5.25

Planning Ages for 65-Year-Olds from the Longevity Illustrator

Health Classification Chance of Survival	MALE						Social Security 2013 Period Life Table
	Non-smoker			Smoker			
	Excellent	Average	Poor	Excellent	Average	Poor	
90%	72	71	70	68	68	67	70
75%	80	78	76	73	72	71	76
50%	87	85	83	81	78	76	83
25%	94	92	90	88	85	83	89
10%	98	97	95	94	91	89	94

Health Classification Chance of Survival	FEMALE						Social Security 2013 Period Life Table
	Non-smoker			Smoker			
	Excellent	Average	Poor	Excellent	Average	Poor	
90%	75	74	72	70	69	68	73
75%	83	81	79	76	75	73	79
50%	90	88	86	84	82	80	86
25%	96	94	93	92	89	87	92
10%	101	99	97	97	95	93	96

Source: The Longevity Illustrator, www.longevityillustrator.org.

of longevity will wish to assume a longer time horizon and behave more conservatively. This is a more straightforward way to incorporate longevity risk aversion into a retirement income plan. Trying to develop a plan around survival probabilities by age is more complex.

The use of survival probabilities is probably best limited to those working with more mathematical utility models to analyze retirement spending decisions. But the complexities of such models mean their insights are best used to describe potential caveats or adjustments for the conclusions derived from the more straightforward approach of using a fixed planning age. When using survival probabilities, the risk of a long life is mitigated by planning to reduce spending with age to account for the reduced likelihood of living beyond a certain age.

◉ Are Retirees More Flexible with Asset Allocation?

The basic asset allocation framework for safe withdrawal rate studies is to assume a few basic asset classes held in fixed proportion over retirement. William Bengen's original research used large-capitalization US stocks and intermediate-term government bonds. Later he also incorporated small-capitalization stocks into the mix and looked at different types of bond investments. Occasionally, we also see some basic attempts at including international diversification in the asset allocation. Expanding asset class choices can support a higher sustainable spending rate. As for asset allocation glide paths, a fixed asset allocation over retirement has been standard. But it is worth exploring further about the implications of declining or rising equity allocations throughout retirement as well.

Broader Diversification Is Possible

Safe withdrawal rates are connected in vitally important ways to underlying asset class choices and their return/volatility characteristics. Often, retirees are limited to accepting whatever a researcher assumes about market returns in order to obtain guidance about sustainable spending rates. I talked about why I found this troubling in my article "Capital Market Expectations, Asset Allocation, and Safe Withdrawal Rates," from the January 2012 *Journal of Financial Planning*. It provides a framework for connecting these pieces together, in turn letting retirees move beyond existing research assumptions to identify a more personalized safe withdrawal rate.

Reconciling the assumptions underpinning safe withdrawal rate studies with your own capital market expectations and constraints is a daunting task. My article proposed a general framework for determining a safe withdrawal rate for a given retirement duration, acceptable failure probability, asset allocation, and capital market expectations. Retirees do not need to be constrained by the assumptions and choices of others.

Most researchers use one set of capital market expectations to study aspects of safe withdrawal rates. Often, they base their analyses on US historical data going back to 1926. This is far from a perfect solution. When determining a forward-looking safe withdrawal rate, the most important factor is our expectations about future market returns as driven by their underlying components: income, growth, and changes in valuation multiples. If current bond yields are noticeably lower than usual, the average historical bond return will likely be of little relevance.

But not all research is based on historical averages. Sometimes researchers use different assumptions, either because they want to illustrate a particular concept with basic assumptions, or because they have incorporated their own capital market expectations.

Still, a general problem remains: safe withdrawal rates research leaves unanswered questions about what would happen if different asset classes were included, or if different assumptions were made about returns, volatilities, and correlations. My research generalized the framework for safe withdrawal rates, presenting a structure that incorporates user-specified capital market and retirement assumptions. I used Monte Carlo simulations to calculate the combinations of real portfolio arithmetic returns and volatilities that would support different withdrawal rates for various retirement durations and acceptable failure probabilities.

From there, it is a matter of determining the portfolio's expected return and volatility based on our assumptions about asset classes and their expected returns, volatilities, and correlations. In order to find the optimal asset allocation, these assumptions can be transformed into an efficient frontier. Overlaying the efficient frontier onto my exhibits lets you find the point corresponding to the highest maximum sustainable withdrawal rate. The asset allocation for the optimal point can then be determined separate from the underlying efficient frontier characteristics. This provides you with a recommended withdrawal rate and recommended asset allocation for your own specifications.

My article also described a secondary finding: that a wide range of asset allocations support withdrawal rates nearly as high as the optimal asset allocation. Many retirees will be able to support a withdrawal rate within 0.1 percentage points of the optimum with a markedly lower stock allocation. Conservative retirees need not be pressured into uncomfortably aggressive asset allocations, such as the recommendations for 50 to 75 percent stocks found in prominent research articles by Bill Bengen and others.

Exhibit 5.26 provides capital market assumptions for five asset classes: US stocks, US REITs, the MSCI EAFE for international stocks, US bonds, and US bills. These include the arithmetic real returns, compounded returns, volatilities, and correlations. These are not my recommended assumptions—they are a case study about the process. Assuming that these values align with a retiree's viewpoints and choices for asset allocation, Exhibit 5.26 provides the ingredients to study sustainable spending rates.

To assess the importance of these different capital market expectations, I compute an efficient frontier for this set of assumptions. Software is available to make such computations, as this task is generally not done by hand. Mean-variance optimizer software uses inputs to find the efficient

Exhibit 5.26

Hypothetical Long-Term Capital Market Expectations (in Real US Dollar Terms)

	Arithmetic Means	Geometric Means	Standard Deviations	US Stocks	US REITS	MSCI EAFE	US Bonds	US Bills
US Stocks	6.5%	4.50%	20%	1.0	0.7	0.6	0.1	0.1
US REITs	5.5%	4.22%	16%	0.7	1.0	0.5	0.3	0.4
MSCI EAFE	6.5%	4.08%	22%	0.6	0.5	1.0	-0.1	-0.1
US Bonds	0.7%	0.46%	7%	0.1	0.3	-0.1	1.0	0.7
US Bills	-0.3%	-0.38%	4%	0.1	0.4	0	0.7	1.0

Note: These are hypothetical numbers used to illustrate the framework for expanding the asset allocation that can be used with sustainable spending studies. They do not represent actual forecasts.

frontier of asset allocations that provide the most return for a given volatility or the least volatility for a given return.

The efficient frontier can then be plotted onto the grid framework relating withdrawal rates to returns and volatilities for an acceptable failure probability and retirement duration. In Exhibit 5.27, I overlaid the efficient frontier (a lighter color for only considering US stocks and bonds, black for all five asset classes in Exhibit 5.26) onto the withdrawal rate charts for a thirty-year retirement duration and a 10 percent acceptable failure probability (different charts can be made for different assumptions about retirement length and the acceptable failure rate). Each diagonal line (technically an "isoquant") shows the combination of rates of return and standard deviations that will support a given sustainable withdrawal rate.

From this overlay, we determine where the efficient frontier reaches the highest withdrawal rate. The thin parts of the curves identify the entire efficient frontier of asset allocations. The circles identify the points reaching the highest sustainable withdrawal rate. The thick parts of the

Exhibit 5.27

Sustainable Withdrawal Rates with 10% Failure for 30-Year Retirement Horizon

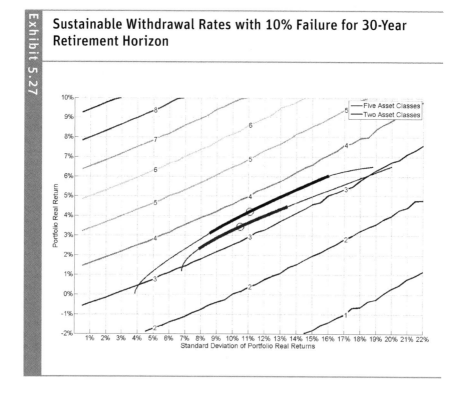

curves identify the range of portfolio allocations supporting withdrawal rates within 0.1 percentage points of the maximum. Returning to the mean-variance optimization results, we find the asset allocation corresponding to this optimal point. The optimal asset allocation can then be compared to the retiree's investment constraints and risk tolerance to determine its acceptability. If it is found to be unacceptable, other points on the efficient frontier that support progressively lower withdrawal rates can be investigated until a suitable asset allocation is found.

Exhibit 5.28 provides further detail. When using all five asset classes (the black efficient frontier), the optimal asset allocation supports a 3.61 percent withdrawal rate over thirty years with a 10 percent chance for failure. The optimal asset allocation is shown. Meanwhile, when only two of the asset classes are used, the withdrawal rate is 3.34 percent with an optimal asset allocation of 47.2 percent stocks and 52.8 percent bonds. The asset allocations provided in Exhibit 5.28 cannot be seen in the visual found in Exhibit 5.27, but they do exist behind the scenes within the software.

Exhibit 5.28

Sustainable Withdrawal Rates with 10% Failure for 30-Year Retirement Horizon

Asset Classes	Withdrawal Rate	Real Portfolio Return	Portfolio Standard Deviation	Asset Allocation
US Stocks	3.34%	3.4%	10.5%	47.2%
US Bonds				52.8%

With Five Asset Classes

Asset Classes	Withdrawal Rate	Real Portfolio Return	Portfolio Standard Deviation	Asset Allocation
US Stocks	3.61%	4.2%	11.1%	14.9%
US REITS				30.5%
MSCI EAFE				20.4%
US Bonds				34.2%
US Bills				0.0%

This case study illustrates how the framework for incorporating your own capital market expectations works. Of course, formulating appropriate capital market expectations is hard. Volatility especially complicates the process. A common view is that future stock returns will be lower than historical averages, but what about stock volatility? Would lower stock returns be accompanied by lower volatility, or is it reasonable to keep volatility the same? Might we even expect volatility to increase? The withdrawal rate lines in Exhibit 5.27 are upward sloping, making pinpointing the precise combination of expected returns and volatilities especially important; if you forecast lower volatility, you can spend more for a given level of returns.

This framework can be used to estimate sustainable withdrawal rates for a given failure rate and retirement duration for most any kind of capital market expectations. The purpose here is to demonstrate how retirees can translate their own expectations into an understanding about how to choose a withdrawal rate and asset allocation strategy.

Dynamic Asset Allocation Strategies

A second common assumption for withdrawal rate studies is that the asset allocation remains fixed throughout retirement and is rebalanced to the targeted allocation every year. For this discussion, we will relax the assumption that retirees maintain the same fixed asset allocation throughout their retirement, but, we will remain firmly within the realm of total-return investing. In chapter 7, we will also consider time segmentation as a different way to justify a dynamic asset allocation in retirement.

Changing asset allocation over retirement within the context of a total-return investment portfolio can be understood as an attempt to reduce portfolio volatility at key points in retirement in order to reduce the retiree's exposure to sequence-of-returns risk. Even if the average market return is decent, retirees are especially vulnerable to the impact of bad market returns in early retirement. Sequence risk is uniquely caused by the attempt to spend a constant amount each year from a volatile investment portfolio. Sequence risk can be dampened by either letting spending fluctuate or reducing portfolio volatility. For now, we'll focus on reducing volatility.

Outside of just using a low-equity allocation throughout retirement (which comes with its own sets of risks in terms of being unable to support a spending goal beyond the bond yield curve), we can identify three major ways to reduce portfolio volatility when it counts the most. These methods have three goals:

1. To reduce volatility when most exposed to absolute wealth losses (rising equity glide path),
2. To reduce volatility when most exposed to "predictable" market losses (valuation-based asset allocation), or
3. To reduce volatility when financial goals are most at risk (funded ratio).

We will address each in turn.

1. Rising Equity Glide Path

First, rising equity glide paths for retirement aim to reduce portfolio volatility in the pivotal years near retirement when a retiree is most vulnerable to losing the most dollars of wealth with a given market drop. This discussion is based on an article I wrote with Michael Kitces titled "Reducing Retirement Risk with a Rising Equity Glide Path," which was published in the January 2014 issue of the *Journal of Financial Planning*.

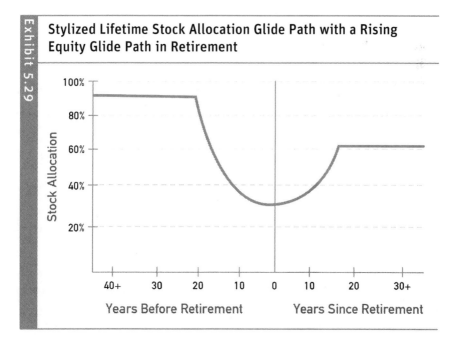

Exhibit 5.29

Stylized Lifetime Stock Allocation Glide Path with a Rising Equity Glide Path in Retirement

People are most vulnerable and have the most at stake when their wealth is largest, which generally happens around retirement. The suggested lifetime stock allocation path thus becomes U-shaped: stock holdings are higher when young, at their lowest around the retirement date, and higher again later in retirement. Exhibit 5.29 illustrates this general pattern.

The idea of a rising equity glide path in retirement is counterintuitive, as conventional wisdom says that stock allocation should decline with age. On account of this counterintuitive surprise, the rising equity glide path concept has been popular with personal finance writers. The rising equity glide path is intended to be treated as a risk management technique in retirement. It may help support spending and wealth in retirement at times when retirement goals may be most at risk.

To understand the concept of rising equity glide paths, it is worthwhile to consider four general economic environments retirees may face. First, financial markets may do well throughout the entire retirement period. In this case, retirement should be successful regardless of asset allocation strategy, though more aggressive strategies will support a larger legacy. Next, the entire retirement may be confronted by poor market returns. In this case, no allocation strategy can save retirement. A rising stock allocation would at least fare better than a more aggressive asset allocation throughout. Third, financial markets may perform well in early retirement but poorly later in retirement. In this case, sequence risk will not manifest, and the sustainable withdrawal rate will be high. Rising equity glide paths will work, but they may leave less legacy than otherwise. Finally, the rising stock glide path excels in scenarios that have historically led to the worst outcomes for retirees. That is, markets fare poorly early in retirement and then recover later in retirement. These scenarios have created the lowest withdrawal rates for past retirees, and this is where a rising equity glide path can make a difference in supporting better retirement outcomes.

While the rising equity glide path idea is meant as a risk management technique, there are obvious real-world implications that may limit its usefulness. Primarily, it may be that as people age, it becomes increasingly difficult to stay the course in response to market volatility, and retirees who have experienced a period in early retirement where they dealt with less volatility may not be prepared to deal with volatility again late in life. Perhaps the best implication from research along these lines is to at least not think about continuing to reduce stock allocations throughout retirement, and also that it may be okay to start retirement with a lower stock allocation than the traditional withdrawal rate studies suggest.

2. Valuation-Based Asset Allocation

A second approach to dynamic asset allocation is to use valuation-based asset allocation. The idea for this approach is to reduce the stock allocation when the portfolio is the most vulnerable to experiencing a big decline in value, which historically has happened when measures such as Robert Shiller's cyclically adjusted price-earnings (PE) ratio have risen to levels well above their averages (i.e., 1929, the mid-1960s, and 2000).

A related possibility is to modify asset allocation based on current market valuations. For instance, in an April 2012 *Journal of Financial Planning* article titled "Withdrawal Rates, Savings Rates, and Valuation-Based Asset Allocation," I investigated a case study comparing a 50/50 fixed asset allocation for stocks and bonds against a strategy that keeps 50 percent stocks as a baseline but switches to 25 percent stocks when Shiller's PE ratio rises above four-thirds of its historical average up to that point, and rises to 75 percent stocks when Shiller's PE ratio falls below two-thirds of its historical average up to that point. In rolling historical thirty-year periods using Robert Shiller's data for large-capitalization US stocks and ten-year US government bonds, the valuation-based strategy raised the SAFEMAX withdrawal rate from 3.93 percent to 4.58 percent.

Another article of mine, "Retirement Risk, Rising Equity Glide Paths, and Valuation-Based Asset Allocation," linked the concept of rising equity glide paths with valuation-based asset allocation by focusing more on the interplay between different glide paths and valuation-based asset allocation. There, my coauthor Michael Kitces and I clarify that the rising equity glide path does not necessarily have to be used as a universal solution. However, the current investing environment in 2017 reflects the circumstances when the rising glide path is most useful. That is, the stock market is highly valued and is more vulnerable to a decline. This is when the rising glide path works to lower the stock allocation to serve as a guide through the years when the retiree is most vulnerable to a market drop. Presuming such a drop occurs at some point, it will then shift to a higher stock allocation later in retirement when markets are less highly valued.

In other words, the rising glide path approximates a valuation-based asset allocation strategy.

When markets are not highly valued, retirees might look more carefully at just holding a higher stock allocation or using a valuation-based asset allocation strategy. If markets are undervalued, the traditional type of declining equity glide path in retirement can look more attractive, as it provides a closer approximation to what would be done with a valuation-based strategy.

In a highly valued market environment (like 2017), retirees can reduce their vulnerability to the effects of a big drop in the stock market by using a lower equity allocation. This can be accomplished by using either a preset rising equity glide path (as an inverse of what today's target-date funds do for the preretirement period), a valuation-based strategy, or some combination of the two.

It must be noted that implementing a valuation-based allocation strategy requires a certain disposition, as it is a contrarian strategy requiring lower stock allocations when people are most giddy about stocks, and requiring higher stock allocations when panic has set in for the typical investor. The fact that the strategies "worked" historically does not guarantee future success. Nonetheless, this research proposes a potential asset allocation approach for retirees wishing to incorporate valuations into their asset allocation choices, but also wishing to maintain a formal commitment to an asset allocation decision framework that will hopefully help prevent hasty, emotion-based decisions. At the very least, these findings can help support the psychological discipline to stay the course and not buy high and sell low.

3. Funded Ratio

Finally, asset allocation can be based on a retiree's funded ratio. The point of calculating an individual's funded ratio is to treat personal retirement planning in the same manner as a corporate pension fund. Are the lifetime values of assets large enough to meet the lifetime liabilities? The answer to this question is measured through the funded ratio. A funded status of 100 percent means that a household has just enough assets to meet liabilities. Overfunded and underfunded individuals have more or less than this.

This approach seeks to reduce portfolio volatility when retirees have enough assets to just get by with meeting their retirement spending goals using a low-volatility portfolio. Once retirees have excess "discretionary" wealth beyond what is needed to safely lock in their goals, they can invest more aggressively with a volatile portfolio. In other words, reduce volatility when the possibility of meeting your financial goals is most vulnerable to the impacts of a negative market.

Determining your funded status is an important method to help get a feel for whether your retirement plan is on track. Chapter 8 will provide more details about using the funded ratio in practice. A key point for now is that the funded ratio can be used to guide asset allocation, as being overfunded for retirement can provide the capacity to use a more aggressive asset allocation.

Further Reading

Basu, Somnath. 2005. "Age Banding: A Model for Planning Retirement Needs." *Journal of Financial Counseling and Planning* 16 (1): 29–36.

Bernicke, Ty. 2005. "Reality Retirement Planning: A New Paradigm for an Old Science." *Journal of Financial Planning* 18 (6): 56–61.

Bernstein, William. 1998. "The Retirement Calculator from Hell." [http://www.efficientfrontier.com/ef/998/hell.htm]

Blanchett, David. 2014. "Exploring the Retirement Consumption Puzzles." *Journal of Financial Planning* 27 (5): 34–42.

Bengen, William P. 2006. *Conserving Client Portfolios during Retirement*. Denver: FPA Press. [http://amzn.to/2soKFLF]

Bogle, John C. 2009. *Enough: True Measures of Money, Business, and Life.* Hoboken, NJ: John Wiley. [http://amzn.to/2tqSzJk]

Campbell, J. Y., and R. J. Shiller. 1998. "Valuation Ratios and the Long-Run Stock Market Outlook." *Journal of Portfolio Management* 24 (2): 11–26.

Cotton, Dirk, Alex Mears, and Cary Cotton. 2016. "Competing Risks: Death and Ruin." *Journal of Personal Finance* 15 (2): 34–40.

Curtis, Robert. 2006. "Monte Carlo Mania." In *Retirement Income Redesigned: Master Plans for Distribution*, edited by Harold Evensky and Deena B. Katz. New York: Bloomberg Press. [http://amzn.to/2uOwI8v]

Jacobs, David B. 2006. "Is Failure an Option? Designing a Sound Withdrawal Strategy." Unpublished draft paper (October).

Jaconetti, Colleen. 2012. "Investing for Income in Today's Environment." The American College–New York Life Center for Retirement Income Video Series. https://retirement.theamericancollege.edu/video-library/investing-income-todays-environment.

Kitces, Michael E. 2008. "Resolving the Paradox—Is the Safe Withdrawal Rate Sometimes Too Safe?" The Kitces Report (May).

Kitces, Michael E., and Wade D. Pfau. 2015. "Retirement Risk, Rising Equity Glide Paths, and Valuation-Based Asset Allocation." *Journal of Financial Planning* 28 (3): 38–48.

Kinniry, Francis M., Colleen M. Jaconetti, Michael A. DiJoseph, and Yan Zilbering. 2014. "Putting a Value on Your Value: Quantifying Vanguard Advisor's Alpha." Vanguard Research Paper.

Pfau, Wade D. 2010. "An International Perspective on Safe Withdrawal Rates: The Demise of the 4% Rule?" *Journal of Financial Planning* 23 (12): 52–61.

Pfau, Wade D. 2011. "Safe Savings Rates: A New Approach to Retirement Planning over the Lifecycle." *Journal of Financial Planning* 24 (5): 42–50.

Pfau, Wade D. 2012. "Capital Market Expectations, Asset Allocation, and Safe Withdrawal Rates." *Journal of Financial Planning* 25 (1): 36–43.

Pfau, Wade D. 2012. "Withdrawal Rates, Savings Rates, and Valuation-Based Asset Allocation." *Journal of Financial Planning* 25 (4): 34–40.

Pfau, Wade D., and Michael E. Kitces. 2014. "Reducing Retirement Risk with a Rising Equity Glide Path." *Journal of Financial Planning* 27 (1): 38–45.

Roy, Katherine, and Sharon Carson. 2015. "Spending in Retirement." J. P. Morgan Asset Management Retirement Insights (August).

Society of Actuaries, www.longevityillustrator.org.

Stein, Michael. 1998. *The Prosperous Retirement: Guide to the New Reality. Emstco Press.* [http://amzn.to/2o3jYhl]

CHAPTER 6

Managing Sequence Risk with Variable Spending Strategies

William Bengen's 1994 article introduced the concept of the 4 percent rule for retirement withdrawals. He defined the sustainable spending rate as the percentage of retirement date assets that can be withdrawn, with this amount adjusted for inflation in subsequent years, such that the retirement portfolio is not depleted for at least thirty years. Specifically, Bengen found that a 4 percent initial spending rate would have been sustainable in the worst-case scenario from US historical data over rolling thirty-year periods with a stock allocation of between 50 and 75 percent. Bengen used a number of simplifying assumptions (understandably) in an attempt to illustrate the importance of the sequence of investment returns to retirement spending outcomes. Among these is the previously mentioned constant inflation-adjusted spending assumption. It was a simplification to obtain a general guideline about feasible retirement spending.

While this assumption may reflect the *preferences* of many retirees to smooth their spending as much as possible, real-world individuals inevitably vary their spending over time in response to their portfolio's performance. Retirees will not play the implied game of chicken by keeping their real spending constant as their portfolios plummet toward zero. It is an unrealistic assumption.

Being flexible with spending matters a great deal. Constant spending from a volatile portfolio is a unique source of sequence-of-returns risk that can be partially alleviated by reducing spending when the portfolio drops in value. With flexibility, the initial withdrawal rate can increase by more than one might think on account of the synergies created through decreasing sequence risk. In this regard, estimates obtained with a constant inflation-adjusted spending assumption may be overly conservative for those willing and able to adjust their spending over time.

In the previous chapter, we altered the inflation-adjusted spending assumption by considering other preplanned retirement spending patterns such as David Blanchett's retirement spending smile. The focus in this chapter differs because now we will consider different spending rules that will adjust spending in response to portfolio performance rather than in a preplanned way.

◉ Evaluation Criteria for Variable Spending Strategies and the PAY Rule™ to Calibrate Retirement Spending

Our attention now shifts to variable spending strategies for retirement. We still focus on probability-based strategies, which rely on a total-return investment approach, where the principal value of the portfolio may be spent as needed in addition to any interest and dividends generated by the portfolio. The mechanism for managing sequence risk, though, is to allow spending to fluctuate over time. Reducing spending in the event of a market decline provides a release valve for sequence-of-returns risk that can allow the initial withdrawal rate to increase. This is because the current withdrawal rate does not have to be increased by as much when the portfolio loses value. Managing sequence-of-returns risk in this manner allows synergies to develop, making it possible to keep spending at a higher average level than a constant inflation-adjusted strategy without any flexibility, while maintaining the same overall risk for portfolio depletion.

Sustainable spending rates for retirees depend on many factors: asset allocation, present market valuations (particularly, current interest rates), the desired spending pattern over time, the degree of budget flexibility to adjust spending in response to market performance, the desire to preserve a portion of the portfolio over long periods of time, and the length of the planning horizon. The assumptions that went into creating the 4 percent rule represent a number of simplifications for research purposes; the matter explored in great depth now is what happens when spending is not kept constant in inflation-adjusted terms.

A sustainable spending strategy will generally seek to provide a proper balance among three goals:

1. Preserve some portion of the underlying portfolio (in inflation-adjusted terms),
2. Maximize spending to meet current budgetary needs, and
3. Stabilize spending to keep pace with inflation and meet future budgetary needs with low risk of significant spending cuts.

Many retirees place a great deal of importance on preserving the underlying value of their assets so they can support distributions for many years to come. At the same time, current budgetary needs call for the freedom to spend as much as possible at the present. With a long-term perspective, retirees seek to spend as much as they can on a sustainable basis without risking drastic cuts to future budgets.

There are trade-offs between these objectives. Most obviously, spending more today creates risk for future asset preservation and future spending goals. In addition, a lack of flexibility to adjust spending from a volatile portfolio uniquely amplifies sequence risk. With inflexibility to adjust spending, a more conservative spending rate is the primary risk management technique for a total-return investment portfolio.

This spending lever may lead to an unnecessarily low lifestyle in retirement, and it is also not an efficient solution to sustaining spending. In an investments world, even a little discretion to adjust spending can go a long way toward boosting retirement spending. The idea is to start with a higher withdrawal rate, with the idea in mind to reduce spending if needed at some future point. Flexibility with spending allows for a higher initial spending rate.

How exactly should retirees adjust their spending in response to changes in the value of their retirement portfolios? Countless variations on spending rules are discussed everywhere from research papers to Internet discussion boards. I want to bring clarity to the discussion by identifying and classifying key variable spending strategies, and developing simple metrics to evaluate and compare the strategies on an equal basis. The goal is to assist in the process of figuring out which sort of variable spending strategy will be most appropriate for your personal situation.

When comparing different spending strategies, there are a number of useful metrics to consider. Of primary importance is the range of spending outcomes over time and the value of remaining wealth at the end of the planning horizon. For these aspects, strategies will be calibrated to have comparable downside risk using the PAY Rule described below. It is also important to consider the direction of spending over retirement: Does a strategy tend to keep spending level? Does spending start *high* and decrease over time? Does spending start *low* and increase over time? The final consideration is the degree of spending volatility created by a strategy. How much does spending change on a year-to-year basis? Those with fixed budgets may be willing to accept lower average spending in order to create more stability for annual expenditures.

Variable spending rules are rarely evaluated with matching data and assumptions, making it difficult to adequately compare the downside risks for different strategies. If one rule suggests a 6 percent withdrawal rate while another suggests a 3 percent withdrawal rate, it doesn't necessarily mean the first rule is twice as powerful. The first rule might simply be based on higher market return assumptions. In order to properly compare different strategies, we must begin with the same set of capital market assumptions.

We should also look at where we are situated in the distribution of possible spending and wealth outcomes. Building a retirement income strategy involves numerous trade-offs, and one metric (such as the probability of failure) cannot summarize the overall performance of a strategy. Higher spending upfront means running a greater risk of having less to spend later. More aggressive asset allocation means greater upside potential for spending growth and legacy, but downside risk would increase as well. Naturally, greater spending means fewer assets for a legacy. Spending evolves differently depending on the random sequence of market returns, and retirees have to decide where to focus their concerns.

Failure Rates (or Success Rates)

The traditional failure rate (which calculates the probability of portfolio depletion) often employed by safe withdrawal rate studies cannot be used to compare variable spending strategies, as it only tracks portfolio depletion.

Different variable strategies may imply different spending levels just prior to depletion. For instance, a 6 percent variable spending strategy may cause spending to fall to $20,000 per year as portfolio depletion nears, while the 3 percent strategy might maintain spending at $50,000 until depletion. Failure rates ignore this important distinction and focus solely on the depletion event. This reflects a general theme in variable withdrawal rate literature: the more retirees are willing to let their spending drop in retirement, the higher the initial spending rate they may use. Technically, some variable spending strategies will *never* fail. For instance, when spending is always calculated as a percentage of remaining assets, even a 99 percent withdrawal rate never runs out (though it may be tough to slice up that last remaining penny).

In addition, portfolio failure rates do not account for other income generating assets you might have available. Cutting spending from a portfolio may not be disastrous if you already receive plenty of income from other sources such as Social Security, pensions, and annuities. The bottom line should be how potential spending reductions from a portfolio will impact the overall lifestyle of the retiree, with all nonportfolio sources of income taken into consideration. Failure—defined strictly as investment portfolio depletion—is not the whole story.

The failure rate is an extreme outcome measure that only considers financial wealth depletion. Retiree spending potential is irrelevant. Retirees must find an appropriate personal balance between spending more and making potentially larger subsequent cutbacks in the event of a long life and poor market returns. By focusing only on the failure rate, retirees could end up leaving behind an unintentionally large legacy and not enjoying retirement as much as possible.

The PAY Rule™

As an alternative to failure rates, I suggest calibrating the downside risk across strategies in order to match them for a level of risk the retiree is comfortable taking. This calibration is done with a customized PAY Rule that I first outlined in my article "Making Sense out of Variable Strategies for Retirees" from the October 2015 issue of the *Journal of Financial Planning* (in that article it went by the name "XYZ formula").

The original PAY Rule as stated in that article was as follows: Retiree Accepts an **X%** Probability that *spending* falls below a threshold Amount of **$Y** (in inflation-adjusted terms) by Year **Z** of retirement. Where a failure rate might simply say retirees accept a 10 percent chance of failure within the first thirty years of retirement, a PAY Rule would instead say that retirees accept a 10 percent chance that their spending level will fall below an inflation-adjusted $60,000 by the thirtieth year of retirement. This can incorporate Social Security and other income sources as well, and it provides a way to compare strategies while otherwise dealing with the reality that higher initial spending rates can be justified if spending is subsequently allowed to drop more steeply. The formula provides a controlled anchor for those spending drops. When it is combined with consistent market assumptions and a view of the entire distribution of outcomes, we can compare different variable strategies on an equal footing.

Since publishing that article, I have come to realize that calibrating $Y to *wealth* instead of *spending* will work better. Attempting to calibrate downside spending can easily create a situation in which no spending rule works, which was an issue in my published article. Higher spending rates caused spending to fall too far, while lower spending rates impeded spending from rising enough. If the initial spending rate is too high, spending will plummet too quickly without recovery on the downside, and the $Y spending threshold cannot be reached. At the same time, if spending is too low initially, it may never rise sufficiently in the bad luck scenarios to meet the needed threshold. There may not be any level of initial spending that can work. A happy medium was not always available, but defining $Y as wealth instead of spending corrects for this.

As well, a number of spending rules include sudden and large discrete changes to spending throughout retirement. With an approach like the traditional 4 percent rule, when the portfolio is depleted, someone starting with $1 million may spend $40,000 one year and $0 the next. This can make it harder to compare different spending strategies, since the PAY Rule may calibrate to a spending strategy that changes dramatically in the year following Z. By shifting the focus to remaining wealth, we also reduce the incidence of these discrete shifts to spending.

The PAY Rule works very well when defined as follows:

The PAY Rule acts as a behind-the-scenes constraint to calibrate shortfalls between the strategies, allowing for a better overall understanding of the distribution of potential spending afforded by the strategies.

An important remaining issue, though, is how individuals decide on the parameters for the PAY Rule. These three parameters should be considered:

1. Length of the planning horizon,
2. Safety margin for remaining wealth at the planning horizon, and
3. Allowed probability for falling below the safety margin by the planning horizon.

A more conservative retiree would choose:

- A lower probability for **X%** in order to better avoid the bad outcome,
- A higher threshold for **$Y** in order to preserve more wealth as a safety margin to cover contingencies, including the possibility of outliving the planning horizon, and
- A longer retirement horizon for **Z** in order to plan for a time period with a smaller chance to outlive.

These three variables are chosen jointly, leading to an overall level of risk for the spending plan. If each parameter is chosen to be extra cautious, the overall degree of plan conservativeness will be high, with the implication that retirement spending must be less in order to meet the requirements of the downside risk threshold. Not all variables need to be overly conservative. For instance, a higher value for $Y means that there is still a larger safety margin for wealth to cover unexpected longevity, which in turn could justify a smaller value for Z. Alternatively, if X% is already quite low, then perhaps there is more discretion to justify a lower value for $Y or a lower number of years for Z.

Ultimately, individuals must find a formulation that creates an acceptable level of downside risk—making each plan comparable—so that the focus can then be shifted to evaluating the overall distribution of spending, the direction of spending over retirement, and the degree of spending volatility. Factors to consider in choosing parameters for the PAY Rule include flexibility to reduce spending, fear of outliving the planning horizon, legacy goals, and the availability of other contingency assets or insurance to protect from spending shocks.

Direction of Spending

After calibrating different spending strategies with the PAY Rule, we can compare the distributions of outcomes using different performance metrics. First, for the direction of spending, different strategies will lead to different patterns of spending over time. Generally, for strategies that adjust spending in response to portfolio performance, the pattern of spending in retirement will relate to what is shown in Exhibit 6.1. With strong portfolio performance, the standard of living (spending amount) can rise during retirement, while average returns may keep the living standard more consistent, and poor returns will lead to a reduced standard of living.

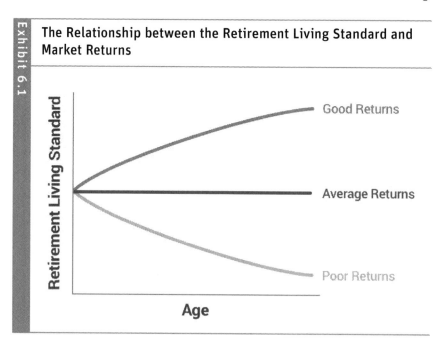

Exhibit 6.1

The Relationship between the Retirement Living Standard and Market Returns

Beyond this, different variable spending strategies will allow for different manifestations of this trend in retirement. Three general patterns for spending in retirement are illustrated in Exhibit 6.2. Some strategies may allow for a higher initial level of spending, with a spending path that decreases on average over time (at least in real terms). For a simple example, a strategy that calls for spending a fixed amount without inflation adjustments will represent such a pattern. Other strategies may leave spending more stable in inflation-adjusted terms, at least on average. If the spending level exceeds what the yield curve for interest rates can support, then the strategy seeks to "amortize the upside" with the hope that subsequent market returns can justify keeping the higher spending level constant. Finally, strategies might start with lower spending to reflect what the bond yield curve can support and then work to increase spending over time if and when upside growth materializes. These patterns connect closely to the initial withdrawal rate in retirement, as spending patterns that will include more spending reductions over time can start with a higher withdrawal rate, while spending patterns that are more likely to rise over time must begin with a lower withdrawal rate.

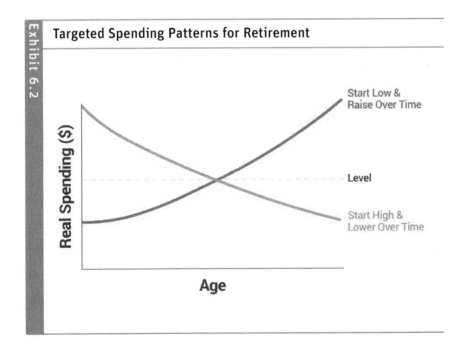

Acceptable Degree of Spending Volatility

A final important consideration is how much fluctuation in annual spending can be expected with a strategy. Spending could increase or decrease over time, but the risk metric of greatest concern is the extent to which annual spending may need to be reduced. The amount of spending volatility a retiree can accept is based on several factors, including:

- simple willingness to make spending cuts,
- an ability to reduce spending without dramatically impacting lifestyle,
- the need for inflation adjustments for the retirement budget, and
- access to other income sources from outside the investment portfolio.

The measure I will use for spending volatility looks at the average reduction in year-on-year spending over the retirement horizon. If there is never a decrease in spending, then the volatility measure is zero. If a thirty-year retirement experiences four spending reductions (in inflation-adjusted terms)—once at 10 percent, once at 5 percent, once at 3 percent, and once at 2 percent—then the measure is the average of these reductions over thirty years (total of 20 percent over thirty years, for a measure of –0.67 percent downside spending volatility).

Spending volatility could be measured more generally as annual spending changes, including increases and decreases, but we do not wish to penalize

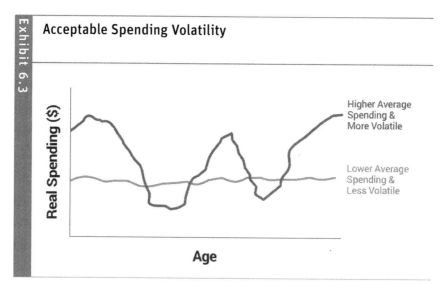

Exhibit 6.3

Acceptable Spending Volatility

Real Spending ($)

Higher Average Spending & More Volatile

Lower Average Spending & Less Volatile

Age

a strategy that supports spending increases over time. This is the reason for focusing only on the spending reductions.

Risk-averse retirees will accept a strategy with lower but more stable spending over retirement, compared to a strategy that might support higher average spending, but with greater volatility and more occasions for annual spending to dip to uncomfortably lower levels. Two spending patterns like this are displayed in Exhibit 6.3. The more risk averse will prefer the lower average, less volatile path, while those with more flexibility and risk tolerance might be willing to accept the higher average but more volatile spending path.

◉ Overview of Variable Spending Strategies

By reviewing existing research on variable spending, we can identify and describe key representative variable spending strategies from the countless possibilities and classify them into a general taxonomy. I identify three general categories for variable spending strategies:

1. Decision rule methods,
2. Actuarial methods, and
3. Dynamic programming methods.

Key examples from the first two categories are shown in Exhibit 6.4. The third category, based on complex dynamic programming computational methods, moves beyond our scope of coverage and is not widely used in personal finance. That being said, I have created an appendix for the chapter to provide a basic introduction about dynamic programming methods within the context of how they compare to decision rules and actuarial methods.

Though numerous exceptions exist, we can try to generalize a few important distinctions for these methods. Among these, decision rule methods frequently share elements of the probability-based school of thought, while advocates of actuarial methods (and dynamic programming methods) often identify more with the safety-first school.

Decision rule methods will demonstrate more willingness to start spending at a higher level than justified by the bond yield curve, with an expectation

Exhibit 6.4

Variable Spending Strategies in Retirement

Decision Rule Methods

1. Bengen's Constant Inflation-Adjusted Spending
2. Fixed-Percentage Withdrawals
3. Endowment Formula: Weighted Average of Methods 1 and 2
4. Endowment Formula: Fixed Percentage of Three-Year Moving Average Portfolio Balance
5. Bengen's Dollar Floor-and-Ceiling Withdrawals
6. Vanguard's Percentage Floor-and-Ceiling Withdrawals
7. Kitces's Ratcheting Rule
8. Guyton and Klinger's Decision Rules
9. Zolt's Glide Path Spending Rule

Actuarial Methods

10. Modified Required Minimum Distribution (RMD) Spending Rules Apply PMT Formula (with different returns, longevity, and spending smoothing)
    Monte Carlo PMT Formulas:
    - Frank, Mitchell, and Blanchett's Age-Based 3-D Model
    - Blanchett, Maciej, and Chen's Mortality-Updating Constant Probability of Failure
    - Blanchett's "Simple Formula"

that future portfolio growth from stocks can be counted on to justify a higher spending rate now. Meanwhile, with actuarial methods, spending may start at a lower level, and spending will only increase in the event that upside potential has been realized. There is a greater recognition of the notion that stock investments are still risky even after long holding periods, so efforts to "amortize the upside" through higher spending may backfire.

Decision rules will generally try to keep spending at a steadier level and only make spending adjustments when deemed essential, while actuarial methods may call for more frequent spending adjustments. Actuarial advocates suggest that those seeking smoother spending should at least use a less volatile portfolio. For actuarial methods, spending volatility is more directly linked to investment volatility. Less volatile spending requires a less volatile portfolio. However, some actuarial methods may seek to smooth spending as well without reducing portfolio volatility by applying a rule that spending is not allowed to adjust too much on a year-by-year basis. Any effort to keep spending constant from a volatile portfolio creates risk for even greater subsequent spending declines.

Beyond these differing views of market risk, decision rule methods will generally adopt a conservative planning horizon beyond life expectancy (such as thirty or forty years), while actuarial methods will make decisions based on a dynamically adjusting time horizon linked to the remaining life expectancy as retirement progresses. Finally, decision rule methods will generally be more comfortable in formulating their spending parameters using historical market data, whereas actuarial methods will be more willing to incorporate updated market return expectations as the spending plan is updated regularly throughout retirement. With this overview, we now consider ten strategies in greater detail.

Bengen's Constant Inflation-Adjusted Spending Strategy

The first method to be tested is the original constant inflation-adjusted withdrawal strategy introduced in William Bengen's 1994 article, "Determining Withdrawal Rates Using Historical Data." This will serve as a baseline for subsequent comparison with other strategies. Bengen's rule says to adjust spending annually for inflation and maintain constant inflation-adjusted spending until the portfolio depletes. Annual spending increases by the previous year's inflation rate and does not otherwise adjust for market returns or the present size of the underlying investment portfolio. The withdrawal rate is defined only in terms of the first year of the plan, and subsequent spending rates are no longer tracked as an input to guide spending. Spending continues to adjust for inflation, regardless of portfolio size, unless and until the underlying portfolio is fully depleted. We have already analyzed how this method performs in historical data. A 4 percent initial spending rate survived all of the rolling historical periods when using a 50/50 portfolio. Exhibit 6.5 shows how this plays out, with sixty-two lines (on top of one another, in this case) with real spending of $4 from an initial portfolio of $100, reflecting the sixty-two rolling historical thirty-year periods in the data set for which the rule could provide a consistent real income.

The bottom part of the exhibit shows remaining wealth throughout retirement for each of the sixty-two rolling historical periods in the data set. In contrast with the smooth income provided, remaining wealth is much more volatile. It runs as low as $3.36 after thirty years for the 1966 retiree (whose portfolio will deplete in year thirty-one) and up to $463.9 after thirty years for the 1982 retiree. The volatility in remaining wealth is a byproduct of keeping spending at the same level regardless of portfolio performance. (These numbers are all scalable, as you can just multiply the assumed $100 initial wealth by the factor needed to obtain actual wealth to know the implications for spending and remaining wealth from a different starting point. For instance, spending $4 from wealth of $100 is the same as spending $40,000 from wealth of $1,000,000.)

The benefits of Bengen's strategy are numerous:

1. It provides smooth and consistent income as long as wealth remains.
2. The upcoming budget is more predictable, especially when account balances remain strong.
3. Those whose lifestyle goals work with a sufficiently low spending rate (whether that be 4 percent or some other number) and who have a taste for market volatility can meet their goals with a high likelihood for success.
4. It may be possible to create a large legacy with this strategy through the combination of a low spending rate and an aggressive asset allocation.

But it suffers from a number of disadvantages, too, primary among which is the retiree's vulnerability to wealth depletion. Spending remains consistent until wealth hits zero. If the retiree has insufficient income sources outside the investment portfolio, this could have devastating implications. Not only could the retiree's preferred lifestyle be unattainable, but a minimally acceptable standard of living could prove to be too expensive after portfolio depletion. This strategy is particularly risky for those lacking sufficient resources elsewhere to cover basic needs.

This strategy also uniquely increases sequence-of-returns risk by calling for constant real spending from a volatile investment portfolio. Safety-first advocates would argue that this strategy is inherently flawed—those seeking constant spending should use a less volatile retirement strategy,

Exhibit 6.5

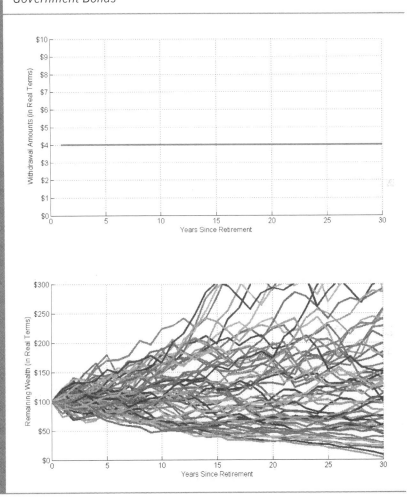

Time Path of Real Spending and Wealth
Constant Inflation-Adjusted Spending Strategy
For 4% Initial Spending Rate, 50/50 Asset Allocation, Rolling
30-Year Retirements
Using SBBI Data, 1926–2016, S&P 500 and Intermediate-Term
Government Bonds

and those who accept portfolio volatility should also accept spending volatility. A progressively lower spending rate is required to manage the increased sequence risk. As the portfolio declines, a reduction in spending is essential to prevent the discrete drop-off in spending power when the portfolio reaches zero.

The constant spending strategy is also extremely inefficient. If market performance is better than whatever would be considered a "worst-case" scenario when a spending rate is chosen, spending will fall well below what would be feasible and sustainable. Your wealth will continue to grow unabated as your current spending rate drops (a constant spending amount from an increasing portfolio means a lower subsequent spending rate). On the upside, in good market scenarios, legacy wealth ends up being greater than with most other strategies because there is no mechanism to allow for spending increases in retirement.

While the constant inflation-adjusted spending strategy provides a useful benchmark and baseline for analyzing sustainable retirement spending strategies, it should probably not be viewed as a realistic or reasonable retirement income strategy. Efficient retirement strategies must adjust spending at least somewhat for portfolio volatility. The remaining strategies provide variations on how to make such adjustments.

Fixed-Percentage Withdrawals

The fixed-percentage withdrawal strategy is the polar opposite of constant inflation-adjusted spending. Subsequent strategies we consider will strive to strike a balance between these two. The fixed-percentage strategy calls for retirees to spend a constant percentage of the remaining portfolio balance in each year of retirement.

The first advantage of this strategy is that, since it always spends a *percentage* of what remains, it never depletes the portfolio. Of course, spending could fall to uncomfortably low levels, but the concept of portfolio failure rates is incompatible here. In addition, spending is allowed to increase when market returns outpace the retirement distributions and the portfolio grows.

A third advantage of this rule is that it completely eliminates sequence-of-returns risk, as Dirk Cotton first pointed out in 2013 at his Retirement Café blog. The fixed-percentage approach provides a clear mechanism for reducing spending after a portfolio decline, thus removing such a risk. As with investing a lump sum of assets, the specific order of returns makes no difference to the final outcomes realized with this strategy. As such, we can expect the sustainable spending rate to be higher than with constant inflation-adjusted withdrawals.

As for disadvantages, when combined with volatile investments, spending can become extremely volatile with this strategy, making it difficult for retirees to budget in advance. For a fixed retirement budget, managing retirement with this rule could be a particular challenge. Those considering this rule should probably be thinking in terms of applying it to discretionary expenses that allow more flexibility for spending reductions that will not completely derail a retiree's standard of living.

Exhibit 6.6 shows how this rule performed with the same 50/50 portfolio in the sixty-two rolling historical periods from US history since 1926 for a 4 percent initial withdrawal rate. Occasionally the popular press will mistakenly define the 4 percent rule this way (withdraw 4 percent of the remaining account balance each year), but the accepted definition of the 4 percent rule is the constant inflation-adjustment spending strategy defined earlier. To be clear, with constant inflation-adjusted spending, the withdrawal rate will change throughout retirement as the portfolio value changes. The withdrawal rate adjusts, while spending stays the same. But with the fixed-percentage rule, the withdrawal rate stays the same, while spending adjusts.

Spending is naturally more volatile with the fixed-percentage strategy. After thirty years, spending ranges from $2.67 to $9.10 in real terms, relative to the initial $4.00 spent from a $100.00 portfolio. At the same time, remaining wealth is less volatile than before, as the range after thirty years is $76.71 to $230.74. In both cases, spending and wealth were lower in the worst cases from the middle part of retirement, approaching low points of $2.00 from a portfolio with $50.00 left. In the historical data, poor market environments in early retirement (which led to these low points) were followed by better market environments in the latter part of retirement. Because spending declined along with the portfolio as the spending rate remained constant at 4 percent, portfolio losses were not locked in to the same extent, and the spending rate was not forced upward to meet the spending goal, thus avoiding sequence-of-returns risk, helping preserve the portfolio, and letting it subsequently grow. The disadvantage, as the exhibit clearly reveals, is that spending paths were quite volatile with this strategy throughout history.

On the retirement spending strategy spectrum, these first two strategies represent the opposite extremes. The fixed-percentage rule experiences volatile spending but a portfolio that technically cannot be depleted. The

Exhibit 6.6

Time Path of Real Spending and Wealth
Fixed-Percentage Withdrawals
For 4% Initial Spending Rate, 50/50 Asset Allocation, Rolling 30-Year Retirements
Using SBBI Data, 1926–2016, S&P 500 and Intermediate-Term Government Bonds

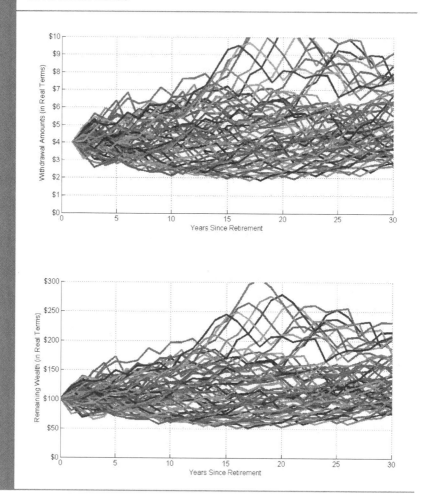

constant inflation-adjusted spending rule offers predictable spending (as long as assets remain), but a portfolio that can be depleted, reducing spending to zero.

In reality, neither end of the spectrum is an ideal place for most retirees. The other strategies we will discuss seek a compromise between these two extremes by including a mechanism to smooth spending adjustments made in response to market volatility. Many strategies seek to obtain some advantages of the fixed-percentage rule, while also reducing the frequency and size of spending adjustments and placing bounds on how far spending can increase or decrease.

Endowment Formulas for Retirement Spending

Endowment policy—a general term referring to the spending decisions facing endowment funds, foundations, family offices, and other related institutions—has confronted questions about sustainable spending for many years. Endowment funds have shifted to the probability-based methods discussed here since the 1970s, as previous ideas about only spending interest from a fixed-income portfolio were slowly abandoned for not providing enough income and inflation protection.

Endowment spending policy is an active area of research, with the latest policies of different university endowments often guiding the way for others. It is interesting that research on endowment spending policies has evolved separately from research on spending policies for retirees. Each area developed its own tools for balancing the trade-off between the desire to keep spending growth consistent with inflation and the fact that poor market returns might eventually trigger a need to reduce spending. The balance to strike is how and when to reduce spending to avoid creating too much spending volatility and uncertainty, while simultaneously maintaining future potential spending and avoiding even bigger subsequent cuts. Retirees can easily apply endowment spending rules to their own personal situations. Generally, endowment spending rules can be classified into two categories: hybrid rules and moving average rules.

First, hybrid rules provide a way to combine the constant amount and fixed-percentage strategies. A simple example is illustrated in Exhibit 6.7. In this case, annual spending is determined as the average of constant inflation-adjusted spending based on the initial balance at retirement, and a percentage of the remaining account balance. For a 4 percent withdrawal rate and a $100 initial balance, annual spending is half of $4 on an inflation-adjusted basis, and half of 4 percent of the remaining account balance throughout retirement.

This hybrid strikes a balance between trying to stabilize spending and allowing it to fluctuate in response to portfolio performance. Real spending drops to about $3 (a 25 percent decrease from the initial level) in the historical data, which is midway between a constant $4 and the $2 threshold reached with the pure fixed-percentage strategy. Similarly, wealth balances are less strained than with the constant spending rule but fall behind what is left with the pure fixed-percentage strategy.

Exhibit 6.7

Time Path of Real Spending and Wealth
Endowment Formula—Hybrid
For 4% Initial Spending Rate, 50/50 Asset Allocation, Rolling 30-Year Retirements
Using SBBI Data, 1926–2016, S&P 500 and Intermediate-Term Government Bonds

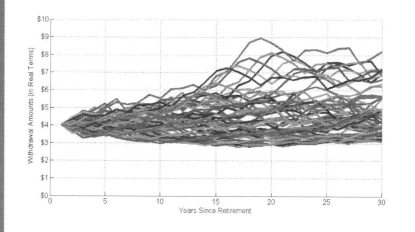

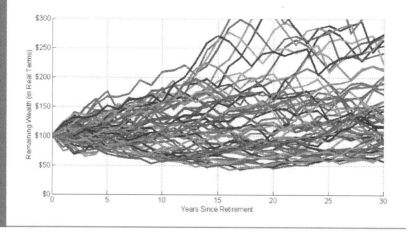

Hybrid rules lead to more stable spending than fixed-percentage rules, but they increase the risk that assets can be depleted as well. For this reason, the sustainable spending rate associated with hybrid rules generally falls between the spending rates for the other two rules. This allows income fluctuation and some response to market conditions, but not as much as with the fixed-percentage rule. Also, wealth can still run out, though not as soon as with the constant inflation-adjusted withdrawal rule.

The second type of endowment policy rule bases spending on a percentage of the moving average of the remaining account balance. The most common smoothing rules for endowment spending are moving average rules. Rather than define the spending rate only in terms of the initial year of the plan, the spending rate is a constant value over time. But rather than spending a constant percentage of the remaining portfolio balance each year—resulting in a great deal of spending volatility—moving average rules seek to spend a constant percentage of the average portfolio balance over the previous few years. Most frequently, the average portfolio value over the previous three years or twelve quarters is multiplied by a spending rate to determine the feasible spending amount for a given year. This approach allows spending to adjust somewhat more gradually over time than with a pure fixed-percentage rule. Exhibit 6.8 provides an example of a 4 percent spending rule based on the average remaining portfolio balance during the previous three years. In practical terms, this rule ends up behaving closely to the fixed-percentage rule. Volatility for spending will be slightly less, but a very similar overall experience can be observed in the historical data.

Bengen's Hard-Dollar Floor-and-Ceiling Approach

In a May 2001 *Journal of Financial Planning* article titled "Conserving Client Portfolios in Retirement, Part IV," William Bengen offered a new balance between the constant amount and fixed-percentage strategies with his "floor-and-ceiling" spending approach. This method begins by applying the fixed-percentage rule, which allows greater spending when markets are up and forces spending reductions when they are down. While he still allows spending to fluctuate considerably, Bengen's new strategy implements limits in both directions with hard-dollar ceilings and floors. Exhibit 6.9 provides a baseline example for this family of rules. The ceiling is set at 20 percent above the real value of the first year's withdrawal, and the floor is 15 percent below that same value (unless wealth depletes).

Exhibit 6.8

Time Path of Real Spending and Wealth

Endowment Formula—Three-Year Moving Average
For 4% Initial Spending Rate, 50/50 Asset Allocation,
Rolling 30-Year Retirements Using SBBI Data, 1926–2016,
S&P 500 and Intermediate-Term Government Bonds

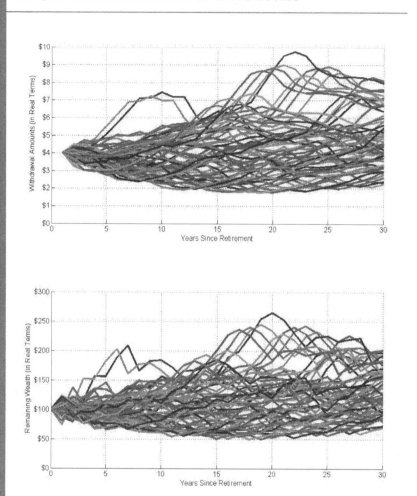

With an initial real withdrawal of $4.00 from $100.00, the floor and ceiling are set at $3.40 and $4.80, respectively. This smooths fluctuations by keeping spending from drifting too far from its initial level.

While the hard-dollar floor ensures spending never drops too low, it is important to recognize that it also restores the possibility of portfolio

Exhibit 6.9

Time Path of Real Spending and Wealth

Bengen's Hard-Dollar Floor-and-Ceiling Rule
For 4% Initial Spending Rate, 50/50 Asset Allocation,
Rolling 30-Year Retirements Using SBBI Data, 1926–2016,
S&P 500 and Intermediate-Term Government Bonds

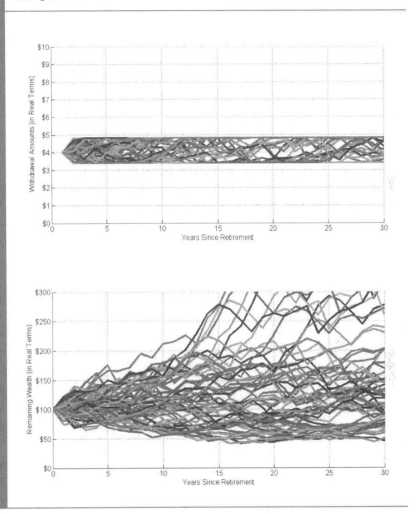

depletion, which the fixed-percentage rule seeks to eliminate. In addition, the failure rate comparison for this rule will be less meaningful if spending is already lower in the period before wealth depletion than with constant inflation-adjusted spending. Bengen determined that the floor-and-ceiling rule increased the historical worst-case initial spending rate by 10 percent, thanks to its allowance to cut spending when markets perform poorly.

Exhibit 6.9 illustrates what happens when initial spending remains at 4 percent and spending fluctuates only within the band allowed by the rule.

Remaining wealth is better supported on the downside as a result of the 15 percent spending reductions. In poor market environments, the reduced spending helps preserve the portfolio balance, so about 50 percent of the initial portfolio balance remains after thirty years. With the constant inflation-adjusted spending rule, some scenarios put the portfolio on the verge of depletion after thirty years, so this spending rule has made a substantial contribution to preserving wealth in the worst-case scenarios. A willingness to reduce spending by up to 15 percent from the initial level provides a great deal of support for sustaining the investment portfolio in retirement. Placing a ceiling on spending will preserve sustainability by saving more for future rainy days. While including a floor on how far spending can fall opens the possibility of wealth depletion, it becomes increasingly unlikely as the minimal floor decreases.

Bengen noted that the choice of the ceiling value really does not have much impact on sustainable spending. If the portfolio does well enough for spending to grow to the level of the ceiling, sequence risk does not manifest, and the current withdrawal rate declines. It becomes unlikely that portfolio depletion will be a concern. The important variable is the floor location. The lower the floor, the higher the initial withdrawal rate. With an appropriate choice of floor, it may be possible for spending to start higher but to never fall below the supported amount for the constant inflation-adjusted strategy.

Vanguard's Percentage Floor-and-Ceiling Approach

In a 2013 Vanguard research paper titled "A More Dynamic Approach to Spending for Investors in Retirement," a research team headed by Colleen Jaconetti developed an alternative form of the floor-and-ceiling spending rule that relies on percentages rather than hard-dollar amounts. With their framework, the ceiling refers to a maximum *percentage* increase in spending each year, while the floor refers to a maximum percentage drop in spending for each year. The baseline case they describe is a 5 percent ceiling and a 2.5 percent floor, illustrated in Exhibit 6.10.

To determine spending, they say to first apply a fixed-percentage spending rule to the remaining account balance. For the baseline, if

Exhibit 6.10

Time Path of Real Spending and Wealth
Vanguard's Percentage Floor-and-Ceiling Rule
For 4% Initial Spending Rate, 50/50 Asset Allocation,
Rolling 30-Year Retirements Using SBBI Data, 1926–2016,
S&P 500 and Intermediate-Term Government Bonds

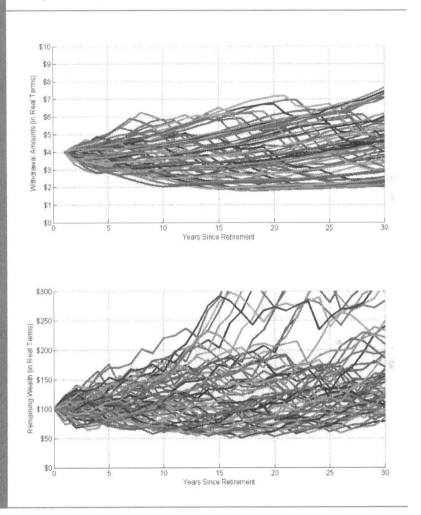

the spending amount would be more than 5 percent greater than that of the previous year, then the new spending amount is capped at 5 percent growth. Meanwhile, if the spending amount would drop by more than 2.5 percent, then spending for the year is limited to a 2.5 percent decrease. Each year the rule is applied again to the previous year's spending level.

The narrower the range between the floor and ceiling, the more this spending rule acts as a constant amount rule with a fixed spending growth rate. As the range increases, the rule behaves more like a fixed-percentage rule, because you become less likely to reach the binding constraints on either end. Despite the lack of a hard-dollar floor, this method is also susceptible to portfolio depletion. Spending may not always drop quickly enough to preserve the portfolio.

Kitces's Ratcheting Rule

In 2015, Michael Kitces proposed a ratcheting rule for retirement spending that shared the basic framework of constant inflation-adjusted spending while also allowing spending to increase if the portfolio performs well in retirement. As with many of these rules, the ratcheting rule could be implemented in numerous ways.

In the baseline case for Kitces's rule, spending adjusts for inflation throughout retirement, with the option to increase by an additional 10 percent any time the nominal value of the portfolio jumps more than 50 percent above its initial level. To limit spending increases, the 10 percent spike is only allowed once every three years when the portfolio remains consistently above the 150 percent level.

Kitces notes that this version of the rule might ultimately be too conservative in creating the conditions to allow for spending increases, but it nonetheless provides a basic idea of how to structure rules of this nature. The natural fear with increasing spending is that it will force larger subsequent cutbacks. But as William Bengen found when analyzing thresholds for the floor-and-ceiling rule, the ceiling threshold has little impact on sustainable spending. Historical data shows that when retirement started well, spending increases did not jeopardize the spending plan.

Exhibit 6.11 shows the historical paths of spending and wealth when implementing this rule with a 4 percent initial spending rate. Real spending remains above the initial 4 percent level in any simulation, though just as with constant inflation-adjusted spending, some cases show wealth on the edge of depletion. In other cases, real spending more than doubled by the end of thirty years.

Exhibit 6.11

Time Path of Real Spending and Wealth
Kitces's Ratcheting Rule
For 4% Initial Spending Rate, 50/50 Asset Allocation,
Rolling 30-Year Retirements
Using SBBI Data, 1926–2016, S&P 500 and Intermediate-Term
Government Bonds

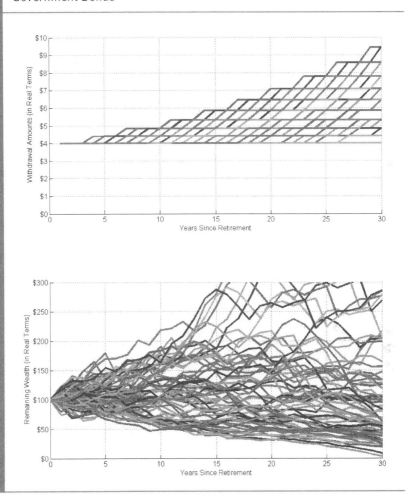

The spending path supported by this rule may not appeal to many retirees, as it starts spending low and increases it throughout retirement when justified. By not allowing for downward spending adjustments, it forces the initial spending rate to similarly low levels as the constant inflation-adjusted spending rule. Spending can only increase later in retirement when such increases may be less needed. However, Kitces merely aimed to reveal the superiority of a ratcheting rule to constant inflation-adjusted spending. When retirements are not on track toward worst-case outcomes, spending can increase, and the ratcheting rule provides a systematic mechanism for managing such spending increases.

Guyton and Klinger's Decision Rules

The next decision rule approach provides the name for this category of methods. The Guyton and Klinger spending decision rules derive from an October 2004 *Journal of Financial Planning* article by Jonathan Guyton titled "Decision Rules and Portfolio Management for Retirees: Is the 'Safe' Initial Withdrawal Rate Too Safe?" and from a follow-up article in the journal he wrote with William Klinger in 2006 titled "Decision Rules and Maximum Initial Withdrawal Rates."

The modern form of the rules, as they are generally understood and implemented today, is found in the latter article. In it, the authors use Monte Carlo simulations based on the underlying data from 1973 to 2004 and 1928 to 2004 to analyze three retirement asset allocations—50 percent, 65 percent, and 80 percent stocks—over forty-year retirement spending horizons.

Four decision rules comprise this approach. They allow spending to increase faster than inflation when markets are doing well and to drop, even in nominal terms, when the portfolio is losing value.

1. **Portfolio management rule:** This rule addresses where withdrawals are taken from and is not something I model in my simulations. With this rule, a cash reserve is created to cover spending needs. Following years with negative returns, asset allocation can change as withdrawals from equities are avoided if sufficient assets remain in cash and fixed income to cover withdrawals.

2. **Withdrawal rule:** Annual spending increases with inflation except in years after the portfolio experienced a negative return. After negative return years, spending stays the same. There is no makeup in subsequent years for a missed spending increase. This rule is only applied if the year's withdrawal rate (current spending divided by remaining assets) is higher than the initial retirement date withdrawal rate.

Exhibit 6.12

Time Path of Real Spending and Wealth

Guyton and Klinger's Decision Rules
For 4% Initial Spending Rate, 50/50 Asset Allocation,
Rolling 30-Year Retirements Using SBBI Data, 1926–2016,
S&P 500 and Intermediate-Term Government Bonds

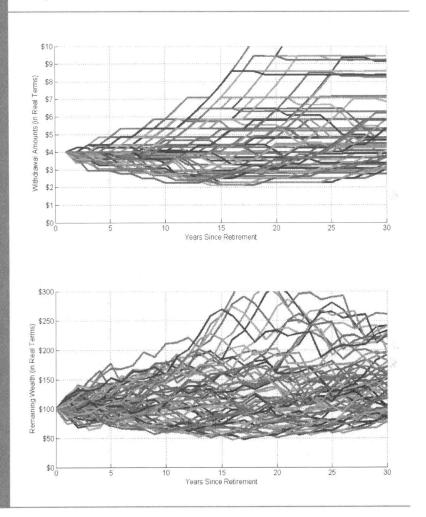

3. **Capital preservation rule:** Spending is cut 10 percent if the current withdrawal rate rises to 20 percent more than its initial level and the planning age is still more than fifteen years away. So for a thirty-year horizon, the rule only applies for the first fifteen years of retirement. For example, if the initial withdrawal rate is 5 percent, then a spending

cut would take place whenever the current withdrawal rate exceeds 6 percent of remaining assets in the first fifteen years of retirement.

4. **Prosperity rule:** Spending is increased 10 percent in any year that the current withdrawal rate falls to 20 percent below its initial level. For example, if the initial withdrawal rate is 5 percent, a spending increase would take place whenever the current withdrawal rate falls below 4 percent of remaining assets.

The modern version of their rules drops Guyton's original inflation rule, which capped spending increases at 6 percent when inflation exceeded that amount. It also adjusts the withdrawal rule to prevent spending freezes when the current withdrawal rate falls below the initial withdrawal rate.

Exhibit 6.12 illustrates the historical performance of the withdrawal, capital preservation, and prosperity rules using a 50/50 asset allocation.

Zolt's Glide Path Rule

A final example in the decision rules category is the Target Percentage Adjustment method introduced by David Zolt in his January 2013 *Journal of Financial Planning* article, "Achieving a Higher Safe Withdrawal Rate with the Target Percentage Adjustment." The basic premise of his rule is that retirees are willing to forgo an inflation increase but will never want to accept a decrease in their nominal spending. They will have a certain lifestyle in mind that will rarely necessitate increasing spending in real terms, so there is no need for such an option. Essentially, retirees would like to increase spending with inflation but will forego some increase when necessary. This works in the opposite direction of the Kitces ratcheting rule, since it holds that spending never increases in real terms, but it can decrease in real terms. (Remember that keeping spending level when there is inflation means that real spending has declined.)

With this perspective, the question becomes when it is or is not acceptable to take a full inflation adjustment for spending. Zolt's method relies on building a capital needs analysis to determine a glide path for wealth throughout retirement. Full spending increases for inflation are made in years when actual remaining wealth exceeds required remaining wealth at that point of time, and full inflation adjustments are not made in years when actual remaining wealth falls below the required amount as determined by the glide path at that point.

Exhibit 6.13 illustrates the required wealth glide path for the baseline example provided in Zolt's 2013 article. To be clear, other glide path assumptions could be developed. He illustrated an assumed 4 percent initial spending rate, 3 percent inflation throughout retirement, and a forty-five-year planning horizon. With this desired spending path, a 6.1 percent compounded return is required to ensure that spending goals can be met and that remaining wealth precisely depletes after the withdrawal at year forty-five. With these assumptions, the figure shows that wealth continues to grow until year twenty-four of retirement, when it reaches $129.00 from an initial base of $100.00. Then, wealth declines for the remainder of retirement before reaching $0.00 at the end. The $4.00 initial spending amount grows to $14.69 after forty-five years of 3 percent compounding inflation. Again, this wealth glide path is used to determine the types of spending adjustments made throughout retirement. In years when remaining wealth exceeds the glide path level, a full inflation increase is made. But when wealth falls below this required level, the full increase is not made.

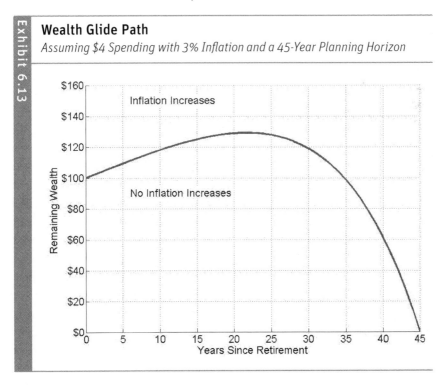

Exhibit 6.13

Wealth Glide Path

Assuming $4 Spending with 3% Inflation and a 45-Year Planning Horizon

Zolt looks at a number of different ways to adjust spending at a slower rate when wealth is falling below its glide path level. He sought spending rules that would allow a larger increase in initial spending with a lower expected subsequent decrease in real purchasing power over time. From the tables in his paper, the spending rule that looks most favorable—and that I will treat as a baseline representation of his approach—is to keep spending level, with

Time Path of Real Spending and Wealth
Zolt's Target Percentage Adjustment Rule
For 4% Initial Spending Rate, 50/50 Asset Allocation,
Rolling 30-Year Retirements Using SBBI Data, 1926–2016,
S&P 500 and Intermediate-Term Government Bonds

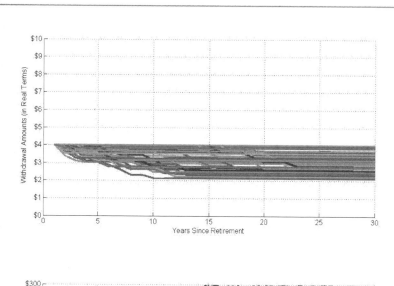

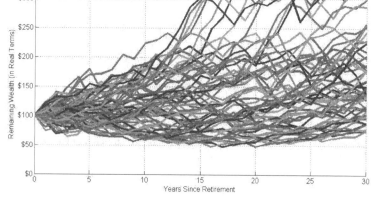

no partial inflation adjustment when wealth falls below the glide path. In any year when remaining wealth is higher than the critical number from the glide path, spending adjusts for inflation. However, in any year that wealth falls below that number, no inflation adjustment is made. Throughout retirement, sometimes spending adjusts for inflation, and sometimes it stays fixed. Exhibit 6.14 illustrates how this rule performed in the historical data when using the glide path defined earlier.

Required Minimum Distributions (as a Representation of Actuarial Methods)

One final spending rule serves as a reasonably easy way to implement an actuarial method for retirement spending. Actuarial methods generally have retirees recalculate their sustainable spending annually based on the remaining portfolio balance, remaining longevity, and expected portfolio returns. These are the factors that enter into the PMT formula: PMT(rate,nper,pv,fv,type).

This formula provides the sustainable spending amount when you have an expected return for investments (*rate*), the planning horizon (*nper*), the current size of the financial portfolio (*pv*), the desired amount of remaining wealth at the end of the planning horizon (*fv*), and a value of 1 for type if withdrawals are made at the start of the period. If the *rate* is expressed in inflation-adjusted terms, the answer would imply an inflation-adjusted spending level. In addition, *fv* could be a value less than zero (to reflect a distribution at the end date) if the retiree wants to leave a bequest or to preserve a portion of the portfolio for other purposes.

Though the formula provides an ongoing sustainable spending amount, this calculation could be repeated annually, reflecting ongoing changes in *rate, nper,* and *pv*, which would then provide retirees with updated sustainable spending amounts for each year of retirement. The remaining portfolio balance will evolve over time, and circumstances may also call for a change in expected market returns. A dynamic measure of remaining life expectancy is also important, as withdrawal rates can increase as the remaining time horizon shortens. For various actuarial methods, differences center primarily on appropriate assumptions for market returns and remaining longevity, as well as whether additional smoothing factors should be applied to control how quickly spending adjusts to new circumstances.

A simple form for the actuarial method is to use the Internal Revenue Services' required minimum distribution (RMD) rules as a more general guide for sustainable spending. In an effort to get those benefiting from tax deferral to eventually pay taxes, the RMD rules indicate a by-age percentage that must be withdrawn from tax-deferred accounts. Two research articles from 2012 (David Blanchett, Maciej Kowara, and Peng Chen's "Optimal Withdrawal Strategy for Retirement-Income Portfolios" in the *Retirement Management Journal* and Wei Sun and Anthony Webb's "Should Households Base Asset Decumulation Strategies on Required Minimum Distribution Tables?" from Center for Retirement Research at Boston College) both studied the RMD rule as a spending option and found it to be a reasonable strategy that roughly approximates more sophisticated attempts to optimize spending.

The RMD rule contains the actuarial components of spending a percentage of remaining assets, which is calibrated to an updating remaining life expectancy, covering the *nper* and *pv* aspects of the PMT formula. Its deficiency is that it does not provide a mechanism for users to adjust the value of *rate* beyond whatever government policy makers initially assumed when developing the by-age RMD rates. The RMD rules assume investment returns of 0 percent, so they do not reflect asset allocation or other market return assumptions. With this conservative return assumption, some retirees may decide the RMD strategy provides overly conservative spending rates. The RMD rules also assume that the value of the portfolio can fall to zero by the end of life, setting aside the possibility of an intended safety margin or legacy.

A straightforward application of the RMD rule would not allow us to calibrate remaining wealth for our PAY Rule. I will modify the RMD rates so this calibration may take place. In order to accomplish this, I must find the appropriate factor to adjust all RMD percentages so the PAY Rule threshold is reached. Or, in the context of the examples I have been discussing thus far with decision rules, the initial spending rate is always 4 percent. My modified RMD rule simply multiplies all RMD percentages by 1.24 so that the sixty-five-year-old RMD percentage of 3.23 percent is adjusted upward to 4 percent. Subsequent spending rates are based on a percentage of remaining assets required by the rule and multiplied by the same calibration factor. While RMDs do not generally apply until age 70.5, distribution rates are published for younger ages, as they are relevant for inherited IRAs.

Exhibit 6.15 provides the historical outcomes for spending and wealth with this modified RMD rule. The most notable aspect of this rule is how it pushes down remaining wealth at the end of the time horizon, even when markets perform well. This results from the increased percentage of remaining assets spent as one ages. This strategy works efficiently to spend down remaining assets in retirement, as none of the historical rolling periods allowed for real wealth to be higher than its initial level

Exhibit 6.15

Time Path of Real Spending and Wealth
Modified Required Minimum Distribution Rule (RMDs Multiplied by 1.24)
For 4% Initial Spending Rate, 50/50 Asset Allocation,
Rolling 30-Year Retirements Using SBBI Data, 1926–2016,
S&P 500 and Intermediate-Term Government Bonds

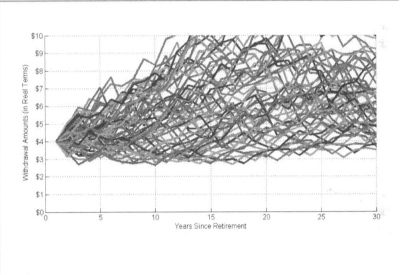

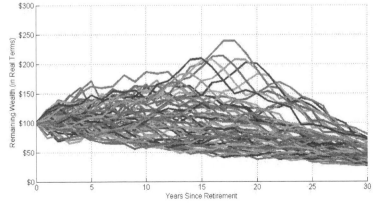

after thirty years. But the modified RMD rule also leads to variable spending. Spending rates increase with age, and if these rates increase too quickly, spending may fall.

Many other actuarial methods will require increasing sophistication in developing assumptions to apply to the RMD formula. Other examples of actuarial methods include the "annually recalculated virtual annuity" (ARVA) approach from the hubristically named "The Only Spending Rule Article You Will Ever Need," by M. Barton Waring and Laurence B. Siegel, in the January/February 2015 issue of the *Financial Analysts Journal,* and the "actuarial approach" described by Ken Steiner in the fall 2014 issue of the *Journal of Personal Finance* in an article named "A Better Systematic Withdrawal Strategy—the Actuarial Approach." As well, members of the Bogleheads Forum collectively developed a variant of this approach described in various discussion threads and on their wiki, which they call "variable percentage withdrawal."

These approaches recognize that the amount someone can spend in each year of retirement can be determined through a simple annuity calculation for a spending rate assuming a fixed portfolio return and remaining time horizon. Their calculations can be updated annually for the new portfolio balance, any changes to the expected return, an adjustment for remaining longevity, and other rules to limit spending adjustments.

There are also a number of other more sophisticated actuarial methods that incorporate Monte Carlo simulations to calibrate spending based on a specified probability of success or failure. David Blanchett from Morningstar has been involved with many of these efforts, and his joint work was distilled into a simple formula for retirement withdrawals that he published as "Simple Formulas to Implement Complex Withdrawal Strategies" in the September 2013 issue of the *Journal of Financial Planning.* His spreadsheet that accompanied the article allows users to input their preferred asset allocation, expected portfolio returns, level of portfolio fees, remaining life expectancy, and targeted probability of success, in order to obtain a customized withdrawal rate. The genesis of this work began in the age-based, three-dimensional distribution model he developed with Larry Frank and John Mitchell in a series of three articles published in 2011 and 2012 issues of the *Journal of Financial Planning,* with Larry Frank as the lead author. Though these methods are more sophisticated to allow for a probability of failure, the underlying PMT formula remains as the philosophical core of the spending recommendations.

◎ Summarizing the Performance of Variable Spending Rules in the Historical Data

Thus far, we have compared the historical performance of various spending strategies when the initial spending rate is 4 percent. We have not yet applied a PAY Rule or considered how spending may be impacted by the low interest rate environment facing retirees. But before getting to that, it is worthwhile to introduce an exhibit that summarizes the information about the distribution of spending and wealth outcomes.

Exhibit 6.16 compares 4 percent initial spending rates for each of the spending rules using the historical data that we have just analyzed visually. This exhibit allows us to see how spending evolves over time at different percentiles of the distribution, as well as remaining wealth, direction of spending over time, and the average spending reductions over time. It also summarizes and quantifies the previous visuals about how spending and wealth evolved in each of the rolling historical periods.

For each strategy, the initial spending rate is shown, with the assumption that retirement wealth is equal to $100,000. Results are scalable for other wealth amounts. The distribution for real spending amounts is shown for ten, twenty, and thirty years into retirement. The distribution of remaining real wealth is shown after the thirtieth year of retirement. Considering spending and wealth are both important—as retirees should not be narrowly focused on a singular goal to avoid financial wealth depletion—financial goals for retirement can essentially be reduced to two competing objectives: to support as much spending as feasible, and to maintain a reserve of financial assets to support risk management objectives such as protecting from spending shocks or otherwise provide a legacy.

Three additional spending metrics are included at the right of the exhibit.

1. The *change in real spending after thirty years* for that strategy relative to its initial spending level. Positive numbers mean that spending increases over retirement, while negative numbers imply spending declines. These numbers are provided for each percentile of the distribution.

2. The next column *(year 30 spending relative to baseline)* provides year thirty spending relative to the initial spending supported by the baseline constant inflation-adjusted strategy. These numbers provide a sense of how spending evolves relative to the baseline strategy to help determine the overall outcomes for spending. This column will be relevant after we later apply a PAY Rule that lets the initial spending rate differ for each strategy. A strategy that starts at a higher initial spending level may experience a large drop relative to that level, but it may still remain above where spending would have been at the baseline, and this column aids in understanding this possibility.

3. The final column reflects *downside spending volatility.* This provides a measure of the potential annual spending decreases over retirement. This volatility measure does not apply for spending increases. Rather, for each simulation, the sum of spending decreases over the thirty years is calculated and divided by 30. If the average spending decline is 3 percent, it means that over the thirty years of retirement, real spending decreased by 3 percent per year on an average annual basis.

In presenting outcomes, each spending strategy is represented by twenty-two numbers. The most important number is not universal, as individual considerations will vary. Retirees will surely wish to consider the implications for when markets do well and when markets do poorly. To demonstrate the range of possibilities, outcomes for spending and remaining wealth will be shown for the ninetieth percentile (markets do well), fiftieth percentile (the midrange outcome in which half can expect to do better and half worse), and the tenth percentile (markets do poorly). Beyond this, the exhibit allows users to consider the initial spending level, the evolution of spending, the impact on legacy, and downside spending volatility.

As you can see, the constant inflation-adjusted spending rule creates the smallest range for spending adjustments and the largest range for remaining wealth after thirty years. From a retirement date portfolio of $100,000, spending remains constant across the distribution over time at $4,000. The range of remaining wealth after thirty years is $27,830 at the tenth percentile and $322,310 at the ninetieth percentile. At the median, wealth has grown to $127,010 in real terms. If spending stays constant, and this is the baseline strategy, the remaining measures about the direction of spending, spending relative to the baseline, and spending volatility are all 0 percent.

Exhibit 6.16

Time Path of Real Spending and Wealth

Sustainable Spending Rates from an Investment Portfolio over 30 Years
For a 65-Year-Old (Which Is Relevant Only for the RMD Rule)
For 4% Initial Spending Rate, 50/50 Asset Allocation,
Rolling 30-Year Retirements Using SBBI Data, 1926–2016,
S&P 500 and Intermediate-Term Government Bonds
Retirement Date Wealth Level = $100,000

Spending Strategy	Initial Spending Rate	Percentile of Distribution	Real Spending in 10 Years	Real Spending in 20 Years	Real Spending in 30 Years	Real Remaining Wealth After 30 Years	Change in Real Spending at Year 30	Year 30 Spending Relative to Baseline	Downside Spending Volatility
Constant Inflation-Adjusted Spending (BASELINE)	4.00%	90th	$4,000	$4,000	$4,000	$322,310	0%	0%	0%
		50th	$4,000	$4,000	$4,000	$127,010	0%	0%	0%
		10th	$4,000	$4,000	$4,000	$27,830	0%	0%	0%
Fixed-Percentage Withdrawals	4.00%	90th	$6,010	$7,730	$7,760	$202,690	94%	94%	-3%
		50th	$4,170	$4,440	$4,800	$120,280	20%	20%	-4%
		10th	$2,570	$2,420	$3,250	$87,480	-19%	-19%	-5%
Endowment Formula—Weighted Average—Hybrid	4.00%	90th	$5,100	$6,470	$6,870	$256,830	72%	72%	-2%
		50th	$4,090	$4,180	$4,340	$124,270	9%	9%	-2%
		10th	$3,230	$3,160	$3,380	$73,200	-16%	-16%	-3%
Endowment Formula—3-Year Moving Average	4.00%	90th	$5,100	$6,560	$7,110	$186,160	78%	78%	-2%
		50th	$3,860	$4,110	$4,460	$120,040	12%	12%	-2%
		10th	$2,580	$2,230	$2,900	$84,940	-28%	-28%	-3%
Bengen's Dollar Floor-and-Ceiling Withdrawals	4.00%	90th	$4,800	$4,800	$4,800	$288,960	20%	20%	0%
		50th	$4,170	$4,400	$4,760	$122,810	19%	19%	-1%
		10th	$3,400	$3,400	$3,400	$68,760	-15%	-15%	-3%
Vanguard's Percentage Floor-and-Ceiling Withdrawals	4.00%	90th	$5,130	$5,780	$6,420	$318,970	61%	61%	0%
		50th	$3,820	$3,570	$4,230	$132,200	6%	6%	-2%
		10th	$2,560	$2,070	$2,240	$94,920	-44%	-44%	-3%
Kitces Ratcheting Rule	4.00%	90th	$4,840	$6,440	$9,430	$231,710	136%	136%	0%
		50th	$4,000	$5,320	$7,090	$81,430	77%	77%	0%
		10th	$4,000	$4,000	$4,000	$25,900	0%	0%	0%
Guyton and Klinger's Decision Rules	4.00%	90th	$5,320	$7,970	$8,730	$223,940	118%	118%	0%
		50th	$4,000	$4,300	$4,660	$126,180	17%	17%	-1%
		10th	$2,770	$2,590	$3,070	$86,690	-23%	-23%	-2%
Zolt's Glide Path Spending Rule	4.00%	90th	$4,000	$4,000	$4,000	$364,000	0%	0%	0%
		50th	$3,750	$3,540	$3,530	$154,540	-12%	-12%	-1%
		10th	$2,740	$2,360	$2,360	$87,600	-41%	-41%	-1%
Modified RMD Rule (Spending Rate = 1.24 × RMD %)	4.00%	90th	$7,490	$11,610	$10,170	$70,160	154%	154%	-4%
		50th	$5,200	$6,670	$6,290	$41,630	57%	57%	-5%
		10th	$3,210	$3,640	$4,260	$30,280	6%	6%	-7%

As for other strategies, we can discuss them in terms of the trends for each of the measures. Regarding how spending evolves over time, spending can reach the highest levels at the ninetieth percentile with the modified RMD rule, the Kitces ratcheting rule, Guyton and Klinger's decision rules, and the fixed-percentage rule. As for the median level of spending after thirty years, spending is the highest with the Kitces ratcheting rule, the modified RMD rule, and the fixed-percentage rule. At the tenth percentile, spending after thirty years is the highest with the modified RMD rule, constant inflation-adjusted spending, and the Kitces ratcheting rule. The Vanguard floor-and-ceiling and Zolt glide path rules lead to the lowest levels of spending after thirty years.

Remaining wealth after thirty years is the highest at the ninetieth percentile for constant inflation-adjusted spending and Zolt's glide path rule. These rules do not allow for any spending increases in retirement, even when markets do well, which allows for more remaining wealth when initial withdrawal rates are the same. The modified RMD rule, which increases the withdrawal rate over time to match declining longevity, is the most efficient at spending down assets over retirement. It is the only rule with a decline in remaining real wealth at the ninetieth percentile. At the median, Zolt's glide path rule maintains the largest remaining wealth on account of spending decreases without any possibility for increases. At the tenth percentile, remaining wealth is the largest for Vanguard's floor-and-ceiling rule.

In terms of changes in spending at the ninetieth percentile, the modified RMD rule provided the largest spending increase. This was followed by the ratcheting rule and the Guyton and Klinger decision rules. Meanwhile, at the median, the ratcheting rule offered the largest spending increase of 77 percent after thirty years. This was followed by the modified RMD rules.

The only strategy to experience a decline in spending at the median was Zolt's glide path spending rule. At the tenth percentile of outcomes, the modified RMD rule was the only strategy that allowed for a spending increase even in these poor market environments. Spending was 6 percent higher at the tenth percentile after thirty years.

In terms of strategies that experience the biggest reductions to spending, Vanguard's floor-and-ceiling percentages strategy experienced a 44 percent decline in spending at the tenth percentile, while Zolt's glide path strategy experienced a 41 percent decline in spending.

The next column (year 30 spending relative to baseline) shows the year thirty spending for a strategy relative to the initial spending from the baseline constant inflation-adjusted spending strategy. For this particular exhibit, all were strategies recalibrated to an initial 4 percent spending rate rather than using a PAY Rule. Thus, for this exhibit, the spending relative to the baseline strategy is the same as the spending for the strategy itself. Again, this is because all strategies in this particular exhibit start at retirement with a 4 percent withdrawal rate.

The final column in the exhibit is downside spending volatility. This is the average of spending decreases experienced over the thirty-year period. The strategy with the most downside spending volatility is the modified RMD rule. At the ninetieth percentile, it experienced an average decrease in spending of 4 percent. At the median, the decrease is 5 percent, and at the tenth percentile, the decrease is 7 percent. The fixed-percentage withdrawal strategy is next on the list of those with the most downside spending volatility. Other strategies with noticeable downside volatility include the two endowment formula strategies and the Vanguard floor-and-ceiling percentages strategy. Since wealth was never depleted in this exhibit, the constant inflation-adjusted strategy and the ratcheting strategy are the only two that never experienced any downside volatility. Neither of these strategies experiences a spending decrease unless the portfolio becomes depleted.

◉ Comparing Strategies in Different Market Environments

With this overview of how the different variable spending strategies performed historically, it is worthwhile to put a bit more effort into understanding the relative performance of these strategies in different market environments. Toward this end, I chose the years 1966 (poor retirement environment), 1982 (great retirement environment), and 1946 (average retirement environment) to demonstrate the evolution of spending and wealth with the strategies.

First, 1966 represents a tough year to enter retirement, as this year triggered the lowest sustainable spending rate of just over 4 percent for the constant inflation-adjusted strategy. Exhibit 6.17 provides the path of spending and wealth for each of the ten strategies for the years 1966–1995. We can observe that the constant inflation-adjusted spending

Exhibit 6.17

Time Path of Real Spending and Wealth

Performance for All Strategies, 1966 Retiree
For 4% Initial Spending Rate, 50/50 Asset Allocation,
Rolling 30-Year Retirements Using SBBI Data, 1966–1995,
S&P 500 and Intermediate-Term Government Bonds

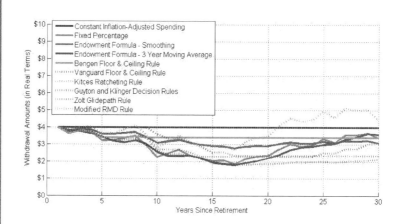

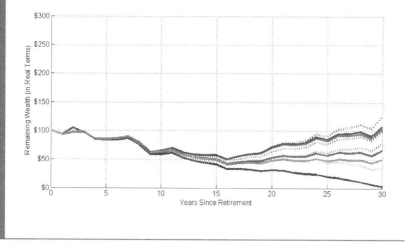

strategy and Michael Kitces's ratcheting strategy both sustained real spending at the initial $4 throughout the thirty-year horizon. During these years, the ratcheting strategy was never afforded an opportunity to increase spending. With both of these strategies, wealth is on the verge of depletion by the end, and both strategies would deplete assets in year thirty-one of retirement.

The other eight strategies led to reduced spending early on and throughout retirement. For the fixed-percentage, moving-average endowment formula, and Vanguard's floor-and-ceiling rule, real spending fell by 50 percent about fifteen years into retirement. After this point, the Vanguard strategy kept spending at the lower level, as it was difficult for the strategy to reach the wealth triggers needed to allow subsequent spending increases. This allowed real wealth to grow the most by the end of the retirement horizon, exceeding its initial level in real terms.

As for other strategies, Bengen's floor-and-ceiling rule quickly found its way to the hard-dollar floor and did not subsequently increase during retirement. The smoothing endowment formula, Guyton and Klinger's decision rules, and Zolt's glide path rule all kept spending and wealth within the middle range of the strategies. The modified RMD rule is the only strategy to eventually allow for real spending to increase above its initial $4 level. This happened by year twenty-one of retirement, at an assumed age of eighty-six, as withdrawal percentages increased at a fast enough pace to counteract declining wealth.

Next, Exhibit 6.18 provides the results for the 1982 retiree, which experienced the highest sustainable withdrawal rate in the historical period for the constant inflation-adjusted spending strategy. All the strategies either keep real spending level (constant inflation-adjusted spending and Zolt's glide path rule) or increase it over time. The most aggressive spending increases are seen with the modified RMD rule, the fixed-percentage rule, and Guyton and Klinger's decision rules. The modified RMD rule is the only strategy that experienced a decline in real wealth by year thirty as spending levels rose dramatically. This strategy works most efficiently to spend down remaining assets.

Finally, Exhibit 6.19 shows the spending path for the ten strategies beginning from 1946, a more typically average year to retire. For this retirement year, the variable strategies experienced a reduction in spending in the early part of retirement that was overcome later in retirement when spending typically increased.

By year thirty, most strategies experienced spending at close to the same real level as it started. The ratcheting strategy is the only strategy with significantly higher spending at year thirty. The modified RMD rule strategy

Time Path of Real Spending and Wealth
Performance for All Strategies, 1982 Retiree
For 4% Initial Spending Rate, 50/50 Asset Allocation,
Rolling 30-Year Retirements Using SBBI Data, 1982–2011,
S&P 500 and Intermediate-Term Government Bonds

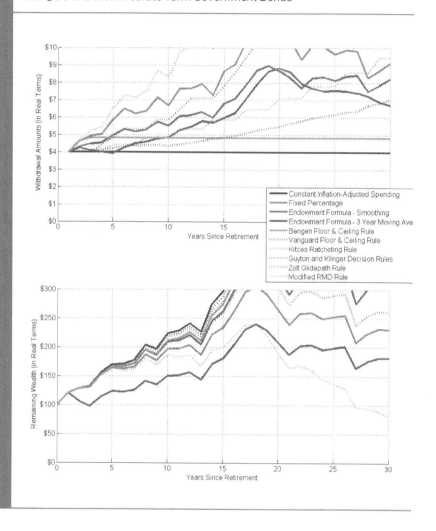

experienced the highest spending in the middle part of retirement, but with reductions in the portfolio balance that led to lower spending by year thirty. Remaining wealth after thirty years is the lowest with the modified RMD strategy. Other strategies tend to have wealth levels between 75 and 100 percent of the initial retirement amount.

Exhibit 6.19

Time Path of Real Spending and Wealth

Performance for All Strategies, 1946 Retiree
For 4% Initial Spending Rate, 50/50 Asset Allocation,
Rolling 30-Year Retirements Using SBBI Data, 1946–1975,
S&P 500 and Intermediate-Term Government Bonds

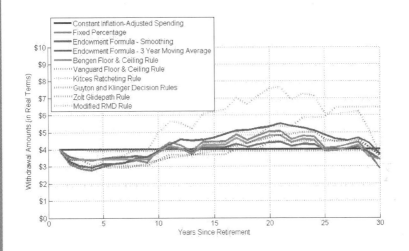

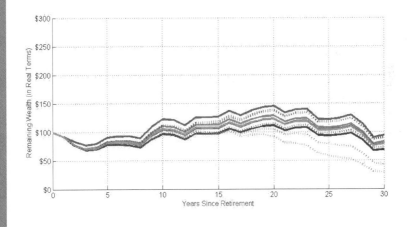

⊙ Applying the PAY Rule™ with the Historical Data

Thus far, we have looked at applying a 4 percent initial withdrawal rate to the different retirement spending strategies. In such cases, we did not use a PAY Rule to calibrate the level of downside risk, as the initial spending rate was always the same.

Now, we are ready to consider the impact of controlling downside wealth outcomes and allowing the initial withdrawal rate to vary to maintain the same downside risk across strategies. Exhibit 6.20 provides results for the various spending strategies using a PAY Rule that allows for a 10 percent chance that real wealth has fallen below $15,000 from an initial $100,000 by year thirty of retirement.

This analysis is again conducted using a 50/50 portfolio of stocks and bonds and is based on rolling periods from history. For constant inflation-adjusted spending, the supported initial spending rate is 4.18 percent. To be clear, this is higher than the SAFEMAX value of 4.03 percent. This is because the PAY Rule is not that spending falls to zero with 100 percent probability by year thirty of retirement, but that there is a 10 percent chance that wealth falls below $15,000 by year thirty. It is a different criterion. Spending can be higher because we allow for a 10 percent chance that real wealth will fall below a threshold that is not too high to offset the higher accepted downside probability risk.

For constant inflation-adjusted spending, spending stays at this initial level in real terms throughout retirement across the distribution. Remaining wealth after thirty years ranges from just below the $15,000 limit allowed in year thirty at the tenth percentile to as much as $310,000, or three times more than the initial wealth balance, in the ninetieth percentile. In the median outcome, real wealth has grown by about 10 percent.

For this baseline strategy, spending does not increase or decrease in any of the scenarios, as wealth has not been depleted for the circumstances shown in the exhibit. Therefore, changes in real spending, changes in spending relative to the baseline, and downside spending volatility are all zero.

The next strategy in the exhibit is fixed-percentage withdrawals. The initial spending rate for this strategy can be 9.49 percent, which is more than double the constant inflation-adjusted spending strategy. This initial spending level is higher because our focus is on calibrating downside exposure to wealth losses. In this case, the initial spending rate of 9.49 percent preserves remaining wealth after thirty years at just under $15,000 in the tenth percentile as the PAY Rule requires.

Because the initial spending rate is high, there is a tendency for spending to decline with this strategy across the distribution of outcomes. By year thirty, the ninetieth percentile real spending level is only $3,340. At the median, it is $2,060, and at the tenth percentile it is $1,400.

These are noticeable drops relative to both the initial spending level for this strategy and the spending supported by the baseline constant inflation-adjusted spending of $4,180. This strategy experiences the highest initial withdrawal rate and the most significant spending decreases across the distribution. This is a clear example of the trade-off of allowing for a higher initial spending rate resulting in less spending for later in retirement. With this strategy, real spending has fallen by 65 percent in the ninetieth percentile, 78 percent at the median, and 85 percent in the tenth percentile. In terms of downside spending volatility, this strategy experiences relatively high average spending reductions. The averages for spending reductions range from 3 percent at the ninetieth percentile and median to 4 percent at the tenth percentile.

The next strategy is the endowment formula that provides a weighted average in which half of spending evolves with the constant inflation-adjusted strategy and the other half evolves with a fixed-percentage withdrawal of the remaining account balance. This strategy is a form of compromise between the two extremes previously discussed. The initial spending rate is 5.45 percent.

With this strategy at the ninetieth percentile, spending can increase in retirement. It is 28 percent higher by year thirty. However, at the median and tenth percentiles, retirees can expect a reduction in their spending potential. It is 22 percent less at the median and 41 percent less at the tenth percentile. Relative to the baseline strategy, spending with this endowment strategy is 67 percent higher at the ninetieth percentile, 1 percent higher at the median, and 24 percent less at the tenth percentile. This strategy reduces downside volatility relative to the fixed-percentage strategy, as it also has a component of spending that uses constant inflation-adjusted spending. Across the board, average downside reductions to spending averaged 2 percent over the thirty-year period.

Next, the second endowment formula is based on a three-year moving average. The initial spending rate of 9.42 percent is just slightly below the initial spending rate with the fixed-percentage withdrawals. In practical terms, this strategy behaves similarly to fixed-percentage withdrawals but with slightly less volatility. In all cases, spending is reduced throughout retirement due to the high initial spending level. It is 63 percent less at the ninetieth percentile ranging to 86 percent less at the tenth percentile. In addition, because of the significant spending reductions over time across the distribution of spending, spending will be less by year thirty of retirement compared to the baseline constant inflation-adjusted spending strategy. The strategy has significant volatility on the downside as well, averaging 3 percent reductions in spending on a year-by-year basis over the thirty-year retirement period across the distribution of outcomes.

The next strategy is Bengen's dollar floor-and-ceiling withdrawal strategy. This strategy is based on allowing a ceiling that is 20 percent higher than the initial withdrawal rate level and a floor that is 15 percent less than the initial withdrawal level in dollar terms. The initial spending rate is 4.84 percent. Spending with this strategy is held within the range mentioned. It can reach as high as $5,810, which it does at the ninetieth percentile at subsequent points in retirement. This represents a 20 percent increase over initial spending. On the downside, spending can drop as low as $4,110, which is 15 percent below the initial retirement date spending level. By year thirty, spending has fallen to this floor at both the median and tenth percentiles. It is interesting that downside spending is only slightly less than with the constant inflation-adjusted baseline.

Bengen's dollar floor-and-ceiling rule allows initial spending to increase while also providing the ability to adjust spending in a way that reduces the sequence risk. In this way, even when the floor is reached, spending remains at about the same level as it was with the constant inflation-adjusted baseline strategy.

In this sense, the floor-and-ceiling strategy dominates the constant inflation-adjusted baseline strategy by providing the potential for higher spending throughout retirement. On the downside, it creates circumstances in which spending would be only slightly less than the baseline strategy. By allowing for higher spending, the floor-and-ceiling strategy ends up reducing the balance of remaining wealth after thirty years of retirement.

At the ninetieth percentile, spending is 20 percent higher than its initial level and 39 percent higher than the baseline level. At the median, spending is 15 percent below the initial level and 2 percent less than the baseline. The same is also true at the tenth percentile. This strategy allows for *some* variability in spending and spending reductions. The average spending reduction at the median is 1 percent, while it is 3 percent at the tenth percentile.

The next strategy in the exhibit is Vanguard's percentage floor-and-ceiling withdrawal strategy. This strategy is more variable in nature and has a bit more in common with the fixed-percentage withdrawal strategy than with the constant inflation-adjusted spending strategy. It's a floor-and-ceiling method that behaves more like a fixed-percentage strategy.

The initial spending level is 7.46 percent, and with this strategy, spending also tends to decrease by year thirty across the distribution of outcomes. It is 7 percent less at the ninetieth percentile, 64 percent less at the median, and 80 percent less at the tenth percentile. These are dramatic spending reductions, though they are not as dramatic as with a fixed-percentage spending strategy.

Relative to the baseline constant inflation-adjusted spending strategy, spending after thirty years is 65 percent higher at the ninetieth percentile, but it is 34 percent less at the median and 64 percent less the tenth percentile. Downside spending volatility is noticeable with a 1 percent average decrease at the ninetieth percentile and a 3 percent average decrease at the median and tenth percentiles.

Next, Exhibit 6.20 shows the outcomes for the Kitces ratcheting rule. This is a rule that allows for spending increases but not decreases. As such, the initial spending rate is the same as with baseline, and at the tenth percentile of outcomes, spending will stay the same. Where this strategy differs is when markets do well. At the ninetieth percentile, real spending increases by 136 percent after thirty years, and it is 61 percent higher at the median. There is no downside spending volatility.

Sustainable Spending Rates from an Investment Portfolio over 30 Years

PAY Rule: Allow for a 10% Chance That Real Wealth Has Fallen Below $15,000 by Year 30 For a 65-Year-Old Couple, 50/50 Asset Allocation, Rolling 30-Year Retirements, Using SBBI Data, 1926–2016, S&P 500 and Intermediate-Term Government Bonds

Retirement Date Wealth Level = $100,000

Spending Strategy	Initial Spending Rate	Percentile of Distribution	Real Spending in 10 Years	Real Spending in 20 Years	Real Spending in 30 Years	Real Remaining Wealth After 30 Years	Change in Real Spending at Year 30	Year 30 Spending Relative to Baseline	Downside Spending Volatility
Constant Inflation-Adjusted Spending (BASELINE)	4.18%	90th	$4,180	$4,180	$4,180	$304,500	0%	0%	0%
		50th	$4,180	$4,180	$4,180	$112,670	0%	0%	0%
		10th	$4,180	$4,180	$4,180	$14,340	0%	0%	0%
Fixed-Percentage Withdrawals	9.49%	90th	$8,390	$5,990	$3,340	$34,640	−65%	−20%	−3%
		50th	$5,820	$3,440	$2,060	$20,560	−78%	−51%	−3%
		10th	$3,590	$1,880	$1,400	$14,950	−85%	−67%	−4%
Endowment Formula—Weighted Average—Hybrid	5.45%	90th	$6,400	$7,330	$7,000	$152,830	28%	67%	−2%
		50th	$5,170	$4,620	$4,230	$56,710	−22%	1%	−2%
		10th	$4,120	$3,580	$3,190	$14,510	−41%	−24%	−2%
Endowment Formula—3-Year Moving Average	9.42%	90th	$8,520	$5,930	$3,470	$34,350	−63%	−17%	−3%
		50th	$6,370	$3,610	$2,100	$21,130	−78%	−50%	−3%
		10th	$4,200	$1,910	$1,350	$14,820	−86%	−68%	−3%
Bengen's Dollar Floor-and-Ceiling Withdrawals	4.84%	90th	$5,810	$5,810	$5,810	$210,440	20%	39%	0%
		50th	$4,650	$4,200	$4,110	$75,330	−15%	−2%	−1%
		10th	$4,110	$4,110	$4,110	$12,660	−15%	−2%	−3%
Vanguard's Percentage Floor-and-Ceiling Withdrawals	7.46%	90th	$8,110	$7,620	$6,910	$84,350	−7%	65%	−1%
		50th	$5,640	$3,880	$2,770	$34,780	−63%	−34%	−3%
		10th	$3,630	$2,060	$1,500	$12,960	−80%	−64%	−3%
Kitces Ratcheting Rule	4.18%	90th	$5,060	$6,730	$9,860	$217,780	136%	136%	0%
		50th	$4,180	$5,310	$6,730	$68,760	61%	61%	0%
		10th	$4,180	$4,180	$4,180	$14,340	0%	0%	0%
Guyton and Klinger's Decision Rules	6.34%	90th	$6,970	$8,550	$9,270	$94,030	46%	122%	0%
		50th	$5,270	$4,590	$4,500	$47,850	−29%	8%	−1%
		10th	$3,530	$2,840	$2,900	$11,280	−54%	−31%	−2%
Zolt's Glide Path Spending Rule	6.89%	90th	$6,240	$5,370	$5,080	$230,620	−26%	22%	−1%
		50th	$5,160	$3,660	$3,240	$61,810	−53%	−22%	−2%
		10th	$3,670	$2,210	$1,690	$14,710	−75%	−60%	−2%
Modified RMD Rule (Spending Rate = 1.6 × RMD %)	5.17%	90th	$8,550	$10,870	$6,790	$34,530	31%	62%	−4%
		50th	$5,930	$6,240	$4,200	$20,490	−19%	0%	−5%
		10th	$3,660	$3,400	$2,840	$14,900	−45%	−32%	−6%

212   How Much Can I Spend in Retirement?

Guyton and Klinger's series of decision rules provide the next approach in the exhibit. This strategy supports an initial spending rate of 6.34 percent. After thirty years, spending grows by an additional 46 percent at the ninetieth percentile, though spending decreases can be expected at the median (–29 percent) and tenth percentile (–54 percent). Relative to the baseline, spending is 122 percent higher at the ninetieth percentile, 8 percent higher at the median, and 31 percent lower at the tenth percentile. Annual spending reductions average 1 percent at the median and 2 percent at the tenth percentile.

Zolt's Target Percentage Adjustment rule is next, and this rule supports a 6.89 percent initial spending rate. After the first year, real spending never increases, but it may decrease. Spending falls by 26 percent after thirty years at the ninetieth percentile, and by 53 percent at the median and 75 percent at the tenth percentile. Relative to the baseline, real spending is 22 percent larger at the high end, 22 percent less at the median, and 60 percent less at the tenth percentile. Average spending reductions range from 1 to 2 percent.

The final strategy is the modified RMD rule. The PAY Rule calibration allows for distribution rates to be 1.6 times that shown in the government's RMD tables. This provides a 5.17 percent initial withdrawal rate. After thirty years, real spending grows by 31 percent at the ninetieth percentile and falls by 19 percent and 45 percent at the median and tenth percentile. Relative to the baseline, median spending is quite close to the same, while spending is 62 percent higher at the top and 32 percent lower at the bottom. This strategy effectively spends down assets in the same way as the fixed-percentage strategy, and it leads to the largest downside spending reductions, which average from 4 to 6 percent.

◉ Applying the PAY Rule™ with Monte Carlo Simulations for the Current Market Environment

Next, I simulate these strategies with Monte Carlo simulations for stock and bond returns using current market environment as a starting point. This approach is described in the technical appendix to chapter 3. I believe the results in Exhibit 6.21 are much more realistic than historical data for today's retirees. These simulations reflect the lower bond yields available to retirees today, but a mechanism is included for interest rates to gradually increase over time, on average. Bond returns are calculated from the simulated interest rates and their changes, and stock returns are calculated by adding a simulated equity premium on top of the simulated interest rates. All strategies are simulated with the same asset allocations and portfolio returns for the sake of comparison. Strategies are simulated with annual data, assume withdrawals are made at the start of each year, and use annual rebalancing to restore the targeted asset allocation. The tax implications for different spending strategies are not otherwise considered.

The PAY Rule used to create Exhibit 6.21 is the same as with Exhibit 6.20: The retiree accepts a 10 percent chance that real wealth falls below $15,000 (based on an initial $100,000) by year thirty of retirement. Spending levels in Exhibit 6.21 are generally lower than found with historical data, even though spending patterns are largely similar. Due to the similarities, I will not go into great detail in describing the numbers.

That being said, the starting points merit some discussion. For instance, Bengen's baseline constant inflation-adjusted spending rule supports an initial spending rate of 2.78 percent as a starting point—noticeably lower than the 4.18 percent found with historical data, but it is the implication of retiring in a low interest rate world. For the $100,000 initial portfolio, this supports $2,780 in real spending across the entire distribution of Monte Carlo simulations for as long as wealth remains.

The fixed-percentage strategy allows initial spending to increase to 6.60 percent, with noticeable spending reductions and aggressive wealth depletion over time. Again, the smoothing endowment formula provides a compromise with a 3.71 percent initial spending rate, and the initial spending rate for the moving average endowment formula is identical to that for the fixed-percentage rule.

Bengen's floor-and-ceiling rule allows the initial withdrawal rate to increase to 3.20 percent and helps keep downside spending at a level close to the baseline amount. Vanguard's floor-and-ceiling rule again behaves closer to a fixed-percentage strategy, though it preserves wealth at a stronger pace. Next, the Kitces ratcheting rule has the lowest initial spending rate of 2.69 percent, but it allows for significant upside spending potential while keeping the downside risk similar to the baseline.

Exhibit 6.21

Sustainable Spending Rates from an Investment Portfolio over 30 Years

PAY Rule: Allow for a 10% Chance That Real Wealth Has Fallen Below $15,000 by Year 30

For a 65-Year-Old Couple, Using a 50/50 Portfolio of Stocks and Bonds

1,000 Monte Carlo Simulations Based on Current Market Conditions

Retirement Date Wealth Level = $100,000

Spending Strategy	Initial Spending Rate	Percentile of Distribution	Real Spending in 10 Years	Real Spending in 20 Years	Real Spending in 30 Years	Real Remaining Wealth After 30 Years	Change in Real Spending at Year 30	Year 30 Spending Relative to Baseline	Downside Spending Volatility
Constant Inflation-Adjusted Spending (BASELINE)	2.78%	90th	$2,780	$2,780	$2,780	$360,480	0%	0%	0%
		50th	$2,780	$2,780	$2,780	$109,950	0%	0%	0%
		10th	$2,780	$2,780	$2,780	$14,880	0%	0%	0%
Fixed-Percentage Withdrawals	6.60%	90th	$6,990	$6,140	$5,460	$83,710	-17%	96%	-3%
		50th	$4,490	$3,180	$2,360	$34,690	-64%	-15%	-3%
		10th	$2,980	$1,620	$1,020	$14,980	-85%	-63%	-4%
Endowment Formula–Weighted Average–Hybrid	3.71%	90th	$4,500	$5,100	$6,030	$230,710	63%	117%	-1%
		50th	$3,500	$3,370	$3,250	$74,000	-12%	17%	-2%
		10th	$2,900	$2,460	$2,160	$14,950	-42%	-22%	-3%
Endowment Formula–3-Year Moving Average	6.60%	90th	$7,030	$6,270	$5,650	$88,000	-14%	103%	-2%
		50th	$4,810	$3,210	$2,410	$36,370	-63%	-13%	-3%
		10th	$3,200	$1,640	$1,040	$14,970	-84%	-63%	-4%
Bengen's Dollar Floor-and-Ceiling Withdrawals	3.20%	90th	$3,840	$3,840	$3,840	$294,850	20%	38%	-1%
		50th	$3,000	$2,970	$3,050	$94,270	-5%	10%	-1%
		10th	$2,720	$2,720	$2,720	$14,740	-15%	-2%	-3%
Vanguard's Percentage Floor-and-Ceiling Withdrawals	5.07%	90th	$6,050	$6,030	$6,240	$152,000	23%	124%	-2%
		50th	$4,170	$3,260	$2,750	$52,750	-46%	-1%	-3%
		10th	$2,920	$1,830	$1,120	$14,940	-78%	-60%	-3%
Kitces Ratcheting Rule	2.69%	90th	$3,250	$4,330	$5,770	$323,530	114%	108%	0%
		50th	$2,690	$3,250	$4,330	$94,080	61%	56%	0%
		10th	$2,690	$2,690	$2,690	$14,670	0%	-3%	0%
Guyton and Klinger's Decision Rules	4.47%	90th	$5,410	$6,350	$7,190	$177,510	61%	159%	0%
		50th	$3,880	$3,590	$3,660	$56,940	-18%	32%	-1%
		10th	$2,670	$1,930	$1,890	$15,110	-58%	-32%	-2%
Zolt's Glide Path Spending Rule	4.64%	90th	$4,480	$4,350	$4,310	$244,030	-7%	55%	0%
		50th	$3,670	$3,170	$2,960	$67,360	-36%	6%	-1%
		10th	$2,860	$2,080	$1,470	$14,920	-68%	-47%	-2%
Modified RMD Rule (Spending Rate = 1.11 × RMD %)	3.60%	90th	$6,350	$9,460	$10,810	$83,770	200%	289%	-3%
		50th	$4,080	$4,900	$4,670	$34,720	30%	68%	-4%
		10th	$2,700	$2,500	$2,030	$14,990	-44%	-27%	-6%

Both the Guyton and Klinger decision rules and the Zolt rule allow initial spending to rise about 4 percent to 4.47 percent and 4.64 percent, respectively, though their subsequent evolution varies as before. Finally, the modified RMD rule is calibrated to the PAY Rule by using a 1.11 multiplication factor for the RMD rates, and it again leads to large upside spending potential and the most downside spending volatility.

◉ Choosing a PAY Rule™ and Spending Strategy

The analysis thus far has been based on one manifestation of the PAY Rule (allow a 10 percent chance that real wealth falls below 15 percent of its initial level by year thirty of retirement) and one asset allocation (50/50 portfolio of stocks and bonds). We have not yet delved into the more complex and personalized issue of how to choose a PAY Rule and asset allocation. I will try to provide more guidance on this topic in this final section. I would describe the scenario I've used thus far as a moderate choice for retirees. To give a more complete overview, I will add exhibits providing guidance for more conservative and aggressive retirees as well.

A natural guideline for the retirement spending decision is to first determine what spending rate would satisfy your overall lifestyle goals. Beyond this, it is important to consider the following:

1. Your degree of spending flexibility to make cuts if necessary,
2. Your general view about whether your spending may need to keep pace with overall consumer price inflation, and
3. Whether you want to maintain a safety margin for assets.

Armed with this information, you can then consider the broad range of variable spending strategies and choose the one that seems to best match your goals and manage your risks. My research in this area seeks to develop a framework to help with the decision-making process.

How should a retiree choose a spending method and parameterize the initial spending rate? I have provided a framework to think about the important issues, such as spending flexibility, feelings about upside spending growth versus downside spending risks, the possibility of a minimum spending threshold to be protected, the desired direction of spending (for instance, whether to decrease spending over time), the appropriate planning horizon, and any legacy goals.

A broader set of issues to consider when deciding on a withdrawal rate and asset allocation relate to a Retirement CARE Analysis. Answers to the following questions will help guide these decisions:

(C)apacities:
- Do you have sufficient retirement income from reliable sources that will not be diminished by market downturns?
- How would you adjust your lifestyle if you had to spend less? Is your answer reasonable?
- Are your portfolio distributions flexible enough that you could reduce them after a market downturn without adversely affecting your standard of living in retirement (either because it is easy to make simple lifestyle changes or because you have sufficient reliable income sources like pensions and annuities available outside your portfolio)?
- Do you have insurance to protect from dramatic spending shocks related to health, long-term care, or an unexpected death?
- Related to your funded status, do you have reserve assets that could be deployed to cover spending after a market downturn (that are not earmarked to meet retirement spending goals)? Is the value of these assets correlated with the stock market?

(A)spirations:
- What are your retirement spending goals? How are they divided between basic and discretionary expenses?
- Do you expect your lifestyle spending goals to keep pace with inflation? Are your spending needs sensitive to inflation?
- How long do you want your money to last?
- Do you want to build in a margin of safety for remaining assets?
- What are your legacy objectives?

(R)eturns:
- What are reasonable expectations for different asset classes during retirement?

(E)motional Comfort:

- How much short-term market volatility can you stomach before it starts affecting your sleep with undue stress or causes you to panic and sell stocks after a market downturn?
- What is your longevity risk aversion? How worried are you about outliving your assets? How strongly do you wish to avoid spending reductions in the event you live well beyond your life expectancy?
- Can you stick to the spending and investment objectives for your financial plan without being strongly tempted to overdo things or arbitrarily change course?
- Are you vulnerable to making other behavioral mistakes that could harm the long-term prospects for your financial plan?
- How complex is the financial plan? Can it run on autopilot or be facilitated by a trusted financial professional, or does it require ongoing complex decision-making on your part?
- How financially savvy are different members of your household? Would surviving household members be able to carry on financially if you were incapacitated due to illness or death?

In answering these Retirement CARE questions, a more conservative retiree will experience some of the following characteristics:

- fewer reliable income sources outside the investment portfolio to help cushion the impact of market volatility on lifestyle,
- lower flexibility to make spending reductions because spending goals are fixed and adjust with inflation,
- fewer reserves, buffer assets, or insurance policies to help cushion spending shocks,
- a greater desire to build in a margin of safety for the financial plan,
- greater worry and stress about short-term market volatility, and
- greater worry and stress about outliving your retirement assets.

Meanwhile, a more aggressive retiree will tend to fall in the opposite direction on these matters, highlighting the highly personal and complex nature of determining asset allocation for retirement. I will discuss the matter in more detail in chapter 8.

For now, with decisions made about these issues, retirees can decide on an appropriate PAY Rule and then compare the distributions of spending and wealth created by variable spending rules. I now aim to provide guidance about determining the implications of being conservative, moderate, or aggressive with regard to retirement income decisions. Exhibit 6.22 outlines three different stylized PAY Rules to represent these different retirement preferences. A conservative retiree uses a more conservative asset allocation (such as 25 percent stocks) and seeks greater safety within his or her choices for PAY: there is a smaller chance that wealth falls to low levels by late in retirement (5 percent chance that real wealth falls below $20 from an initial $100 by year 30). A moderate retiree reflects our earlier baseline by being comfortable with 50 percent stocks and accepting a 10 percent change that real wealth falls below $15 by year 30. Finally, an example for a more aggressive retiree is using a 75 percent stock allocation and accepting a 20 percent change that real wealth falls below $10 by year 30.

Exhibit 6.22

Three PAY Rules for Retirees

Based on Initial Retirement Assets of $100

Retiree Type	PAY Rule	Asset Allocation (Stocks/Bonds)
Conservative	Accepts a 5% chance that real wealth falls below $20 by year 30	25/75
Moderate	Accepts a 10% chance that real wealth falls below $15 by year 30	50/50
Aggressive	Accepts a 20% chance that real wealth falls below $10 by year 30	75/25

The moderate case was provided earlier in Exhibit 6.21. In the baseline constant inflation-adjusted spending case, the sustainable spending rate was 2.78 percent. Exhibit 6.23 provides the results for a more conservative retiree using a lower stock allocation and seeking greater safety with the retiree's PAY Rule. In this case, the baseline withdrawal rate falls to 2.15 percent, with other withdrawal rates reduced across the board. The lower

Exhibit 6.23

Sustainable Spending Rates from an Investment Portfolio over 30 Years

PAY Rule (Conservative Case): Allow for a 5% Chance That Real Wealth Has Fallen Below $20,000 by Year 30
For a 65-Year-Old Couple, Using a 25/75 Portfolio of Stocks and Bonds
1,000 Monte Carlo Simulations Based on Current Market Conditions
Retirement Date Wealth Level = $100,000

Spending Strategy	Initial Spending Rate	Percentile of Distribution	Real Spending in 10 Years	Real Spending in 20 Years	Real Spending in 30 Years	Real Remaining Wealth After 30 Years	Change in Real Spending at Year 30	Year 30 Spending Relative to Baseline	Downside Spending Volatility
Constant Inflation-Adjusted Spending (BASELINE)	2.15%	90th	$2,150	$2,150	$2,150	$217,730	0%	0%	0%
		50th	$2,150	$2,150	$2,150	$93,220	0%	0%	0%
		10th	$2,150	$2,150	$2,150	$28,290	0%	0%	0%
Fixed-Percentage Withdrawals	4.61%	90th	$4,810	$4,460	$4,120	$88,760	−11%	92%	−3%
		50th	$3,410	$2,610	$2,190	$46,580	−52%	2%	−3%
		10th	$2,360	$1,570	$1,130	$24,030	−75%	−47%	−4%
Endowment Formula–Weighted Average–Hybrid	2.86%	90th	$3,200	$3,460	$3,670	$161,020	28%	71%	−1%
		50th	$2,660	$2,520	$2,460	$71,900	−14%	14%	−1%
		10th	$2,260	$2,030	$1,810	$25,560	−37%	−16%	−2%
Endowment Formula–3-Year Moving Average	4.48%	90th	$4,830	$4,520	$4,310	$98,190	−4%	100%	−2%
		50th	$3,470	$2,680	$2,230	$49,280	−50%	4%	−3%
		10th	$2,420	$1,610	$1,130	$25,100	−75%	−47%	−3%
Bengen's Dollar Floor-and-Ceiling Withdrawals	2.48%	90th	$2,980	$2,980	$2,980	$187,260	20%	39%	0%
		50th	$2,230	$2,110	$2,110	$85,270	−15%	−2%	−1%
		10th	$2,110	$2,110	$2,110	$27,940	−15%	−2%	−2%
Vanguard's Percentage Floor-and-Ceiling Withdrawals	4.14%	90th	$4,530	$4,290	$4,090	$102,620	−1%	90%	−2%
		50th	$3,260	$2,560	$2,210	$51,500	−47%	3%	−3%
		10th	$2,330	$1,600	$1,120	$24,410	−73%	−48%	−3%
Kitces Ratcheting Rule	2.11%	90th	$2,320	$3,090	$4,110	$207,030	95%	91%	0%
		50th	$2,110	$2,320	$3,090	$84,590	46%	44%	0%
		10th	$2,110	$2,110	$2,110	$28,100	0%	−2%	0%
Guyton and Klinger's Decision Rules	3.36%	90th	$3,700	$4,050	$4,460	$135,590	33%	107%	0%
		50th	$2,910	$2,650	$2,700	$61,420	−20%	26%	−1%
		10th	$2,100	$1,720	$1,700	$25,070	−49%	−21%	−2%
Zolt's Glide Path Spending Rule	2.56%	90th	$2,560	$2,560	$2,560	$188,410	0%	19%	0%
		50th	$2,560	$2,560	$2,560	$75,660	0%	19%	0%
		10th	$2,440	$2,010	$1,760	$25,730	−31%	−18%	−1%
Modified RMD Rule (Spending Rate = 1.11 × RMD %)	2.52%	90th	$4,050	$6,170	$8,010	$88,740	218%	273%	−2%
		50th	$2,870	$3,610	$4,260	$46,570	69%	98%	−3%
		10th	$1,990	$2,170	$2,190	$24,030	−13%	2%	−5%

Exhibit 6.24

Sustainable Spending Rates from an Investment Portfolio over 30 Years

PAY Rule (Aggressive Case): Allow for a 20% Chance That Real Wealth Has Fallen Below $10,000 by Year 30
For a 65-Year-Old Couple, Using a 75/25 Portfolio of Stocks and Bonds
1,000 Monte Carlo Simulations Based on Current Market Conditions
Retirement Date Wealth Level = $100,000

Spending Strategy	Initial Spending Rate	Percentile Distribution	Real Spending in 10 Years	Real Spending in 20 Years	Real Spending in 30 Years	Real Remaining Wealth After 30 Years	Change in Real Spending at Year 30	Year 30 Spending Relative to Baseline	Downside Spending Volatility
Constant Inflation-Adjusted Spending (BASELINE)	3.71%	90th	$3,710	$3,710	$3,710	$584,570	0%	0%	0%
		50th	$3,710	$3,710	$3,710	$127,850	0%	0%	0%
		10th	$3,710	$3,710	$0	$0	-100%	-100%	-23%
Fixed-Percentage Withdrawals	9.36%	90th	$9,950	$7,120	$5,860	$60,000	-37%	58%	-3%
		50th	$5,470	$3,180	$1,940	$20,670	-79%	-48%	-4%
		10th	$2,980	$1,350	$710	$7,500	-92%	-81%	-5%
Endowment Formula–Weighted Average–Hybrid	4.88%	90th	$6,640	$7,560	$9,800	$312,020	101%	164%	-2%
		50th	$4,620	$4,400	$4,120	$73,820	-16%	11%	-3%
		10th	$3,500	$2,890	$0	$0	-100%	-100%	-9%
Endowment Formula–3-Year Moving Average	9.14%	90th	$10,030	$7,780	$6,310	$65,920	-31%	70%	-3%
		50th	$6,050	$3,420	$2,050	$21,760	-78%	-45%	-3%
		10th	$3,410	$1,410	$690	$6,970	-92%	-81%	-4%
Bengen's Dollar Floor-and-Ceiling Withdrawals	4.20%	90th	$5,040	$5,040	$5,040	$468,740	20%	36%	0%
		50th	$4,030	$4,040	$4,020	$101,050	-4%	8%	-2%
		10th	$3,570	$3,570	$0	$0	-100%	-100%	-18%
Vanguard's Percentage Floor-and-Ceiling Withdrawals	6.00%	90th	$7,590	$8,000	$9,330	$246,150	56%	151%	-2%
		50th	$5,060	$4,140	$3,190	$50,940	-47%	-14%	-3%
		10th	$3,420	$1,810	$0	$0	-100%	-100%	-8%
Kitces Ratcheting Rule	3.56%	90th	$4,310	$6,310	$8,390	$525,070	136%	126%	0%
		50th	$3,560	$4,740	$5,730	$101,770	61%	54%	0%
		10th	$3,560	$3,560	$0	$0	-100%	-100%	-21%
Guyton and Klinger's Decision Rules	5.77%	90th	$7,680	$9,290	$11,890	$213,580	106%	220%	-1%
		50th	$4,890	$4,490	$4,400	$48,840	-24%	19%	-2%
		10th	$2,850	$2,040	$510	$0	-91%	-86%	-4%
Zolt's Glide Path Spending Rule	5.80%	90th	$5,360	$5,190	$5,130	$423,790	-12%	38%	0%
		50th	$4,440	$3,640	$3,320	$78,390	-43%	-11%	-1%
		10th	$3,500	$2,040	$0	$0	-100%	-100%	-14%
Modified RMD Rule (Spending Rate = 1.58 × RMD %)	5.10%	90th	$10,090	$12,810	$11,900	$59,810	133%	221%	-4%
		50th	$5,550	$5,730	$3,950	$20,610	-23%	6%	-6%
		10th	$3,020	$2,430	$1,440	$7,480	-72%	-61%	-10%

stock allocation and the greater safety sought means that spending must be more conservative. Even with flexible spending strategies, spending can still be higher than otherwise, but it is still quite limited relative to what was feasible for the moderate retiree.

Finally, Exhibit 6.24 shows what is feasible for a more aggressive retiree. Now the baseline spending strategy supports a 3.71 percent withdrawal rate, which is getting closer to the traditional 4 percent rule even in the current lower interest rate environment. Other spending rules support higher spending as well on account of the more aggressive asset allocation and the greater flexibility to allow wealth to fall to lower levels than otherwise.

My Retirement Dashboard (www.retirementresearcher.com/dashboard) provides ongoing updates for a few of these strategies as economic conditions change over time. It is worthwhile to check this more up-to-date resource. These three stylized cases for conservative, moderate, and aggressive retirees can provide a better idea about the feasible spending patterns that can be expected with these variable spending strategies. It then becomes up to the retiree to decide on the best course of action for his or her personalized case.

Further Reading

Bengen, William P. 1994. "Determining Withdrawal Rates Using Historical Data." *Journal of Financial Planning* 7 (4): 171–180.

Bengen, William P. 2001. "Conserving Client Portfolios during Retirement, Part IV." *Journal of Financial Planning* 14 (5).

Bengen, William P. 2012. "How Much Is Enough?" *Financial Advisor* (May).

Blanchett, David M. 2013. "Simple Formulas to Implement Complex Withdrawal Strategies." *Journal of Financial Planning* 26 (9): 40–48.

Blanchett, David, Maciej Kowara, and Peng Chen. 2012. "Optimal Withdrawal Strategy for Retirement-Income Portfolios." Retirement Management Journal 2 (3): 7–20.

Bogleheads Forum. "Variable Percentage Withdrawal." https://www.bogleheads.org/wiki/Variable_percentage_withdrawal.

Cotton, Dirk. 2013. "Clarifying Sequence of Returns Risk (Part 2, with Pictures!)." *Retirement Café* (blog), September 20.

Cotton, Dirk, Cary Cotton, and Alex Mears. 2016. "Competing Risks: Death and Ruin." *Journal of Personal Finance* 15 (2): 34–40.

Fan, Yuan-An, Steve Murray, and Sam Pittman. 2013. "Optimizing Retirement Income: An Adaptive Approach Based on Assets and Liabilities." *Journal of Retirement* 1 (1): 124–135.

Frank, Larry R., John B. Mitchell, and David M. Blanchett. 2011. "Probability-of-Failure-Based Decision Rules to Manage Sequence Risk in Retirement." *Journal of Financial Planning* 24 (11): 44–53.

Frank, Larry R., John B. Mitchell, and David M. Blanchett. 2012. "An Age-Based, Three-Dimensional Distribution Model Incorporating Sequence and Longevity Risks." *Journal of Financial Planning* 25 (3): 52–60.

Frank, Larry R., John B. Mitchell, and David M. Blanchett. 2012. "Transition through Old Age in a Dynamic Retirement Distribution Model." *Journal of Financial Planning* 25 (12): 42–50.

Guyton, Jonathan T. 2004. "Decision Rules and Portfolio Management for Retirees: Is the 'Safe' Initial Withdrawal Rate Too Safe?" *Journal of Financial Planning* 17 (10): 54–62.

Guyton, Jonathan T., and William J. Klinger. 2006. "Decision Rules and Maximum Initial Withdrawal Rates." *Journal of Financial Planning* 19:49–57.

Irlam, Gordon, and Joseph Tomlinson. 2014. "Retirement Income Research: What Can We Learn from Economics?" *Journal of Retirement* 1 (4): 118–128.

Jaconetti, Colleen M., Francis M. Kinniry, and Michael A. DiJoseph. 2013. "A More Dynamic Approach to Spending for Investors in Retirement." Vanguard Research Paper (October).

Kitces, Michael. 2015. "The Ratcheting Safe Withdrawal Rate – A More Dominant Version Of The 4% Rule?" Nerd's Eye View (blog), June 3.

Pfau, Wade D. 2015. "Making Sense out of Variable Strategies for Retirees." *Journal of Financial Planning* 28 (10): 42–51.

Steiner, Ken. 2014. "A Better Systematic Withdrawal Strategy—the Actuarial Approach." *Journal of Personal Finance* 13 (2): 51–56.

Sun, Wei, and Anthony Webb. 2012. "Should Households Base Asset Decumulation Strategies on Required Minimum Distribution Tables?" Center for Retirement Research at Boston College Working Paper WP 2012-10 (April).

Waring, M. Barton, and Laurence B. Siegel. 2015. "The Only Spending Rule Article You Will Ever Need." *Financial Analysts Journal* 71 (1): 91–107.

Zolt, David. 2013. "Achieving a Higher Safe Withdrawal Rate with the Target Percentage Adjustment." *Journal of Financial Planning* 26 (1): 51–59.

Appendix: **Dynamic Programming Methods for Retirement Income**

A third type of variable spending model, in addition to the methods we've discussed, uses dynamic programming methods. These methods rely on complex computing power and mathematical equations to integrate spending and asset allocation decisions more completely over the life cycle. Dynamic programming provides a road map at each point in time for optimal spending and asset allocation, which have been determined by first considering optimal future behavior stemming from today's decisions.

Because of the complexity of solving for what is optimal today based on how today's decisions will affect what happens tomorrow (and tomorrow's tomorrow, and so on), mathematical simplifications have been developed that basically involve working backward through time. Optimal end-of-life decisions are determined, which then feed into making optimal decisions at each younger age.

Due to their mathematical complexity, dynamic programming methods are mostly discussed in the realm of academia and have not yet become a common part of the toolkit for individual retirees. Gordon Irlam's AACalc (aacalc.com) and Laurence Kotlikoff's E$Planner (esplanner.com) are two software programs based on dynamic programming that are available for household use.

Gordon Irlam and Joseph Tomlinson's 2014 article "Retirement Income Research: What Can We Learn from Economics?" in the *Journal of Retirement* tries to make dynamic programming methods more accessible to those outside of academia. It is hard to generalize about the solutions for dynamic programming methods, but Irlam and Tomlinson provide an example based on a case study in their article. In terms of understanding their findings, we can think about dynamic programming as a different way to choose an evaluation criterion. I have been discussing the choice of a PAY Rule and a visual comparison of the results as a way for individuals to decide on a retirement income strategy.

For dynamic programming, individuals would not make these decisions directly. Instead, a utility function would be determined, which provides a link to the satisfaction the individual derives from different amounts of spending and legacy. This utility function would build in a degree of spending flexibility about how willing the individual is to spend more today with the trade-off that this could require less spending in the future. Given the mathematics of this trade-off, the remainder of the strategy will follow from the dynamic programming methodology about how much to spend each year and how to adjust asset allocation each year as circumstances evolve. The results are meaningful to the extent that the mathematical function expressing the trade-offs between spending certainty and the average level of spending—as well as between spending and legacy—adequately reflects the preferences of the individual using the model.

Irlam and Tomlinson build a case study for a conservative individual with $500,000 of financial assets, $20,000 of Social Security benefits, and no particular desire to leave a legacy. They compare outcomes for the solution offered by the dynamic programming methodology to the outcomes for various decision rule and actuarial methods and asset allocation strategies. For spending, they consider constant inflation-adjusted spending strategies, a fixed-percentage strategy, and a strategy similar to the RMD rule spending. For asset allocation, they consider fixed allocation strategies, age in bonds, age minus ten in bonds, and target-date funds.

Among the other strategies, they find that the closest match to their optimal dynamic programming solution is the RMD-styled strategy with a fixed 90 percent stock allocation. Next is a 6.8 percent fixed-percentage strategy with a 90 percent stock allocation. In third is a constant inflation-adjusted spending strategy with a 60 percent stock allocation. All the other asset allocation strategies result in worse outcomes because they lack sufficient aggressiveness. It is interesting that the variable spending strategies are accompanied by higher stock allocations, the reason being that varying withdrawals provide a safety value for stock volatility. With constant inflation-adjusted spending, a lower stock allocation to reduce volatility is the only avenue for alleviating sequence risk.

For readers who are interested in further exploring the mathematics of dynamic programming, Samuel Pittman, Yuan An Fan, and Steve Murray provide a simplified example in their 2013 article, "Optimizing Retirement Income: An Adaptive Approach Based on Assets and Liabilities," also from the *Journal of Retirement*. In it, they use dynamic programming to create a retirement income strategy for a simplified world with three time periods and two investment outcomes.

CHAPTER 7

Managing Sequence Risk with Bonds

Bonds can be incorporated directly into a retirement strategy in three broad ways:

1. An assets-only approach as part of the asset allocation to build a total-returns investment portfolio,
2. Matching the duration of bond funds to the duration of the retirement liability, and
3. Holding individual bonds to maturity to generate the desired cash flows to fund expenses on an ongoing basis throughout retirement.

The two latter methods put the retirement liability (meeting an ongoing spending goal in retirement) at the forefront and try to choose bonds to best protect the spending plan from interest rate volatility.

(As an aside, another use for bonds—or, more likely, shorter-term cash instruments—with sufficiently low volatility is as a source of liquidity to provide for short-term and contingency expenses. The discussion in this chapter focuses on using bonds specifically to meet budgeted retirement expenses.)

The first approach is the standard investing philosophy for accumulation that does not really consider how the nature of risk changes upon retirement. In short, it uses modern portfolio theory to choose an asset allocation strategy that includes bonds as part of a total-returns investment portfolio. Bonds, with their lower expected returns and volatility, provide a way to reduce the portfolio's overall volatility to an acceptable level while still maintaining a sufficient overall portfolio return. Asset allocation in this framework is generally determined in terms of assets-only considerations to build a diversified portfolio with the highest expected return for the accepted level of risk. To the extent that retirement income needs are considered, it is generally to find an asset allocation that will minimize the probability of failure for the financial plan. Looking back to William Bengen's original work in the 1990s about sustainable spending rates, the best worst-case historical spending rates could be achieved with an overall bond allocation of 20 to 65 percent. He also found that intermediate-term US government bonds provided a sweet spot in terms of return/volatility trade-offs, keeping worst-case historical spending rates at the highest possible level.

The second and third methods take a more nuanced approach to incorporating bonds. In the second, a bond fund (a mutual fund or an ETF) can be chosen specifically so that its "duration" matches the duration of the retirement liability. I will explain this in greater detail later. The third route involves holding individual bonds to maturity to provide the desired income to fund annual expenses on an ongoing basis throughout retirement. In this method, maturing bonds and bond coupon payments provide a steady and known stream of contractually guaranteed income to meet planned expenditures.

Scholars and practitioners have numerous disagreements about the best way to incorporate bonds into a real-world retirement income plan. We will be delving into these controversies as well.

The discussion builds toward an eventual consideration of time segmentation—a hybrid strategy that invests differently for short-term and long-term expenses rather than use a total-return approach. Time segmentation is often described as a way to help manage sequence-of-returns risk, though this point is controversial. Though a myriad of strategies can be devised that would fall under the umbrella of time segmentation, the easiest way to approach this topic is to include a rolling retirement income bond ladder as a tool for income planning. Sequence risk may be mitigated by holding individual bonds to maturity. A retirement income bond ladder may be constructed to cover early retirement expenses, with a more aggressive portfolio of assets earmarked for longer-term expenses, in order to reduce the risk of selling assets at a loss.

⊙ Understanding How Bonds Work

Before we can discuss bonds in depth, it is important that we establish a common understanding of what bonds are and how they work. As a starting point, a bond is a contractual obligation to make a series of specific payments on specific dates. Typically, this includes interest payments made on a semiannual basis until the maturity date and the return of the bond's face value. Bonds are issued by both governments and private corporations to raise funds, and they are purchased by investors seeking an investment return on their capital.

Treasuries are issued by the US government. Technically, Treasuries with maturities of a year or less are called "bills," while those with maturities of more than a year up to ten years are called "notes." "Bonds" typically refers to Treasuries with maturities of more than ten years. In my discussion, I will use the term "bond" generically to represent all of these cases. Bank CDs also function as a type of bond in terms of providing specified cash flows at specified dates, though they are not traded on secondary markets.

Bond interest rates—both coupon rates and the yields subsequently provided to investors—are determined by the interaction of supply and demand for the bonds as they continue to be traded. An increase in demand—such as that triggered by a "flight to quality" when investors are panicked by the falling prices of risky assets—will push up the price of these bonds. Conversely, a stretched government seeking to raise funds through an increasing supply of new bond issues will reduce the price of bonds.

Newly issued bonds are sold on the primary market, but many go on to be traded on secondary markets. A bond that sells at par value can be purchased for the same price as its face value. Bonds may also sell at a premium (higher than face value) or discount (lower than face value). Bond prices are quoted in terms of bid and ask prices. *Bid* is the price the bond can be sold for, and *ask* is the price at which it can be purchased. The difference in prices is the spread made by the party helping conduct the exchanges between buyers and sellers. Household investors will experience lower bid and higher ask prices than reported in newspapers, because the newspapers report the wholesale prices for institutions placing trades in excess of $1 million.

Rising interest rates will lower prices for existing bonds so the subsequent return to the new purchaser can match the higher returns available on new bonds with higher interest rates. Conversely, lower interest rates will increase the price existing bonds can sell for. If sold at their face value, these older bonds offer higher returns than newly issued bonds, and their owners will want to hold them. An agreeable selling price cán only be found if the bond sells at a premium, and then the new purchaser receives a subsequent return on their purchase price that is in line with newly issued bonds. The price of a bond on the secondary market will fluctuate in the opposite direction of interest rates.

In the universe of bonds, there is not one single interest rate. Differences in interest rates among bonds reflect several factors:

- the time to maturity for the bond (longer-term bonds will experience more price volatility as interest rates change),
- the credit risk of the bond (bonds that are more likely to default on their promised payments are riskier and will have to reward investors with higher yields),
- liquidity (bonds that are more actively traded may offer lower yields), and
- the tax status of the bond (municipal bonds from state and local government agencies are free from federal income taxes and thus offer lower interest rates).

Bonds may also feature other options that affect the price an investor is willing to pay. For instance, if the bond is "callable" (meaning the issuer retains the right to repay it early if interest rates decline), the potential capital gains are reduced, which in turn lowers the price investors are willing to pay.

US government Treasuries are generally seen as having the lowest credit risk, and they will generally offer lower yields than corporate bonds with the same maturity date. They are less likely to default and create problems for borrowers to receive what is owed. They are backed by the full faith and credit of the US government. Treasuries are also free from state and local taxes.

In recent years, financial innovation has led to the creation of many new types of fixed-income instruments with varying risk and return potential, but the retirement income planning discussion here is about using traditional government or noncallable (face value cannot be repaid early) high-quality corporate bonds to support a retirement income strategy.

◉ Bond Pricing 101

As a bond provides a contractual right to a series of future payments received at specified points of time, the price for a bond is simply the present discounted value of the future cash flows. The face value of a bond will be repaid at maturity.

A *zero-coupon* bond provides only a bond's face value, and it will be sold at a discount to the face value in order to provide a return and compensate for the risks related to holding it. A *coupon bond* provides the face value at maturity in addition to a series of *coupon payments* (often on a semiannual basis) until the maturity date. The coupon rate is contractually defined as a percentage of the face value.

The *yield to maturity* is the internal rate of return an investor will earn by holding a bond to maturity and receiving its cash flows. The yield to maturity for a new investor differs from the coupon rate whenever the bond sells for a different price than its face value.

Exhibit 7.1 provides a simple example to understand the pricing process for bonds. The bond being considered is a ten-year coupon bond with a face value of $1,000 and a coupon rate of 2 percent. In this simple example, one coupon payment of $20 (2 percent of $1,000) is made at the end of each year for ten years to the bond's owner(s) on those dates, and the face value is paid in full at the end of the tenth year. These can be seen in the exhibit's "Cash Flows" column. The next three columns provide the discounted value of these cash flows for different interest rates: 2 percent, 2.5 percent, and 3 percent. When the discount rate is 2 percent, we see that the total discounted cash flows add to $1,000, which is the same as the face value. This is an important point: When the interest rate is the same as the bond coupon rate, the price of a coupon bond will match its face value.

Let's be clear about what the discounted value of the payments means. In year ten, for instance, the discounted value of the payment with a 2 percent interest rate is $836.76. Imagine placing this amount in a bank account that earns an annually compounded 2 percent return each year. After ten years, it will grow to be $1,020, which is the amount of the cash payment provided in year ten. In other words, an investor would need to set aside $836.76 today in order to have $1,020 in ten years if the funds grew at a 2 percent annually compounded return.

If interest rates in the economy are 2.5 percent, then an investor would not be willing to pay $1,000 for this bond that provides only 2 percent coupon payments. The investor would prefer a new bond that presumably is now offering a 2.5 percent coupon. To entice an investor to purchase the bond in this exhibit, the bond would have to be sold for a lower price. In a competitive and active market, bonds with the same maturity and risk characteristics must offer the same potential return for both parties to agree to a trade. In this case, the future cash flows are discounted at 2.5 percent, and the sum of these discounted cash flows (and potential selling price) is $956.24.

Exhibit 7.1

Basic Pricing for a 10-Year Coupon Bond

Coupon Rate: 2%
Face Value: $1,000

Interest Rates:		2%	2.5%	3.0%
Year	Cash Flows	Discounted Cash Flows		
1	$20.00	$19.61	$19.51	$19.42
2	$20.00	$19.22	$19.04	$18.85
3	$20.00	$18.85	$18.57	$18.30
4	$20.00	$18.48	$18.12	$17.77
5	$20.00	$18.11	$17.68	$17.25
6	$20.00	$17.76	$17.25	$16.75
7	$20.00	$17.41	$16.83	$16.26
8	$20.00	$17.07	$16.41	$15.79
9	$20.00	$16.74	$16.01	$15.33
10	$1,020.00	$836.76	$796.82	$758.98
Bond Price:		$1,000.00	$956.24	$914.70
Price Change:		0.0%	−4.4%	−8.5%

Whoever owns the bond is entitled to the predefined cash flows of $20 per year plus $1,000 more in the final year. These cash flows do not change with interest rates. What changes is the selling price of the bond. For an investor who pays $956.24 for the bond, the yield to maturity received by the investor on this smaller investment is 2.5 percent. Note that a 0.5 percent increase in interest rates reduced the selling price of the bond by 4.4 percent. If the investor sold the bond, the return received by the previous owner is defined in terms of any coupon payments received less the capital loss associated with the interest rate rise. This is why increasing interest rates lower the prices for existing bonds. The same phenomenon is also shown for an interest rate of 3 percent. In this case, the bond's price would have to be set at $914.70 to adequately entice an investor. The 8.5 percent price reduction provides a yield to maturity of 3 percent to the new purchaser that then matches the overall higher interest rate in the economy.

The yield to maturity can differ from the coupon rate as bonds are bought and sold at prices other than face value, exposing the investor to *interest rate risk*—the risk that a bond price will fall due to rising interest rates.

Coupon rates are one of the most confusing aspects of bonds for people to understand. When the bond is issued, it pays a set coupon rate. For a regular Treasury bond, if the coupon rate is 2 percent and face value is $1,000, then the bond pays coupons of $20 per year. Usually these are paid semiannually—two coupon payments of $10 in this case. Note: the coupon rate *never* changes. Interest rates can change, but that will affect the yield, not the coupon rate. If interest rates rise, then the price the bond can be sold at will decrease, raising the underlying yield to maturity to match the increasing interest rate. But if I buy a $1,000 face value bond on the secondary market for only $700 and it has a 2 percent coupon, it is important to understand that my coupon income will be based on 2 percent of $1,000, not 2 percent of $700. Though this may seem basic and simple as I explain it, it has proved to be a major source of confusion.

The *yield* is the yield to maturity based on the ask price paid by the investor—the return the investor would get for buying the bond today and holding it to maturity. If the ask price matches the face value, then the yield will be the same as the coupon. If the ask price is higher, then the yield will be less than the coupon, and if the ask price is lower, then the yield will be higher than the coupon. Why? This gets back to the point I was stressing before about how the coupon rate never changes. The bond provides a promise for a fixed set of payments. It pays all the fixed coupon amounts and repays the face value at the maturity date. These payments do not change. But bonds can be sold and resold on secondary markets prior to the maturity date. If I pay $900 for a bond providing a fixed set of promised payments, then I'm going to get a higher return on my $900 investment than if I paid $1,100 for the same set of promised payments. Lower ask prices imply higher yields, and vice versa.

◉ Bond Duration

Bond prices are sensitive to interest rate changes, and bond duration is a measure of just how sensitive. For instance, in Exhibit 7.1, an increase in interest rates for the simple bond from 2 percent to 3 percent caused the bond's price to fall by 8.5 percent. This bond has a duration of 8.5, meaning that a 1 percent rise in interest rates leads to an 8.5 percent drop in price. The bond duration is measured in years, and the weighted-dollar average for the time when the cash flows are received in this example is 8.5 years.

Exhibit 7.2 uses the same basic setup as Exhibit 7.1 to provide more insight about how bond prices relate to interest rates and time to maturity. Again, the basic scenario is that we have purchased a bond with a $1,000 face value and 2 percent annual coupon payments. The current interest rate for a comparable bond is also 2 percent. Sometime shortly after purchase, interest rates change, with the exhibit showing new potential interest rates from 1 to 5 percent. The exhibit shows the new price that bonds with different maturities could sell for after the rate change. The bottom section of the exhibit shows the percentage change in price resulting from the rate change. Here we can clearly see how bond prices move counter to interest rates, and how price fluctuations are more dramatic for longer-term bonds, demonstrating their higher duration. At the extreme, the thirty-year bond would experience a capital gain of 25.8 percent if interest rates *fell* by 1 percent, and a 19.6 percent capital loss if interest rates rose by 1 percent. Price risk increases with time to maturity. If interest rates rose to 5 percent, the capital loss for a thirty-year bond would be 46.1 percent—comparable to a major stock market drop. Despite their reputation as reliable and predictable, bonds can be risky.

Exhibit 7.2

Basic Prices and Interest Rates

Current Bond Value:	$1,000
Coupon Rate:	2% (annual)
Current Interest Rate:	2%

New Interest Rates	1.0%	1.5%	2.0%	2.5%	3.0%	3.5%	4.0%	4.5%	5.0%
Years to Maturity									
1	$1,009.90	$1,004.93	$1,000.00	$995.12	$990.29	$985.51	$980.77	$976.08	$971.43
5	$1,048.53	$1,023.91	$1,000.00	$976.77	$954.20	$932.27	$910.96	$890.25	$870.12
10	$1,094.71	$1,046.11	$1,000.00	$956.24	$914.70	$875.25	$837.78	$802.18	$768.35
20	$1,180.46	$1,085.84	$1,000.00	$922.05	$851.23	$786.81	$728.19	$674.80	$626.13
30	$1,258.08	$1,120.08	$1,000.00	$895.35	$804.00	$724.12	$654.16	$592.78	$538.83

New Interest Rates	1.0%	1.5%	2.0%	2.5%	3.0%	3.5%	4.0%	4.5%	5.0%
Years to Maturity									
1	1.0%	0.5%	0.0%	-0.5%	-1.0%	-1.4%	-1.9%	-2.4%	-2.9%
5	4.9%	2.4%	0.0%	-2.3%	-4.6%	-6.8%	-8.9%	-11.0%	-13.0%
10	9.5%	4.6%	0.0%	-4.4%	-8.5%	-12.5%	-16.2%	-19.8%	-23.2%
20	18.0%	8.6%	0.0%	-7.8%	-14.9%	-21.3%	-27.2%	-32.5%	-37.4%
30	25.8%	12.0%	0.0%	-10.5%	-19.6%	-27.6%	-34.6%	-40.7%	-46.1%

While more complex bonds can have some unusual duration properties, the basic noncallable coupon and discount bonds we consider for a retirement income plan define duration in a straightforward way. A bond's duration is essentially the effective maturity of a bond—an average of when the bond's payments are received, weighted by the discounted size of those cash flows. A zero-coupon bond provides one payment at the maturity date, so its duration is the same as the time to maturity. The further away the maturity date, the higher the bond's duration, making it more sensitive to interest rate changes. A coupon bond will have a shorter duration than the time to the maturity date, because coupon payments are received before the maturity date. Higher coupon rates push relatively more cash flows sooner, which otherwise lowers the duration for a bond with the same maturity date. Also, lower interest rates mean the future cash flows from a bond are discounted less relative to nearer-term cash flows, and so bond duration increases when interest rates are low. An implication for this point is that our low interest-rate environment increases the interest rate risk for holding bonds, as a rate increase can result in a bigger capital loss.

An observant reader of Exhibit 7.2 might note that duration is not symmetric. For a thirty-year bond, a 1% increase in interest rates to 3% percent results in a capital loss of 19.6 percent, while a 1 percent decrease in interest rates to 1 percent results in a capital gain of 25.6 percent. The duration measure works best for small interest rate changes because it is a linear approximation to a shape that is actually curved. The term *convexity* describes price sensitivity to interest changes more precisely. Bond prices are more sensitive to rate decreases (prices rise more) than to equivalent rate increases (prices fall by less). These differences are accounted for by the fact that changing interest rates also impact duration. The duration for a given bond rises as interest rates fall, and future cash flows are discounted by less. But for a household retiree, duration provides a close enough approximation to this relationship, and only those with a greater interest in the mathematics of bond pricing should worry about further adding bond convexity to their discussion.

Though somewhat technical, this discussion of bond duration is important because the concept also applies to retirement spending liabilities and, therefore, the ability to meet retirement goals. Retirement spending has a duration that can be defined in the same way as an effective maturity for those cash flows. It is an average of when expenses must be paid, weighted by the size of the discounted values of those expenses.

Individual bonds have a duration. A bond fund, which is a collection of bonds, also has a duration equal to the average duration of each holding weighted by its proportion in the fund. Retirement liabilities have a duration, too. If the duration of the bonds and the spending liabilities can be matched to the same value, then the retiree has "immunized" his or her interest rate risk. Rising interest rates would lower the value of bond holdings, but rising rates also lower the present value of the future spending obligations. When durations are the same, both the asset and liability values are reduced by the same amount, and the retiree remains equally well-off in terms of the ability to meet liabilities. This is the meaning of immunizing interest rate risk.

However, if the durations do not match, then the retiree is exposed to interest rate risk. This is especially relevant for the case of holding bonds in bond funds. If the duration of the bond fund is less than the duration of the retirement liability, then rising interest rates may actually put the retiree into a better position, as the cost of retirement falls by more than the value of assets. On the other hand, if interest rates fall, the present value of cost-of-retirement liabilities increases by more than the value of the assets intended to fund those expenses, leaving the retiree in a worse position. For many retirees, the duration of their retirement liability may naturally tend to be higher than the duration of their bond holdings, creating a greater risk exposure to interest rate declines.

Meanwhile, if the duration of the bond portfolio is larger than the duration of the retirement liability, then rising rates will cause the bond value to drop by more than the retirement liability, leaving the retiree less able to fund retirement. Falling rates, in this case, would allow the value of bond holdings to rise by more than the cost of the liability, making it easier to fund retirement. We will return to this point again later, because it is the source of the controversy about selecting between individual bonds and bond funds for matching retirement expenses.

◉ The Yield Curve

Understanding the relationship between bond risk and time to maturity and duration of a bond provides the basis for understanding the bond yield curve. The yield curve shows the yields to maturity for a series of bonds—typically US Treasury bonds—with the same credit quality but different maturity dates, along with the term structure for interest rates.

Exhibit 7.3 shows the yield curve for Treasury STRIPS (Separate Trading of Registered Interest and Principal of Securities) from January 3, 2017. STRIPS represent a collection of zero-coupon bonds that are sold at a discount of their face value. The return they provide is reflected as the growth rate on price paid, and the face value is received at the maturity date. The price of a zero-coupon bond slowly gravitates toward its face value as the maturity date approaches.

The Treasury facilitates the creation of STRIPS by "stripping" the coupon payments and face value payment from Treasury bonds and selling them as separate securities. Each coupon payment becomes a standalone zero-coupon security providing the one coupon payment at its specified date (Coupon STRIPS). The return of the face value at the maturity date also becomes a zero-coupon security (Principal STRIPS).

Exhibit 7.3

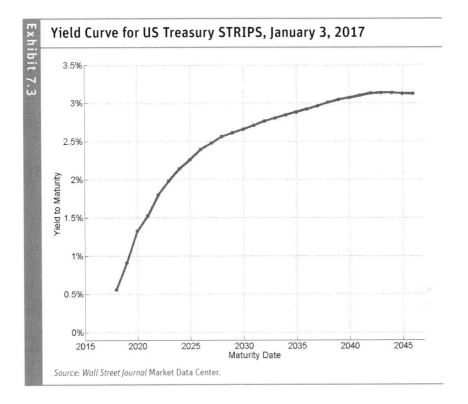

Yield Curve for US Treasury STRIPS, January 3, 2017

Source: *Wall Street Journal* Market Data Center.

Bonds with more distant maturity dates typically offer higher interest rates than bonds with earlier maturity dates. While that is not always the case, Exhibit 7.3 shows us it was true in January 2017, as thirty-year STRIPS were yielding 3.1 percent. Longer-term bonds experience bigger price fluctuations as interest rates change, which explains why the 2046 yield is noticeably higher than earlier maturities. When interest rates increase, the price of existing bonds on the secondary market falls in order to calibrate the yield investors will receive from owning existing bonds with the yields being offered by newly issued bonds at the higher interest rates. Bonds that mature sooner are less exposed to this price risk. Thus, shorter-term US Treasury securities are generally considered to be among the lowest-risk investment assets when annualized volatility represents the measure of risk, which means they tend to be offered at a lower yield. Higher yields accompany longer-term bonds, as investors need an added incentive to accept the higher price risks.

The shape of the yield curve is molded by two theories. First, expectations theory suggests that the shape of the yield curve should be reflected by beliefs about future short-term interest rates. Investing in bonds over ten years can be done in two ways:

1. Buy a ten-year bond, or
2. Buy a one-year bond and then reinvest in a new one-year bond after one year, continuing with a succession of ten one-year bonds.

For markets to be in balance, these two strategies should offer the same expected return to an investor, meaning that the combined impact of one-year rates over ten years should match the rate for a ten-year bond. An inverted yield curve where short-term rates exceed long-term rates can be understood as a clear expectation that short-term interest rates will fall in the future. Since interest rate fluctuations are extremely difficult to predict, the expectations theory alone would probably leave the average yield curve relatively flat.

The other theory to determine yield curve shape is the liquidity preference theory, which suggests a need for a risk premium to be offered for longer-term bonds to account for their increased interest rate risk and price volatility, as discussed. Longer-term bonds are less liquid, as well, since this price risk could force them to be sold at a loss if an unexpected expense arose. With this risk premium added to the expectations theory, the typical or neutral shape for the yield curve becomes upward sloping (like in Exhibit 7.3).

The bond yield curve provides a reality check on retirement spending. Spending beyond what the bond yield curve can support introduces the risk that future spending will need to be cut if higher returns are not realized.

● Treasury Inflation-Protected Securities (TIPS)

The United States began issuing Treasury Inflation-Protected Securities (TIPS) in 1997. Backed by the full faith and credit of the US government and assurances that inflation cannot eat away at their value, TIPS provide a risk-free asset for US-based investors.

The face value and coupon payments are both indexed to keep pace with inflation and preserve purchasing power, and their yields are quoted in real inflation-adjusted terms. Whenever positive inflation (as opposed to deflation) is expected, real yields will be less than the nominal yields quoted on traditional (i.e., not inflation adjusted) bonds. As an approximation:

real interest rate = nominal interest rate – expected inflation rate

Or, more precisely, the exact formula to relate these variables is:

(1 + nominal interest rate) = (1 + real interest rate) ×
(1 + expected inflation rate)

Nominal interest rates are determined by compensation expected to keep pace with inflation plus a real rate of return for the investor. Of course, supply and demand affect bond prices and interest rates. Real interest rates can be negative.

Investors may expect a positive nominal return on their investment (otherwise, there is no reason to invest), but that return may not be able to keep pace with inflation. Unlike traditional bonds, TIPS yields are quoted as real interest rates.

Their nominal yields are not known in advance, because they depend on the subsequently realized inflation experience. Conversely, we know nominal yields for traditional bonds, but their real yields can only be known after observing the realized path of inflation up to the maturity date.

Inflation adjustments for TIPS are linked to the Consumer Price Index for All Urban Consumers (CPI-U). These adjustments are tracked in terms of the "accrued principal," which is a unique term for TIPS. Accrued principal is the inflation-adjusted value of the initial face value since the TIPS was issued. For TIPS, inflation adjustments are realized by having the coupon rate be paid on the value of the accrued principal, not the nominal initial face value.

As well, at the maturity date, the investor receives the accrued principal back, not the nominal face value. A real coupon rate is paid on an inflation-adjusted amount, and an inflation-adjusted amount is returned at the maturity date.

If there is deflation, the accrued principal can decrease, but it is protected from falling below its initial par value. This means that TIPS on the secondary markets with lower accrued principal will be able to provide better protection from a deflationary episode, other factors being the same.

Otherwise, deflation that is not significant enough to cause the accrued principal to fall below its initial par value will hurt TIPS relative to traditional bonds. Generally, the purpose of TIPS is to provide protection from unexpectedly high inflation, and buying TIPS with a lower relative accrued principal is a secondary consideration when choosing specific TIPS to purchase.

It is important to note that TIPS are purchased in nominal dollars. On the secondary market, the ask price for TIPS is quoted in real terms, represented as a percentage of the inflation-adjusted accrued principal. The price paid is the ask price times the accrued principal divided by 100.

TIPS notes and bonds have been issued since January 1997. Until mid-2002, each auction for TIPS of the various maturities provided an initial real yield above 3 percent. Lucky investors in 1998 and 1999 could have purchased thirty-year TIPS yielding close to 4 percent, and yields on ten- and twenty-year TIPS exceeded 4 percent in 1999 and 2000. Since this time, TIPS yields have fallen.

An auction for a five-year note held in October 2010 made headlines as the real yield dipped below zero (to −0.55 percent) for the first time. Purchasers of those issues locked in yields that will not keep pace with inflation. Though surprising at the time, negative yields for TIPS have become much more the norm in recent years.

Exhibit 7.4 shows the TIPS yield curve for January 3, 2017. Yields are negative for TIPS maturing prior to 2022 and positive beyond that, although the longest ones do not even reach 1 percent. The Treasury stopped issuing thirty-year TIPS in the early 2000s, and in 2009 they switched from issuing new twenty-year TIPS back to issuing new thirty-year TIPS. That is why you see gaps in the yield curve—represented by dashed lines in the exhibit—with no TIPS maturity in 2030–31 and 2033–39.

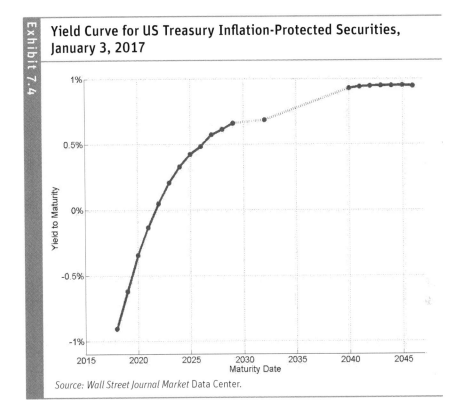

Yield Curve for US Treasury Inflation-Protected Securities, January 3, 2017

Source: Wall Street Journal Market Data Center.

Before the introduction of TIPS, real interest rates were less transparent. They could be estimated only by first estimating what people believed inflation would be in the future.

Exhibit 7.5 provides the historical paths for ten-year Treasury rates and the estimated real interest rates on ten-year Treasuries since 1981, using the Cleveland Federal Reserve Bank's estimates of inflation expectations. Notice how the movement of the curves is almost parallel. The difference between them is the expected inflation rate. In 1981, real interest rates were close to 8 percent, while nominal interest rates exceeded 15 percent. Both have consistently decreased since that time, with real rates reaching their lowest levels in 2013.

With TIPS, we now have a better idea of market expectations for future inflation, though I would not call it perfect. TIPS offer a break-even inflation rate, defined as the difference in yields on the same maturity of traditional Treasuries and TIPS. TIPS yields may not reflect the true

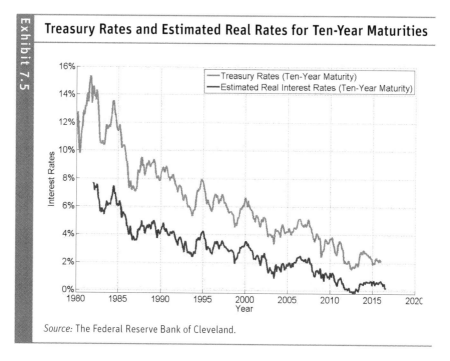

Treasury Rates and Estimated Real Rates for Ten-Year Maturities

Exhibit 7.5

Treasury Rates (Ten-Year Maturity)
Estimated Real Interest Rates (Ten-Year Maturity)

Source: The Federal Reserve Bank of Cleveland.

underlying real interest rate, because they have a few other components built into their pricing.

TIPS yields can be broken down into three components:

1. An implied nominal yield consisting of an underlying real interest rate and expected inflation,
2. An illiquidity premium, and
3. An inflation-protection premium.

According to Jennifer Roush, William Dudley, and Michelle Steinberg Ezer of the New York Federal Reserve Bank, since the introduction of TIPS, all three of these components have boosted TIPS yields relative to conventional bonds in ways that cannot be expected to continue in the future. In particular, when TIPS were first introduced, they offered a substantial premium to compensate for this illiquid new market. The authors discuss one set of estimates that suggests as much as 200 basis points (2 percent) of the yield for early ten-year TIPS derived from this premium.

As markets became more established, the illiquidity premium declined, bringing TIPS yields down with them, suggesting that the days of 3–4 percent yields may now be a relic of history, as this premium will likely never return.

The *inflation-protection premium* is the yield investors are willing to sacrifice for the unique protection TIPS provide against unexpected inflation—similar to an insurance premium. Roush and co-authors cite several studies that believe inflation-protection premiums have been low since the introduction of TIPS, as investors may not have been too worried about inflation in these years. If true, this would also cause TIPS to sell for lower prices, meaning higher yields and a lower break-even inflation rate than otherwise possible. If inflation becomes a bigger concern in the future, then investors may be more willing to pay for an inflation-protection premium, resulting in lower TIPS yields and a higher perceived break-even inflation rate. Rather than waiting to buy TIPS until everyone starts worrying about inflation, a natural time to purchase is before inflation becomes a major concern.

Despite the other factors of TIPS pricing, the difference between Treasury and TIPS rates for the same maturity represents a reasonable market estimate of future inflation expectations. Exhibit 7.6 returns us to January 3, 2017, to find this difference.

Consider the thirty-year maturity. A thirty-year Treasury bond provides its owner a nominal 3.04 percent yield. Its real yield is unknown and depends on realized future inflation. Meanwhile, a thirty-year TIPS offers a real yield of 0.94 percent. Its nominal yield is unknown, as it also depends on realized future inflation. The difference between these yields is the implied break-even inflation rate: 2.1 percent. Without a liquidity or inflation-protection premium, this represents the market's equilibrium estimate of future inflation. Over the next thirty years, the markets have priced in expectations for inflation of only around 2 percent.

If realized annual inflation exceeds 2.1 percent over the next thirty years, then TIPS will outperform Treasuries. But if it falls short, TIPS will underperform. If enough traders thought inflation would be higher than this, they would *buy* TIPS and sell Treasuries, raising the price of TIPS, and giving us lower TIPS yields, higher Treasury yields, and a larger break-

Exhibit 7.6

US Government Yield Curve for Constant Maturity Bonds, January 3, 2017

Maturity	Treasury Yield	TIPS Yield	Implied Break-Even Inflation Rate
1 Year	0.89%	−0.91%	1.80%
5 Years	1.94%	0.08%	1.86%
10 Years	2.45%	0.47%	1.98%
20 Years	2.78%	0.78%	2.00%
30 Years	3.04%	0.94%	2.10%

Source: US Department of the Treasury.

even inflation rate. Such trading would continue until the market reaches the equilibrium we observe.

Traditional bonds are priced around the objective of getting a return that exceeds expected inflation. If inflation is unexpectedly high, then the real return on nominal bonds is less. TIPS, on the other hand, keep pace with higher inflation, because it triggers a higher nominal return above their underlying real interest rate. Essentially, TIPS provide protection from unexpected inflation. They outperform Treasuries when inflation exceeds the implied break-even inflation rate.

This is a valuable attribute when spending for your retirement income plan is expected to grow with inflation. Traditional bonds outperform if inflation is unexpectedly low. Low inflation also makes it easier to meet retirement spending goals, so this outcome is less in need of protection. Retirees generally get more use from insurance that protects from high inflation, making TIPS a more natural candidate for retirement portfolios. In short, TIPS provide retirees with reliable, inflation-adjusted income that will maintain its real purchasing power.

In 2003, Zvi Bodie and Michael J. Clowes published the book *Worry-Free Investing: A Safe Approach to Achieving Your Lifetime Financial Goals,* in which they argued that typical retirement-oriented investors should rely primarily on TIPS for their retirement savings. Of course, other financial assets should be included in retirement portfolios, but, they said, only once you have enough savings (after accounting for any income expected from Social Security and other defined-benefit pensions) to cover your planned retirement expenditures without these riskier assets. In an interview in the February 2010 issue of *Journal of Financial Planning,* Bodie confirmed his continued endorsement of this strategy. He also indicated that his personal retirement portfolio is 100 percent in TIPS.

TIPS tend to be the preferred choice in academic approaches to retirement income, assuming that spending needs grow with inflation. But not everyone agrees. First, there are issues to consider related to how TIPS provide adjustments for the Consumer Price Index for All Urban Consumers (CPI-U). The CPI-U often doesn't match the actual inflation experience of any individual household purchasing a different basket of goods. The Bureau of Labor Statistics has also created an experimental CPI for the elderly that suggests their consumption basket cost may grow at a faster overall rate. As we have already also explored, it's safe to assume that the spending of many households will not keep pace with inflation.

Another reason TIPS are not universally adored is that while they are exempt from state and local taxes (like all Treasuries), the inflation adjustments provided for their coupon payments and principal are taxable at the federal level. This tax will need to be paid on an ongoing basis for the inflation adjustments on the accrued principal, even though you won't see a penny of it until the maturity date. Calculating taxes for this "phantom income" can be especially complex, so many retirees prefer to hold their TIPS in qualified retirement accounts.

TIPS are presented by some as the perfect hedge for the retirement spending liability, but that is only true if a retiree's spending grows at the same rate as the CPI-U. Another negative is that TIPS tend to have a higher duration than traditional Treasuries because of their lower real coupon rates and because the cash flows received from TIPS will weigh more heavily toward payments with bigger inflation adjustments made closer to the maturity date.

Michael Zwecher suggests in his 2010 book, *Retirement Portfolios,* that he is not dogmatic about seeking inflation protection. He views the higher yield on traditional bonds as a premium for writing a call option on inflation. As indicated, traditional bonds lose out when inflation is unexpectedly high. Some retirees may be willing to accept this risk in return for the higher yield that traditional bonds provide otherwise. This could be especially true of households who are not as exposed to this inflation risk either because their spending will not keep pace with inflation or because they have inflation protection from other assets.

Overall, there is no single answer to the choice of TIPS versus traditional Treasuries. I tend to lean toward TIPS as a default choice, but individual circumstances could certainly warrant a more mixed approach. Individuals who can live comfortably on their inflation-adjusted Social Security benefit, for instance, may have little need for TIPS.

◉ Using Duration-Matched Bond Funds

In basic asset allocation for wealth accumulation, matching assets to liabilities is not a priority. The retirement liability (the desire to meet a spending goal in retirement) is not part of the analysis. Investment decisions made in an assets-only wealth management framework (where the goal is to maximize wealth subject to an acceptable volatility) often differ from those made when the goal is meeting ongoing spending needs. In an assets-only framework, a bond portfolio's duration is more likely to be determined by the investor's willingness to accept volatility and the risk-return trade-offs for increased duration.

The goals of this chapter are ultimately to find a way to match the bond portfolio to retirement expenses and to look in depth at how bonds can be used to meet retirement goals. Hence, our discussion of bond funds (mutual funds or ETFs), which can be chosen in such a way that their duration matches that of the retirement liability, is about helping immunize the retiree against interest rate risk and bond price volatility.

When choosing a bond fund, it is important to note that bond returns are primarily driven by their term/duration and credit risk. Active management for bonds generally does not add returns, especially after accounting for fund fees. The best choice is a low-cost fund with appropriate duration and credit risk for your situation.

Series I Savings Bonds

Any discussion of TIPS requires an additional mention of Series I Savings Bonds. I Bonds can be purchased in taxable accounts from Treasury Direct without paying any fees or commissions. They work like a CD, as they are not tradable on secondary markets. I Bond yields are quoted in terms of a real interest rate, and then they earn realized inflation on top of that. Like TIPS, they offer constant real returns but variable nominal returns.

I Bonds must be held for at least one year. If sold within five years, there is a penalty of three months' worth of interest. Beyond this point, they can be sold at any time, and they accumulate interest for up to thirty years. There are no coupon payments, as accumulated interest is received when the I Bonds are sold. This interest is all tax-deferred until the bonds are sold, despite being held in a taxable account. Like all US Treasuries, they are exempt from state and local taxes.

They offer such a great deal that the government limits the annual purchase amount to $10,000 per Social Security number, plus an extra $5,000 allocated from a tax refund.

Unlike TIPS, I Bonds are not exposed to interest rate risk. There are no capital losses if rates rise, but also no capital gains if they drop. If rates rise, it might be tempting to sell your I Bonds in order to buy new higher rate I Bonds, but the annual purchase limit puts a damper on such plans.

For long-term planning, a thirty-five-year-old couple could begin purchasing $20,000 of I Bonds per year for the next thirty years. Then, at age sixty-five, they would already have a thirty-year ladder of an annual inflation-adjusted $20,000 of real purchasing power as part of their reliable income for retirement. Those with less time before retirement could make adjustments to this strategy accordingly.

Bond funds provide advantages through greater diversification of bond maturities, as well as the possibility of trading more cheaply within the fund without having to pay retail markups. Bond funds may also provide easier handling for taxes and simpler reinvestment of interest payments.

On the matter of diversification, it is not an issue for Treasuries. Credit risk is minimal, and any such risk would likely affect Treasuries in a similar way. For corporate and municipal bonds, however, diversification within the fund will help mitigate credit risk. In addition, funds may enjoy better pricing as institutional traders, since trading costs for individual investors in these markets may be higher. For typical household investors, holding individual bonds for Treasuries is more practical and beneficial than for corporate or municipal bonds.

This approach presents one major difficulty: determining the duration of the retirement liability. With each passing year, remaining life expectancy decreases, but not on a one-to-one basis. In practice, duration matching for a retired household will be highly complex and not necessarily practical, making immunization from interest rate risk an insurmountable obstacle for a household to accomplish on their own through the use of bond funds instead of holding individual bonds. It requires constant monitoring and rebalancing of the bonds to match the desired duration as interest rates change and bonds mature. As it is, these concepts have not fully penetrated the wealth management world, and decisions about holding bond funds are still typically made on an assets-only basis.

That being said, at least two companies have created mutual funds to provide duration matching with bonds. First, Dimensional Fund Advisor's Target-Date Retirement Income Funds define the retirement liability specifically as a goal to support inflation-adjusted spending for twenty-five years after the target date. Using TIPS to support the inflation-adjustment goal, they can create a portfolio with a duration that matches their defined liability from a given target date and hedges inflation and interest rate risk.

The other company is BlackRock, whose CoRI Retirement Indices are based on a bond portfolio that hedges the price of a lifetime income annuity with a 2.5 percent cost-of-living adjustment, locking in the potential amount of income available from annuitizing a portion of your portfolio without actually purchasing an annuity. Income goals are survival-weighted rather than fixed at twenty-five years, and they grow with a 2.5 percent COLA rather than the CPI. But the underlying concept of hedging interest rate risk by defining a retirement liability and then matching its duration to that of the supporting assets is the same.

◉ Target-Date Retirement Income Funds

Dimensional Fund Advisors (DFA) takes a more direct approach to immunizing retirement liabilities through their target-date retirement income funds. These funds provide a useful case study for understanding the role bond funds play in meeting retirement expenses.

One of the defining distinctions for retirement income planning as opposed to traditional wealth management is that the focus shifts to meeting an ongoing spending objective. Traditional target-date funds (TDFs) are designed to increase nominal account balances while managing account balance volatility—they are not built to meet a spending objective. They provide an assets-only investing framework. However, a stable account balance does not necessarily translate to stable income thanks to daily fluctuations in interest rates. DFA bridges this divide by providing a target-date fund with a more complete risk management framework that manages volatility of expected affordable retirement spending.

The essential point to understanding how target-date retirement income funds differ dramatically from traditional target-date funds is to realize that *controlling account balance volatility and controlling spending volatility are two entirely different matters.* It is easy to overlook this point in our world, where something like the 4 percent rule tends to be the default retirement strategy. Its success is justified because it worked historically or can be expected to work on average—not because of how current interest rates or capital market expectations relate to sustainable retirement spending.

Traditional target-date funds focus on controlling portfolio volatility as the target-date (retirement) approaches. This focus may be due either to the belief that capital preservation becomes the primary concern of the retiree near their target date, or a naïve belief (because something like the 4 percent rule is in the back of one's mind) that reduced portfolio volatility is equivalent to sustainable and nonfluctuating spending power.

To understand why a stable account balance does not necessarily translate into sustainable income, we must take a step back to view the spending objective for retirement.

Target-date funds, by design, must be generalized to provide a reasonably close approximation of typical investor needs, so first, DFA sets the spending objective for their target-date income fund of providing support for twenty-five years of inflation-adjusted spending beginning at the target date. Twenty-five years extends beyond the life expectancy for sixty-five-year-olds, but plenty of people live past the age of ninety. However, lengthening time frames requires spending less to stretch assets further, and DFA views twenty-five years as a reasonable compromise between supporting longevity and supporting higher income for the typical investor. Note that defining the retirement goal in this way will allow for a duration to be calculated on the retirement liability. This is an essential ingredient to matching durations and immunizing interest rate risk.

The next step is to recognize which variables have the largest impact on the amount of wealth needed to support twenty-five years of inflation-adjusted spending. General market volatility may be the common focus, but it is important to also assess interest rates and inflation. This is where traditional target-date funds fail to support a retirement spending objective. They rarely coordinate investments sufficiently to provide proper hedging for interest rate and inflation variability.

DFA illustrates this situation by comparing a portfolio of Treasury bills with a portfolio of Treasury Inflation-Protected Securities (TIPS). The former are short-term nominal investments, while the latter—as we discussed earlier—are specifically designed to have a duration that matches the duration of the twenty-five-year spending objective. For a portfolio of Treasury bills, nominal wealth remains fairly stable, with growth provided through short-term interest rates as they fluctuate over time. However, volatility is clearly present when you look at the amount of real retirement spending a portfolio of Treasury bills can sustain. Rising inflation and decreasing real interest rates will decrease the amount of real spending the portfolio can support over twenty-five years. High inflation means that required spending may grow faster than the portfolio balance, and decreasing real interest rates increase the present value of the spending stream. Since the value of Treasury bills does not grow sufficiently when interest rates drop, sustainable spending falls. Though Treasury bills can keep nominal wealth stable, the real spending they can support is actually quite volatile.

Contrast that with a portfolio of TIPS with the same duration as the spending goal. TIPS provide inflation protection, so if inflation rises, they support greater income to match what is needed for the real spending goal. When the TIPS portfolio has the same duration as the spending objective, interest rate fluctuations are also hedged. When interest rates decrease, the cost of the spending objective increases, and the value of the TIPS portfolio rises accordingly. If interest rates rise, then the TIPS portfolio loses value, but the cost of meeting the spending objective also decreases.

For a portfolio of long-term TIPS, the account balances may be quite volatile as inflation and interest rates fluctuate, but the sustainable amount of inflation-adjusted spending remains reasonably level. Exhibit 7.7 illustrates these ideas: Treasury bills support low *wealth* volatility but high *spending* volatility, while TIPS support low spending volatility but high wealth volatility. TIPS users accept price risk to meet the spending goal.

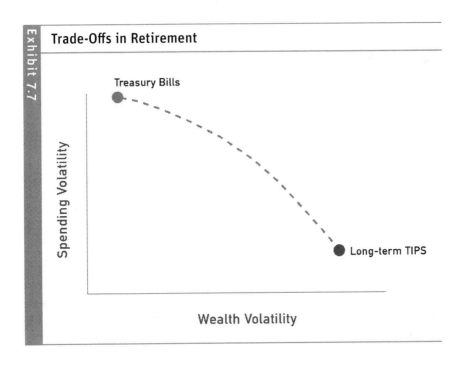

Exhibit 7.7

Trade-Offs in Retirement

Treasury Bills

Long-term TIPS

Spending Volatility

Wealth Volatility

The next step is to understand the objectives of the retirement saver. As our world has transitioned from defined-benefit pensions to defined-contribution pensions, the focal point of retirement has gone from a monthly or annual income amount to a portfolio value. Typical target-date fund investors seek a sustainable income in retirement, but the number they see on their financial statements is the aggregate wealth in their account. As we just reviewed, aggregate account balances do not directly translate to sustainable spending. The portfolio can remain quite stable, while sustainable income fluctuates in ways most investors do not realize.

Traditional target-date funds reflect this same problem. As they generally transition from stocks to nominal bonds as the retirement date approaches, their objective is to provide some stability for portfolio fluctuations while also seeking growth. But without the efforts to provide inflation protection or duration matching through the growing fixed-income portion of the portfolio, the ability for an account balance to support the spending objective is hampered.

This is where DFA's target-date retirement income funds enter the scene as an alternative to traditional TDFs. These funds share the same philosophy as TDFs preretirement in terms of accounting for the relative size of human capital and financial capital over time and reducing the stock allocation as human capital decreases with age. A globally diversified portfolio of stocks and bonds is designed to grow the portfolio and the sustainable income base. But rather than transitioning from stocks into duration-mismatched nominal bonds as the target date approaches, DFA's funds transition into a portfolio of TIPS with the same duration as a twenty-five-year real spending objective beginning at the target date. This allows the investments to better lock in an inflation-adjusted income stream for retirement. It also provides a more effective way for typical TDF investors to support their retirement spending by managing the risks related to inflation and interest rate fluctuations, while still leaving some assets to focus on growth.

Exhibit 7.8 provides a generalized illustration for the allocation of household wealth over the investor's lifetime using target-date retirement income funds. When the investor is far from the target date, household wealth is presumably held primarily as human capital—that is, future labor earnings. For the smaller investment portfolio, the asset allocation focuses on growth, primarily with global equities. For example, at the end of 2016, DFA's 2060 Target Date Retirement Income Fund was invested 94 percent in global equities and 6 percent in global bonds and other assets. As the retiree gets within twenty-five years of the target date, global equities begin to give way to more fixed income, and this is when the TIPS investments play a larger role. For instance, DFA's 2030 target-date retirement income fund had an allocation of 60 percent global equities, 15 percent global bonds, and 25 percent TIPS by the end of 2016. At the target date, asset allocation is designed to be 25 percent global equities and 75 percent TIPS. There are no global bonds at this point. Human capital is also depleted, and household wealth is primarily held in the investment portfolio. The equity allocation still seeks wealth growth to support more future income, while the fixed-income assets are specifically designed to support a twenty-five-year inflation-adjusted spending objective.

DFA's target-date retirement income funds have grown out of efforts to provide a seamless way for investors to receive a defined-benefit styled income from their defined-contribution account using a mutual fund. This gives us a clear example of how to use bond funds to try to immunize interest rate risk for retirement planning.

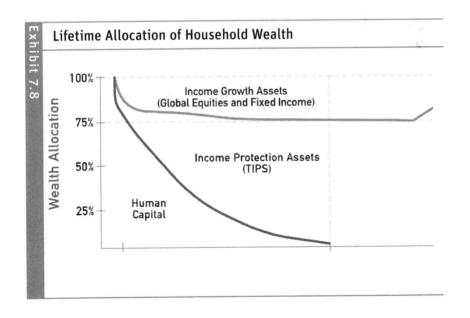

Exhibit 7.8

Lifetime Allocation of Household Wealth

Wealth Allocation

Income Growth Assets
(Global Equities and Fixed Income)

Income Protection Assets
(TIPS)

Human
Capital

100%
75%
50%
25%

◉ BlackRock's CoRI Retirement Indexes

Another example of a bond fund that seeks to immunize interest rate risk for those approaching retirement is BlackRock's series of CoRI Retirement Indexes.

The CoRI Retirement Indexes are gauged to help retirees understand the cost of one dollar of cost-of-living adjusted (COLA) income for the remainder of their lives. They provide the indexes for those aged fifty-five to seventy-four. For the fifty-five to sixty-four indexes, the goal is to put together a collection of bond investments that can track the evolving cost of purchasing a single-premium immediate annuity (SPIA) with a 2.5 percent COLA at age sixty-five. After sixty-five, the indexes are meant to track the evolving cost of purchasing a SPIA.

These indexes provide retirees with a clear way to understand how much sustainable income they could expect to obtain with their savings. For instance, on January 3, 2017, the CoRI Index for a fifty-six-year-old planning to retire at sixty-five was $14.96. Someone who saved $100,000 and invested in this fund could expect to obtain $6,684 ($100,000 / $14.96 = $6,684) in cost-of-living adjusted income for life starting at age sixty-five should they sell the fund at that time and buy an annuity. For a sixty-five-year-old, the CoRI index was priced at $20.91. One divided by this number gives us a spending rate, which in this case is 4.8 percent. This reflects the median price of commercial SPIAs with unisex mortality assumptions (as required for ERISA qualified retirement plans) and the 2.5 percent COLA. The CoRI index is priced higher for the sixty-five-year-old because there is no deferral period for the investment to earn interest before income begins. After sixty-five, the index value decreases because the present value of a lifetime income shrinks in relation to the remaining time horizon at more advanced ages.

The planning notion is that assets in the CoRI index could be used to purchase a SPIA at sixty-five, and the investments track the cost of this SPIA. The investment comes with no guarantees, as the fund managers are essentially using bonds to track the hypothetical cost of a deferred-income annuity. By properly matching the duration of the bond investments with the duration of the underlying projected income, the index should be immune to interest rate risk and should do a good job tracking its objective. Eliminating this interest rate risk hedges the costs of retirement, which should reduce the impact of sequence risk as retirement nears. It provides an alternative option to purchasing a deferred-income annuity in the years leading up to retirement for those seeking to take market risk off the table.

The BlackRock indexes also aim to shift the focus to lifetime income rather than wealth maximization. The ultimate goal of individual investors is to fund retirement spending. The CoRI indexes let retirees get a better feel for how an income annuity works, but without actually locking in the purchase. Retirees can test-drive a SPIA through age seventy-five before making an irrevocable commitment to annuitize or not. CoRI provides an effective and intuitive way for individuals to think about the cost of retirement and how they can translate their savings into sustainable spending.

◉ Laddering with Individual Bonds

Outside of these professionally managed mutual fund solutions, those seeking a do-it-yourself approach to duration matching with bond funds may underestimate the difficulty of the task. Duration matching is not straightforward when shares of the bond fund must be sold to meet ongoing retirement expenses. If rates have risen, shares of the bond fund may need to be sold at a loss, with more shares sold to meet a given spending objective. This triggers sequence risk and locks in losses. Immunization only works if interest payments can be reinvested at a new higher interest rate to compensate for capital losses. But not all the funds are fully reinvested when a spending goal is met, so reinvestment risk and interest rate risk do not get neutralized. The return on remaining assets would need to be even higher to keep the retirement liability funded. Immunization is harder when there is also a spending goal to support.

An alternative approach is to use individual bonds in a retirement income plan. A retirement income bond ladder can be structured so the cash flows provided through coupons and maturing face values will provide a steady and known stream of contractually guaranteed income for the ongoing expenditure needs in retirement. Cash flows from the bonds are matched to fund desired expenses at desired dates. Interest rate risk can be ignored for the retirement expenses that have been matched with these dedicated assets. Sequence risk is reduced because there is less risk of assets being sold at a loss. Rebalancing may be required in terms of extending the length of the bond ladder as time passes to cover future expenses, but the complexities involved in an ongoing effort to match durations can be better avoided.

Retirement income bond ladders generally take the form of Treasury bonds to minimize the possibility of default risk. But for those seeking higher yield by accepting some credit risk, newer mutual funds such as Franklin Templeton's Retirement Payout Funds and ETFs such as Guggenheim Bulletshares and iShares term-maturity funds have cropped up as a pool of corporate bonds sharing the same maturity date.

For a household retiree, maximizing investment returns is not the goal; the goal is to meet expenses. Paper losses on individual bonds do not have to be realized if the bond is held to maturity. While the retiree misses out on the opportunity to buy the bond at a lower price later, this cannot be known in advance. It is always unfortunate to buy bonds and then see the price drop due to rising rates. But if the initial purchase allows the retiree to meet his or her retirement objective, then it is a successful purchase, no matter what interest rates subsequently do. Retirees who realize that it is nearly impossible to predict interest rate fluctuations can take comfort in knowing that individual bonds allow them to enjoy retirement and ignore subsequent interest rate fluctuations. Ignoring interest rate fluctuations is not possible with a bond fund strategy that has to make frequent adjustments to the portfolio's duration in order to immunize against interest rate risk.

The difference between a traditional bond ladder as an accumulation tool and a retirement income bond ladder is that with a traditional ladder, the cash flows received as coupons and face value are *reinvested* to purchase new replacement bonds at prevailing prices that extend the ladder and keep its length relatively constant over time. With a retirement income bond ladder, the cash flows received are spent on planned retirement expenses. A retirement income ladder will naturally wind down if other assets from outside the ladder are not used to extend it further as time passes.

When an investor purchases an individual bond and holds it to the maturity date, the return is precisely equal to the prevailing interest rates at the time of purchase. This is because the price paid to purchase a bond fluctuates so the return it provides to the investor matches the yields provided by bonds with similar characteristics for maturity date, credit risk, liquidity, and tax status.

Many investors would prefer to own bonds through mutual funds or exchange traded funds (ETFs), rather than making outright purchases of individual bonds. The returns of such funds are based on two factors: current interest rates and future changes in interest rates. If interest rates are low, bond returns will follow suit, both because the bonds in the fund are offering low yields, and because interest rates may be more likely to move up, rather than down, which would result in capital losses for the bonds held in the funds.

As we have discussed, changing interest rates lead, in turn, to capital gains or losses for investors. For professional bond traders, rising interest rates would be a serious problem for someone who had just purchased a long-term bond. Most traders have no intention of holding bonds to maturity and will realize capital losses on the subsequent sale. Interest rate increases might also force retirees owning bond funds into a position of selling shares at a loss in order to meet retirement expenses. For a bond portfolio that is not fully immunized, this triggering of sequence-of-returns risk can create irreparable harm for retirees.

I would argue that it is much easier for a retiree to ignore unrealized capital losses on an individual bond than for a professional trader or retiree needing to sell bond shares to meet expenses, because the individual bond is bought with the purpose of being held to maturity to provide a desired amount of income at that date.

Exhibit 7.9 quantifies this point. If interest rates are at 2 percent when a thirty-year bond is purchased, but then subsequently rise permanently from 2 percent to 3 percent during the first year the bond is held, the retiree is sitting on an unrealized capital loss for the next twenty-nine years. After one year, the bond price falls to $816, representing an 18.4 percent loss. Nevertheless, the bond continues to pay its 2 percent coupon payments and at maturity will repay the $1,000 face value. As the maturity date slowly approaches, the unrealized losses slowly dissipate. The bond price gradually returns to match its face value. The full recovery will happen at the maturity date when the final cash flows are received as expected. In this way, a household investor can be justified in ignoring

Exhibit 7.9

30-Year Maturity Bond with 2% Coupons and $1,000 Face Value
Ongoing Price of Bond if Interest Rates Stay at 2% and if Interest Rates Rise to and Stay at 3%

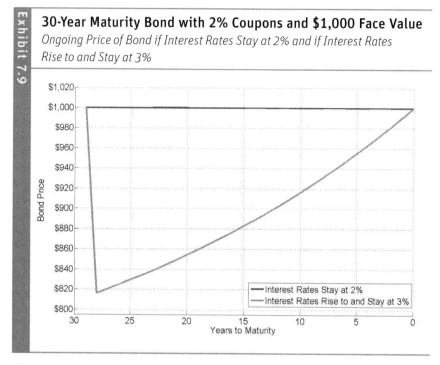

those unrealized capital losses on the bond, as they will not be realized if the bond is held to maturity.

When it comes to retirement income bond ladders, Joe Tomlinson created a taxonomy of different types in his 2014 *Advisor Perspectives* column, "Why the Risk Reduction Benefits of Bond Ladders Have Been Overstated." His list inspired me to create a more extended version in Exhibit 7.10.

Retirement income bond ladders are divided between one-time ladders and rolling ladders. "One-time ladders" are divided into three types differentiated by the length of the ladder. The shared characteristic between all types of one-time ladders is that they can be spent down over time. The bond ladder is not extended as bonds mature, gradually reducing the length of the bond ladder as time passes.

A short-term bond ladder might be used for something like building a Social Security delay bridge for someone looking to temporarily generate more retirement income for the period that they wait before collecting Social Security benefits. As a part of delaying benefits to age seventy, a sixty-two-year-old might build an eight-year bond ladder that generates

Exhibit 7.10

Taxonomy of Retirement Income Bond Ladders

Types of Bond Ladders	Potential Use
One-Time Ladders	
Fixed Short Term	Build a Social Security delay bridge
Fixed Medium Term	Twenty-year bond ladder followed by deferred-income annuity to cover remainder of lifetime
Fixed Long Term	Thirty-year bond ladder as source of "lifetime" retirement income
Rolling Ladders	
Automatic	Each year purchase a new bond to extend the horizon by one more year as bond matures, keeping ladder length constant over time
Market-Based	Allow ladder length to fluctuate based on market performance. For example, extend ladder by more when the stock market has performed well or market valuations are high, but let ladder length decrease without extension after poor market performance or low market valuations
Personalized	Conduct a capital needs analysis for how much wealth should remain in each year of retirement to meet goals. Extend ladder when actual wealth exceeds the requirement. Let ladder length decrease when actual wealth is falling short.

income equivalent to the reduced age sixty-two Social Security benefit level. This extra income is not needed after Social Security benefits begin, so the ladder is allowed to wind down naturally.

For a medium-term one-time bond ladder, the classic example is to combine a bond ladder with longevity insurance through a deferred-income annuity. Bond ladders expose retirees to longevity risk if you live past the ladder's end date. To account for this, S. Gowri Shankar developed an alternative of combining a twenty-year TIPS ladder with a deferred immediate annuity

(DIA) that begins payments twenty years after the retirement date in his 2009 article, "A New Strategy to Guarantee Retirement Income Using TIPS and Longevity Insurance." He did this to provide longevity protection with a smaller amount of annuitized assets. With this strategy, the bond ladder is again allowed to wind down, because the deferred-income annuity replaces the lost income precisely when the bond ladder terminates.

Finally, a full thirty-year bond ladder could be created with the idea of generating "lifetime" income. A thirty-year bond ladder is as long as can be constructed with available bonds (it does not *truly* provide lifetime income). The bond ladder would be spent down entirely by year thirty, creating a problem for someone still alive in year thirty-one. For this reason, not all assets should be used to construct such a ladder. It is important to set something aside for unplanned contingencies and the prospect of living longer than thirty years. For unplanned expenses, while the bond ladder is liquid, selling portions of it to meet unexpected expenses directly means sacrificing some of the assets earmarked for later retirement spending. Also, retirees selling individual bonds prior to their maturity dates face interest rate risk, as a rise in interest rates would force capital losses to be realized in these cases. For someone considering a thirty-year retirement income bond ladder, it is important to also take a serious look at income annuities as a cheaper and more secure way to generate lifetime income.

The next category of bond ladders consists of different ways to build bond ladders extended over time to keep the length relatively constant as time passes. Rolling bond ladders are not meant to be fully wound down. As bonds mature with the proceeds spent, new bonds are purchased with other financial assets to extend the ladder length. Rolling ladders provide the basis for time segmentation strategies.

Possibilities for designing rolling ladders include to automatically extend the ladder length by one additional year as each year passes (automatic), or to develop a strategy to only extend the ladder when certain conditions are met (market-based). Possible decision criteria for extending a rolling ladder could be stock market valuations, current interest rates, recent market performance, or the individual's personal situation with respect to being adequately funded as determined by a capital needs analysis (personalized). We will discuss different strategies in more detail when we get to the topic of time segmentation. But first we will consider how to construct an actual retirement income bond ladder.

How to Buy Individual Bonds

Bonds can be purchased on both primary (when bonds are first issued) and secondary (subsequent trading) markets. There are wholesale markets for large institutions (with trades of at least $1 million) and retail markets for individual households.

TreasuryDirect.gov is available for purchases of traditional US Treasuries, TIPS, and I Bonds, in taxable accounts, without any transaction costs. When newly issued bonds are purchased at an auction, buyers receive the same wholesale pricing as large institutions and more deflation protection for TIPS because the accrued principal has not increased yet. There are no markups for pricing. The downside is that auctions provide less flexibility in maturity dates, and you have to wait for the next auction. The secondary market will also be needed to construct a complete ladder, as only a few maturities might be available at any given auction. Many brokerage accounts will also make new issues available for their typical brokerage charges.

Brokerage accounts have to be used for purchases in IRAs or other qualified retirement accounts. They can also be used to make purchases on the secondary markets for either taxable or tax-advantaged retirement accounts. For secondary markets, there can be large markups on pricing due to a lack of pricing transparency and lack of liquidity, especially outside the markets for Treasury debt.

The bid-ask spread creates a wedge for bond pricing. Wholesale prices are provided daily by the *Wall Street Journal* for Treasury bonds. The bid price is how much the bond can sell for, while the ask or offer price is how much one pays to buy the bond. A markup is the additional amount that the broker-dealer intermediary adds to the wholesale ask price in order to sell the bond to an individual investor. Investors may have no idea what the markup is, as it is not transparent. Those individuals selling bonds may also need to pay a markdown to the intermediary that is below the wholesale bid price. Markups and markdowns are generally smaller for frequently traded Treasuries, but they can get quite high for less liquid bonds. Nonetheless, an advantage of individual bonds is that a markup on purchase is only a one-time expense, and there are no ongoing fees as are charged on a bond fund.

● Building a Retirement Income Treasury STRIPS Ladder

Building bond ladders for retirement income is an important but understudied topic. Especially since we are at a point when many are worried about future interest rate increases, bond mutual funds risk locking in capital losses when shares are sold to meet expenses, while a bond ladder will still provide the obligated cash flows, no matter what happens with interest rates. Rather than purchasing bond mutual funds, an individual could build a ladder of bonds with some maturing each year to provide the income needed to cover annual expenses.

The *Wall Street Journal's* Market Data Center provides information on all outstanding Treasury bonds, STRIPS (zero-coupon bonds) and Treasury Inflation-Protected Securities (TIPS). Though creating an initial bond ladder with any of these asset subclasses is relatively straightforward, coupon payments increase the complexity, especially when it is time to extend the bond ladder as time passes. For this reason, we will first focus on US Treasury bond STRIPS.

Treasury STRIPS are zero-coupon bonds that only provide their face value on the maturity date. They sell for less than their face value, and the implied investment return from holding them to their maturity date can be calculated based on the pricing discount from their stated face value paid at maturity, as well as the length of time to maturity.

Using data from the *Wall Street Journal* for January 3, 2017, I've calculated the cost of building a ladder of Treasury STRIPS for up to thirty years, using the bond that matures at the earliest date each year (2017–2046). For the first year, cash is held for expenses rather than purchasing a bond that will mature in a few weeks. The results are in Exhibit 7.11.

Yields range from 0.56 percent for bonds maturing in 2018, up to 3.12 percent for bonds maturing in 2046. The bond ladder is designed to provide $40,000 of income in the first year, with 2 percent annual growth to approximate inflation. Without TIPS, built-in cost-of-living adjustments can only be applied in such a way. Future realized inflation could differ from the assumption used to build the ladder, leading the real value of the cash flows to fluctuate in unpredictable ways. Only TIPS can hedge unexpected inflation outside of what is assumed for the COLA.

Exhibit 7.11

Constructing Retirement Income Bonds Ladders Using Treasury STRIPS on January 3, 2017, for an Annual Income of $40,000 with a 2% Annual Cost-of-Living Adjustment

Maturity Date	Ask Price	Yield to Maturity (%)	Targeted Spending Amount	# of Shares Purchased	Cost of Shares	Cumulative Cost to Build Bond Ladder of This Length	Implied Portfolio Bond Allocation for Wealth of $1 Million
2017	$1,000.00	n/a	$40,000	40.00	$40,000	$40,000	4.0%
2018	$988.92	0.56%	$40,800	40.80	$40,348	$80,348	8.0%
2019	$973.16	0.91%	$41,616	41.62	$40,499	$120,847	12.1%
2020	$948.56	1.33%	$42,448	42.45	$40,265	$161,112	16.1%
2021	$927.15	1.52%	$43,297	43.30	$40,143	$201,255	20.1%
2022	$898.43	1.80%	$44,163	44.16	$39,678	$240,932	24.1%
2023	$871.42	1.99%	$45,047	45.05	$39,254	$280,187	28.0%
2024	$844.01	2.14%	$45,947	45.95	$38,780	$318,967	31.9%
2025	$817.67	2.26%	$46,866	46.87	$38,321	$357,288	35.7%
2026	$789.14	2.40%	$47,804	47.80	$37,724	$395,012	39.5%
2027	$764.08	2.48%	$48,760	48.76	$37,256	$432,268	43.2%
2028	$737.88	2.57%	$49,735	49.73	$36,698	$468,967	46.9%
2029	$715.10	2.61%	$50,730	50.73	$36,277	$505,244	50.5%
2030	$692.37	2.66%	$51,744	51.74	$35,826	$541,070	54.1%
2031	$669.55	2.71%	$52,779	52.78	$35,338	$576,408	57.6%
2032	$646.19	2.77%	$53,835	53.83	$34,787	$611,195	61.1%
2033	$624.55	2.81%	$54,911	54.91	$34,295	$645,490	64.5%
2034	$603.32	2.85%	$56,010	56.01	$33,792	$679,282	67.9%
2035	$582.40	2.89%	$57,130	57.13	$33,272	$712,555	71.3%
2036	$562.14	2.92%	$58,272	58.27	$32,757	$745,312	74.5%
2037	$541.57	2.96%	$59,438	59.44	$32,190	$777,502	77.8%
2038	$520.80	3.01%	$60,627	60.63	$31,574	$809,076	80.9%
2039	$501.64	3.04%	$61,839	61.84	$31,021	$840,097	84.0%
2040	$484.01	3.07%	$63,076	63.08	$30,529	$870,626	87.1%
2041	$466.26	3.10%	$64,337	64.34	$29,998	$900,624	90.1%
2042	$448.89	3.13%	$65,624	65.62	$29,458	$930,082	93.0%
2043	$434.40	3.14%	$66,937	66.94	$29,077	$959,160	95.9%
2044	$421.17	3.14%	$68,275	68.28	$28,756	$987,915	98.8%
2045	$409.67	3.13%	$69,641	69.64	$28,530	$1,016,445	Not Feasible
2046	$397.56	3.12%	$71,034	71.03	$28,240	$1,044,685	Not Feasible

Wholesale Cost for 30-Year Bond Ladder: **$1,044,685**

Initial Income Receipt as a Percentage of Cost: **3.83%**

Internal Rate of Return: **2.80%**

Source: Calculated with data from *Wall Street Journal* Market Data Center.

The exhibit shows the cumulative cost (using wholesale prices without any potential markups in pricing for retail consumers) of building $40,000 with 2 percent growth for up to thirty years. To get a clearer understanding of how the exhibit works, consider funding the income goal for 2027. With a 2 percent COLA, you seek to generate $48,760 that year. You want maturing bonds with this face value. The yield on a strip maturing that year is 2.48 percent. Discounting the spending amount to the present, you must set aside $37,256 in the bond today with a 2.48 percent annual return to have $48,760 available from the maturing bond in 2027. The same process works for every date income is desired.

Over the full thirty years, the total ladder cost is $1.045 million. This implies an initial spending rate of 3.83 percent for the $40,000 initial spending goal and an implied internal rate of return of 2.8 percent on the cash flows supported through the initial ladder cost. In other words, 2.8 percent is the fixed investment return required for the initial $1.045 million payment to support the subsequent cash flows over the next thirty years. This is the maximum spending that can be supported by the Treasury STRIPS' yield curve in the current market environment. Efforts to spend at a higher rate with risky investments like stocks will create risk that the goal cannot be met.

The other important detail in the exhibit is the column showing the implied portfolio bond allocation needed to build a STRIPS ladder of increasing length from a portfolio of $1 million. The column reveals that every year of income from the ladder requires an allocation of about 4 percent of the portfolio, though this percentage declines at longer maturities where the yields are higher. With a $1 million portfolio, the initial withdrawal rate to get $40,000 of spending is 4 percent. The full retirement ladder could only support a 4 percent initial spending rate (with the 2 percent COLA for spending) for twenty-eight years, as the portfolio would be fully depleted in year twenty-nine.

The ladder cost is scalable. If you want $100,000 of income, the cost is equal to the cost of $40,000 of income times the ratio of the new income goal: 100,000 / 40,000 = 2.5. Also, this exhibit works to show the cost for building a one-time bond ladder of any length up to thirty years. The total cost for a shorter ladder is simply the cost shown at that point in the cumulative cost column.

○ Building a Retirement Income TIPS Ladder

A TIPS ladder can be constructed similarly to a Treasury STRIPS ladder, also using data from the *Wall Street Journal* Market Data Center, which provides a daily report of wholesale prices from the secondary markets for all outstanding TIPS issues. On January 3, 2017, there were forty outstanding TIPS available, with maturity dates ranging from January 2017 to February 2046. As mentioned before, there are no TIPS maturing in 2030–31 and 2033–39. For these years, we buy extra TIPS for the most recent maturing year (i.e., 2029 for 2030–31 and 2032 for 2033–39) to cover the later spending, assuming those proceeds subsequently grow at a 0 percent real return until they are needed for spending.

TIPS provide coupon payments, which make the calculations a bit more complex than that of STRIPS. To construct a ladder with coupon bonds, we have to work backward from the ladder's end date. Our goal is to construct a TIPS ladder that provides $40,000 of inflation-adjusted income for thirty years between 2017 and 2046. Exhibit 7.12 shows the process for constructing this TIPS ladder.

These columns differ from the STRIPS ladder. In particular, we must make the distinction between real and nominal variables for TIPS trading in secondary markets. The ask price is in real terms. The accrued principal indicates how an original $1,000 has adjusted for subsequent inflation since the TIPS was first issued. Accrued principal is the real value of the bond at the present. Coupon rates are applied to determine coupon amounts, and the current real value of the accrued principal will be returned as the face value at the maturity date. The nominal ask price combines the ask price with the accrued principal (multiply together and divide by one hundred) to let a purchaser know how much must be paid today in order to purchase the TIPS on the wholesale market. This column is relevant for determining the cost of building the TIPS ladder, but it is a nominal number that is not connected to the yield. The real yield to maturity is provided in inflation-adjusted terms, linking the ask price and accrued principal with the coupon payments and maturity to find the inflation-adjusted rate of return for holding the TIPS.

As mentioned, to construct the ladder, we have to start from the end date. Starting at 2046, we need to buy enough shares of TIPS to give us $40,000 of inflation-adjusted income that year. This involves buying the TIPS maturing in 2046, which has a coupon of 1 percent, an asking price of $101.47, a yield of 0.94 percent, and accrued principal of $1,020. In real terms based on today's accrued principal, and with a simplification that the full coupon payment is made once per year instead of twice, on February 15, 2046, this bond will pay $1020 \times (1 + 0.01) = \$1,030.20$ in real interest and principal. We want an income of $40,000, so we need to buy $40000 / 1030.20 = 38.8274$ shares. The nominal price we pay for a share of this TIPS today is $1,034.98. Given the wholesale nominal asking price, these shares

Exhibit 7.12

Constructing a 30-Year TIPS Ladder on January 3, 2017, for an Annual Real Income of $40,000

Maturity Date	Coupon Rate	Ask Price	Accrued Principal	Nominal Ask Price	Real Yield to Maturity (%)	Real Targeted Spending Amount	# of Shares Purchased	Cost of Shares
2017	0.00%	$100.00	$1,000	$1,000	0	$40,000	22.27	$22,266
2018	1.63%	$102.63	$1,153	$1,183	−0.91%	$40,000	19.31	$22,851
2019	2.13%	$105.63	$1,125	$1,188	−0.62%	$40,000	20.11	$23,901
2020	1.38%	$105.25	$1,117	$1,176	−0.34%	$40,000	20.69	$24,322
2021	1.13%	$105.09	$1,104	$1,160	−0.14%	$40,000	21.22	$24,620
2022	0.13%	$100.38	$1,067	$1,071	0.05%	$40,000	22.20	$23,779
2023	0.13%	$99.50	$1,047	$1,042	0.21%	$40,000	22.66	$23,601
2024	0.63%	$102.06	$1,035	$1,056	0.33%	$40,000	22.95	$24,240
2025	0.25%	$98.63	$1,020	$1,006	0.42%	$40,000	23.43	$23,570
2026	0.63%	$101.25	$1,017	$1,030	0.48%	$40,000	23.56	$24,257
2027	2.38%	$117.53	$1,198	$1,408	0.57%	$40,000	20.12	$28,334
2028	1.75%	$112.09	$1,153	$1,292	0.61%	$40,000	21.41	$27,665
2029	2.50%	$121.22	$1,125	$1,364	0.66%	$40,000	70.49	$96,128
2030			NO MATURING TIPS			$40,000	NO MATURING TIPS	
2031						$40,000		
2032	3.38%	$138.94	$1,361	$1,891	0.69%	$40,000	208.53	$394,313
2033						$40,000		
2034						$40,000		
2035			NO MATURING TIPS			$40,000	NO MATURING TIPS	
2036						$40,000		
2037						$40,000		
2038						$40,000		
2039						$40,000		
2040	2.13%	$124.88	$1,118	$1,396	0.93%	$40,000	32.80	$45,796
2041	2.13%	$125.56	$1,103	$1,385	0.94%	$40,000	33.96	$47,026
2042	0.75%	$95.66	$1,069	$1,023	0.94%	$40,000	35.78	$36,587
2043	0.63%	$92.56	$1,051	$973	0.95%	$40,000	36.67	$35,669
2044	1.38%	$110.19	$1,037	$1,143	0.95%	$40,000	37.39	$42,726
2045	0.75%	$95.13	$1,026	$976	0.95%	$40,000	38.31	$37,393
2046	1.00%	$101.47	$1,020	$1,035	0.94%	$40,000	38.83	$40,186

Wholesale Cost for 30-Year Bond Ladder: **$1,069,231**

Initial Income Receipt as a Percentage of Cost: **3.74%**

Internal Rate of Return: **0.76%**

Source: Calculated with data from *Wall Street Journal* Market Data Center.

cost us 38.8274 × 1034.98 = $40,186 today. Paying $40,186 today entitles us to $40,000 of real income in 2046, in addition to $396.04, which is 0.01 × 1020 × 38.83 shares of real coupon payments for each of the years before then. We know the real value based on today's accrued principal. The nominal amount you actually receive in 2046 will be larger to the extent that we experience inflation over the next thirty years.

Now we move to 2045. We want $40,000 of real income for that year, too. The trick is that we have to account for the fact that the 2046 maturing TIPS we just purchased is going to give us coupon payments of $396.04 of income for that year as well. We can subtract that from what we need to purchase. We need an additional $39,603.96 of real income in 2045. To review the process, the 2045 TIPS has a coupon rate of 0.75 percent and accrued principal of $1,026. A share will provide real income of 1026 × 1.0075 = $1,033.70 in 2045. We require 39603.96 / 1033.70 = 38.31 shares of the 2045 TIPS. The ask price is $95.13, so the price we must pay today is 95.13 × 1026 / 100 = $975.98. The total cost for these shares is $37,393.

This process continues, working backward to the present. In 2017, the ladder provides $17,734 of real income as interest payments for bonds maturing in later years. This means that we only need to set aside an additional $22,266 for the $40,000 of spending in the first year.

This is the logic behind constructing the TIPS ladder. Note that to deal with the problem of missing maturities, we bought three years of spending with the 2029 TIPS and eight years of spending with the 2032 TIPS.

It is impossible for a TIPS ladder to have a cumulative cost column that correctly shows the costs for building shorter TIPS ladders in the same manner as we had for Treasury STRIPS. With the thirty-year ladder shown, part of the income available at earlier dates comes from coupon payments from longer-dated bonds that would not be part of a shorter ladder. Because the ladder is constructed beginning at its end, we would have to start from scratch if we chose a different end date. This was not the case for STRIPS, since there was no interest income to complicate the calculations for earlier years in the ladder.

The total cost for this TIPS ladder with wholesale pricing is $1.069 million. For the $40,000 inflation-adjusted spending, this represents an initial withdrawal rate of 3.74 percent. The real internal rate of return on the cash flows as they are spent is 0.76 percent. A thirty-year TIPS ladder is as close as we can get to a real-world "safe withdrawal rate" for thirty years of inflation-adjusted spending. At current interest rates, 3.74 percent is the number. A thirty-year TIPS ladder represents the "risk-free" way to support thirty years of real income. Spending more from an investment portfolio is based on a hope that a higher return can justify and sustain a higher spending rate. This is risky. It is important to note that with this bond ladder, nothing will be left at the end of the thirtieth year. The calculation is "risk free" for thirty years, but the possibility of living beyond thirty years must be considered. A TIPS ladder does not hedge longevity risk.

There is one further relevant point about comparing the TIPS ladder with the STRIPS ladder. The STRIPS ladder was built with a COLA of 2 percent. Its cost was just slightly less than the TIPS ladder. Calibrating the two costs can provide us with a break-even inflation rate between TIPS and STRIPS. A COLA of about 2.17 percent calibrates the costs for the two ladders. In terms of which then provides a better performance for retirees, the TIPS ladder provides more income and inflation protection if realized average annual inflation exceeds 2.17 percent over the next thirty years, while the STRIPS ladder would be able to match actual inflation and provide surplus (in real terms) should the realized inflation experience fall short of 2.17 percent. The choice between ladder types should depend on how you feel about the likelihood of high inflation in the future, as well as a consideration about the impact of different inflation scenarios on your lifestyle. If your inflation expectations exceed what the market has priced in or if high inflation will be more damaging to your lifestyle than low inflation, then this tilts the decision in favor of TIPS over STRIPS. Conversely, if you are not worried about inflation and high inflation will not have a negative impact on lifestyle, then you might choose to construct your bond ladder with STRIPS using a smaller COLA that allows the ladder to be purchased more cheaply.

◉ Time Segmentation

The Financial Planning Association (FPA) divides retirement income strategies into three categories: systematic withdrawals, time-based segmentation, and essential-versus-discretionary income. Thus far, we have focused on systematic withdrawal strategies. Their defining characteristic is that rules are used to take distributions in a systematic manner from an investment portfolio designed with a total-returns perspective. Spending may come from both the income generated by the portfolio and the spenddown of principal. At the other extreme, the essential-versus-discretionary approach incorporates lifetime income guarantees through annuitization. Annuities extend beyond our scope here; they will be my focus in a subsequent volume. We now turn our attention to time-based segmentation, or time segmentation.

Time segmentation differs from systematic withdrawals in that fixed-income assets are held to maturity to guarantee upcoming retiree expenses over the short and medium term. A growth portfolio is also built with more volatile assets having higher expected returns, to be deployed to cover expenses in the more distant future. This is not total-returns investing, since different investing strategies are used to cover different time horizons. Time segmentation also differs from essential-versus-discretionary because it does not build a lifetime income floor. Rather, there is an income front end with contractual protections. The assumption is that people have not saved enough to immunize their entire lifetime of spending. Importantly, time segmentation also accounts for the fact that spending needs may change, and this requires flexibility and the avoidance of irreversible decisions.

Defining time segmentation as it is used in practice is challenging. Time segmentation, also known as bucketing, is used by countless financial advisors, each of whom tends to define their process in a unique way. Differences can be found with regard to the number of time segments and their respective lengths, the choice of asset classes used within each segment, whether individual bonds are used in place of bond funds, the degree to which the overall asset allocation is allowed to change over time, and how and when the different segments are further extended as time passes. These issues may not always be addressed, and critics of time segmentation wonder if there is really a "there there," as Jonathan Guyton questioned in a 2014 *Journal of Financial Planning* column.

At its core, though, time segmentation simply involves investing differently for retirement spending goals falling at different points in retirement. Fixed-income assets with greater security are generally reserved for earlier retirement expenses, and higher volatility investments with greater growth potential are employed to support later retirement expenses.

The most lucid explanation of time segmentation is provided in the 2004 book *Asset Dedication: How to Grow Wealthy with the Next Generation of Asset Allocation,* written by Stephen J. Huxley and J. Brent Burns. Their description serves as a motivation for this discussion, though I must be clear that I am not specifically replicating their specific approach when I test various time segmentation strategies.

Effectively discussing and simulating time segmentation requires defining it in core terms without some of the bells and whistles that occasionally get included. For example, I will consider two time segments rather than six, use individual bonds for the upfront time segment and a large-capitalization stock fund for the growth segment meant to cover later expenses, and include straightforward automated rules to guide how the upfront time segment is to be extended over time with a rolling bond ladder. This latter point is important, because many versions of time segmentation used in practice may treat the process of extending earlier time segments in an ad hoc fashion, or may even neglect it.

Defining Asset Allocation within Time Segmentation

Building bond ladders to cover retirement spending needs is a relatively understudied topic within the retirement income world. Perhaps the best source for education about the logic of holding individual bonds is provided in the work of Stephen Huxley and J. Brent Burns, who developed the concept of asset dedication. They explain asset allocation differently.

A first consideration for time segmentation is its different treatment of asset allocation. Asset allocation is allowed to fluctuate in a dynamic manner because efforts are not made to maintain a fixed ratio of stocks and bonds. Rather, bond holdings are based on the cost of maintaining a bond ladder with the desired length and income level. Stock holdings consist of what is left over after building and updating the bond ladder. An initial stock allocation of 50 percent could easily rise above 90 percent if the growth portfolio performs well, and it could fall to 0 percent with poor growth leading all available assets used to maintain a bond ladder until it depletes as well.

To the extent that time segmentation does not call for portions of a bond ladder to be sold in order to rebalance funds into the growth portfolio, time segmentation can only have one possible direction for portfolio rebalancing: extend the bond ladder with funds from the growth portfolio. Time segmentation provides a way to reallocate funds from stocks to bonds, by moving assets from the growth portfolio to the bond ladder. It does not provide a mechanism to move in the other direction. The only mechanism available to shift toward an increasing stock allocation is to simply avoid extending the bond ladder over time; maturing bonds are spent and are not replaced.

Dramatically fluctuating asset allocations may make retirees uncomfortable. Nonetheless, Huxley and Burns are critical of traditional asset allocation, because other than saying that risk-tolerant individuals can hold more stocks, there is no clear way to decide on the appropriate allocation between stocks and bonds. They reject the usefulness of risk tolerance questionnaires commonly used in practice. With asset allocation, they argue, bond funds are treated as "stocks-lite," in which a volatile bond mutual fund is held that still fluctuates in value, just to a lesser degree than stocks. Huxley and Burns criticize bond mutual funds for behaving as equities but with lower returns and volatility in a retirement portfolio. Given bond funds' volatility, it is hard to explain to retirees why their asset allocation should be 60/40 rather than 50/50 or 70/30. The traditional asset allocation approach is tied up too much in a single-period framework that abstracts from an investor's goal to build a nest egg that will allow for desired spending amounts for as long as retirement lasts. Risk, in their understanding, is not being able to meet retirement goals, rather than simple measures of portfolio volatility.

The time segmentation approach to asset allocation can lead to a much more dynamic asset allocation over time. The bond allocation is determined in terms of the monetary cost of building the desired bond ladder, rather than trying to keep the overall portfolio at a fixed percentage of bonds. Bonds provide the cash flows to match assets to liabilities. Stocks, meanwhile, represent whatever is left after the bond ladder is created and updated. Goals and investment performance drive the asset allocation. If stocks perform sufficiently well, the stock allocation may increase over time. If stocks do not perform well, the stock allocation could creep toward 0 percent as the cost of maintaining the bond ladder takes up an increasing percentage of the remaining portfolio value.

A retiree would understand that his or her bond allocation is 40 percent, for example, if this were the amount needed to lock in spending goals for a targeted eight-year horizon. The important discussion becomes: how much spending and for how long is one comfortable to have locked into place with fixed-income assets? Conservative behavior would be expressed through a desire to build a longer bond ladder in order to lock in more spending. Goals drive asset allocation decisions, instead of questionnaires or other tools that attempt to measure an investor's tolerance for portfolio volatility and potential losses.

The bond allocation is simply the portion of assets required to build the bond ladder with sufficient income and the desired length. More conservative behavior is reflected as wanting a longer upfront bond ladder, which implies a higher allocation to bonds. The fundamental trade-off in choosing the bond ladder length is the degree of certainty versus growth. A longer bond ladder length creates greater income security in retirement, as more years of spending are covered by holding more individual bonds to maturity. However, a shorter bond ladder allows more assets to remain in the growth portfolio; if growth is realized, then the portfolio can support retirement spending for longer than otherwise.

If your desired withdrawal rate is above what the yield curve can support, you can't build a bond portfolio to meet your lifetime spending needs, and bonds will actually serve as a drag on the portfolio, as there will be no chance to get the types of returns needed to meet those lifetime spending goals. If risk-pooling strategies with annuities are not in the cards, one must either cut back on spending ambitions or add more volatile assets offering a greater potential investment return. Some retirees may rely on the assumption of future portfolio growth to justify spending more today than bonds could otherwise support. But these efforts to support greater portfolio growth could backfire, ultimately reducing retirement sustainability relative to what a longer bond ladder could have supported.

At the extreme, we saw before that the current yield curve for Treasury STRIPS could support twenty-eight years of spending at a 4 percent initial spending rate with a 2 percent spending COLA. Creating a twenty-eight-year ladder, then, would ensure twenty-eight years of spending but leave nothing in the growth portfolio for potential expenses beyond this horizon. Shorter ladders allow more to be left in the growth portfolio, creating possibilities that this spending might be supported for more than twenty-eight years as well as possibilities that this spending could ultimately be supported for less than twenty-eight years. Seeking growth means running the risk that the necessary funds will not be available.

The implication of all this is that dynamic asset allocation is not really of any concern. Simply, the portion of assets needed to build the desired bond ladder as the percentage of available assets determines the bond allocation. Retirees can focus on this bond ladder and not worry about their overall asset allocation. If this percentage fluctuates wildly and unpredictably, so be it. Efforts to maintain a less volatile asset allocation would instead require letting the bond ladder length fluctuate more dramatically.

Equity exposure moves you away from the guarantee that your plan will work, but it gives you a chance to meet spending goals that extend beyond what the yield curve can support. By building an income floor at the front end of the portfolio, retirees have assets dedicated to meeting their spending needs over an eight-year (or whatever length is chosen) horizon, and then the remainder of the portfolio is invested for long-term growth. Assets are dedicated to the purpose they are best suited for: bonds generate predictable cash flows, and stocks provide less predictability but more growth potential.

Time Segmentation Is a Probability-Based Approach

As for the debate between the probability-based and safety-first schools of thought for retirement income planning, I view time segmentation as a hybrid between the two that falls closer on the spectrum to the probability-based school. Time segmentation generally relies on the idea of "stocks for the long run," as there is a degree of comfort that the growth portfolio will provide sufficient returns to maintain retirement sustainability. According to advocates, the long-run growth potential of stocks can be expected to materialize in time to keep the bond ladder adequately extended.

To understand this probability-based point of view, Exhibit 7.13 plots the historical worst-case annualized nominal returns for large-capitalization US stocks and intermediate-term US government bonds since 1926. Over shorter holding periods, bonds were less exposed to downside risks. Over one year, for instance, the worst case for bonds was a 5.1 percent drop, while stocks fell by 43.3 percent in their worst year. Over any historical three-year period, bonds provided a positive annualized return. It took fifteen years before stocks historically were always able to provide a positive return. But for holding periods of at least seventeen years, the historical worst-case annualized performance for stocks exceeds that for bonds. Over twenty-year periods, for instance, stocks experienced a worst-case 3.1 percent annualized return, compared to 1.6 percent for bonds. For thirty-year periods, the worst case for stocks was 8.5 percent, compared to 2.2 percent for bonds. And for forty-year periods, stocks' worst performance was an 8.9 percent annualized return, compared to 2.8 percent as the worst for bonds. For historical forty-year periods, even the best case for bonds (8.1 percent) could not beat the worst case for stocks. Because probability-based advocates have confidence that the historical record provides sufficient precedence for what can be expected in the future, this is the basic logic for understanding the view that stocks should be the primary asset designed to cover retirement expenses over the longer term.

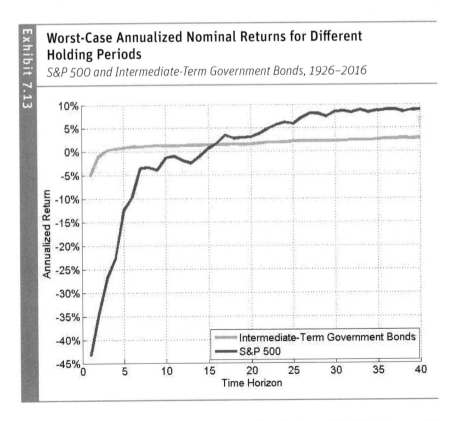

Exhibit 7.13

Worst-Case Annualized Nominal Returns for Different Holding Periods
S&P 500 and Intermediate-Term Government Bonds, 1926–2016

With this optimistic view about stocks in the long run, the objective becomes to maintain a high stock allocation. Prior to the start of constructing a retirement income bond ladder, the argument goes, the stock allocation should be 100 percent. Only enough is taken from the growth portfolio to construct the desired bond ladder. Someone with greater risk aversion can lock in a longer spending stream, which devotes more to bonds, and then allow the remaining stocks a longer time to compound before needing to be sold. To the extent that this provides an improvement over traditional asset allocation, it helps devote as much as possible to growth assets, and it helps avoid having to sell stocks after momentary drops. Nothing will need to be sold until it is necessary to lock in more spending. Only the minimal amount needed to lock in spending should go to specific individual bonds, and the rest should be earmarked for growth.

Behavioral Benefits of Time Segmentation

Advocates of time segmentation argue that it can lead to better retiree behavior because it is more easily understood. Time segmentation can be more intuitive than the blender approach of the total-returns portfolio, as it's easier for people to understand that certain assets are to be used for different time horizons in retirement. It is a form of mental accounting. The approach is simple and clear to explain and understand.

But with traditional asset allocation, different asset classes are mixed into a single portfolio, and individuals experience difficulty relating to why they have a particular asset allocation or what the different parts of their portfolio are aiming to do. Bonds are used to dampen volatility, which leaves them behaving as sluggish stocks.

This lack of understanding of asset allocation could make a retiree vulnerable to panic and stock selling after a market decline. The argument is that when retirees instead have a front-end bond ladder, they know there is time for stocks to recover before they need to be sold. This provides the courage to leave stocks alone and to focus on a more long-term investing approach. To the extent that this helps a retiree to stay the course and to avoid panic selling of growth assets after a market decline, this can be a strong justification for time segmentation even if it is not necessarily a superior investing strategy for a fully rational investor.

Time Segmentation and Sequence-of-Returns Risk

A selling point for time segmentation is that it avoids short-term sequence-of-returns risk, as the volatile growth assets will not need to be sold immediately after a market drop in order to support retirement spending. The bond ladder does not have to be replenished every year. The retiree can wait for markets to recover before selling stocks in order to extend the bond ladder.

However, this point is controversial, as a fully functioning framework must extend the bond ladder at some point. That could trigger sequence risk. We must determine whether dynamic asset allocation is what is responsible for time segmentation outcomes. But first, it is worthwhile to explore sequence risk for individual bonds and bond funds a bit more, since this point is often confused during retirement.

As noted, the value of the bond ladder does fluctuate over time with changing interest rates, but this is immaterial to the success of the plan if the bonds are held to maturity. At maturity they pay the full expected value, and earlier unrealized gains or losses do not materialize. Investors financing a retirement goal can happily ignore the fluctuating value of their individual bonds, knowing that the desired cash flows will be provided from bond coupon payments and the return of principal at maturity. When laddered bonds are held to maturity, cash flows are known, and there is no realized interest-rate risk. In fact, rising interest rates could even help with issues such as reducing the overall IRS required minimum distribution (RMD) amounts for bonds in tax-deferred accounts.

With a bond fund, the concept of duration implies an investor is made whole after a rate increase once a time period matching the fund's duration has passed, because that investor is able to reinvest coupon payments at higher interest rates to offset the capital losses on bonds. However, that conclusion assumes the portfolio is not funding a spending goal. If those coupons are being used for spending and if some shares of the bond fund are sold to cover spending, then the bond portfolio will not be able to recover through its ability to reinvest cash flows at a new higher interest rate. Portfolio returns would need to be even higher to offset the loss in ability to fully reinvest funds at higher rates. This makes duration matching for household investors using constant-duration bond funds much more difficult in practice. Only a few commercial solutions exist.

Time segmentation does provide a practical way for retirees to duration-match their spending goals. But the idea that time segmentation reduces sequence risk is less clear-cut. Time segmentation is a probability-based approach in that its advocates are confident that sufficient upside growth will take place before growth assets need to be sold to support spending. The safety-first side reminds us that there is no guarantee this will actually happen. Growth assets may still have to be sold at a loss, depending on the mechanics for when it becomes necessary to rebalance into bonds. The bond ladder may be depleted before the growth portfolio has recovered sufficiently. Sequence risk may still materialize if assets are sold at a loss. We need to empirically investigate the importance of this matter, which we will now do.

Choosing How to Extend the Ladder over Time

If a time segmentation approach does not offer clear rules about the method for extending the bond ladder over time, then it is not a true retirement income plan that can be tested and analyzed.

I will investigate examples of three different methods for choosing when to extend the bond ladder as retirement progresses. These are based on the three methods for creating rolling bond ladders mentioned earlier in Exhibit 7.10: (1) automatic, (2) market-based, and (3) personalized.

Automatic rolling ladders, which Huxley and Burns call "rolling horizon," keep the same time horizon perpetually by automatically rolling out the ladder length each year as a bond matures. This is done for as long as the growth portfolio has sufficient assets to extend the ladder length. An initial ladder length is chosen, and the ladder is built. At the end of each year, the ladder is extended by one year so that the ladder length remains fixed over time. If the growth portfolio is 100 percent stocks, then this strategy involves taking ongoing distributions from a 100 percent stock portfolio. The only recourse is that the distribution amount is not the full value of spending, but rather the discounted value of the bonds to be purchased based on current interest rates. If and when the growth portfolio depletes, the ladder will continue to provide income without being further extended until it is wound down completely and all assets are depleted.

Exhibit 7.14 provides the outcomes for one Monte Carlo simulation for stock returns and bond yields to show how an automatic rolling ladder

Exhibit 7.14

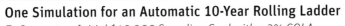

One Simulation for an Automatic 10-Year Rolling Ladder
To Support an Initial $40,000 Spending Goal with a 2% COLA

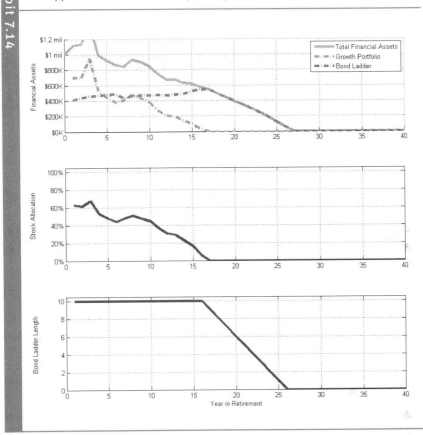

might perform in practice. This retiree seeks to support an initial $40,000 spending goal with an annual 2 percent cost-of-living adjustment for as long as possible in retirement. The retiree has $1 million at the start of retirement to divide between a bond ladder and a stock portfolio. The retiree seeks to maintain a ten-year bond ladder providing the desired annual spending throughout retirement. With a 2.45 percent initial bond yield and assuming a flat yield curve, building the initial bond ladder requires 39.2 percent of the asset base. The other 60.8 percent of assets are left in stocks. While I allow interest rates to fluctuate randomly over time, I do simplify by assuming a flat yield curve. Relative to an upward sloping yield curve, a flat yield curve lowers the costs of short-term spending and raises the costs of long-term spending. But these factors will tend to offset one another, and with low interest rates, the differing assumptions will lead to relatively minor differences in ladder costs.

In this particular Monte Carlo simulation, a total-returns investment portfolio that uses annual rebalancing to maintain a fixed 60.8 percent stock and 39.2 percent bond allocation would have supported spending until year thirty of retirement. With an automatic rolling ladder, wealth depletes in year twenty-seven. Because the growth portfolio experiences early losses, the automatic replenishing of the bond ladder each year pushes the stock allocation downward over time. In year seventeen, the last remaining assets in the growth portfolio are transitioned to the bond ladder. At this point, the bond ladder can support nine more years of full income along with a portion of the tenth year's income. Assets are fully depleted in year twenty-seven. In this simulation, early stock losses raised the necessary distribution rate to support rebalancing, creating too much pressure on the growth portfolio. Time segmentation did not support a better outcome.

Next, Exhibit 7.15 provides a sense of the range of possibilities for the dynamic asset allocation generated by ten-year automatic rolling ladders. Twenty random simulations are shown with thin lines, along with the tenth, fiftieth, and ninetieth percentiles across the distribution. The median stock allocation stays relatively close to its initial level with only slight upward drift. At the tenth percentile, the stock allocation falls dramatically as the growth portfolio is spent down to extend the bond ladder over time. The growth portfolio depletes by year fifteen. On the other hand, the growth portfolio grows dramatically at the ninetieth percentile, so that the stock allocation continues rising even as the bond ladder extends. This rising equity glide path is triggered by strong stock market performance expanding the growth portfolio at a rapid pace that exceeds the distributions needed to keep the bond ladder fully funded.

Next, market-based and personalized approaches are both part of the category that Huxley and Burns call flexible horizons. Market-based rules for extending the ladder could be based on triggers such as positive stock growth, high stock market valuations, or high interest rates. Noting whether the market has grown is objective, but there is a degree of subjectivity involved in deciding whether stock market valuations or interest rates are

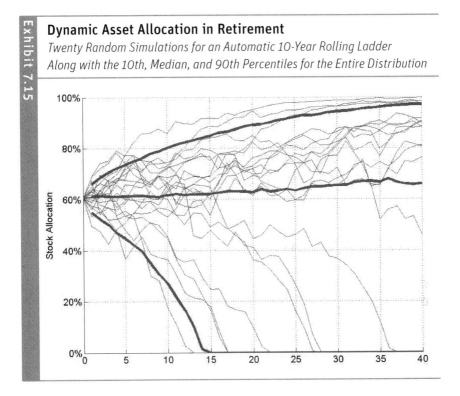

Exhibit 7.15

Dynamic Asset Allocation in Retirement

Twenty Random Simulations for an Automatic 10-Year Rolling Ladder
Along with the 10th, Median, and 90th Percentiles for the Entire Distribution

high. It is important not to fall into the trap of using market timing to make these decisions.

For an example of a market-based approach, I will use a simple rule that is similar to how the life insurance industry describes the use of cash value life insurance and how Barry and Steven Sacks decide when to draw from a reverse mortgage line of credit. That is, if the stock market produced a negative return in the previous year, then the bond ladder is not extended in the current year. If the stock market produced a positive return in the previous year, then the ladder is extended back to the full targeted length when there are sufficient assets in the growth portfolio to achieve this. For example, if the target ladder length is ten years, then two years of negative returns would reduce the ladder length to eight years. If a positive return is experienced in the third year, then the ladder is extended by three years to account for that year's spending and the two years that the ladder was not extended, in order to get back to the desired ten-year target length. If the growth portfolio depletes, the ladder is no longer extended, and retirement income ends once the ladder is wound down.

Exhibit 7.16 provides the outcome for the market-based rolling ladder for the same Monte Carlo simulation used previously. In this case, we can see that until year twenty-one, there are cases where the ladder length is allowed to decrease after years of negative stock returns. This slows down the pace of the reduction in stock allocation. However, the growth portfolio also depletes in this scenario in year twenty-one. Then the bond ladder begins to wind down, and assets are fully depleted by year thirty. This market-based ladder provides slightly less total spending than could have been achieved with the fixed 60.8/39.2 asset allocation total-returns portfolio, since less of the year thirty spending goal can be met. But compared to a total-returns portfolio that used the same dynamic asset allocation as this market-based strategy as observed in the exhibit, the

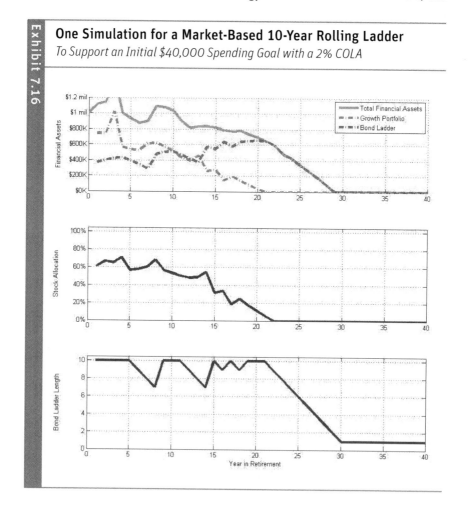

Exhibit 7.16

One Simulation for a Market-Based 10-Year Rolling Ladder

To Support an Initial $40,000 Spending Goal with a 2% COLA

bond ladder version did perform slightly better. The total-returns version with matching asset allocation could have only supported the same income into year twenty-nine.

As before, Exhibit 7.17 indicates the range of possibilities for the dynamic asset allocation generated by the market-based ten-year rolling ladder. Again, twenty random simulations are shown with thin lines, along with the tenth, fiftieth, and ninetieth percentiles across the distribution. The pattern of asset allocation is similar to before, though the median stock allocation does rise more quickly to about 75 percent by the end of the time horizon. The ability to let the bond ladder length decrease after a stock decline does help preserve the portfolio a bit longer than otherwise, while also increasing stock allocations slightly compared to the automatic ladder. Again, effort is made to preserve the bond ladder length as much as possible, which does lead the stock allocation to decline after bad market outcomes. This happens at a slower pace than before, though, as the market-based approach provides more flexibility for short-term bond ladder reductions as well.

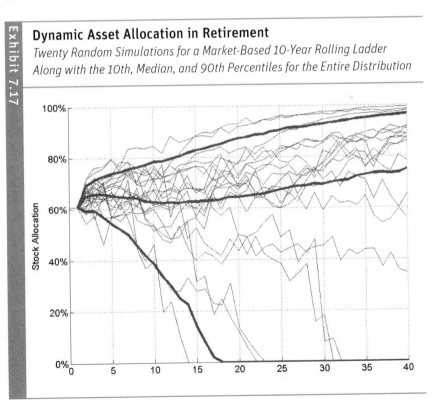

Exhibit 7.17

Dynamic Asset Allocation in Retirement
*Twenty Random Simulations for a Market-Based 10-Year Rolling Ladder
Along with the 10th, Median, and 90th Percentiles for the Entire Distribution*

Finally, personalized rules can be based on a "critical path" for retirement wealth. Within retirement income planning research, I have observed three cases in which a "critical path" is used to help guide decisions around retirement spending. First, Huxley and Burns used a critical path to help decide when to extend the bond ladder in their Asset Dedication book. Second, a team of researchers at Texas Tech University used a critical path to determine when to take distributions from an investment portfolio and when to take distributions from a reverse mortgage line of credit. I discussed that method in my book *Reverse Mortgages: How to Use Reverse Mortgages to Secure Your Retirement*. Third, David Zolt used the critical path to decide whether or not a retiree should take a full inflation adjustment for spending during each year of retirement. This variable spending strategy was discussed in chapter 6.

The "critical path" helps determine if the portfolio is on target to meeting the retirement goal. First, a retiree determines an end goal for the portfolio in terms of how long the portfolio should last, as well as how much spending it should support. Examples of portfolio end goals could be to deplete the portfolio by age 105, to maintain $100,000 at age 90, and so on. Next, these numbers are combined with the current portfolio value to determine a portfolio return assumption that will allow the end goal for the portfolio to be met. Third, this information is combined to determine a glide path for the value of remaining wealth throughout retirement, showing the wealth needed to remain precisely on track to meet the spending and portfolio end value goals. The critical path compares where the portfolio is and where it should be in dollar terms to be on track.

Volatility is not an appropriate measure of risk for personal financial planning. When one is in the safety zone above the critical path, volatility may not be risky, but a low-volatility portfolio may be quite dangerous when one has fallen below the critical path and the portfolio is plummeting toward zero. Portfolio volatility is not the same as risk; while they are related, the real risk in personal finance is witnessing the wealth level fall below the critical path. In a sense, high volatility when above the critical path is less risky than low volatility when below the critical path.

Exhibit 7.18 provides an example of a critical path for retirement wealth. This individual has $1 million at retirement. She seeks to support $40,000 of spending with a 2 percent COLA for a forty-five-year retirement period. Wealth is allowed to be depleted at the end of forty-five years. She determines that a 5 percent return is needed to support this retirement spending goal with her portfolio. The exhibit tracks the path of her remaining wealth with a 5 percent return to let her know where she should be during each year of retirement to be on a sustainable path toward meeting her retirement goal. Having wealth above the glide path represents a safety zone, while retirement is in more dangerous territory whenever wealth falls below its critical path value.

In each year of retirement, the retiree can compare the current value of her remaining wealth to the critical path value of wealth. If her actual wealth exceeds the critical path, then she is in good shape with extra discretionary wealth. But when her actual wealth falls below the critical path, she is falling behind in terms of being able to meet her full retirement goal. In the context of this discussion, the bond ladder can be extended further when wealth is above the critical path, but the ladder is not extended during years when wealth falls below the critical path. One instead seeks

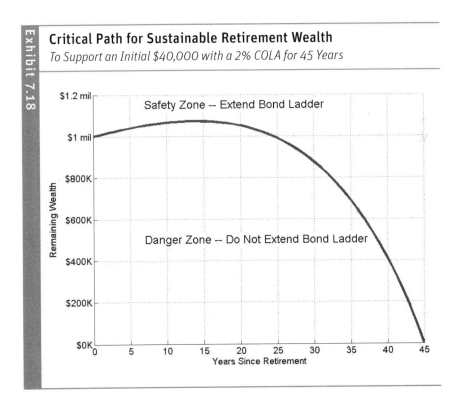

Exhibit 7.18

Critical Path for Sustainable Retirement Wealth
To Support an Initial $40,000 with a 2% COLA for 45 Years

hope for growth assets to recover and get one back above the critical path before extending the bond ladder.

This action is designed to relieve the stress on the growth portfolio and allow it a better chance to recover before taking further distributions from it. It is predicated on faith in "stocks for the long run." Unlike the other two ladder extension strategies, this one moves the portfolio toward 100 percent stocks when the portfolio is in danger.

Exhibit 7.19 provides the outcomes using a critical path approach to bond ladder extension based on the same Monte Carlo simulation as used previously. In this case, we can observe that remaining financial assets quickly fall below the glide path threshold, leading the bond ladder to be less than ten years for much of the retirement period. The bond ladder dissipates by year thirteen of retirement, as the critical path threshold for extending the ladder is not passed again after the fourth year. Unlike with the other strategies, this pushes asset allocation to 100 percent stocks as the bond ladder depletes before the growth portfolio. To signify growth portfolio depletion, I show that the asset allocation drops to 0 percent stocks once no assets remain. For this simulation, retirement spending was fully supported for thirty years, and the growth portfolio is depleted in year thirty-one.

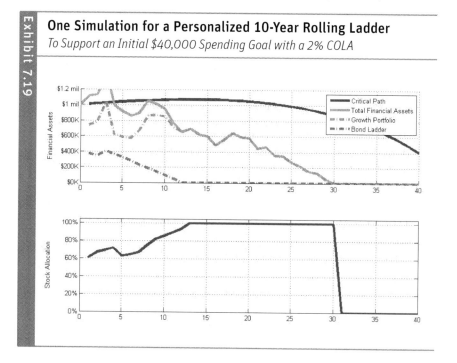

Exhibit 7.19

One Simulation for a Personalized 10-Year Rolling Ladder
To Support an Initial $40,000 Spending Goal with a 2% COLA

Exhibit 7.20 provides the corresponding analysis showing the distribution for asset allocation over time, along with the stock allocation paths for twenty random simulations. We can observe clearly how this strategy pushes the stock allocation higher than the other strategies, since it leads to the bond ladder depleting prior to the growth portfolio. The stock allocation at the tenth percentile rises almost immediately as well, unlike in the other cases. The median stock allocation continues to rise, surpassing 80 percent within the first ten years of retirement.

Is Time Segmentation a Superior Investing Strategy?

Determining whether time segmentation is a superior investing strategy to total-returns investing is controversial, though the general consensus is that there is no reason to believe that time segmentation is a uniquely better way to invest. To be a better investment strategy, it would need to be able to reduce sequence risk in a unique way relative to a total-returns portfolio with the same asset allocation. The basic controversy is around asset allocation and how to compare two different strategies. A time segmentation strategy

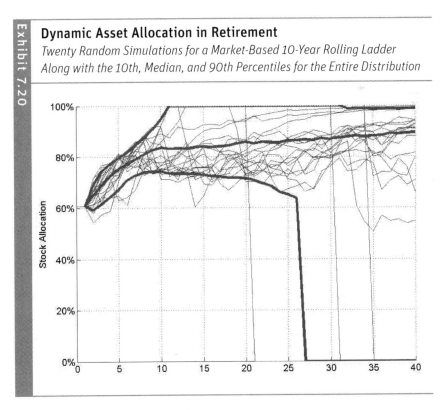

Exhibit 7.20

Dynamic Asset Allocation in Retirement
Twenty Random Simulations for a Market-Based 10-Year Rolling Ladder
Along with the 10th, Median, and 90th Percentiles for the Entire Distribution

justifies a dynamic asset allocation with a potentially higher average stock allocation, and it cannot easily be compared to a total-return investing strategy with a static allocation. Whether time segmentation is a better strategy depends on the interactions of three issues:

- Because asset allocation is allowed to fluctuate, a time segmentation approach can have a very different asset allocation path than a total-returns investing approach. Is this acceptable to the retiree who has always been told that a more static (or at least a slowly changing) allocation is the right way to invest?
- Time segmentation approaches introduce varying degrees of effort in attempting to avoid selling stocks at inopportune times.
- By holding individual bonds to maturity, fixed-income assets do not need to be sold at a loss to support retirement income.

Exhibit 7.21 provides the ongoing probabilities of success for seven different strategies in supporting the retirement spending goal (spend $40,000 initially with 2 percent cost-of-living adjustments in subsequent years) for up to forty years of retirement. The analysis is based on ten thousand Monte Carlo simulations starting from today's low bond yields with the capacity for rates to increase over time (as described in the technical appendix to chapter 3). Three of the strategies are the time segmentation rolling ladder approaches previously described with bond ladder lengths targeted at ten years. Ladders are extended either automatically, in years after positive market returns, or when remaining wealth exceeds the critical path level for that year of retirement.

The other four strategies are for total-returns investment portfolios. The first of these maintains a fixed 60.8 percent stock allocation throughout retirement, which matches the initial stock allocation after constructing a ten-year bond ladder at the start of retirement. This strategy is worthwhile to include because retirees using total-returns portfolios are more likely to maintain a relatively stable asset allocation in retirement. However, this strategy is not directly comparable to the time segmentation strategies because the asset allocation will be so different in subsequent years. The other three total-returns strategies use dynamic asset allocations designed to match the asset allocation generated by the time segmentation strategies for each Monte Carlo simulation in each year of retirement. Though real retirees would be unlikely to use such dynamic asset allocation strategies, since they would have no basis to know what these allocations should be, these are important to include because they help control for the effects of dynamic asset allocation in order to see better about the specific role of the bond ladder portion of a time segmentation strategy as opposed to holding an equivalent amount of bond funds.

We can learn a lot from the exhibit. First, after about twenty-seven years of retirement, the personalized time segmentation approach with the critical path offers the highest probabilities of success. However, we can see that the total-returns investing approach with an identically matching asset allocation provides almost identical success rates. This suggests that the success of the strategy can be attributed to its generally more aggressive asset allocation, rather than any unique contribution provided by the bond ladder. Nonetheless, the higher success rate is notable.

Moving down, a simple fixed asset allocation total-returns approach shows up next in terms of its ability to support retirement income. This is important to note, since this strategy is more indicative of what a retiree may use if not choosing a time segmentation approach.

Next we observe the market-based time segmentation approach. While it underperforms relative to the fixed asset allocation total-returns case, the time segmentation version does noticeably better than its total-returns counterpart with the same asset allocation. This suggests that the market-based approach is providing a unique way to reduce sequence risk relative to an equivalent total-returns portfolio. It avoids selling stocks after a stock market downturn.

Finally, the automatic rolling ladder time segmentation approach performs noticeably worse than other strategies, including a total-returns strategy with a matching dynamic asset allocation. The reason is that this strategy more quickly drains the growth portfolio, reduces the stock allocation, and increases the sequence-of-returns risk as more pressure is placed on distributions for the growth portfolio.

We can understand this by considering distribution rates for the second year of retirement while including a simple assumption that the market return in the first year of retirement was sufficient to precisely offset the first-year distribution, and that interest rates do not change from their initial 2.45

percent level in year two. These simplifying assumptions will illustrate the point without a loss of generality. For the total-returns portfolio, the portfolio distribution in year two after the 2 percent COLA is $40,800. This represents 4.08 percent from a $1 million portfolio. Meanwhile, for the time segmentation strategy, after building the bond ladder, the growth portfolio has $608,000 left. The distribution from this portfolio is the amount needed to support spending in year eleven. This is $40,000 with eleven years of 2 percent COLAs, then discounted for ten years by the 2.45 percent discount rate. This is $39,043, which reflects a much higher 6.42 percent distribution rate from the remaining growth portfolio. The automatic rolling ladder approach does not provide discretion to avoid extending the bond ladder, and for the example illustrated here, it ends up forcing too much distribution pressure on the remaining growth portfolio to be an effective strategy. It actually enhances sequence-of-returns risk.

The total-returns approach with matching dynamic asset allocation performs a bit better since it does not force the distribution rate as high so quickly, but this asset allocation cannot support spending as well as a fixed 60.8 percent stock allocation. When the portfolio is endangered, the strategy pushes the stock allocation down, which is effectively locking failure into place for a greater number of the simulated market scenarios.

It is difficult to argue that time segmentation by itself provides a superior investing strategy for retirees. The superior results appear to be attributed to the dynamic asset allocation that results from coupling the critical path to a time segmentation strategy to create a personalized rolling ladder. However, the results are nearly equivalent for a total-returns approach with the same dynamic asset allocation. That suggests that the more aggressive asset allocation is primarily responsible for the overperformance. This strategy could be recommended for retirees who would otherwise reject a more aggressive total-returns investing approach but are comfortable with the argument that a more aggressive allocation is justified when the bond ladder is implemented. Of course, in some cases with this strategy, the bond ladder depletes, and the retiree may be left with 100 percent stocks in the latter part of retirement (though heirs may be fine with that). For investors who are unpersuaded by this argument and the empirical tests that confirm it, the strategy is tough to recommend.

Exhibit 7.21

Probability of Success for Different Investment Strategies in Retirement

To Support an Initial $40,000 Spending Goal with a 2% COLA

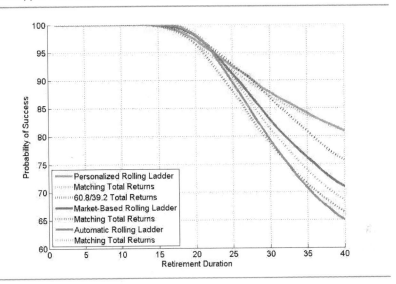

In the end, appeals to time segmentation should be based as strongly on the behavioral aspects of the strategy as on its performance. For retirees who may struggle to stay the course with a total-returns investing approach, the appealing logic of time segmentation could help them maintain better investment discipline in retirement. While time segmentation by itself may not provide a superior investing strategy when compared to a total-returns approach with matching dynamic asset allocation, it is a viable strategy deserving of its place in the retirement income toolkit. Retirees must understand, however, that its implementation will mean dynamic asset allocations and that a clear rule must be implemented for when to extend the bond ladder during retirement.

Further Reading

Bodie, Zvi, and Michael J. Clowes. 2003. *Worry-Free Investing: A Safe Approach to Achieving Your Lifetime Financial Goals.* Upper Saddle River, NJ: Financial Times Prentice Hall. [http://amzn.to/2nDmETg]

Guyton, Jonathan. 2014. "Mirror, Mirror on the Wall..." *Journal of Financial Planning* 24 (10): 28–30.

Huxley, Stephen J., and J. Brent Burns. 2004. *Asset Dedication: How to Grow Wealthy with the Next Generation of Asset Allocation.* New York: McGraw-Hill. [http://amzn.to/2nDsi7J]

Lee, Shelley A. 2010. "Zvi Bodie on Financial Planners and 'First, Do No Harm.'" *Journal of Financial Planning* 20 (2): 16–19.

Roush, Jennifer, William Dudley, and Michelle Steinberg Ezer. 2008. "The Case for TIPS: An Examination of the Costs and Benefits." New York Federal Reserve Bank Staff Reports No. 353 (October).

Shankar, S. G. 2009. "A New Strategy to Guarantee Retirement Income Using TIPS and Longevity Insurance." *Financial Services Review* 18:53–68.

Sit, Harry (The Finance Buff). 2010. *Explore Tips: A Practical Guide to Investing in Treasury Inflation-Protected Securities.* La Vergne, TN: CreateSpace. [http://amzn.to/2mItzph]

Tomlinson, Joseph. 2014. "Why the Risk-Reduction Benefits of Bond Ladders Have Been Overstated." *Advisor Perspectives* (November 18).

Zwecher, Michael J. 2010. *Retirement Portfolios: Theory, Construction, and Management.* Hoboken, NJ: John Wiley. [http://amzn.to/2wh4dI6]

CHAPTER 8

Theory Meets Practice: Developing a Sustainable Spending Strategy

We have covered a number of important topics to help inform decisions about sustainable spending rates from investments and the factors that influence these decisions. But what is the right withdrawal rate and the appropriate asset allocation to use in retirement? The answer obviously depends on personal circumstances. There is no one-size-fits-all solution. This point should be clear throughout the book, and the closest I have come to providing any type of personalized advice thus far was at the end of chapter 6 when I introduced the Retirement CARE Analysis™ and discussed the parameters for PAY Rules that could be applied for conservative, moderate, and aggressive retirees.

This chapter extends the discussion about personalization for your withdrawal rate by explaining how theory meets practice at McLean Asset Management. I will discuss the framework that Alex Murguia, managing principal at McLean Asset Management, and I have developed to advance our clients through the necessary steps to build an efficient retirement income strategy. This includes deciding on a withdrawal rate and asset allocation. Later in this chapter, I will explain the overall logic and thought process of our Retirement Income Optimization framework used to build your personalized RIO-Map™. We have designed this to guide our clients toward personalized solutions. I always stand ready with McLean Asset Management to help readers work through our framework, if you seek personalized assistance beyond what can be provided in book form. Please see http://www.retirementresearcher.com/rio-book for more details.

Remember, the process of building a retirement income strategy involves determining how to best combine retirement income tools to optimize the balance between meeting your retirement goals and *protecting* those goals from the unique risks of retirement. Retirement risks come in many forms, including unknown planning horizons, market volatility, inflation, and spending shocks that can derail your plan. Each of these risks must be managed by combining different income tools and tactics with different relative strengths and weaknesses. No single solution can cover every risk. It requires a framework that incorporates your capacities, flexibility, and emotional comfort. The objective becomes to flesh out the details for how each income tool could contribute to your personal situation, quantify the advantages and disadvantages of different strategies, and determine how to best develop your overall plan. Then we are able to step back and make the decisions about withdrawal rates and asset allocation.

◉ Taking Portfolio Spending out of the Vacuum

Before describing our RIO-Map framework, it is necessary to properly address one further aspect about the research on sustainable spending rates. The Trinity study established the idea of focusing on success rates and failure rates, building into our psyche the idea that one's retirement is a failure if the investment portfolio depletes. This has put too much emphasis on the portfolio and on spending conservatively to keep failure rates low. This is not the whole story for retirement income. Certain circumstances, which we will explore, may allow retirees to accept a higher probability of "failure" and, thus, spend more aggressively from their investment portfolio. Depleting the investment portfolio is not always catastrophic.

We must evaluate the trade-off between reducing spending today to better protect future spending potential and seeking to enjoy the highest possible living standard today even if that creates greater risks for having to make cutbacks later in retirement. Withdrawal rate studies have typically focused on the probability of depleting the portfolio while still alive, without considering what is lost in terms of life satisfaction by using a lower withdrawal rate and spending less. The fact is that when using low withdrawal rates, retirees will typically leave behind a large pot of wealth (unless their retirement returns sequence matches the worst-case scenario). This is not usually included in the analysis, other than to recommend using a higher stock allocation to increase the average legacy.

When taking portfolio spending out of the vacuum, there are four inter-related factors that we must consider:

- Longevity risk aversion: how fearful are you about outliving your investment portfolio in retirement? This is an emotional characteristic unrelated to whether you may outlive your portfolio in an objective sense.
- Reliable income sources: what proportion of your retirement spending is covered through reliable income sources from outside the investment portfolio?
- Spending flexibility: is it possible to reduce portfolio distributions without harming your standard of living in a significant way?
- Availability of reserves: what other resources are available that have not been earmarked to manage spending and can be used to cover contingencies?

These factors all relate to what is an acceptable probability of success, or probability of failure, for the retirement plan. For someone who worries and loses sleep about outliving his or her portfolio, does not have much additional income from outside the portfolio, mostly faces fixed expenses without much room to make cuts, and does not have much in the way of backup reserves, it may be necessary to plan for a quite high probability of success. This will imply using a lower stock allocation and a lower spending rate. However, for someone who has less fear about outliving his or her portfolio, has a number of additional income sources from outside the portfolio, has the flexibility to cut portfolio spending without adversely impacting lifestyle, and has sufficient additional reserves, a higher spending rate accompanied by a lower probability of success could be quite satisfactory and "optimal."

The first to explore this were Moshe Milevsky and Huaxiong Huang in their March/April 2011 *Financial Analysts Journal* article titled "Spending Retirement on Planet Vulcan: The Impact of Longevity Risk Aversion on Optimal Withdrawal Rates." By referring to Planet Vulcan from Star Trek, they mean to discuss the decisions made by a fully rational investor when facing longevity risk but not market risk. The individual does not know how long he or she will live, but the investment returns are known in advance. The retiree has to decide how much to spend from the portfolio each year in the face of an uncertain lifespan. The authors summarize the rational investor's decision-making process as follows: "Wealth managers should advocate dynamic spending in proportion to survival probabilities, adjusted up for exogenous pension income and down for longevity risk aversion."

Several important points are packed into that sentence. The first idea is that retirees should intentionally plan to spend more when they are sure to be alive, while planning for reduced spending later on when survival is less certain. Since survival probabilities decline with age, it is rational (on Planet Vulcan) to spend more earlier on while you are more likely to be alive, and to spend less later on when the probability of still being alive is lower. You should intentionally plan to decrease spending as you age to account for the lower probability of living to each subsequent age. Otherwise, retirees sacrifice too much by cutting spending in early retirement to allow for the same spending much later on when the odds of still being alive are low. With lower future spending, the initial withdrawal rate can be increased. This idea will resonate with some readers, and it will sound like a terrible idea to other readers. Simply, a greater desire to reject this notion implies that someone has greater longevity risk aversion. Even if the probability is low, this person does not want to be in a position to make significant spending cuts or to become a burden to his or her children at an advanced age.

As well, most retirees will have income streams available from outside their financial portfolios ("exogenous pension income"), such as Social Security and other defined-benefit pensions or annuities. These income streams reduce the lifestyle impact of depleting the investment portfolio, which could make a retiree more comfortable with the idea of spending more aggressively than a "safe" spending rate analysis would suggest. Finally, both of these factors will be tempered somewhat to the extent that a retiree is particularly fearful of outliving his or her financial portfolio. Greater longevity risk aversion requires spending less in order to maintain the portfolio over a longer time horizon.

To be more explicit about what all of this means, we must distinguish between "safe" withdrawal rates and "optimal" withdrawal rates. Previous chapters have discussed how the 4 percent rule may be too high for those focused on identifying a sustainable withdrawal rate that will not deplete the portfolio over a thirty-year period. This does not necessarily forbid

Understanding Longevity Risk Aversion

Moshe Milevsky coined the term *longevity risk aversion* to describe the emotions related to how one feels about the possibility of outliving one's investment portfolio in late retirement.

To understand longevity risk aversion, consider which of these statements resonates more with you:

(1) To get the most enjoyment out of retirement, it is optimal to frontload spending and to enjoy a higher standard of living while one is still able to do so.

(2) The thought of needing to significantly reduce my living standard or burdening my children at an advanced age is sufficiently alarming that I would rather maintain a more conservative lifestyle today to better protect against this possibility.

Answering (1) implies low longevity risk aversion, while answering (2) implies high longevity risk aversion. With low longevity risk aversion, the focus is on maximizing today's lifestyle. With higher longevity risk aversion, the focus shifts to protecting lifestyle in the future.

Longevity Risk Aversion

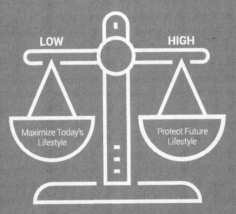

People with high flexibility and low longevity risk aversion are quite willing to let their spending decrease over time to reflect the low probability of survival as they age. Spending starts higher this way. As tolerance to endure spending reductions decreases, initial retirement spending declines in order to raise late-in-life retirement spending. There will be less frontloading of spending.

the use of a 4 percent or higher withdrawal rate. Retirees may still choose higher withdrawal rates as a part of downplaying the potential impact of investment portfolio depletion.

I was part of a research effort with Michael Finke and Duncan Williams to explore these issues in a March 2012 article in the *Journal of Financial Planning* titled "Spending Flexibility and Safe Withdrawal Rates." We also investigated withdrawal rates after adding other income sources from outside the retirement portfolio (such as Social Security and pensions). Also, instead of focusing on the traditional objective of worrying only about using a low failure rate, we sought a better balance between the competing trade-offs for wanting to spend and enjoy more while one is still alive and healthy, against not wanting to deplete the investment portfolio and having to rely only on nonportfolio income sources in later retirement. What we call "spending flexibility" shares a lot with what Milevsky and Huang call "longevity risk aversion," as both concepts are about identifying a willingness to reduce spending if necessary at advanced ages. We also brought asset allocation and randomized investment returns into the mix, seeking to determine both optimal withdrawal rates and optimal asset allocations for different retiree circumstances.

In practical terms, being more longevity risk averse and less flexible with spending means one has a desire to smooth spending over retirement. These retirees care less about increasing spending if markets perform well and instead wish to focus on keeping spending stable if their retirement circumstances combine a long life and a poor sequence of market returns.

We find that people with flexibility about how much they can spend and with more outside sources of income may be willing to accept rather high failure rates as a part of balancing these competing trade-offs. Our study was based on historical US data, which generally leads to a conclusion that 4 percent is a "safe" withdrawal rate because it assumes higher bond yields than are available at present. But we found that with those capital market expectations, the 4 percent retirement withdrawal rate strategy may only be appropriate for more risk-averse retirees with moderate guaranteed income sources. The ability to accept greater failure probabilities means that risk-tolerant retirees will prefer a higher withdrawal rate and a riskier retirement portfolio. A risk-tolerant retiree may prefer a withdrawal rate of between 5 and 7 percent with a guaranteed income of $20,000. As well, the optimal allocation to stocks increases by between ten and thirty percentage points, and the (withdrawal rate increases by between one and two percentage po retirees with a guaranteed income of $60,000 instead of $20,000.

Again, there is an important point to reemphasize here. In one case in the article, we identify a 7 percent withdrawal rate as "optimal." That is not a "safe" withdrawal rate. With the market assumptions in the article, the 7 percent withdrawal rate has a 57 percent chance of failure over a thirty-year retirement. Though it is not safe, it does maximize the overall expected lifetime satisfaction for a fairly flexible retired couple who has a secured income base of $20,000 from Social Security. In our analysis, 7 percent is how the couple could best balance the trade-off between spending more in early retirement and the possibility of then having to spend less later in retirement.

In April 2017, David Blanchett published an article in the *Journal of Financial Planning* titled "The Impact of Guaranteed Income and Dynamic Withdrawals on Safe Initial Withdrawal Rates." His article provides more recent further confirmation for this discussion, and his objective was to quantify the relative impact of different factors on initial spending rates and acceptable probabilities of failure. He investigates how optimal initial withdrawal rates are impacted by the amount of guaranteed income, the extent that the household can adjust spending, the risk of the investment portfolio, the return assumptions used for projections, and the degree of income stability desired by the retiree.

Blanchett finds that the level of guaranteed income is by far the most important factor in explaining optimal spending rates from investments. Withdrawal rates can be up to four percentage points higher across the range of guaranteed income levels he examines. Other findings include that withdrawal rates should be lowered for spending needs that are more fixed in nature and for those with a preference to seek stable spending over time (these are the two aspects of spending flexibility), and withdrawal rates can be higher with higher stock allocations and higher return assumptions. They can be more aggressive because they can afford to have their portfolios fall to zero.

Withdrawal rates, in turn, are linked to probabilities of success. Optimal acceptable success rates do vary quite a bit based on individual circumstances, but as a general rule of thumb, he finds that a 75 percent success rate is generally a more acceptable target than a 90 percent or 95 percent success rate. Again, the most important factor is the level of guaranteed income, as more income from outside the portfolio supports a greater ability to accept a lower success rate for the investment portfolio. It can make sense to choose a retirement income strategy with a much higher failure rate for the investment portfolio than is commonly considered in safe withdrawal rate studies.

A simple focus on a retirement income strategy that applies a low failure rate for the investment portfolio is woefully incomplete. This narrow focus ignores the lost potential enjoyment from spending more even if it means having to cut back later, it ignores how much flexibility retirees may have to cut their spending at a later date, it ignores the availability of other spending resources outside the financial portfolio, it ignores the lowered survival probabilities in late retirement, it ignores any goals to leave a bequest, and it ignores how long the "failure" condition may last. An overreliance on only spending at a "safe" withdrawal rate may unduly sacrifice lifestyle in early retirement. The end result will be that in the majority of cases, retirees will die with a lot of unspent money that they had intended to use to support their lifestyle. Bequests will be unintentionally large at the cost of fully enjoying retirement. Retirees need to be thinking about a more complete model that incorporates all of this when developing their retirement income strategies. Our RIO-Map provides this framework.

◎ Real-World Solutions: The RIO Questionnaire and RIO-Map™ Construction

We have finished covering the relevant theory. Now we are ready to implement a practical framework to develop a retirement income strategy. At McLean Asset Management, we have developed the RIO Questionnaire and RIO-Map as our practical framework for achieving retirement success. RIO stands for Retirement Income Optimization. This RIO framework effectively guides the decision-making process for our clients. It is worth explaining this process and framework, as it provides a practical approach for answering the very personalized questions related to choosing an appropriate withdrawal rate and asset allocation strategy.

The process starts by taking the RIO Questionnaire. This is done online. There are a lot of questions, but they can be answered quickly based on your instincts and perceptions. The whole questionnaire should take about thirty minutes to complete. At this stage there is no need to refer to any financial statements. That can come later when we further explore your funded ratio (more on this later). It is amazing how much can be learned by just answering questions based on your instincts, views, priorities, and knowledge base. The RIO Questionnaire is not a quest for perfection but a first concrete step to make sure you get moving in the right direction. It provides the information needed to build your road map and to find the relevant tools and tactics to investigate more carefully in order to craft a complete and effective retirement income strategy. Exhibit 8.1 provides screenshots for a sampling of the various components within the RIO Questionnaire.

After you complete the RIO Questionnaire, we will use your answers to achieve the following:

1. Determine and prioritize your financial goals in retirement between longevity, lifestyle, liquidity, and legacy. Your goal prioritization will

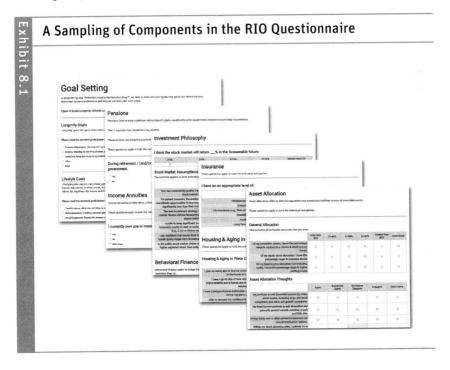

Exhibit 8.1

A Sampling of Components in the RIO Questionnaire

help you know whether you identify more with probability-based or safety-first retirement approaches as outlined in chapter 1.

2. Investigate the relevance, the use, and your knowledge about a variety of tactics and tools related to reliable income, the diversified portfolio, reserves, and retirement income funding.

3. Identify your exposure to various retirement risks. These risks are categorized as personal risks, external risks, and capital market risks.

4. Outline the strengths and weaknesses within your current approach.

5. Provide the foundation that, along with the funded ratio that quantifies assets and liabilities, allows for the construction of your RIO-Map.

6. Identify potential gaps in your retirement income plan and suggest next steps to make sure you have a clear path ahead in terms of developing a unified strategy based on best practices for retirement income to meet your retirement goals and manage your retirement risks.

The RIO-Map also provides a documented plan to help survivors who may have less financial sophistication than the one generally in charge of the family finances.

While every map will be different in terms of the sizes and holdings within the different boxes, Exhibit 8.2 shows the general structure of the RIO-

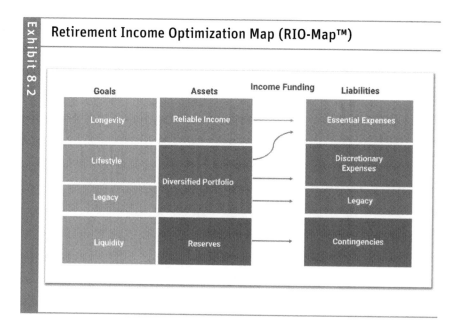

Exhibit 8.2

Retirement Income Optimization Map (RIO-Map™)

Goals	Assets	Income Funding	Liabilities
Longevity	Reliable Income		Essential Expenses
Lifestyle	Diversified Portfolio		Discretionary Expenses
Legacy			Legacy
Liquidity	Reserves		Contingencies

Map. We break the map down into four parts: (1) Your Goals, (2) Assets, (3) Income Funding Plan (the arrows), and (4) Liabilities.

The RIO Questionnaire guides you through a series of components to touch on all the pieces of the RIO-Map. We consider these pieces as follows.

Goals

We start with your financial goals for life. This framework is about being purposeful with your retirement; hence we start with where you want to go. There are countless possible financial goals, which we simplify into the "Four Ls of Retirement."

First, longevity goals center on the lifetime sustainability of the core or essential expenses in retirement. These goals largely relate to housing, health care, basic living expenses, and maintaining a basic level of financial independence without becoming a burden to others.

Next, lifestyle goals relate to how you want to live your life and maintain your desired overall standard of living in retirement. Components of lifestyle may be a bit more discretionary in nature, including items such as travel and leisure, self-improvement activities, social engagement, and vicarious enjoyments such as helping with tuition for family members. These goals require maximizing your spending power in such a way that your spending can remain consistent and sustainable within an accepted degree of risk that these expenses may need to be scaled back at certain points in retirement. For these goals, there may be a sense of seeking more upside growth potential at the risk of downside losses at a level that exceeds what is feasible with the longevity goals.

Third, legacy goals typically relate to any financial impact you wish to leave on your family and community. These goals include leaving assets for subsequent generations or to charities. This also involves being able to contribute in other significant ways with your time and talent to impactful activities. The thought of "leaving behind" a legacy is a consistent theme. As a caveat, legacy goals can also be met while you are living.

Finally, liquidity goals relate to the objective to maintain additional assets not earmarked for other goals that can be tapped quickly to provide funds for unexpected contingencies. Such contingencies relate to anything falling outside the planned retirement budget. Possibilities include supporting family members during emergencies, major repairs or home improvement necessities, resources to help with an unexpected illness or death, potential long-term care needs, renovating your home to allow for aging in place, and other life transitions.

The questionnaire guides you toward prioritizing the relative importance of these four goals in your life. Once you prioritize these goals, you can assess and prioritize the tactics for your RIO-Map to best meet the goals and manage their risks.

Assets and Liabilities

The next column of the RIO-Map is for household assets. Assets consist of more than just investment accounts, as we include every resource at the household's disposal for meeting retirement liabilities. Assets will be the means to connect your goals to your liabilities. We need to properly position these assets with different tactics and tools. The goals can be mapped directly to liabilities, and the available assets are what we use to build the map and meet retirement expenses as expressed through the goals. While liabilities represent the fourth column on the RIO-Map, we do not need a separate section about them. Liabilities are simply the numerical quantification of the retiree financial goals. We will focus instead on how assets match to these goals/liabilities. This bigger picture makes clear that we are focusing on more than just the investment portfolio. Those without adequate reliable income and reserves may, in effect, have to behave like more risk-averse investors with regard to the investment portfolio, but it is important to move beyond investments with the planning.

Assets are divided among reliable income, the diversified portfolio, and reserves. Reliable income resources are used to draw consistent income to meet longevity goals and to cover essential expenses. Reliable income answers the question, "How can I create a base of secure income in retirement that is safeguarded from market volatility?" Tactics within this section include Social Security claiming, annuities, traditional pensions, bond income ladders, and potentially continued employment. In some cases, access to home equity through a reverse mortgage may also be a source of reliable income. In combination, these tactics make up what we refer to as the "safety-first" portion of your assets. Those worried about longevity will place a greater focus here.

The RIO Questionnaire determines your knowledge about, use of, and relevance of these different tactics for supporting reliable income. If your longevity goals are a high priority, then you want to make sure you have a well-thought-out reliable income section within your RIO-Map and that you have filled in any gaps to protect essential spending in retirement from market volatility. As relevant, we will work together to analyze the possibilities and your decisions related to six basic reliable income sources, including Social Security claiming, annuities, company pensions and other employer benefits, bond income ladders, employment or other income-earning opportunities in retirement, and the potential role of a reverse mortgage. We are looking for complementary tactics to meet your needs, and it would be a rare case when all of these tactics are implemented at the same time.

The next asset section of the RIO-Map is the diversified portfolio. The diversified portfolio can be used most effectively to meet lifestyle and legacy goals, which translate into the liabilities related to discretionary expenses and legacy. Here we review your investments as well as your views, attitudes, and knowledge about investing. While there are numerous investment strategies and many ways to construct a diversified portfolio, you want to make sure yours is compatible with the framework needed when investing for retirement income.

There is more at stake here than just identifying an asset allocation. We seek to determine how well you are positioned to effectively capture market rates of return, how you have practically managed your portfolio in the past, and what are your strengths and weaknesses in investment knowledge or application that could lead to good or poor outcomes. Specifically, we need to consider:

1. *Investment philosophy:* What is your investment philosophy, and how has it been applied to your portfolio? It is important to have a good understanding of the long-term determinants of market returns based on scientific foundations, not consumer misinformation. Have you paid attention to investment costs and tax efficiency? Have you focused on lower-cost passive investments that support a better

chance for success, or have you instead focused on chasing returns and on whatever is in vogue? How informed are you about investment principles, and have you effectively put your knowledge into practice? Have you shifted your mind-set from wealth accumulation to retirement income distribution and how the goals shift from maximizing wealth to ensuring consistent spending in the face of reduced risk capacity?

2. *Investment behaviors:* How aware and prone are you to various human biases that can negatively affect your investment behaviors? We consider both knowledge and vulnerability. While we may be aware of the proper investment philosophy to have, implementing it in light of our own biases and human tendencies is another matter. You want to acknowledge, to the best of your ability, how your behavioral biases may or may not affect your investment decision-making for retirement income. We discuss some of these potential behavioral biases in chapter 9. Does your portfolio have the right level of risk to help you better manage your biases?

3. *Asset allocation views:* What are your views on constructing a properly diversified portfolio and your ability to put these views into practice? Although your investment philosophy may cover a wide range of thoughts, you need to know how to put it all together to construct an actual portfolio specifically for retirement income. You want to make sure you are positioned to effectively capture the market rates of return you need through proper exposure of the various sources of investment risk. It is important to have a clear strategy and not just a collection of funds assembled in an ad hoc and piecemeal fashion. Also, are you placing your investment holdings inside the proper account structures to maximize tax efficiency? Do you have any concentrated positions that need to be diversified?

4. *Practical application of investment management:* How well can you manage your portfolio on an ongoing basis? This specifically involves the ability to maintain the original intention of the portfolio over time and to periodically adjust the portfolio according to changes in your life. This includes rebalancing, active tax management for asset location and distribution management, assessing style drift, and other factors that slowly creep up and cause unnecessary friction in your portfolio if they are not frequently monitored and adjusted.

The diversified portfolio portion of the RIO-Map is about making sure that you have a unified strategy that maximizes your retirement preferences. It needs to be well coordinated with your reliable income and reserves. It is important to get an early start in making sure that the portfolio is in proper shape for retirement, but we should also consider final tweaks about the overall asset allocation after all the other components of the RIO-Map have been fully implemented.

The final component of assets is the reserves. We identify how well positioned you are to absorb any potential external shocks to your retirement income streams and how well you have planned asset transfer strategies. Reserves are aimed to meet the goal of supporting liquidity, which can be used to meet contingencies in retirement. Reserves are unique as well in that many types of reserve assets we analyze may serve to reduce the potential size of the contingency liability box rather than simply increase the size of the reserve asset box. As long as the size of the reserve asset box is aligned with the size of the contingency liability, the absolute size of these two boxes is less relevant. The idea is that reserve assets can be used to limit the impact of different potential contingencies in retirement. As a simple example, a long-term care insurance policy can offset a portion of the spending associated with experiencing a long-term care need, reducing the size of this contingency. Contingencies include external shocks ranging from unexpected job loss, an unexpected death in the household, a chronic illness diagnosis, a long-term care need, and more. Those highlighting liquidity as a high retirement priority will focus on how to best deploy their reserves.

The spending shocks that can accompany these contingencies can disrupt a retirement plan if there are not sufficient reserves in place to manage such risks and costs. Reserve assets may include varying combinations of cash and income, insurance policies, housing and the ability to age in place, family assistance and obligations, taking care of one's health, having a team of retirement professionals, and having estate planning basics covered. Having extra investment assets available beyond what is earmarked to cover other goals is also a source of reserve assets. It is important to understand that for an asset to be available to fund contingencies, it cannot be earmarked to cover a different liability. Otherwise, if it is spent on something unexpected, it will no longer be available to cover what was originally intended.

There is another subtle point about the importance of reserves that relates to longevity risk aversion. When relying on an investment portfolio to cover retirement expenses, another reason why people may spend less could be that they have a somewhat amorphous mental account in their mind about using assets. They have earmarked the same pool of investments to cover both lifestyle and liquidity, not clearly distinguishing how these objectives can be separated. Thus, in a sense, they worry that all of their investments must provide liquidity for contingencies, and they spend less in response. They want a very high probability of success for their spending plan, because they fear dipping into this pool of assets for contingencies as well, in a way not modeled within their financial plan. With the RIO-Map framework, we can be more explicit about the available reserve assets, which may allow retirees to feel more comfortable to go ahead and spend to support their lifestyle goals more completely.

As mentioned, some of the reserve assets we analyze are intended to help reduce the potential size of the contingency liability box, rather than purely increasing the size of the reserve asset box. For instance, having a strong network of family and community support in place reduces the need for large expenditures for care in the event of various health, cognition, or frailty shocks. Likewise, taking care of your health and considering your family health history are another set of important factors that affects the size of potential health expenses. Laying a foundation to support aging in place can help reduce the potential costs of late-in-life institutional living. As well, maintaining proper insurance coverage for health, long-term care, property, and one's life also can limit the impact of spending shocks related to these events. Being able to view these reserves within the RIO-Map could help with any psychological angst one feels about "not having enough."

Two other matters we consider within reserves may not sound like "reserve assets," though they also help control risks related to various retirement contingencies. These include having a team of financial professionals in place, and taking care of basic estate planning tasks. For financial professionals, a financial advisor is able to serve as a "quarterback" to coordinate actions between various providers in order to ensure a consistent strategy on all fronts. Other professionals who may be part of this team include accountants, elder-law attorneys, and long-term care coordinators. As for estate planning, aspects to consider include reviewing one's values and objectives for a legacy plan, having a streamlined financial plan in place for survivors, properly titling assets and reviewing beneficiary designations, and having proper legal documents in place including a will and medical power of attorney. We consider these matters as part of reserves because of their role in managing potential contingencies and preventing costly mistakes from being made.

The RIO Questionnaire prioritizes the importance of reserves in your thinking, and it also surveys your use of, knowledge about, and relevance of these various tactics and tools for your plan.

Retirement Income Funding

The RIO Questionnaire next covers the retirement income funding portion of the RIO-Map, which is expressed in the next column as a series of arrows connecting the retirement assets to the retirement liabilities. This is where you assess the path to your destination. Here you want to explore how well it all comes together, whether you are "on track," and what changes, if any, need to be made to your retirement journey. This is the financial planning portion of your RIO-Map. It is the map's compass to help set you on your course to determine if your preferred tactics are more probability-based or safety-first. It is about making sure that assets are used efficiently to meet goals and cover liabilities. It is also about making sure that you are ready to make any necessary changes over time as your situation and plans evolve.

This analysis moves well beyond just considering the investment portfolio and its asset allocation. For the retirement income funding portion, specific issues we look at include your flexibility about changing your spending habits to achieve other objectives (retirement income flexibility), your outlined plan for success and the coordination of your chosen tactics (retirement funding analysis), your current views about the various financial planning strategies and tactics used to fund retirement income (goal funding strategies), and your understanding of the link between your retirement income strategy and your goals (financial planning context).

How do your chosen tactics complement each other in your retirement income framework? Have you optimized the tactics within reliable income in light of the other sections of the RIO-Map and their underlying tactics? You really want to take a step back and see the bigger picture here to get a better sense of how all the moving pieces can best fit together.

Because retirees generally will still have a number of lifestyle and legacy goals that they want to accomplish otheir RIO-Map, it is frequently important to maintain investments in the stock market. However, proper planning will include a layering in of other income sources to provide alternative methods of retirement income funding that help to derisk the retirement from the impact of sequence-of-returns and longevity risks. Only focusing on the investment portfolio can lead to suboptimal outcomes. With this retirement income funding framwork in place, you no longer have to hope for the best from your investments. Although market returns are still important, the RIO-Map has identified ways to buffer market volatility and other external shocks while still achieving your retirement income success.

⊚ Next Steps for the RIO Questionnaire Results and the RIO-Map™

Especially for retirement income funding, the RIO Questionnaire provides a beginning of the journey rather than the destination. More work is to be done. The RIO-Map is not just used at the start of the journey, but it is a continuing reference point that shifts as your priorities, needs, and desires evolve over time.

Scoring the RIO Questionnaire

After you complete the RIO Questionnaire, we will analyze your answers to determine where you stand with respect to various aspects of retirement income planning. As a part of this, we first apply sensitivity filters to your answers. It is possible for two households to answer their RIO-Map questions in a similar manner but still have different scores, strengths, weaknesses, and RIO-Maps. This is because we apply sensitivities such as your goal priorities, age, marital status, proximity to retirement, and other factors to ensure your map is specific to you. Your score will depend on the various milestones in your life. As a quick example, someone who is fifty-five will have different views toward Social Security than someone who is sixty-one, and that should be reflected in your scoring.

Exhibit 8.3

Scoring the RIO Questionnaire

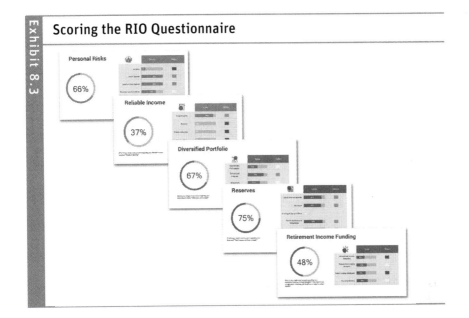

Your RIO numerical scores generally translate into one of three outcomes. For a given tactic or risk, you either are on track, have the potential for improvement, or can otherwise rule out the issue or option as not being applicable to your situation. For instance, if you do not have a traditional company pension, you would receive a low score for the tactic, but we would be clear that this just is not an option for your case. Nonetheless, without a company pension, it would be important to further consider other sources of reliable income.

After applying the sensitivity filters, we are able to score each subsection individually and then combine them to find your retirement income optimization score for each section. Because we take into account your personal situation, objectives, implementation, and knowledge of these topics, we are able to determine the values for each question in a manner that maximizes your retirement income opportunity set. This provides us with a standardized view of where you stand on every tactic, tool, or factor within the retirement income framework. Exhibit 8.3 provides one example of what this may look like.

Determining Strengths and Weaknesses

The RIO scores determine your relative strengths and weaknesses, and these will then be presented in the order of prioritization of your personal goals. In other words, if your goal priorities center on longevity, we will first review your strengths and weaknesses from the reliable income portion of the map, as it is most relevant for you. We will continue to work in this stepwise order until we worked through the RIO-Map. Exhibit 8.4 provides an example of how we present your strengths and weakness.

Once we have identified your strengths and weaknesses, we are ready to start quantifying and building your plan of action. This action plan is your 180-day plan.

Funded Ratio

For a plan of action, we start with the funded ratio, which is used to quantify the actual monetary value and costs of your goals, assets, and liabilities. This sets the size of the boxes on your RIO-Map, and it sets the stage for moving into the retirement income funding analysis by quantifying any gaps between the related asset and liability components in the map. The purpose of the funded ratio is to determine, on a lifetime basis, whether the retirement assets are large enough to meet the retirement liabilities.

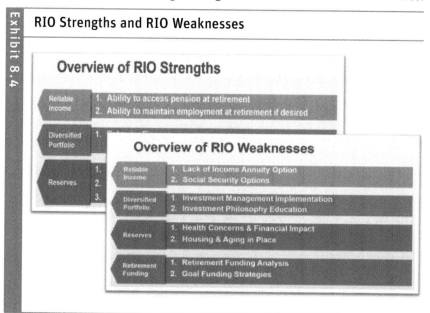

Exhibit 8.4

RIO Strengths and RIO Weaknesses

Overview of RIO Strengths

| Reliable Income | 1. Ability to access pension at retirement |
| | 2. Ability to maintain employment at retirement if desired |

Diversified Portfolio 1.

Reserves 1. 2. 3.

Overview of RIO Weaknesses

Reliable Income	1. Lack of Income Annuity Option
	2. Social Security Options
Diversified Portfolio	1. Investment Management Implementation
	2. Investment Philosophy Education
Reserves	1. Health Concerns & Financial Impact
	2. Housing & Aging in Place
Retirement Funding	1. Retirement Funding Analysis
	2. Goal Funding Strategies

This also helps match the reality of whether your assets are sufficient to meet your retirement goals.

At this stage, you will begin to determine your planned retirement budget. How will it differ from preretirement, how will it adjust for inflation, and how is it divided between essential and discretionary expenses? We will also need to determine the appropriate planning age for your retirement journey based on objective factors like your health status and subjective factors like your longevity risk aversion. We also need a proper accounting of the available assets and the legacy goals, and we can provide estimates about potential contingencies based on your RIO scores. Since there is a great deal of uncertainty about potential contingencies, we will also apply scenario analysis to see how the funded status would be impacted by various spending shocks in retirement. This helps create a more complete retirement balance sheet.

A funded ratio of one means that a retiree has just enough assets to meet his or her liabilities, while overfunded and underfunded individuals have more or less than this, respectively. A nice feature of the funded ratio is that our calculations are made with a simple assumption that investment assets are only allocated to inflation-protected bonds. This lets us see whether you are able to meet your goals without taking market risk, which can provide better context about how much investment risk you may desire or need when determining the right asset allocation for your plan. If you have already won the game by having sufficient assets without taking risk, this can be helpful in deciding just how much risk to take. The funded ratio does not use Monte Carlo simulation. Such simulation comes later when we develop your personal benchmark analysis.

We can consider your funded measures both from the perspective of the overall RIO-Map and for different subcomponents of the map. An important output of this analysis is that it also provides the relative sizes of the different components of RIO-Map. This allows us to look for gaps, such as whether there is sufficient reliable income to cover essential expenses, or whether sufficient reserve assets are available to cover contingencies. This will guide further analysis within retirement income funding to find strategic allocations to help balance and optimize your RIO-Map.

Portfolio Structure and Implementation

It is important to get an early start to identify the appropriate market risk factors and build your diversified, low-cost, passively managed multi-asset-class investment portfolio for retirement. Even if your portfolio was set up with proper care in the past, has it slowly evolved and transformed away from what is appropriate for you now? And does it need further refinements as part of the transition into retirement? Determining asset allocation should really be the last step in the process of fully completing the Retirement CARE Analysis and the retirement income funding portion of the RIO-Map. But it is important make sure the portfolio is mostly right for you as other steps are being completed. At the end of the process, it will still be possible to engage in any additional fine-tuning.

This section provides an overview of the important types of questions to answer about portfolio construction and implementation as a part of the diversified portfolio section of the RIO-Map. For instance, are you comfortable with your portfolio and its potential volatility? Can you stick with it during market downturns? Specifically, how did you respond to the financial crisis of 2008? In March 2009 were you still holding on to your stock positions, or had you abandoned them? This is important for determining the right exposure to market volatility with regard to your emotional comfort and ability to implement your knowledge about investing.

As well, was your portfolio developed with a clear intent and purpose, or was it built in a piecemeal fashion over time without any clear direction or overall strategy for guiding its component pieces? Are there any concentrated positions, or is the portfolio properly diversified? Is it worthwhile to consolidate the number of your investment accounts and vehicles in order to simplify matters? Especially, if you have invested in a variety of actively managed funds, they almost surely are averaging out to underperform market indexes due to their fees and lack of coherent aggregate strategy. What fees are you paying on your underlying investment vehicles? Have you invested in lower-cost passive investments, or in higher-cost actively managed investments that generally end up underperforming over time due to their higher costs?

Have you addressed tax efficiency with your portfolio decisions? In terms of preparing your portfolio for retirement income, we must consider the cost basis and tax implications of any portfolio changes. This may require a gradual implementation of changes to reduce the tax impact. For tax efficiency, we consider how to best locate assets between taxable, tax-deferred, and tax-free accounts, as well as where to take distributions from in order to best manage taxes. Tax efficiency in retirement also requires careful implementation of tax bracket management, which involves not wasting space to pay taxes when it is possible at a relatively low tax bracket, in order to avoid having to pay taxes later at a higher tax bracket. We must also consider RMDs as part of a long-term plan to manage taxes. Strategies include potentially converting IRA assets to a Roth IRA and taking portfolio distributions in such a manner that tax-free resources are used to obtain additional distributions that would otherwise be taxed at a higher rate.

Personal Benchmark Analysis©

Another step in the journey is to develop your Personal Benchmark Analysis. This is how we approach the common topic of using Monte Carlo simulations to test a financial plan. To expand on the funded ratio analysis, the Personal Benchmark Analysis tests whether the distributions required from your investment portfolio to meet your spending goals will be sustainable to your planning age under different simulated market return sequences. This step incorporates market volatility and asset allocation to test the overall viability of your financial plan. It reports probability of success, and various strategic allocations for the RIO-Map can potentially change this probability of success. With the inStream software originally developed at McLean Asset Management, your investment performance is aggregated, and your Personal Benchmark Analysis is rerun behind the scenes on a nightly basis with the daily market updates. Your advisor is provided with an alert if anything about your financial plan falls outside of the thresholds you set. If you tend to worry about the markets, this may help to reduce your worry, because you can be confident that the plan is being tested daily, and you will be notified if there is some corrective action that should be taken.

Strategic Allocations for the RIO-Map™

Strategic allocations for the RIO-Map is a broad and important process of using the RIO scores to identify where further attention is needed to improve your retirement plan. The issues we will investigate were described earlier when discussing the different components of the RIO-Map, and this will not be reviewed again in detail here. Briefly, though, we further analyze the role for different tools and tactics in your RIO-Map for assets (reliable income, diversified portfolio, reserves) and for retirement income funding.

Though not all tactics will be relevant for each retiree, the possibilities for reliable income consist of Social Security, annuities, pensions and employer benefits, bond ladders, continued employment, and a reverse mortgage. The diversified portfolio is covered with the early portfolio structure and implementation steps and will again be revisited at the end of the process with the Retirement CARE Analysis. As for reserves, we review cash and excess financial assets, insurance, housing and aging in place, family assistance and obligations, your health outlook, a team of financial planning professionals, and estate planning basics. Then we revisit the steps of retirement income funding. We assess these tools and tactics in a complementary manner to look for potential efficiencies and improvements within your plan. We also evaluate and address gaps within your RIO-Map as identified with the funded ratio analysis.

The 180-Day Progress Plan

We want to be as efficient as possible in order to hit the ground quickly and get some wins under your belt. Working through the entire process will take time. To prevent procrastination and also to prevent a sense of being overwhelmed, we will provide a series of steps to accomplish in the first 180 days. This helps you address the more salient items on your journey. Exhibit 8.5 provides an example of how this may look.

Exhibit 8.5

The 180-Day Progress Plan

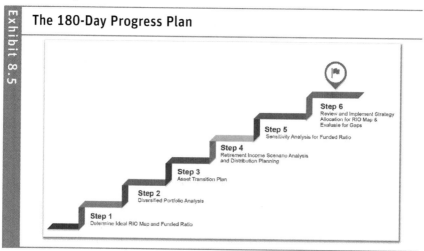

Step 6
Review and Implement Strategy Allocation for RIO Map & Evaluate for Gaps

Step 5
Sensitivity Analysis for Funded Ratio

Step 4
Retirement Income Scenario Analysis and Distribution Planning

Step 3
Asset Transition Plan

Step 2
Diversified Portfolio Analysis

Step 1
Determine Ideal RIO Map and Funded Ratio

Exhibit 8.6

The Retirement CARE Analysis™

Capacities (Resiliencies)

Reliable income	What proportion of your spending goals are covered through reliable income sources from outside the investment portfolio that will not be diminished by market downturns?
Spending flexibility	Is it possible to reduce portfolio distributions by making simple lifestyle adjustments without significantly harming your standard of living?
Funded ratio	Are there sufficient assets to meet retirement goals without taking market risk? Is there excess discretionary wealth, or are you underfunded with respect to goals?
Availability of reserves and exposures to spending shocks	How much exposure is there to large and uncertain expenses? What insurance policies or other reserves are available to manage these shocks? Are there buffer assets? How is home equity used within the plan?

Aspirations (Goals)

Lifestyle	What is the retirement budget? How does it change over time? How closely connected is it to consumer price inflation?
Legacy	What are the legacy goals? How important is legacy relative to other goals?

Returns (Assumptions)

Capital market expectations	What are reasonable market return assumptions for different asset classes and inflation to guide simulation of the retirement income plan? How are returns impacted by investor behavior, fees, taxes, and investment vehicle choices?

Emotional Comfort (Constraints)

Traditional risk aversion	How much short-term portfolio volatility can you stomach before it affects your sleep and leads you to panic and change course if markets are down?
Longevity risk aversion	How fearful are you about outliving your investment portfolio? Greater concern means more longevity risk aversion, implying that one should choose a higher planning age.
Financial tool aversion	Are you willing to consider different types of retirement tools, such as annuities and reverse mortgages, or are some tools simply nonstarters for you?
Susceptibility to behavioral mistakes	When it comes to investing and long-term planning for complex situations, how prone are you to making a variety of behavioral mistakes? Will you be able to stick to your financial plan?
Financial plan complexity	What is the acceptable degree of complexity and involvement needed to manage your finances? Do you enjoy the planning process, or would you prefer to outsource management to others? Would you prefer more simple set-it-and-forget-it types of solutions?
Financial savvy of all household members	How is financial planning knowledge and savvy distributed among household members? What is the degree of vulnerability of others in the household if the more financially savvy member experiences cognitive decline or an unexpected death?

⊙ Retirement CARE Analysis™: Reviewing Asset Allocation in the Context of the Overall Retirement Plan and RIO-Map™

How should a retiree choose an initial spending rate and asset allocation? Thus far, I have discussed the remaining theory related to thinking about the investment portfolio within the context of the retiree's overall asset base. This built on previous chapters, which investigated the classical withdrawal rate studies and the implications of changing various assumptions within those studies. Then I described the practical framework we developed at McLean Asset Management to guide real retirees through this process.

In chapter 6, I introduced the Retirement CARE Analysis as the way to begin thinking about an appropriate personalized withdrawal strategy in retirement. To conclude this chapter, it is worthwhile to revisit the Retirement CARE Analysis, as it effectively summarizes everything we have discussed. It provides the details for how to decide on the aggressiveness of both spending and asset allocation within a retirement income plan. Because these matters have already been discussed, at this time I will simply review the Retirement CARE Analysis in Exhibit 8.6. This is a listing of the important factors to consider.

These matters are highly personalized, and personalized advice cannot be provided through a book. However, this chapter has outlined a framework, in both theoretical and practical terms, for how to think about the decisions regarding sustainable spending rates from investments and appropriate asset allocation for retirement. If you seek additional guidance, I would encourage you to give the RIO Questionnaire a try (http://www.retirementresearcher.com/rio-book).

Further Reading

Blanchett, David M. 2017. "The Impact of Guaranteed Income and Dynamic Withdrawals on Safe Initial Withdrawal Rates." *Journal of Financial Planning* 30 (4): 42–52.

Finke, Michael, Wade D. Pfau, and Duncan Williams. 2012. "Spending Flexibility and Safe Withdrawal Rates." *Journal of Financial Planning* 25 (3): 44–51.

Milevsky, Moshe A., and Huaxiong Huang. 2011. "Spending Retirement on Planet Vulcan: The Impact of Longevity Risk Aversion on Optimal Withdrawal Rates." *Financial Analysts Journal* 67 (2): 45–58.

CHAPTER 9

Value of Good Financial Decision-Making in Retirement

In the previous chapters, I sought to provide context for how a retirement income strategy can extend beyond traditional wealth management to better manage the many risks of retirement.

As we approach the end of this story, this final chapter will turn more toward the process of good financial decision-making for retirement and the benefits it can provide to retirees. I will start by explaining more about my own background within the financial services profession, including the roles I play as an educator at the American College of Financial Services and my Retirement Researcher website, and my role in providing financial planning services as a principal at McLean Asset Management.

My career decisions do incentivize me to encourage readers to work with financial planners. However, my primary focus is on education, and this is true going back to the days when I started the Retirement Researcher blog while still working as an economics professor in Japan with no connection to the financial services world. I am glad to guide readers toward high-quality advisors who can provide net positive impacts on their personal finances. I am also glad to empower and educate readers on how to do this on your own.

I continue the chapter by describing how good decisions impact a financial plan relative to poor decisions. Then I will describe the challenges that we as humans must overcome to make good financial decisions. I have made an effort to provide sufficient information for individuals to construct retirement income plans on their own. However, I recognize that some readers may decide they do not have the time, patience, or inclination to do it all on their own. Thus, I also explain how the financial advisory profession works and what McLean Asset Management is able to do to help you build an efficient retirement income plan.

● How I Fit into the Financial Services Profession

From 2003 to 2013, I worked as an economics professor in Tokyo, at a university that primarily served graduate students who worked as government officials in developing and emerging market countries. My research during those years centered on public pension systems in countries such as Vietnam, Thailand, and Pakistan. My interest in finance was mostly prompted by managing my own personal finances, and reading books like *A Random Walk Down Wall Street* led me to become a passive investor with a focus on low costs and a long-term mind-set.

By 2009, I started to become serious about moving my family back to the United States. I started studying for the CFA examinations in 2009 as a way to make myself more marketable for US employers. In 2010, I obtained access to a data set that provided financial market returns from a variety of countries extending back to 1900. I don't recall exactly how I first came across William Bengen's 4 percent rule for retirement income, but I believe it was mentioned briefly in the CFA curriculum. I thought it could be interesting to see how the 4 percent rule would have performed in other countries and not just the United States. I finished an article on the topic in September 2010 as my first entry at my new Retirement Researcher blog and submitted it for review at the *Journal of Financial Planning*.

The article was published in December 2010. For a traditional academic, this publication was remarkable for two reasons. First, publication took place three months after submission, which is extremely fast compared to the academic world, where it could take journals one to three years to publish articles. Second, I received reader feedback, indicating that the article was actually being read and not just collecting dust on university library bookshelves. I was hooked and made a full transition from economics to personal financial planning. I published a number of additional research articles about retirement income in the *Journal of Financial Planning* in 2011 and 2012 and even won the journal's award for the most influential article published in 2011, while still living and working in Japan.

The American College of Financial Services

As a part of my ongoing efforts to return to the United States, I interviewed with the American College in August 2012. I accepted an offer to become a professor of retirement income, teaching primarily in the new PhD program on financial and retirement planning, starting in April 2013. The American College was building the Retirement Income Certified Professional (RICP) designation and making the relatively new field of retirement income into a top priority for the future. I believe that my job title at the American College is unique.

Originally created by Solomon Huebner, a University of Pennsylvania professor in the Wharton School who sought to professionalize the life insurance industry, the American College dates back to 1927. The American College created the CLU designation for insurance agents, and for many years most of its students were from the insurance industry. In recent years, the American College has expanded to provide education for all of the financial services profession, though the university still carries an aura of being intertwined with the insurance industry, and certainly many of its students and funding come from the insurance side of financial services profession.

The American College pioneered the RICP designation for financial advisors later in 2012. It provides fair and comprehensive coverage to the different schools of thought and philosophies about retirement income planning, including investments and insurance approaches. I know this because I helped develop the curriculum. The American College is also one of the leading educators for the CFP program, which historically is connected more to the investments and fiduciary side of the ongoing financial services debate. Today, the American College serves both sides of the financial services profession and seeks to provide ongoing leadership in retirement income planning.

McLean Asset Management

In late 2012, I also began a correspondence with Alex Murguia, who is the CEO of McLean Asset Management, headquartered in McLean, Virginia. At first, he brought me in to work with inStream Solutions, an independent financial planning software company he developed for advisory firms when he was not satisfied with any of the existing financial planning software available for financial advisors. The software can dramatically improve the efficiency of financial advisors and help ensure that all of their clients' financial plans are updated and monitored on a daily basis.

Though inStream is fully independent of McLean, I worked and still work as director of retirement research at the company, having helped build a safe savings rate module, create distribution rules to guide retirement withdrawals, develop ways to compare financial plans with metrics going beyond the simple probability of failure, build reasonable capital market assumptions to guide the Monte Carlo simulations, and implement a Social Security calculator.

As I worked with inStream, I learned more about McLean and came to understand that McLean is a fee-only fiduciary firm that truly understands the retirement income problem. They understand the need to build efficient retirement income strategies that may reduce assets managed in the short term but will help their clients the most in the long term. McLean also shares my interest in education, as Alex holds a PhD himself. In 2014, I joined McLean Asset Management as a principal at the firm. Working with McLean provides the resources to strengthen my Retirement Researcher website and help get my message out to a wider audience, with an understanding that education is the primary goal.

Retirement Researcher

I created my Retirement Researcher blog in September 2010. As my blog has developed over the years, I have still tried to maintain the original mission stated on earlier versions of the site: RetirementResearcher.com provides independent, data-driven, and research-based information about retirement income planning. The website is geared toward providing unbiased information about building efficient retirement income strategies and is willing to cross between the various silos of the financial services profession. I outlined in chapter 1 how there are two completely different schools of thought about retirement income planning: the probability-based approach and the safety-first approach. My website seeks to provide an understanding about both so readers can better determine the best approach for their personal circumstances, and McLean Asset Management shares this objective with me. Originally, I thought my website would be of most interest for sophisticated consumers who are approaching retirement and have a good understanding of the basics of investments and insurance. But I have found that this education is equally valued by financial advisors, and so my audience is split between the two groups.

There are plenty of financial education websites aimed at consumers, but they tackle it from a different angle. My aim is to build a website that empowers readers about retirement income and further expands into other areas important for an effective retirement. The key is to provide readers with a clearinghouse of knowledge, which allows them to take the best of what is empirically valid in a cohesive manner and digest at their own pace what they need. So, let's take a step back and seek to better quantify the value of good financial decision-making.

● The Value of Good Financial Decision-Making

Good financial planning decisions extend well beyond where and how you invest. Two major research efforts have attempted to quantify how good financial decision-making can enhance your lifetime standard of living. It is important to understand what this research means, because it may not always equal a higher portfolio return in the short term.

The research identifies how good decision-making can enhance sustainable lifetime income on a risk-adjusted basis. The ability to spend more than you could have otherwise means your assets are generating a higher net return after accounting for taxes, fees, and good decision-making, which makes the higher spending possible.

In the field of finance, the term *alpha* identifies how a fund manager can combine securities into a portfolio that provides excess returns to investors above the appropriate related benchmark for those investments on a risk-adjusted basis. In simple terms, achieving alpha means earning more money than a risk-appropriate index would have provided. Generally, this is achieved through either timing market trends correctly or picking winning individual securities. If a fund manager charges a fee of 1 percent of assets under management and produces alpha of 2 percent, the investor enjoys an overall net gain of 1 percent. After fees, the investor earned 1 percent more than he or she would have had he or she invested directly in the benchmark index.

In practice, it is very difficult to achieve alpha consistently from market timing and security selection, though many investment managers still seem to believe otherwise. Some investment managers are able to beat the market, but it is difficult to separate skill from luck, and even more difficult for those managers to subsequently continue to outperform. The difficulty in generating investment alpha can help explain the rise of indexing in recent years as a more effective alternative. Low-cost index funds generally perform better than the majority of actively managed funds, at least after accounting for management fees. As a side note, many readers may not even realize they are paying fees on mutual funds, since the fees do not appear on portfolio statements and investors never receive a receipt. It is important to look for the ongoing expense ratio and loads charged at the time of purchase or sale.

After fees, alpha is typically negative for actively managed funds. Mathematically, the average fund must earn the average market return before fees. Some do better and some worse, but the average is the average. After fees, though, the average fund will fall behind the market. Those who understand this point can dramatically simplify their portfolio by filling it with strategic well-diversified, low-cost funds and generally avoiding trading except for rebalancing, tax reasons, or generating distributions for retirement spending.

In this regard, investing has now mostly been commoditized, at least when investing is done without regard for the overall financial plan. Financial advisors solely focused on selecting investments will struggle to add value for clients. Unfortunately, asset selection is all many advisors do, and the public is often unaware of the existence of advisors who do much more than just manage investments.

Another development from this changing investment world is that for good advisors, investing does not occur in a vacuum. The old investing framework went something like this: "Let's invest, see how it goes, and then determine what you can spend." The new methodology for good advisors is to first figure out what you want to accomplish with your wealth and then build a low-cost strategy to achieve this. Your goals provide the context for how to structure and deploy assets. The structure, process, and ongoing plan adjustment to accommodate life's ever-changing desires and goals becomes the method for adding value to the financial plan.

There is immense value in comprehensive financial planning and good financial decision-making. It is important to remember and easy to forget that the end goal of comprehensive financial planning goes beyond choosing investments.

The term *alpha* has been shown to be insufficient when it comes to financial planning, since it only refers to investing in a vacuum. Two articles sought to replace it with a term that represents more than merely beating the market. Vanguard proposes the term *Advisor Alpha* to explain this broader concept. David Blanchett and Paul Kaplan at Morningstar settled on *Gamma.* One thing is certain; as it pertains to investing, *alpha* is really just a Greek word for "myth."

Vanguard's Advisor Alpha

Vanguard developed their Advisor Alpha concept in 2001. Their infographics show their overall estimate for Advisor Alpha as 3 percent on a net basis (4 percent less an assumed 1 percent advisory fee). In the introduction of their report, they explain that their objective is to shift the focus away from "traditional beat-the-market objectives" (i.e., traditional alpha) toward what they view as the "best practices of wealth management."

These best practices are separated into several categories, shown in Exhibit 9.1, that focus on tax efficiency, costs, risk management, and making good investment decisions.

Suppose a good comprehensive financial advisor who does all these things charges a fee of 1 percent of assets under management. An investor who can do all of the above on his or her own can keep that fee. However, investors who don't know how to effectively implement everything above becomes these steps or choose to devote their time and energy elsewhere—miss this extra Advisor Alpha. Even though they saved the 1 percent fee, they will likely end up worse off for not implementing all these other important aspects of a good financial plan.

Justin Wagner from Vanguard offers the following example for this important point. Suppose the overall market return is 8 percent. Without good financial decision-making, the combined impact of fees, taxes, and poor investment decisions is around 4 percent. This leaves a net return of

Exhibit 9.1

Components of Vanguard's Advisor Alpha: Impact on an Investor's Returns

1. Build a customized investment plan aimed at achieving goals and meeting constraints for risk tolerance and risk capacity

>0%	Suitable asset allocation with broadly diversity investments
0 – 0.45%	Focus on low-cost investments (low expenses ratios)
0 – 0.75%	Locating assets properly in taxable and tax-advantage accounts
>0%	Focus on total-returns investing instead of income investing

2. Minize risk and tax impacts

0 – 0.35%	Rebalancing to the stategic asset allocation
0 – 0.7%	Deciding where to draw assets from (tax-deferred or taxable) to meet spending

3. Behavioral coaching

>1.5%	Providing support to stay the course in times of market stress

Overall net impact of good advice: about 3%

4 percent to the investor. However, for investors working with a capable advisor, they eliminate poor investment decisions, minimize taxes, and only pay the 1 percent fee, leaving a net return of 7 percent. These higher net returns can then be translated into an improved retirement lifestyle and a better ability to meet financial goals. That is the Advisor Alpha. The value added by good advice can greatly exceed the fees, which leaves the investor in a much better position even after paying the advisor. It is incorrect to view advisory fees as a zero-sum game that the advisor wins at the expense of the client; both can be winners.

Morningstar's Gamma

David Blanchett and Paul Kaplan at Morningstar created a similar study about the value of good decision-making. Their results and approach are different from those of Vanguard, but the goal is the same: to quantify the costs of poor and good decision-making. Naturally, many assumptions must be made regarding good financial decisions and the impact of poor financial decisions. The Morningstar research is more directly focused on how retirees can achieve higher income, which they call "gamma." They left out issues like behavioral coaching and included other matters like dynamic retirement spending. Full details can be found in their article, "Alpha, Beta, and Now... Gamma," published in the Fall 2013 issue of the *Journal of Retirement*.

The dimensions for improving financial decisions considered in their article are broken down into several issues, along with consideration of how a naïve investor might approach each issue and how an improved outcome could be achieved with improved knowledge and education or with the help of a professional.

1. Dynamic Withdrawal Strategy

The issue: Making withdrawal decisions using a variable spending strategy that updates spending to keep a similar probability of failure for the remaining time horizon in retirement.

Naïve investor: Uses the 4 percent rule: takes out 4 percent at retirement, then increases that amount by inflation in subsequent years for as long as possible until wealth is depleted.

Improved outcome: Make dynamic decisions based on a circular process. Every year, determine retirement horizon, asset allocation, and maximum withdrawal percentage for a given target probability of failure. Repeat annually to determine spending.

2. Total Wealth Asset Allocation

The issue: Making asset allocation decisions after considering total wealth including lifetime human capital (future employment earnings).

Naïve investor: Makes asset allocation decisions without considering the role of lifetime human capital.

Improved outcome: Calculate the present discounted value of lifetime earnings to be saved. Determine the characteristics of lifetime income in terms of whether it is more bond-like or stock-like. Consider this as an asset in your portfolio and then figure out the asset allocation for the financial portfolio in order to obtain the final overall desired asset allocation for wealth.

3. Tax Efficiency through Asset Location and Withdrawal Sequencing

The issue: Maximizing tax efficiency by locating assets in the most tax-efficient places and withdrawing assets in a more tax-efficient manner.

Naïve investor: Ignores these issues by keeping the same asset allocation for both tax-deferred and taxable accounts, and then withdraws proportionately from each account in retirement.

Improved outcome: Use efficient asset location by filling tax-deferred accounts with bonds, while stocks would be used in taxable accounts as much as possible. Couple that with efficient withdrawal sequencing, which first spends down taxable accounts, and then move on to tax-deferred accounts.

4. Liability Relative Optimization

The issue: The true risk for a retirement portfolio is not the annual volatility of the asset portfolio, nor is it the performance of the asset portfolio relative to a benchmark. Rather, it is the risk that you won't be able to meet your spending goals.

Naïve investor: Makes asset allocation decisions with no regard for spending goals, focusing instead solely on single-period modern portfolio theory concepts.

Improved outcome: Make investment decisions specifically with spending liabilities in mind. This could result in a portfolio with a lower expected return or higher volatility than a more traditional one, but it might do a better job meeting lifetime spending needs. Adding a liability creates a different efficient frontier with portfolios that would have previously seemed suboptimal. For instance, TIPS might not play a role in an assets-only optimization problem, but they might do a better overall job of meeting spending needs, especially in high-inflation environments.

5. Annuity Allocation

The issue: Using product allocation to devote some financial assets to purchasing guaranteed income products may improve outcomes.

Naïve investor: Views annuities as a gamble on dying too soon and ignores them as a retirement income option.

Improved outcome: View annuities as insurance against outliving your wealth by relying on the guaranteed income for life. Allocate part of the financial portfolio to an income annuity at retirement, while also keeping the same overall amount invested in stocks. In other words, part of the allocation to bonds in the retirement portfolio is transitioned into an income annuity.

6. Social Security Claiming

The issue: Social Security retirement benefits may be claimed between ages sixty-two and seventy, with credits provided for those who delay, yet Americans frequently claim Social Security early.

Naïve investor: Claims Social Security retirement benefits at age sixty-two, as do nearly half of Americans.

Improved outcome: Make joint Social Security claiming decisions based on the potential insurance value of Social Security to provide the most possible lifetime income.

By making these improved financial decisions, retirement income can be increased dramatically. Exhibit 9.2 shows that on a risk-adjusted basis, retirement income is 31.8 percent higher for the individual making good financial planning decisions relative to someone making naïve planning decisions. How much is this worth in alpha terms? In other words, how much would portfolio returns need to be increased to support a 31.8 percent larger spending level?

Over a thirty-year period, those starting with a 4 percent withdrawal rate would need to earn 2.34 percent more per year as alpha (in the median case)—a difficult task indeed—to increase their income by this amount. This is the "gamma-equivalent alpha." For someone who would otherwise make naïve planning decisions, a 1 percent advisory fee is worthwhile if that advisor helps the individual make these improved decisions. The net gain to the individual would still be an additional 1.34 percent in annual market returns, according to the Morningstar research.

Though I use the term *naïve* to describe decisions made without enough attention to good financial planning strategies, it is important to emphasize that many well-informed individuals may fall prey to these decisions.

Exhibit 9.2

Components of Morningstar's Gamma

Financial Behavior	Additional Income Generated	Gamma Equivalent Alpha
1. Dynamic Withdrawal Strategy	9.88%	0.70%
2. Total Wealth Asset Allocation	6.43%	0.45%
3. Tax Efficiency	3.23%	0.23%
4. Liability Relative Optimization	1.65%	0.12%
5. Annuity Allocation	1.44%	0.10%
6. Social Security Claiming	9.15%	0.74%
Good Financial Decision Making:	**31.78%**	**2.34%**

Source: *Journal of Retirement* (Fall 2013) – Factors 1-5; *Journal of Personal Finance* (Fall 2012) – Factor 6

Two things might hold you back: inertia and behavioral finance. It takes discipline to continually make the little adjustments needed to maintain the integrity of the portfolio and subsequent goals. And if you are busy with life, you are probably not going to stay up late on a Wednesday night, for instance, to review or reassess your withdrawal sequencing and asset location. Life can get in the way. It is easy to be an armchair quarterback and think you will not succumb to the naïve decisions because the answers are obvious, but when you are "on the field," that is not always the case.

The Vanguard and Morningstar studies are really just the tip of the iceberg. The studies are naturally somewhat limited in what they can examine quantitatively. There are many other ways financial advisors may add value that are harder to quantify, such as ensuring you make the right beneficiary designations within an estate plan, are properly insured, and are not missing important strategies to save on taxes. One significant mistake in any of these areas could unravel years of good planning.

In this regard, advisors serve as a type of insurance policy. They provide support to avoid normal life mistakes that come with a lack of experience. Life consists of many economic milestones like retirement, as well as spurious "opportunities" like buying into a time-share, and various potential mistakes driven by behavioral considerations. Working with someone who has seen these situations hundreds of times can be helpful to steer you in the right direction and avoid costly mistakes.

With retirement, it is important to consider how declining cognitive skills associated with aging will make it increasingly difficult to self-manage your investment and withdrawal decisions. For households where one person handles money matters, surviving household members will be especially vulnerable to making mistakes when they outlive the family financial manager. Developing a strong relationship with a trusted financial planner can help with both of these matters.

In terms of cognitive decline, a research article by Michael Finke, John Howe, and Sandra Huston titled "Old Age and the Decline in Financial Literacy" outlined the situation well. They provided a financial literacy test to older populations and found that financial literacy tends to decline by about 1 percent per year after age sixty, but financial confidence remains the same. Other research from David Laibson at Harvard University has also revealed reduced numeracy with age. It becomes harder to perform basic arithmetic calculations and understand the nature of risk, not to mention questions such as which number is smaller: 1/100 or 1/1000?

Can a financial advisor be cost-effective? Ultimately, that depends on your answers to a series of important questions:

- Do you have the time, energy, interest, knowledge, and desire to implement all of these decisions on your own? Do you enjoy financial planning?
- Will you overcome the inertia of inaction to put together all the various parts needed to create and implement an effective and coherent overall plan?
- Will you continue to periodically update your plan?
- Have you determined how to make sure your planning will be maintained properly if other family members need to take control of it?
- Are you working with a comprehensive financial planner who does more than just manage investment portfolios and is capable of implementing good financial planning decisions?

Cognitive Decline

Declining abilities to do financial calculations and other types of cognitive impairment make it increasingly difficult to manage a complex investment and withdrawal strategy as you age. It is important to plan ahead and make binding decisions before cognitive impairment sets in. Examples of these binding decisions could include working with a trusted financial planning firm that can be on the lookout for cognitive impairment and help arrange for necessary additional help, or using an income annuity (which David Laibson has called "dementia insurance") to lock in an income stream and reduce the need for portfolio management skills. Since confidence in your financial skills does not decline with age, it is important to plan for these possibilities ahead of time.

If you have the time, interest, energy, knowledge, emotional detachment, and desire to do your financial planning on your own, then you may make an excellent advisor. If your advisor is less than capable, you might be better off saving yourself the fee or taking your business elsewhere. Otherwise, it is worth considering that both of these studies demonstrate how working with a financial advisor can lead to net positive outcomes and be cost-effective, especially as you age. It doesn't take much to improve your standard of living through better decision-making, even after accounting for any fee related to planning advice.

● Behavioral Economics

In the previous section, "behavioral coaching" was suggested to have the biggest impact on real-world investor returns. In Vanguard's analysis, being able to overcome your own behavioral quirks could add more than 1.5 percent to your returns, as opposed to falling victim to your own human tendencies. If an advisor can successfully provide behavioral coaching to clients, stopping them from both losing their cool and taking drastic, hasty actions in times of market stress, then the outcome can still be a net win for the clients after accounting for fees. Even for those who generally always make the right decision regarding their portfolios, a single investment mistake (such as getting out of the stock market in late 2008/early 2009) made near retirement could overturn years of good decision-making. The impact of making a wrong financial decision as you get older or wealthier becomes harder to overcome. Sequence-of-returns risk has a corollary here: the timing of mistakes can lead some to have a bigger impact on the lifetime standard of living than others.

To further quantify this matter, Financial Engines published a study in May 2014 with Aon Hewitt that looked at outcomes for defined-contribution retirement plan participants between 2006 and 2012. The 30.3 percent of participants who elected to receive some form of help with their retirement plan on average earned 3.32 *percent more per year,* net of fees, relative to those not receiving investment help. If you have a $1 million portfolio, that's over $30,000 you're leaving on the table. The study also noted that 60.5 percent of those not receiving help were taking inappropriate amounts of risk, including a large group of near-retirees holding overall portfolios that were more volatile than the S&P 500.

With behavioral coaching being the biggest factor in improving financial outcomes, further exploration is warranted into the types of behaviors that lead investors astray; this can highlight the importance of having someone serve as a sounding board and provide input when working your way through a lifetime of financial decisions. A short introduction to the topic of behavioral finance would be beneficial at this juncture.

Probably the most damaging behavioral mistake made by real-world investors is succumbing to the greed-and-fear cycle that causes someone to buy into the market at its peak and sell out at its lows. This natural cycle happens thus: when markets are doing well, investors get excited and pour more money into the market with the hope that this trend will continue indefinitely. Investors on the sidelines may become jealous of neighbors' gains and may worry that they are missing out. But a prolonged run-up generally leads to market valuations becoming misaligned, and it is reasonable to expect a reversal of fortune with lower returns in the future.

Nonetheless, popular culture will send repeated messages that this time is somehow different—it is a new economy with a new paradigm, the old rules no longer apply, and so on. It is tough to rebalance to your strategic asset allocation when markets are rising, because you have to sell shares of the biggest gainers in order to do so. But it is important to have the discipline to stick with your plans and objectives.

A reversal of the market direction is inevitable, causing market prices to plummet. Investors get nervous, and some, after seeing significant declines, become scared enough that they start selling off holdings.

Staying the course is an even greater challenge if you are experiencing cognitive decline. Unfortunately, this time in life calls for rebalancing to your strategic asset allocation, which would require buying assets with falling prices rather than selling them. This is a challenge, both emotionally and intellectually.

Naturally, weak markets will eventually recover and go up again. However, the timing of the recovery is unpredictable. You cannot time the market. Instead, you must stick with your financial plan and the asset allocation that matches your tolerance for market volatility. Unfortunately, investors in financial markets tend to do the opposite of what happens in most other markets: they buy more when prices are high and sell when prices are low. This causes returns to drag dramatically behind what a "buy, hold, and rebalance" investor could have earned. Staying the course would work better. This is the type of "behavioral coaching" Vanguard refers to in their study.

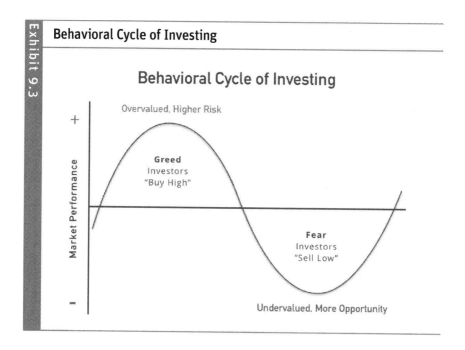

Why do we as humans need to be coached in our behavior? Evolution has designed us not to be effective long-term investors, but rather to seek to avoid short-term dangers. The fields of behavioral finance and behavioral economics have uncovered various biases humans have that are great for day-to-day survival, but somewhat maladaptive for long-term investing. A significant body of research is dedicated to detailing these investor behaviors.

Some of the most common behaviors an advisor helps individual investors with are:

- *Availability Bias/Recency Effect:* **Using recent or current market behavior to predict future market behavior.**

  The most recent events are always freshest in our minds, and we tend to extrapolate recent events into the future, expecting more of the same. Large recent market gains lead us to be optimistic about our chances, while market losses have the opposite effect. It takes discipline to overcome these natural tendencies.

- *Overconfidence:* **Believing you know more than other investors.**

  While investment research increasingly points to the difficulty of beating the market—especially after fees, trading costs, and taxes are taken into account—it is natural to believe we know more than everyone else. This is the "Lake Wobegon effect" in practice. As Garrison Keillor relates in *A Prairie Home Companion,* Lake Wobegon is a place "where all the children are above average." It is all too easy for investors, and even many advisors, to fall into this kind of thinking.

- *Loss Aversion:* **Fearing a loss more than you want to make gains.**

  As human beings, we tend to feel that the pain of experiencing a loss is greater than the joy felt by an equivalent gain. Not recognizing this predisposition can cause people to misjudge their tolerance for risk, making them more likely to bail on their financial plan. Research by Eric Johnson at Columbia University (see the Schlomo Benartzi article for further reading) shows that loss aversion is greater among retirees. Johnson found that retirees feel roughly ten times worse about losing $100 than they feel good about gaining $100. Or, more specifically, the retirees in their research said they would not accept a gamble with a 50 percent chance of winning $100 and a 50 percent chance of losing $10. The general population is loss averse, but generally not to this extent.

- *Hindsight Bias:* **Thinking you can predict market behavior because you believe you know why past market behavior occurred.**

In hindsight, market losses may seem to have an obvious or intuitive explanation. This bias can feed into our overconfidence and cause us to believe we will be able to anticipate such market changes the next time around.

- *Survivorship Bias:* **Underestimating the risk by ignoring the failed companies.**

We may underestimate the degree of market risk if we look only at companies still operating today. This misses out on the lessons of many failed companies no longer on the investment radar. It is like thinking a marathon would be easy to run because you watched a bunch of people cross the finish line. You're ignoring all the people who gave up before reaching the end. This can also feed overconfidence.

- *Herd Mentality:* **Judging your own success or failure based on that of others.**

Sometimes the herd mentality can be rationalized. You don't want to miss out on being rich when everyone else is rich, and perhaps being poor is not so bad when everyone else is also poor. But for a long-term investor, following the herd rarely makes sense.

- *Affinity Traps:* **Taking advice from someone just because you know the person.**

We often take the advice of someone simply based on the fact that we like him or her or share a social circle, regardless of that person's qualifications to speak on investment and personal finance topics.

Further behavioral issues must be considered when it comes to retirement income. Research by Alessandro Previtero at UCLA (see the Schlomo Benartzi article for further reading) shows that recent stock market performance has a big impact on the decision between lump-sum or lifetime income options from pensions. Those making the pension decision after stock market increases over the past six to twelve months are much more likely to select a lump sum instead of guaranteed income, allowing recent market performance to influence this important and irreversible decision. That is recency bias in action.

Research from Jeffrey Brown at the University of Illinois illustrates how the framing of lifetime income can lead to different answers. His research team surveyed more than 1,300 people aged fifty and older and asked them to choose between (1) a life annuity paying $650 each month until death, and (2) a traditional savings account of $100,000 bearing 4 percent interest. These choices are designed to support the same lifetime income after incorporating life expectancies, but the annuity choice in option 1 was expressed in two different ways. With a "consumption frame," option 1 was described as a monthly income of $650 for life. With an "investment frame," option 1 was described as an investment with a $650 return for life. When expressed in terms of consumption, 70 percent of respondents preferred the annuity. But when expressed as an investment, only 21 percent of respondents choose the annuity. Both versions of the question offer the same returns, but the answers elicited differ greatly. Framing an annuity as an investment makes people worry they will die early and "lose" on their investment. When expressed as lifetime consumption, the annuity option sounds less risky and more attractive.

Further research from Professor John Payne at Duke University (see the Schlomo Benartzi article for further reading) demonstrates how retirees gravitate toward options that are easier to understand. He cites how retirees may choose single-life annuities because they offer higher monthly income than joint-life annuities without fully reflecting on the potential impact for spouses. I have also observed this problem with complex annuities like variable annuities with guarantee riders. Retirees frequently misinterpret the roll-up rates offered for the benefit base as a guaranteed return for their money. They may not realize that when this higher hypothetical return number is combined with a lower payout rate later on, the combined outcome may actually leave them worse off. It's important to dig beyond the marquee numbers jumping out of the marketing literature and reflect on what is truly happening when all variables and levers are combined into a cohesive whole.

A final issue is money illusion: the difficulty people have distinguishing between observable dollar amounts over time and the underlying change in purchasing power of wealth. This can complicate retirement planning, since it is important to plan over long time horizons. Even a low inflation rate adds up when compounded over a long time period.

◎ Understanding How the Financial Advisory Profession Works

With the value provided by good financial decision-making and the impediments people face to achieve good financial outcomes for themselves, it is worthwhile discussing more about the advisory profession. How can you find a good advisor?

Though the financial services profession is highly regulated at both the state and national levels, use of the terms *financial advisor* or *financial planner* as job titles is hardly regulated. Regulation generally focuses on the nature of business activities rather than job titles. Pretty much anyone can use these terms without any further oversight about training, competency, education, or qualifications.

Generally, those calling themselves financial planners or advisors represent one of three types: registered investment advisors, stock brokers, or insurance agents.

Of the three types, investment advisors are the only ones required to serve as fiduciaries for their clients, at least when they are wearing their "investment advisor" hat. The fiduciary standard of care requires investment advisors to act in the best interests of clients and disclose any material conflicts of interest to clients for the advice they provide. Fiduciary advisors who serve only as fiduciary advisors are generally part of registered investment advisor (RIA) firms, and they often use the term *fee only* to differentiate themselves from competitors. The National Association for Personal Financial Advisors (NAPFA) is the membership organization for fee-only advisors. A fee-only advisor is paid directly and only by his or her clients, generally as a percentage of assets the advisor manages. That percentage generally decreases as the account size increases. Fees usually cover financial planning advice and investment management.

Some fee-only advisors may have different fee structures. Other possibilities include an hourly charge or fixed retainer fees for services. With other fee arrangements, the advisor is less likely to make trades on the client's behalf. With such fee arrangements, the advisor makes investment recommendations, but the client implements them.

The important point of this fee structure and the meaning of *only* within the term *fee only* is that these advisors are paid only by their clients. They do not receive any commissions or other financial incentives for getting their clients into any particular investments or financial products, which eliminates an obvious source of potential conflicts. Comprehensive financial planners should assist their clients with eight core planning areas: investments, taxes, debt management, education planning, retirement planning, estate planning, insurance, and household budgeting.

As you can see, there is much to do beyond just investment management. Presently, the fiduciary standard of care is not applied to brokers or insurance agents, though new rules from the Department of Labor that went into effect in June 2017 have strengthened requirements for those advising on qualified retirement plans (such as 401(k) and IRA accounts) to serve as fiduciaries. These landmark rule changes could have big impacts over the coming years, since retirement plan assets represent a significant portion of the investment assets held by American households.

Presently, brokers and insurance agents are treated more generally as salespeople, and they are required to use a suitability standard of care with their customers. Any recommended financial products must be "suitable" for the purchaser's situation, though the recommendations do not necessarily need to serve the best interests of the purchaser. For those acting as brokers and insurance agents, their primary professional obligation is to their employer rather than their client. For instance, a suitable investment or insurance product that pays a higher commission to the broker or agent—presumably because it is a more profitable product for the employer—could be recommended under the suitability standard, even if another approach would better serve the customer's interests. Surveys of the public generally reveal that most people do not understand the distinctions between the fiduciary and suitability standards, nor do they understand the differences between investment advisors and brokers. Perhaps a simple example is the analogy of selling cars. When you go to a Honda dealership, you reasonably expect the salesperson to sell you a Honda. The salesperson will probably not suggest that you would be better served by heading over to an unaffiliated Ford dealership.

Consumers understand this about people who sell cars, but they often do not recognize that this same issue exists for brokers and agents. People naturally tend to believe financial advisors are independent and seek to work in their clients' best interests, as they should. Fiduciary investment advisors face little to no conflict in directing client investments, because their compensation is not tied to a specific product. They can essentially recommend you buy the most fitting car from any available car dealership, which is the treatment consumers generally expect from all advisors. But brokers do not have this freedom; they are obligated to sell their sponsoring company's financial products. If another dealership would fit your needs better, they would still encourage you to buy from them instead.

To make matters worse, low-cost products that can better serve consumers carry a lower commission, making them less desirable for brokers to sell. Products that are harder to sell because of their complexity may have reduced effectiveness for clients, but they tend to carry higher commissions in order to incentivize their sale. It's like doctors providing prescriptions based on pharmaceutical company kickbacks rather than the patient's health.

Many advisor websites make it difficult to understand how they are registered and what sort of standard of care they provide. It would be simple if we could just separate the advisors from the brokers, but many advisors are registered as investment advisors and brokers or agents. Dual registration muddles the situation for clients further, as it may not always be clear when advisors are wearing the hat of a fiduciary, and when they are making recommendations under suitability requirements. Because they can also receive commissions, such dually registered advisors should use the term *fee-based* to describe their firms, rather than *fee-only*. However, I'm not sure if all advisors make this distinction between the two terms. Clients could then have a clear understanding of when they are being served under the fiduciary or suitability standard.

○ Concluding Thoughts

We have addressed the question about how much a retiree can spend sustainably from an investment portfolio in retirement, concluding in this chapter with a further look about the value of making good financial decisions and how readers can obtain more help with their financial planning.

This book has focused on the probability-based school for retirement that emphasizes the role of an investment portfolio, without further consideration about the potential role for risk pooling with lifetime income guarantees or other insurance products. My next volume will bring annuities and insurance into the mix. This book's strategies are most appropriate for managing total spending in the probability-based school and for managing the discretionary-spending component in the safety-first school.

I have described the findings of a large body of financial planning research regarding sustainable spending from investment portfolios in the face of a variety of retirement risks. We began with the simple PMT formula that describes the relationship between sustainable spending, investment returns, and time horizon. We discussed how longevity risk and market risk impact decisions about appropriate assumptions for this formula. We then discussed studies that look at the spending decision using historical data and Monte Carlo simulations, such as William Bengen's SAFEMAX and the Trinity study.

We then examined how the analysis changes when we modify the assumptions used in these classic studies. We find that sustainable spending may be less if we consider the international experience, incorporate today's low bond yields and increasing longevity, incorporate investment fees or portfolio underperformance, or use a less aggressive asset allocation. We also find that sustainable spending may be greater if we consider more realistic spending patterns that decline with age, a more diversified investment portfolio, flexibility and the use of dynamic spending strategies, and a capacity and tolerance on the part of the retiree to accept a greater chance of portfolio depletion. We also provided an extensive comparison of using bond funds and individual bonds in a retirement income strategy and how different time segmentation strategies using individual bonds for front-end retirement expenses can impact portfolio sustainability.

Thank you for reading, and please check www.retirementresearcher.com to stay up-to-date with the latest developments in the evolving field of retirement income planning.

Further Reading

Agarwal, Sumit, John C. Driscoll, Xavier Gabaix, and David Laibson. 2009. "The Age of Reason: Financial Decisions over the Lifecycle and Implications for Regulation." Brookings Papers on Economic Activity 2:51–117.

Aon Hewitt and Financial Engines. 2014. "Help in Defined Contribution Plans: 2006 through 2012."

Benartzi, Schlomo. 2010. "Behavioral Finance and the Post-Retirement Crisis."

Blanchett, David. 2012. "When to Claim Social Security Benefits." Journal of Personal Finance 11 (2): 36–87.

Blanchett, David, and Paul Kaplan. 2013. "Alpha, Beta, and Now...Gamma." Morningstar Working Paper. Also published in the Journal of Retirement (Fall 2013).

Brown, Jeffrey R., Jeffrey R. Kling, Sendhil Mullainathan, and Marian V. Wrobel. 2008. "Why Don't the People Insure Late Life Consumption? A Framing Explanation of the Under-Annuitization Puzzle." NBER Working Paper.

Finke, Michael S., John S. Howe, and Sandra J. Huston. 2011. "Old Age and the Decline in Financial Literacy." SSRN Working Paper #1948627 (August 24).

Johnson, Richard. W., Cori E. Uccello, and Joshua H. Goldwyn. 2003. "Single Life vs. Joint and Survivor Pension Payout Options: How Do Married Retirees Choose?" Urban Institute. Final report to the Society of Actuaries and the Actuarial Foundation.

Kinniry, Francis M., Colleen M. Jaconetti, Michael A. DiJoseph, and Yan Zilbering. 2014. "Putting a Value on Your Value: Quantifying Vanguard Advisor's Alpha." Vanguard Research Paper.

Murguia, Alex. "What McLean Can Do For You." McLean E-book Series. [https://www.mcleanam.com/resources/]

GLOSSARY OF ACRONYMS

- AARP: American Association of Retired Persons
- AGI: Adjusted Gross Income
- CD: Certificate of Deposit
- CEO: Chief Executive Officer
- CFA: Chartered Financial Analyst
- CFP: Certified Financial Planner
- CLU: Chartered Life Underwriter
- DIA: Deferred Income Annuities
- FPA: Financial Planning Association
- HECM – Home Equity Conversion Mortgage
- HELOC: Home Equity Line of Credit
- IRA: Individual Retirement Account
- IRS: Internal Revenue Service
- MPT: Modern Portfolio Theory
- MRT: Modern Retirement Theory
- NAPFA: National Association for Personal Financial Advisors
- RIA – Registered Investment Advisor
- RICP: Retirement Income Certified Professional
- SPIA: Single-Premium Immediate Annuities
- STRIPS: Separate Trading of Registered Interest and Principal of Securities
- TIPS: Treasury Inflation-Protected Securities

ABOUT THE AUTHOR

Wade D. Pfau, PhD, CFA, is a professor of retirement income in the PhD program for financial and retirement planning at the American College of Financial Services in Bryn Mawr, Pennsylvania. He also serves as a principal and the director of retirement research for McLean Asset Management and chief planning scientist at inStream Solutions. He hosts the Retirement Researcher website as an educational resource for individuals and financial advisors on topics related to retirement income planning. He holds a doctorate in economics from Princeton University and publishes frequently in a wide variety of academic and practitioner research journals.

Wade is a past selectee for the *InvestmentNews* "Power 20" in 2013 and "40 Under 40" in 2014, the *Investment Advisor* 35 list for 2015 and 25 list for 2014, and *Financial Planning* magazine's Influencer Awards. In 2016 he was chosen as one of the "Icons and Innovators" by *InvestmentNews*. He is a two-time winner of the *Journal of Financial Planning* Montgomery-Warschauer Editor's Award, a two-time winner of the Academic Thought Leadership Award from the Retirement Income Industry Association, and a best-paper-award winner in the Retirement category from the Academy of Financial Services.

He has spoken at the national conferences of organizations such as the CFA Institute, Financial Planning Association, National Association of Personal Financial Advisors, and Academy of Financial Services.

He is also a contributor to the curriculum of the Retirement Income Certified Professional (RICP) designation for financial advisors. He is a coeditor of the *Journal of Personal Finance*. Wade is also a columnist for *Advisor Perspectives*, a RetireMentor for MarketWatch, a contributor to *Forbes*, and an Expert Panelist for the *Wall Street Journal*. His research has been discussed in outlets including the print editions of the *Economist*, *New York Times*, *Wall Street Journal*, *Time*, *Kiplinger's*, and *Money* magazine.

He is also author of the book *Reverse Mortgages: How to Use Reverse Mortgages to Secure Your Retirement*.

Made in the USA
Middletown, DE
17 January 2018